Power Games

Jules Boykoff is the author of *Activism and the Olympics, Celebration Capitalism and the Olympic Games, Landscapes of Dissent,* and *Beyond Bullets: The Suppression of Dissent in the United States,* among others. He is a professor of politics and government at Pacific University in Forest Grove, Oregon.

Power Games

*A Political History
of the Olympics*

Jules Boykoff

VERSO
London • New York

First published by Verso 2016
© Jules Boykoff 2016
Foreword © Dave Zirin 2016

1 3 5 7 9 10 8 6 4 2

Verso
UK: 6 Meard Street, London W1F 0EG
US: 20 Jay Street, Suite 1010, Brooklyn, NY 11201
versobooks.com

Verso is the imprint of New Left Books

ISBN-13: 978-1-78478-072-2
ISBN-13: 978-1-78478-073-9 (US EBK)
ISBN-13: 978-1-78478-074-6 (UK EBK)

British Library Cataloguing in Publication Data
A catalogue record for this book is available from the British Library

Library of Congress Cataloging-in-Publication Data
A catalog record for this book is available from the Library of Congress

Typeset in Sabon by MJ & N Gavan, Truro, Cornwall
Printed in the US by Maple Press

For Kaia Sand and Jessi Wahnetah

Contents

Foreword
By Dave Zirin

My first Olympic memory is of Ronald Reagan. Seriously. Not the 1980 Miracle on Ice US hockey team, Edwin Moses, or Nadia Comaneci but Ronald Reagan. It was the 1984 Summer Games in Los Angeles and the competition was launched with a sunny address from the Gipper, played to rapturous cheers at the LA Coliseum. I cheered as well in my living room: cheering for Reagan was just like cheering for the Olympic heroes I'd read about in *Sports Illustrated*: people like Carl Lewis, Mary Lou Retton, and a spindly twenty-year-old college basketball gravity-defier named Michael Jordan. I had only the most rudimentary idea that the Soviet bloc—our Cold War enemies—were boycotting the Games because we had refused to attend theirs four years earlier. I certainly had no conception that these Olympics had actually harmed people in Los Angeles who had been displaced or locked up in the name of Olympic security. I certainly had no idea about the costs, the corporate underwriting, and the general skullduggery of cash and human flesh passed under tables to keep everyone on the International Olympic Committee happy. I had no idea that there were people who tried to resist these initiatives but found themselves drowned out by the screeching anthems of obedience that are played on repeat, regardless of host country. I had no idea about any of this because there was not a 1980s version of the indispensable Dr. Jules Boykoff.

As a sportswriter who has covered every Olympics and World Cup over the last two decades, I've learned that every mega-event contains debt, displacement, the militarization of public space, and varying degrees of resistance. These Olympic-sized crimes usually garner publicity as a curio about an individual country's corrupt ways. But rarely does anyone mention that these issues afflict every Olympics or World Cup. Rarely is it mentioned that there is a continuity regardless of decade or host country that these mega-events are Typhoid Marys of organized graft.

My guide for understanding the past, present, and future of these struggles has been the work of the indispensable Jules Boykoff. What makes Boykoff so singular is that his starting point is not the internal machinations of the IOC or FIFA. Nor is his starting point ever about the Games themselves and the ways that geopolitical tensions find their way onto the field of play. His jumping-off point is always the people in the host country and how they are affected by the mega-event monolith.

By always beginning with the most beaten down, Boykoff has found himself more capable than any commentator working today of explaining why people have started to stand up, resist the coming Games, and see through the patriotic bombast to the pain the Games can bring. Whether it was the small demonstrations in London, the mass confrontations in Brazil, or the preemptive challenges toward hosting at all in places as disparate as Krakow and Boston, Boykoff tells these untold stories and translates the motivations of an international cast of characters with the lucidity of a great sportswriter and the depth of a scholar and political economist. In *Power Games* he combines meticulous archival research with on-the-ground interviews from Olympic sites and presents it all in a lively, engaging way. In doing so, he offers us the most important, comprehensive book on the Olympic Games that I've come across. This is a political history of the Games that foregrounds themes all too often brushed under the historical rug: the extraordinary privilege that IOC elites have long enjoyed, the wrought-iron ties that the Games have to corporate capitalism, the problematic history the Olympics have with indigenous peoples, and the many ways activists have resisted the Olympic machine.

Jules Boykoff is a mild-mannered individual. He is also dangerous to a lot of powerful people. He is dangerous because he goes to the Olympic cities before the spotlight is turned on, and when the real action is played out in the shadows. He understands how the mega-event industrial complex works, and what people can do to bring it to its knees. Read this book. And if you have friends living in the next Olympic city, send them fifteen copies. These are words as weapons: armaments for those who won't have games played on their backs.

Acknowledgments

In so many ways, this book has been a collective effort. It has been my abundant fortune to have sharp minds and generous spirits on my team. I have numerous people to thank for their assistance, feedback, and encouragement during the writing of this book: Dan Burdsey, Ben Carrington, Tom Carter, Demian Castro, Julian Cheyne, Jeff Derksen, Janice Forsyth, Pete Fussey, Chris Gaffney, Tina Gerhardt, Eva Guggemos, Robin Hahnel, Reg Johanson, Katrina Karkazis, Pam Kofstad, Larissa Lacerda, Isaac Marrero-Guillamón, Cheleen Mahar, Gilmar Mascarenhas, Ian McDonald, Michelle Moore, Tom Mertes, Cecily Nicholson, Christine O'Bonsawin, Christian Parenti, Nicholas Perrin, Jessica Ritter, Matt Seaton, Orlando Santos Junior, Martin Slavin, Cynthia Sloan, Alan Tomlinson, Chris Wilkes, Theresa Williamson, and Dave Zirin.

Thank you to the International Centre for Olympic Studies at Western University in Canada for opening their archives to me. A big thank you goes to Rosemarie O'Connor Quinn, Tom Quinn, and Mark Quinn for their hospitality in Dublin and for supplying a photograph of the remarkable Peter O'Connor. And I am grateful to Aline Luginbühl from IOC Images for her assistance securing photographs. Thanks also to the Artists Rights Society and the Center for the Study of Political Graphics. Am Johal invited me to Simon Fraser University to present my ideas on the Olympics, as did Jennifer Allen and Adam Davis from Oregon Humanities, and David Harvey and Mary Taylor at the City University of New York—thank you all. I appreciate the kindness and courage of people at NoSochi2014, including Dana Wojokh, Tamara Barsik, Lisa Jarkasi, and Zack Barsik. Massive gratitude goes to Emily Van Vleet and Matthew Yasuoka for their remarkable, reliable research assistance over the years. Thanks be to Sue Schoenbeck, Thom Boykoff, and Meg Eberle for being faithful supporters of my work. And an enormous thank you to Andy Hsiao at Verso for believing in this project, for shaping it in important ways, and for helping me see it through. I am also grateful for Jeff Z. Klein's incisive editorial acumen.

Some of the ideas in this book were first aired in the *Guardian, New Left Review,* the *New York Times, Olympika: The International Journal of Olympic Studies, Contemporary Social Science, Human Geography, Sport in Society, Al Jazeera America, Red Pepper, Extra!, CounterPunch, Street Roots,* the *San Francisco Chronicle, Dissent Magazine,* and *The Nation.* Many thanks to the editors I had the good fortune of working with at those publications for their support. And a huge thank you to the many co-authors I have worked with on Olympic politics. This research was supported by a Fulbright research fellowship and a Story-Dondero award from Pacific University in Oregon.

This book would not have possible without the love, support, wit, curiosity, and moxie of Kaia Sand and Jessi Wahnetah. Your ethical metric and inimitable vim buoy my spirit, give me hope, and make everything so much more fun.

Introduction:
"Operation Olympic Games"

Soon after President Barack Obama took office in 2009, the Pentagon unleashed a covert cyber-sabotage attack on Iranian nuclear enrichment facilities aimed at disabling centrifuges designed to purify uranium. Because of a programming error, the operation's cyber-worm slithered errantly out of Iran's Natanz nuclear plant and slinked around the Internet for all to see. Computer security gurus named the cyber-weapon "Stuxnet," but the Pentagon had chosen a different code name for the attack: "Operation Olympic Games."[1] The choice was apt. After all, the process was orchestrated by political elites behind closed doors; it wreaked havoc on the local host; and it cost a bundle, in terms of both political and actual capital. In a nutshell, that describes the state of the Olympics in the twenty-first century: a largely clandestine, elite-driven process with significant impacts on host cities, and all of it coming with an exorbitant price tag. But this has not always been the case. In *Power Games: A Political History of the Olympics*, I chart the evolution of the Olympic Games, from the quixotic dream of a quirky French baron to the domineering colossus it is today. Tracing the political history of the Olympics helps us understand how sport has evolved from pastime to profession, from the ambit of the few to the spectacle of the many. And engaging the history of the Olympics provides an exceptionally useful foundation for comprehending larger cultural, social, and political processes of the last 120 years—and in particular, for understanding class privilege, indigenous repression, activist strategy, and capitalist power.

These are all topics that the International Olympic Committee (IOC) has actively tried to avoid addressing, often by forwarding the notion that the Olympics are not to be politicized. When, for example, IOC president Jacques Rogge was asked about the death of Osama bin Laden, Rogge replied, "What happened to Mr. bin Laden is a political issue on which I do not wish to comment."[2] Throughout his twelve-year tenure as head of the IOC, Rogge—a former orthopedic surgeon, avid yachtsman, and Belgian count—reliably asserted that the Olympic Games could and should sidestep politics, as has every IOC president before and since. But their supposed aversion to politics has always brimmed with hypocrisy. Theirs is "an apoliticism that is in fact deeply political," as the philosopher Theodor Adorno would have put it.[3]

In reality the Olympics are political through and through. The marching, the flags, the national anthems, the alliances with corporate sponsors, the labor exploitation behind the athletic-apparel labels, the treatment of indigenous peoples, the marginalization of the poor and working class, the selection of Olympic host cities—all political. To say the Olympics transcend politics is to conjure fantasy.

Baron Pierre de Coubertin, the French aristocrat who revived the modern Olympics at the end of the nineteenth century, built the Games on a bedrock of contradiction. While he publicly rejected injecting politics into the Olympics, behind the scenes he mobilized political power brokers to help establish and nurture the Games. Coubertin's biographer deems his disavowal of politics "disingenuous in the extreme."[4] From the start, the IOC marinated in politics.

Much later, IOC president Avery Brundage advanced his own brand of Coubertin's duplicitous philosophy. "We actively combat the introduction of politics into the Olympic movement and are adamant against the use of the Olympic Games as a tool or as a weapon by any organization,"[5] he asserted. Brundage pushed this narrative even as South Africa's apartheid system led the IOC to withdraw the country's invitation to the 1964 Tokyo Games and to ultimately expel South Africa from the Olympic Movement in 1970, only to reinstate it in 1992. The IOC, in its role as a supranational sports organization, has also inserted itself into matters of war and peace by hosting meetings between the National Olympic Committees from Israel and Palestine.[6] In the 1990s the IOC began working with the United Nations to institute an "Olympic Truce" before each staging of the Games, whereby countries agree to cease hostilities for the duration of the Olympic competition. This intervention into geopolitics, though unanimously supported, is routinely ignored, as when Russia invaded Crimea in the immediate wake of hosting the 2014 Sochi Winter Games.[7]

Politics were once again at the forefront with the 2008 Summer Olympics in Beijing. The city's bid team explicitly claimed the Games would create a groundswell of democracy in China. Liu Jingmin, the deputy mayor of Beijing, said, "By applying for the Olympics, we want to promote not just the city's development, but the development of society, including democracy and human rights." Liu went still further: "If people have a target like the Olympics to strive for, it will help us establish a more just and harmonious society, a more democratic society, and help integrate China into the world."[8] While in retrospect these claims appear preposterously extravagant, they appealed to the willfully gullible "Olympic family." According to the former IOC vice president Richard Pound, the suggestion that bestowing the Games to China would hasten human-rights progress in the country "was an all-but-irresistible prospect for the IOC."[9] The IOC awarded the 2008 Summer Games to Beijing over Toronto, Paris, and Istanbul.

But does hosting the Olympics really help improve living conditions for residents of the host city? Evidence supporting the claim is scant. Just look at Beijing. Predictions of Olympics-induced human-rights progress in China, it turns out, were greatly exaggerated. When Beijing hosted the Summer Games in 2008 the country ranked 167th on Reporters Without Borders' Press Freedom Index. In 2014 the country dropped to 175th. "The reality is that the Chinese government's hosting of the Games has been *a catalyst* for abuses," said Sophie Richardson of Human Rights Watch.[10] This grim record didn't stop the IOC from selecting Beijing to host the 2022 Winter Olympics, which will make the city the first to stage both the Summer and Winter Games.

The IOC's plea for apoliticism partly arises from the need to safeguard its biggest capital generator, the Games themselves. The Olympic Games have become a cash cow that the IOC and its corporate partners milk feverishly every two years, since the staggering of the Summer and Winter Olympics began in 1994. For the IOC, acknowledging politics might jeopardize their lucre.

In *Barbaric Sport: A Global Plague*, Marc Perelman offers a blistering demolition of sport in general and the Olympics in particular. For him, sport has not only come to be "central to the machine" of capitalism, but "the new opium of the people." Sport, he argues, is actually "more alienating than religion because it suggests the scintillating dream of a promotion for the individual, holds out the prospect of parallel hierarchy." Perelman concludes, "The element of 'protest' against daily reality that even religion (according to Marx) still retained is stifled by the infinite corrosive power of sport, draining mass consciousness of all liberating and emancipatory energy."[11]

While I wholeheartedly agree that sport affords us insight into how capitalism shimmies and schemes—indeed that shimmying is a major leitmotif in this book—a closer look at Marx's original "opium of the people" passage is in order. There's a great deal of empathy embedded in Marx's critique —more than Perelman lets on. Marx noted, "The struggle against religion is therefore indirectly a fight against *the world* of which religion is the spiritual aroma." He added, "Religious distress is at the same time the *expression* of real distress and also the *protest* against real distress. Religion is the sigh of the oppressed creature, the heart of a heartless world, just as it is the spirit of spiritless conditions. It is the *opium* of the people."[12] So, for Marx, religion—and by extension here, sport—was "the heart of a heartless world." We need not eviscerate what provides so many with enjoyment and zest. The chants of the sports fan are not necessarily the blind yammering of monomaniacal naïfs. They can be efforts to make meaning in a cruel capitalist world rigged for the rich—and they can wedge open a path for political conversations we might not otherwise have.

To concede the terrain of sports is to unnecessarily surrender potential common ground for political understanding, and perhaps even action. With that in mind, in this book I'll argue that critical engagement with the politics of sports has historically helped pry open space for ethical commitment and principled action, as evidenced by the Olympic athletes who have taken courageous political stands, the alternatives to the Olympics that have emerged over the years, and the activism that springs up today to challenge the five-ring juggernaut. In short, the Olympics are more than mere opiate.

Sports are remarkably popular. Pope Francis is a lifelong soccer fan from Argentina whose favorite club, San Lorenzo, catapulted in 2013 from the brink of relegation to the league title—divine intervention?[13] Sports can also be the last refuge of the scoundrel. Osama bin Laden marveled at the passion soccer could generate, and he knew it well; in 1994 in London he attended Arsenal Football Club matches on numerous occasions, even purchasing souvenirs for his sons from the club's gift shop.[14] The kind of passion sports generate can be channeled in countless directions, from the radical to the reactionary, from reverence to treachery.

I should acknowledge up front that I come to this book not as some grumpy academic with a penchant for spurning sport, but as someone who dedicated a big part of my life to competitive, high-level soccer. In the late 1980s I earned a slot on the Under-23 National Team—also known as the US Olympic Team—alongside stalwarts like Brad Friedel, Cobi Jones, Joe-Max Moore, Manny Lagos, and Yari Allnutt. My first international match with the Olympic Team took place in France in 1990. Our opponent? The Brazilian Olympic Team, which featured stars like Cafu and Marcelinho. In that same tournament I also suited up against Czechoslovakia, Yugoslavia, and the Soviet Union. The following year I captained the north squad to a gold medal at the US Olympic Festival in Los Angeles, with teammates Brian McBride, Todd Yeagley, Brian Dawson, and Brian Kamler. In short, I am a fan of sport. My personal history is entwined with the political history of the Games.

In his masterful book *Beyond a Boundary*, the West Indian cricketer and essayist C. L. R. James described a pivotal moment in his life. "I was in the toils of greater forces than I knew," he wrote. "Cricket had plunged me into politics long before I was aware of it. When I did turn to politics I did not have too much to learn."[15] Soccer plunged me into politics, but I still had a ton to learn. As the avant-garde poet and union organizer Rodrigo Toscano once wrote, "there's enormous gaps in *my* education."[16] After my experience playing for the US Olympic Soccer Team in France, where we were roundly booed whether we were playing Brazil (understandable), Czechoslovakia (plausible), Yugoslavia (questionable), or the Soviet Union (quizzical), I was eager to start filling in the gaps in my education. In many ways this book is the outcome of that journey.

In April 2015 IOC president Thomas Bach spoke at the United Nations about the Olympic movement's relationship to politics. He evoked a "universal law of sport" that could be threatened by "political interference" undermining "the core principles of fair play, tolerance, and non-discrimination"—traditional IOC language. However, Bach also said: "Sport has to be politically neutral, but it is not apolitical. Sport is not an isolated island in the sea of society."[17] The modern IOC has updated its rhetoric, adding a dose of nuance.

Today the International Olympic Committee is a well-oiled machine, with slick PR, palatial accommodations in Lausanne, Switzerland, and around $1 billion in reserves. National Olympic Committees now outnumber United Nations member states, 206 to 193.[18] The US government references the Games in code names for covert missions. The Olympics are a force to be reckoned with. Let the reckoning begin.

1

Coubertin and the Revival of the Olympic Games

In the early history of the modern Olympic Games medals were awarded not only for feats of athletic prowess, but also for feats of artistic prowess. A "Pentathlon of the Muses" ran astride the athletic events, consisting of competition in architecture, literature, music, painting, and sculpture. The idea was to capture the spirit of the Greeks, who in the ancient Olympics blended physical with artistic aptitude, all to honor the gods.[1]

So it was that at the 1912 Olympics in Stockholm, the literary jury awarded the gold medal in literature to a pair of writers, Georges Hohrod and M. Eschbach, for their stirring poem, "Ode to Sport." The poets, one hailing from France and the other from Germany, seemed to embrace the universalist ambitions of the Olympics by transcending geopolitical rivalry with amity through sport.[2] On the road to literary gold they beat out a gaggle of other poets, including the roguish Gabriele D'Annunzio, whom many critics viewed as the greatest Italian poet since Dante. D'Annunzio went on to become a proto-fascist who inspired Benito Mussolini.[3] But the author of the poem "Ode to Sport" inspired something else entirely: the Olympic Games themselves. Georges Hohrod and M. Eschbach, it turned out, were a collective pseudonym for Baron Pierre de Coubertin, the founder of the modern Olympics.

Coubertin's award-winning verse, which was submitted to the jury in both French and German, is essentially a love poem to sport. "O Sport, pleasure of the Gods, essence of life," the poem begins. "You appeared suddenly in the midst of the grey clearing which writhes with the drudgery of modern existence, like the radiant messenger of a past age, when mankind still smiled." For the Baron, sport was Beauty, Audacity, Honor, Joy, Fecundity, Progress, and Peace—in short, pretty much everything, a divine nectar of righteousness, rectitude, and benevolent possibility: "O Sport, you are Beauty!" he gushed. "O Sport, you are Justice! The perfect equity for which men strive in vain in their social institutions is your constant companion."

Coubertin concluded his panegyric with sweeping optimism, ascribing to the object of his adoration the ability to heal the wounds of war—even prevent it outright: "You promote happy relations between peoples, bringing them together in their shared devotion to a strength which is controlled, organized, and self-disciplined. From you, the young world-wide learn self-respect, and thus the diversity of national qualities becomes the source of a generous and friendly rivalry."[4] For Coubertin, sport was brimming with use value.

The Baron had previously used the pseudonym Georges Hohrod, both for a novella he published in 1899 and for a 1902 collection titled *Le Roman d'un Rallié*; scholars have therefore speculated that the literary judges in Stockholm knew precisely whom they were picking to win the prize.[5] But those questions aside, the poem distills the idealism stoking Coubertin's passion for the Olympics, as well as the contradictions inherent in that idealism.

Coubertin had wanted the Muse's Pentathlon in the competitive mix from the time he founded the Olympic Games in 1896—or the "Olympian Games," as they were more often called in the early days—but he would have to wait several years until it made its way in.[6] Once the Muse's Pentathlon was installed on the official list of Olympic events at Stockholm, the arts held a firm place on the agenda through 1948.[7] Thereafter arts contests fizzled due to lack of spectator interest; the fans preferred competitive sports.[8] Curiously, in his voluminous posthumous writings, Coubertin never alluded to his gold-medal-winning poem.[9] But the Baron had weightier matters on his mind: how to keep his beloved Olympic creation afloat in a sea of skepticism and indifference.

Reviving the Games

In shaping the modern Olympic Games, Pierre de Coubertin saw something indelibly attractive in the Ancient Games of Olympia, which took place from 776 B.C. through 261 A.D. But resurrecting the Panhellenic athletic festival of antiquity was also attractive to the Western powers during a time when French and German archaeological expeditions were unearthing the wonders of Olympia and Delphi.[10] The Coubertin biographer John J. MacAloon writes that the Baron's invocation of Europe's shared Hellenic tradition was "the thinly spread but strong symbolic glue which held nascent international sport together" until Olympism could gain a foothold in the world's imagination.[11]

In the late nineteenth century, the Baron worked tirelessly to chisel the Games from Greek history and revive them in fresh form, helped immensely by his station in the aristocracy.[12] In 1895 the *New York Times* described Coubertin as "a man who comes from the best conservative stock of France, who is deeply interested in the moral regeneration of his country."[13] While the Baron could talk a good populist game, he was irrefutably a product of aristocratic wealth and values. His youth was filled with family stables, Parisian parks, and fencing lessons. His mother proselytized noblesse oblige.[14] The young Baron was a man of banquets and letterheads, pomp and garnish. He had easy access to Europe's aristocracy. To the end he signed his name with the title "Baron."

Coubertin embodied fin-de-siècle cosmopolitanism, with a dash of nobility and sporty panache. He penned a slew of writings on sport, education, and the revival of the Olympic Games. A peripatetic proselytizer, Coubertin crisscrossed Europe gathering allies and refining his talking points. He visited the United States more than once and, like a latter-day Tocqueville, marveled at the Americans' pluck. Gathering support for his "Olympian Games," he highlighted "the distinctly cosmopolitan character" of his enterprise and the idea that sport was "taking the place of unhealthy amusements and evil pleasures in the lives of young men."[15] He claimed "alcoholism has no more powerful antidote than athletics."[16] And he promised, "I shall burnish a flabby and cramped youth, its body and its character, by sport, its risks and even its excesses."[17] For Coubertin, sport was the vigorous key to redemption. "The muscles are made to do the work of a moral educator," he wrote.[18] The Olympics were a vehicle for producing an international band of the moral elite.

The Baron's brand of macho manifesto matched up well with the worldview of US president Theodore Roosevelt. The two men struck up a friendship, marked by flurries of correspondence. In one letter, Roosevelt praised Coubertin's jaunty approach to social uplift. "[I]n our modern, highly artificial, and on the whole congested, civilization," he wrote, "no boon to the race could be greater than the acquisition by the average man of that bodily habit which you describe—a habit based upon having in youth possessed a thorough knowledge of such sports as those you outline, and then of keeping up a reasonable acquaintance with them in later years."[19] The Baron in turn viewed Roosevelt as a kindred spirit, "a firm partisan, an invaluable friend to our cause."[20] Upon Roosevelt's death, Coubertin wrote a personal obituary in which he called the former president "a great man" and "devotee of athletics up to the end of his virile existence," whose tombstone's epitaph should share the motto of the Olympic Institute in Lausanne: "Mens fervida in corpore lacertoso" ("an ardent mind in a trained body").[21] The two men shared a deep affinity for "muscular Christianity" and an inclination to see the marriage of sport, machismo, patriotism, and democracy as a formula for strength.[22]

To capture the spirit infusing his project, Coubertin coined the term "Olympism." For him this meant "an aristocracy, an elite," although "an aristocracy whose origin is completely egalitarian," since it is based on sporting prowess and work ethic.[23] "Olympism," he wrote, "is a state of mind that derives from a twofold doctrine: that of effort, and that of eurythmy."[24] Olympism, "the cult of effort," and "the cult of eurythmy" formed a mystic triumvirate that reverberated through Coubertin's writing.[25] Again drawing from ancient Greece, he dubbed eurythmy a "divine harness," a harmonious balance of athletics and art that was prevalent in ancient times but was now more important than ever in "our nervous age." To him, eurythmy meant a world in "proper proportion," with people living a "eurythmy of life" that blended bonhomie, bonheur, art, and Olympic aesthetics into a potent concoction of possibility.[26]

Theodore Roosevelt recognized the religious impulse in the Baron's project: "I think that you preach just the right form of the gospel of physical development."[27] Like the Greeks, who threaded religion through the ancient Games, Coubertin saw Olympism as "a philosophico-religious doctrine," a non-denominational festival of culture and sport designed to spur reverence and purity.[28] Coubertin was prone to write about the Games as a "sacred enclosure" where athletes served a vital role. The Olympics were a "sanctuary reserved for the consecrated, purified athlete only, the athlete admitted to the main competitions and who became, in this way, a sort of priest, an officiating priest in the religion of the muscles." For Coubertin, the modern Games were "a sort of moral Altis, a sacred Fortress where the competitors in the manly sports par excellence are gathered to pit their strength against each other." The goal of all this was nothing less than "to defend man and to achieve self-mastery, to master danger, the elements, the animal, life."[29]

A patina of religiosity shimmered through the Baron's writings. "Sport to me was a religion, with church, dogmas, services and so on, but especially a religious feeling," wrote Coubertin.[30] To heighten that "feeling," he doggedly installed layer upon layer of Olympic ceremony, elaborate spectacles designed to conjure the "athletic religious concept, the *religio athletae*." In a 1935 speech he expanded on the idea: "The primary, fundamental characteristic of ancient Olympism, and of modern Olympism as well, is that it is a *religion*. By chiseling his body through exercise as a sculptor does a statue, the ancient athlete 'honored the gods.' In doing likewise, the modern athlete honors his country, his race, and his flag."[31] Coubertin and other true believers thought they could add religious fervor to flag-waving nationalism and unproblematically stir them into a potent brew of Olympism.

Internal Contradiction

Coubertin was renowned for his bounteous handlebar mustache—a hirsute gift that kept on giving. He was also famous for his belief that sport could scythe a path away from war and toward peace. "To celebrate the Olympic Games is to appeal to history," Coubertin proclaimed. In turn, history "is the only genuine foundation for a genuine peace."[32] Yet the Baron's views on the role of sport in matters of war and peace were in perpetual tension.

Coubertin was an eccentric Anglophile who saw in the sporting culture of Thomas Arnold's Rugby School the magic formula for Britain's imperial dominance. While in his view the French were mired in physical inertia, softening up like idle dandies, Britons in the mold of Rugby School were mixing rigorous discipline with manly self-display. This led him to ponder "how well it would be for France were we to introduce into our school system some of that physical vitality, some of that animal spirit, from which our neighbors have derived such incontestable benefits."[33] The Baron came to believe that within the British schooling system and its athletic programs lay the means to reinvigorate the French nation after the humiliation of the 1870–71 Franco-Prussian War. Sport, as he put it, was "a marvelous instrument for 'virilization'."[34]

France's brutal defeat had an enormous impact on the young Coubertin. According to the Olympic scholar Jeffrey Segrave:

> Coubertin became obsessed with the idea of creating a new French elite, a new brand of French Tories shaped by English sport and compatible with the Republic. This new elite was a sort of revamped French gentry federated by sports, which would allow France to once again assume leadership status among European nations and, indeed, the world at large in the commercial, military, and colonial realms.[35]

The Baron's muscular nationalism worked in productive tension with his peace-loving internationalism. On one hand, sport was the supreme "peacemaker," a cure that could help quell geopolitical tensions. He believed sport could bring people together to contemplate each other's histories, create meaningful understanding, and surmount social and cultural barriers, making it "a potent, if indirect, factor in securing world peace."[36] Coubertin asserted that "manly sports are good for everyone and under all circumstances,"[37] yet he recognized that there were limits to idealism. "To ask the peoples of the world to love one another," he wrote, "is merely a form of childishness."[38] While athletic activity "will not make angels of brutes," they could, he believed, "temper that brutality, giving the individual a bit of self-control."[39]

But sometimes the Baron went the other direction. He argued that sport was "an indirect preparation for war," and that the skill sets necessary for sport—"indifference towards one's own well being, courage, readiness for the unforeseen"—translated seamlessly to warfare. "The young sportsman is certainly better prepared for war than his untrained brothers," he asserted.[40] A mere year before the outbreak of World War I, Coubertin, in a paroxysm of bellicose prescience, wrote, "People will learn a great lesson from the athlete: hatred without battle is not worthy of man, and insult without blows is utterly unbecoming."[41]

The modern Olympics have always walked a tightrope between chauvinism and internationalism. When Orwell wrote that "international sporting contests lead to orgies of hatred" he had the Olympics in mind. When it comes to international sports mega-events, he argued, "there cannot be much doubt that the whole thing is bound up with the rise of nationalism—that is, with the lunatic modern habit of identifying oneself with large power units and seeing everything in terms of competitive prestige."[42] Coubertin aimed to undercut chauvinism by spreading the Olympic spirit, whereby "applause is vouchsafed solely in proportion to the worth of the feat accomplished, and regardless of any national preference ... all exclusively national sentiments must then be suspended and, so to speak 'sent on temporary holiday'."[43] While Orwell and his intellectual descendants would view this as hooey, Coubertin and his ilk embedded this idea in the high-minded Olympic Charter, the constitution of the Olympic movement. Still the tension between chauvinism and internationalism has persisted through all the Olympiads. It continues to trouble the Games today.

Another set of contradictions marks Coubertin's life and work. While some Olympic historians argue he championed a "moderate political progressivism" based on inclusion and tolerance, many of his views on gender, race, and class were mired in the prejudices of the period.[44] The Olympic Games were supposedly for everyone, but from the outset, numerous athletes were excluded.

Coubertin was a man of many talents, but penning feminist theory was not among them. "The Olympic Games must be reserved for men," he frequently proclaimed. To the Baron, including women's competitions was "impractical, uninteresting, ungainly, and, I do not hesitate to add, improper."[45] The very thought of it induced an "unseemly spectacle" in the mind.[46] "Woman's glory," he said, "rightfully came through the number and quality of children she produced, and that where sports were concerned, her greatest accomplishment was to encourage her sons to excel rather than to seek records for herself."[47] He argued for "the solemn and periodic exaltation of male athleticism ... with the applause of women as a reward."[48] When it came to the Olympics, the role of women "should be above all to crown the victors, as was the case in the ancient tournaments."[49]

These opinions did not fade with time. Even in 1934—three years before he succumbed to a heart attack at the age of 74—the Baron declared, "I continue to think that association with women's athleticism is bad...and that such athleticism should be excluded from the Olympic programme."[50] In 1935 Coubertin was still writing that the vaunted "young adult male" was "the person in whose honor the Olympic Games must be celebrated and their rhythm organized and maintained, because it is on him that the near future depends, as well as the harmonious passage from the past to the future."[51] Even after so many years and the slowly progressing climate of society at large, his views on women and sport had not evolved.

Some Olympic scholars attribute Coubertin's unwavering insistence on the exclusion of women to "nineteenth century thinking," and thus find it understandable.[52] But there were many at the time who were pressing vigorously for women's participation in the Games. If Coubertin's views on women don't make him a card-carrying troglodyte, at the least they are the mark of a man who lacked a moral compass set to true equality.

On matters of race, Coubertin was prone to a Eurocentric brand of racism only slightly relieved by a few liberal impulses. The Baron didn't hesitate to differentiate between "savages" and the "civilized"; sport, he believed, was a prime vehicle to close the gap between the two. As he put it: "Sports means movement, and the influence of movement on bodies is something that has been evident from time immemorial. Strength and agility have been deeply appreciated among savage and civilized peoples alike. Both are achieved through exercise and practice: happy balance in the moral order."[53]

Coubertin's "moral order" made space for the notion that a "superior race" could enjoy "certain privileges," and for the idea of "the natural indolence of the Oriental."[54] His views on the subject sound shocking today. "The theory proposing that all human races have equal rights leads to a line of policy which hinders any progress in the colonies," he wrote; "the superior race is fully entitled to deny the lower race certain privileges of civilized life"—for their own good, of course.[55]

Nevertheless, Coubertin pressed for the admittance of African countries to the Olympic Games in his address to the twenty-second IOC Session in Rome in 1923. But to this liberal push for inclusion he added a hefty dose of colonialism and racist stereotyping:

> And perhaps it may appear premature to introduce the principal of sports competitions into a continent that is behind the times and among peoples still without elementary culture— and particularly presumptuous to expect this expansion to lead to a speeding up of the march of civilization in these countries. Let us think, however, for a moment, of what is troubling the African soul. Untapped forces—individual laziness and a sort of collective need for action—a thousand resentments, and a thousand jealousies of the white man and yet, at the same time, the wish to imitate him and thus share his privileges – the conflict between wishing to submit to discipline and to escape

from it—and, in the midst of an innocent gentleness that is not without its charm, the sudden outburst of ancestral violence … these are just some features of these races to which the younger generation, which has in fact derived great benefit from sport, is turning its attention.[56]

The Baron proceeded to speculate that sport might help Africa "calm down," since it "helps create order and clarify thought." He concluded on an upbeat note: "Let us not hesitate therefore to help Africa join in" the Olympic Movement.[57]

Coubertin sometimes dogwhistled a dim awareness of the prejudices that others held, though certainly not himself. "Anglo-Saxons have some trouble in getting used to the idea that other nations can devote themselves to athleticism, and that successfully," he wrote. "I can understand this, and the feeling is certainly excusable." But he knew that the progressive possibilities of sport outweighed other considerations: "It does not follow that young men of other races, with blood and muscles like their own, should not be worthy of walking in their footsteps."[58]

Many of the Baron's views on race were socially acceptable in the mainstream of his time, but what really got him into trouble were his views on class and amateurism. The Olympic historian John Lucas once characterized the Baron as having an "ever-active mind" that "was grasshopper-like, never lingering for more than a few moments on any one subject."[59] But like it or not, Coubertin was forced to linger on the persistently spiky issue of amateurism.

Coubertin believed reserving the Olympics for amateur athletes was vital to the Games' development. He wrote, "Convinced as I am that amateurism is one of the first conditions of the progress and prosperity of sport, I have never ceased to work for it." He added, "When in 1894 I proposed to revive the Olympian Games, it was with the idea that they would also be reserved to amateurs alone."[60] His problems began when he imported the definition of amateurism that was rampant in class-bound nineteenth-century Britain. Those who performed manual labor for pay, whether tied to sports or not, were considered professionals and were thus sidelined from participation. This meant that if someone did not have an independent source of income outside of actual work—in other words, if they were not independently wealthy—they'd be excluded from the amateur category.[61] Waged workers were out of luck. The Amateur Athletic Club in England took no chances, passing a rule known as "the mechanics clause," which denied amateur status to anyone "who is by trade or employment, a mechanic, artisan, or labourer."[62] As Tony Collins notes in *Sport in Capitalist Society*, amateurism, as a crystalline reflection of British upper- and middle-class values, was deployed as "an ideology of control and exclusion, dressed up as moral imperative for sport."[63] The amateur code allowed the upper and middle classes to regulate working people behind a scrim of rhetorical morality.

The Baron was not keen to exclude people—at least not Anglo-Saxon males—from his Olympics. He preferred a fluffy, non-controversial definition of amateur athletics: "perfect disinterestedness" mixed with "the sentiment of honor."[64] But to get the five-ring engine revving, he had to compromise on the amateur issue, bending toward the British definition, at least in the early days of the Games. His reasoning became excruciatingly conciliatory, reaching such piano-wire tension that it threatened to snap altogether: "Our reaction must be based on adopting a more intelligent, broader, and certainly narrower, definition of an amateur," he wrote in 1901, contradicting himself within a single sentence.[65]

Within a few years the strict British definition of amateurism had to give, in large part because of the pressure and popularity of professional soccer in England.[66] Working-class athletes from the United States also played a pivotal role. In advance of the 1908 Games in London, the *New York Times* pointed out the class bias of Olympic amateurism in discussing the "American oarsmen" who "have been discriminated against" by the Amateur Rowing Association of Great Britain's definition of amateurism. "No artisan, laborer, or mechanic or man who does manual work for a living may compete," the newspaper reported, constituting "a direct slap at American amateurs, most of whom are of the working class."[67]

Writing in 1919, the Baron belatedly declared solidarity with that sentiment, maintaining that he'd wanted workers to be involved all along:

> Formerly the practice of sport was the occasional pastime of rich and idle youth. I have labored for thirty years to make it the habitual pleasure of the lower middle classes. It is now necessary for this pleasure to enter the lives of the adolescent proletariat. It is necessary because this pleasure is the least costly, the most egalitarian, the most anti-alcoholic, and the most productive of contained and controlled energy. All forms of sport for everyone; that is no doubt a formula which is going to be criticised as madly utopian. I do not care.[68]

Coubertin argued that his Games needed to be opened up to the working class "if we do not want civilisation to blow up like a boiler without a valve."[69] Coubertin's gestures toward working-class inclusion should not be confused with radical tendencies. Rather they were a mode of social control, a way to tamp down class conflict and to enforce the status quo. He was a staunch French Republican; to him, socialism was a scourge. "Let us not fall into the utopia of complete communism," he once wrote.[70] As the Olympic historian John Hoberman notes, Coubertin was able to "integrate conservative class interests into a modern ideology of sport" that has demonstrated extraordinary longevity.[71]

Coubertin was not dogmatic when it came to amateurism. He detested "false amateurs who reap fat rewards" for their athletic exploits,[72] but he was also critical of the "rusty" definition of amateurism he inherited from the British, viewing it as "a means of social defense, of class preoccupation."[73] Coubertin wanted a definition of "amateur" that was fair and reasonable. But his push for a more nuanced definition was denied by the IOC Executive Committee in 1922 when it defined an amateur as "an athlete who does not gain any material benefit of his participation in competitions" and a professional as "an athlete who directly/indirectly gains benefit by his personal participation in sports."[74] As we shall see, future IOC presidents were continually forced to deal with the amateurism imbroglio. Avery Brundage, the IOC president from 1952 to 1972, was gripped with an almost religious fervor over the issue; professional athletes were the bane of his presidency. In contrast, Juan Antonio Samaranch, the IOC president from 1980 to 2001, the era of neoliberal capitalism, made professional athletes more than welcome.[75]

Coubertin was a pragmatist who formed strategic alliances to keep his beloved Games moving forward, even if it meant dancing with political devils (he praised both Mussolini and Hitler, host of the 1936 Berlin Games).[76] But the Games always came first, and the Baron strove to imbue them with symbolic ritual, pomp, and pageantry. He added classical-style hymns, banners, and laurel leaves to the Olympic aesthetic. He created the iconic five-ring Olympic symbol in 1913, with the rings symbolic of the five continents and the colors of the rings representing hues found on flags around the world. Coubertin also designed the flag, with his five-ring icon in the center, first unveiling it at the 1914 Olympic World Congress in Paris to celebrate the twentieth anniversary of the IOC. The flag made its Olympic premiere at the 1920 Antwerp Games, where it featured the now-familiar motto "Citius, Altius, Fortius" (Faster, Higher, Stronger).[77] Coubertin moved the IOC headquarters from Paris to neutral territory—Lausanne, Switzerland—in 1915, where it remains today.[78] And he chose effective teammates like Demetrios Vikelas, the affable Greek who eventually became the first president of the IOC. Thanks to the Baron's energy, stamina, talent, and panache, the Games were on.

Party Like It's 1896

In 1894, Coubertin gathered a throng of sports aficionados for an international congress in Paris to discuss the vexing question of amateurism in athletics. In his initial appeal, he did not explicitly mention his plan to revive the Olympic Games, for fear of alienating potential participants.[79] But by the time he issued a preliminary agenda, he tacked on as the eighth and final item "the possibility of restoring the Olympic Games … under what circumstances could they be restored?"[80] By the time the actual congress rolled around, this single bullet point was expanded into three agenda items pertaining to the Games' "advantages from the athletic, moral and international points of view," the selection of specific sports for inclusion at the Games, and the "nomination of an International Committee responsible for preparing their re-establishment."[81]

Some 2,000 witnesses to the proceedings packed the Sorbonne's amphitheater, including seventy-nine official delegates from forty-nine athletic societies based in twelve countries. Luminaries in attendance included representatives of the Paris Polo Club, the French Equestrian Society, and the Society for the Encouragement of Fencing. Numerous royals accepted the invitation: the king of Belgium, the prince of Wales, Grand Duke Vladimir of Russia, Sweden's royal prince, the crown prince of Greece, and more.[82] Early on, the congress was divided into two committees, one that would examine amateurism, and the other, Olympism.[83] Journalists from prominent newspapers—*Le Figaro*, *The Times of London*, the *New York Times*, the *National-Zeitung*—were on hand to cover the action.[84] The stage was set.

The Baron wasn't about to squander the opportunity. He packed the inner circle with dignitaries sympathetic to his Olympic dream. He handpicked an "International Committee for the Olympic Games"—the first iteration of the IOC—that was swiftly ratified by the congress. From the beginning, the IOC carried the whiff of aristocracy, featuring two counts, a lord, and of course the Baron. Professors, generals, and other social and political elites of the day filled out the IOC's roster, even though a number of them hadn't even attended the Paris congress. Coubertin envisioned the original IOC as "three concentric circles." One comprised "a small nucleus of active and convinced members." The second circle was "a nursery of members of good will who were capable of being educated." Lastly, there was "a façade of more or less useful men whose presence satisfied national pretensions while giving some prestige to the group."[85] To charges that the group was elitist and non-democratic, Coubertin replied: "We are not elected. We are self-recruiting, and our terms of office are unlimited. Is there anything else that could irritate the public more?" Was he troubled by such allegations? "We are not in the least concerned about it," he assured a gathering in London in 1908.[86]

Coubertin's goal was to arrange for the inaugural Olympic Games to take place in 1900 in Paris. But the delegates at the Sorbonne decided unanimously to hold the first modern Olympics in Athens only two years after the congress, in 1896.[87] With the Greeks slated to host, Demetrios Vikelas was chosen as IOC president, while Coubertin assumed the post of general secretary.

Vikelas was a University of London–trained author who married a wealthy Greek heiress and enjoyed connections in high places. With only two years to prepare for the first modern Olympics, he led a mad scramble to raise funds to stage the event. But his zeal was tempered by Greek prime minister Charilaos Tricoupis, who didn't believe in anteing up the government's scarce funds for the effort (Coubertin later claimed that Tricoupis "did not believe in the success of the Games").[88] In stark contrast to the Olympics of today, the 1896 Games would have to be financed outside the fiscal system of the national government. Fortunately for the organizers, King George and Crown Prince Constantine of Greece showed considerable enthusiasm for rallying private donors. While the Baron stayed behind in Paris, occupying himself with tasks such as securing sculptor Jules Chaplain to design the Olympic medals, Vikelas scurried around Athens making arrangements, brokering deals, and promising an influx of tourists. He reached out to the foreign press through a stream of telegrams hyping the Games.[89]

To quell the panic over the dearth of funds, Coubertin publicly lowballed the cost of the Olympics, inaugurating a trend that still thrives today. He assured everyone that the Games could be staged for a mere 200,000 drachmas—a figure that the Olympic historian David Young dubbed "ridiculously low," given that the stadium refurbishment alone cost three times that much.[90] Were it not for George Averoff, a wealthy Greek businessman who agreed to finance the stadium building in Athens, the Games might not have happened. (For his munificence Averoff was rewarded with a sizable statue in his likeness that graced the stadium entrance.) The 1896 Olympics also enjoyed the generous support of trade unions and working people across Athens—which was ironic since they would be ineligible to participate in the Games, thanks to the "mechanics clause."[91] Because of the groundswell of local support, the Games were on.

The opening ceremony of 1896 Olympics was said to be the largest assemblage of people for peaceful purposes since antiquity, with 50,000 packed into the stadium and another 20,000 lounging on the hillside above. Young describes the Games as "the grandest sporting event to that point in the history of earth."[92] These first modern Olympics featured forty-three events in nine sports, with thirteen countries sending 311 participants. Nearly three of every four competitors hailed from Greece.[93] The United States sent the largest contingent of foreign athletes, most of them college students from the Eastern seaboard. They fared brilliantly, scooping up a hefty satchel of medals, and punctuated their efforts with rah-rah college-boy cheers that left the assembled Greeks gobsmacked. Blending ignorance with toxic stereotyping, one Athens newspaper explained the Americans' success by claiming they "joined the inherited athletic training of the Anglo-Saxon to the wild impetuosity of the redskin."[94] After competing, Olympic athletes mingled with everyday citizens, making them accessible in ways unthinkable today.[95]

Looking back on the 1896 Olympics, scholars have come to diverse conclusions, from deeming them "a huge success"[96] to the assessment that the Games "are best remembered for the fact that they took place."[97] The Olympics earned mixed reviews in the US press, despite the fact that American athletes shined. One observer deemed the opening of the Games in Athens to be "a delight to the eye and an impressive appeal to the imagination." Pointing to the intrinsic values of the revived sporting competition, the person wrote that the sport festival "has become a good thing of itself, and with all other worthy influences is making for a balanced culture and perfected manhood."[98] Another commentator complained that the event was hardly international, contending that the IOC "failed to attract foreign competitors [and] also failed to attract foreign spectators." Despite Vikelas's rosy predictions, the *New York Times* reported that thanks to a "preposterous" hike in hotel room costs, many tourists who had planned on visiting Athens "abstained from going ... intentionally delaying their visit to Athens till after the termination of the games."[99]

But the Greeks were thrilled with the outcome. At the conclusion of the Games, they were keen to host all future Olympics. At a royal banquet for the athletes and distinguished foreign guests, King George offered a bold toast:

Greece, who has been the mother and nurse of the Olympic Games in ancient times and who had undertaken to celebrate them once more today, can now hope, as their success has gone beyond all expectations, that the foreigners, who have honoured her with their presence, will remember Athens as the peaceful meeting place of all nations, as the tranquil and permanent seat of the Olympic Games.[100]

According to the Games' official report, the king's suggestion elicited "an outburst of hurrahs. The enthusiasm was indiscribable [*sic*]." The idea was ratified by members of the US Olympic team, who wrote an open letter to Crown Prince Constantine stating that "these games should never be removed from their native soil."[101]

Although tactfully taciturn at the time, Coubertin chafed at King George's power move and the Americans' enthusiasm for it. He unsheathed his pen to reassert his vision for the sports festival—to have it circumnavigate the globe to spread the Olympic gospel. Harking back to promises made at the 1894 Paris congress, he firmly insisted, "It was there agreed that every country should celebrate the Olympic games in turn."[102] And the Baron pulled a power move of his own, informing the Greeks that they were welcome to hold their own athletic festivals as long as they didn't use the phrase "Olympic Games." That Greek term densely embedded in Greek history apparently belonged to him.[103]

In the wake of the 1896 Games, Vikelas stepped down as the head of the IOC, and Coubertin ascended from general secretary to president. He held this position until 1925, when at the age of 62 he retired. His extended tenure set the tone for future presidents to remain at the helm of the IOC for long periods of time. To date, the IOC has had just nine presidents in its 120-year history.

Unfairness at the Fair

At the turn of the century the Olympics did not yet enjoy the cachet they have today, so the 1900 Games in Paris and the 1904 Games in St. Louis had to affix themselves to the enormous cosmopolitan institutions of the day—World's Fairs. The early modern Olympics were mere sideshows to the World's Fairs, not the main event on the world stage that we see today.

Early on it was clear that Paris would present challenges to the IOC. Coubertin's French compatriots were anything but eager to host the Games. The Union des Sociétés Françaises de Sports Athlétiques resisted Coubertin's proposal even though the Baron was the general secretary of the group. After considerable finagling, Coubertin was forced to fasten his beloved Games onto the Exposition Universelle in order to get them staged at all. Fair organizers dreaded including the Olympics, partly because French politicians and the professoriat deemed sports a lowbrow pursuit. The Baron responded by calling the Exposition "a vulgar glorified fair: exactly the opposite of what we wanted the Olympic Games to be."[104] When French sport officials performed a volte-face and decided to manage the Games themselves, Coubertin and the IOC found themselves on the outside looking in. As at Athens, local organizers marginalized Coubertin, sometimes even snubbing him. This left a bitter taste in the Baron's mouth.[105]

Attaching the Olympics to the World's Fair meant significant trade-offs. For starters, competition stretched over the many months that the Fair took place—in the case of Paris, some 167 days spanning July through October. Organizers insisted on referring to the sports events as the "Competitions of the Exhibition" rather than the "Olympics Games," a decision that irked Coubertin; he called it "a poor and clumsy title we had to accept for the time being for want of something more elegant and appropriate."[106] Compounding Coubertin's chagrin, sporting competitions were scattered amid an array of unrelated events, leading to confusion among spectators as to what was an Olympic event and what wasn't. Even athletes weren't sure. Some returned home uncertain of whether they had even participated in the Olympics. In 1900, the Luxembourg-born French runner Michel Théato triumphed in the marathon. Yet he only figured out he was an Olympic champion some twelve years later, when Olympic statisticians waded through the mess to sync up their records, deciding which of the events were officially Olympic and which were just part of the Fair.[107]

The Paris Games of 1900 did offer a few bright spots. With Coubertin marginalized, these Olympics were the first in which women were invited to participate, with around twenty women traveling to France to compete in sports like tennis and golf. Charlotte Cooper of Great Britain was the first woman to become an Olympic champion, winning gold in tennis. Cooper, who had already won three Wimbledon tennis tournaments and would go on to win two more, defeated Hélène Prévost of France in straight sets, 6–4, 6–2. Cooper also teamed up with fellow Briton Reginald Doherty to earn the gold medal in mixed doubles, defeating Prévost who joined forces with Harold Mahoney of Ireland. Margaret Abbott became the first woman from the United States to win gold. She beat out nine other women competing in the nine-hole golf tournament. Abbott, a Chicago socialite who had traveled to Paris in 1899 to study art, accompanied by her mother, the novelist and editor Mary Ives Abbott, chalked up her victory in part to the other competitors' sartorial standards, commenting that "all the French girls … turned up to play in high heels and tight skirts." The Games were so disorganized that the twenty-two-year-old golf champion had no idea that the tournament she won was part of the Olympics. She died without knowing she was an Olympic victor.

The uptick in women's involvement was part of a larger trend: six times as many athletes participated in Paris as at

Athens, coming from twenty-six countries and engaging in twenty-four sports. Yet participation was hampered by the prohibitive cost of travel, which gave a leg up to wealthier countries whose national sport committees could defray travel and living expenses. Such unequal participation is bricked into the Olympics to this day.[108]

Coubertin saw the Games' domination by the Universal Exhibition as a disaster. He resolved that the IOC should never again allow the Olympics to get hijacked by a World's Fair, "where their philosophical value vanishes into thin air and their education merit becomes nil." After the 1900 Games, Coubertin decided that Olympism would have to assert its independence and "no longer be reduced to the role of humiliated vassal to which it had been subjected in Paris."[109]

But humiliation was precisely what the Olympics would experience at the 1904 Games in St. Louis, where matters went from bad to worse, despite the backing of the popular US president Theodore Roosevelt. Roosevelt was named honorary president of the 1904 Olympics and even agreed to appear at the Games in person, an apt endorsement from a man the *New York Times* credited with catalyzing "a Nation of brawn and muscle."[110] Despite Roosevelt's imprimatur, the Baron sensed disaster. He reported experiencing "a sort of presentiment that the Olympiad would match the mediocrity of the town." His assessment of St. Louis was blunt: "There was no beauty, no originality." Attaching the Games to the World's Fair only brought him feelings of "repugnance." He didn't even make the voyage to St. Louis.[111]

Neither did many athletes from Europe, leaving the field open for American and Canadian domination—of the 617 competitors who paid the two-dollar entrance fee plus fifty cents per event, 525 were from the United States and forty-one were from Canada. Meanwhile, women's participation declined, with only eight females competing. The World's Fair (officially the Louisiana Purchase Exposition) was once again spread across months, from May through November.[112] The official Olympics lasted a week spanning August and September, but organizers created confusion by referring to all athletic competitions in the wider exhibition as "Olympic events." As one participant from Milwaukee recalled: "The Olympics didn't amount to much then. They were only a little tiny part of the big show in St. Louis. There was not much of an international flavor to the Games. It was largely a meet between American athletic clubs. I ran for the Milwaukee A. C. [Amateur Club] and I never gave any real thought to the idea that I was representing the United States of America."[113]

Worse yet, the St. Louis Olympics were tarnished by the inclusion of the Anthropology Days, a sequence of athletic events in mid-August that allowed social scientists and sport bigwigs to test racist hypotheses. The Anthropology Days were not part of the official Olympic program, but World's Fair organizers often called them the "Special Olympics" and billed them as "the first athletic meeting held anywhere, in which savages were exclusive participants."[114]

The Anthropology Days pitted ethnic and racial groups against one another in events like track and field to see which group, supposedly, was the most athletically gifted. Anthropology Days organizers aimed to whet spectators' appetites for the official Games that would follow, but another motive was to contrast what they called "savages" to the highly trained athletes from the United States and Europe. To do this, they rigged the system to ensure that the savages could be "scientifically proven" to be inferior. Anthropologist Nancy Parezo sums up the affair as "a comedy in bad science" in the service of social Darwinism.[115]

The Anthropology Days were in part inspired by the fledgling field of social science, and it is in that historical context that they are best understood. Academics sought methodological rigor in order to put the "science" in "social science." One form of data that found prominence was anthropometry, whereby researchers used biometric measurements to link race and body type to labels like "natural athlete" and "born criminal." Anthropologists assumed that race existed as a stable category, and that it correlated with specific physical, psychological, and cultural characteristics. Their supposedly objective measures were shaped by politics and used to justify colonialism and racist subjugation.

The organizers of the Anthropology Days at St. Louis were two World's Fair officials, William J. McGee and James E. Sullivan. McGee was an anthropologist and proselytizer of anthropometry. Sullivan headed the Department of Physical Culture for the Exposition. He was a former athlete and prolific writer who penned a glorified account of the proceedings for Spalding's Official Athletic Almanac for 1905 called "Anthropology Days at the Stadium."

Sullivan initially proposed a "Special Olympics" in order to dispel any popular notions that non-whites were "natural athletes" who could compete at the same level as Caucasians. The "utter lack of athletic ability on the part of the savages," as Sullivan put it, would prove that Western athletes were the best in the world.[116] Sullivan and McGee pulled their pool of participants from the nearly 3,000 indigenous people who traveled to St. Louis from around the world to take part in the Fair. A sizable number of them were enticed, cajoled, or bullied into playing along with Anthropology Days.[117] Since the exposition was in the United States, Native groups from the US and Canada predominated, including Arapahos, Chippewas, Kickapoos, Kiowas, Navajos, Nez Perce, Pawnees, Sioux, Wichitas, and First Nations people from Vancouver Island. Even the famous Apache Geronimo was there. Also on hand were indigenous people from the Philippines, recently conquered by the United States in the Spanish-American War: the Bagobos, Igorots, Moros, Negritos, and Visayans. Other indigenous groups included African Pygmies, Argentine Patagonians, and Japanese Ainus.[118]

At the core of McGee's belief system sat the assumption that indigenous peoples and Caucasians were subject to scientific laws governing their physical capabilities. In economic terms, the "Special Olympics" were meant to demonstrate anthropology's use value while conjuring exchange value for his stockpile of anthropological artifacts, which he aimed to sell to procure funding for future research. He also sought to validate his theory that environment determined physical prowess.

Sullivan believed that American athletes and their training methods were unparalleled. As Parezo notes, he "absolutely believed that Caucasians were the best natural as well as the best-trained athletes in the world. Whites (especially those of Northern European heritage) were the superior race and America, because of its racial heritage, was a peerless culture, which would only progress further if it adopted his programs."[119] Both McGee and Sullivan arrived in St. Louis with fully formed conclusions in search of data that would "prove" they were right. If they came across findings in friction with their beliefs, they simply explained them away.[120]

McGee and Sullivan's efforts were thwarted in part by Native Americans like the Ojibwe and Osage, who refused to submit to anthropometric measuring. Others, like the Cocopas, Moros, and Visayans, refused to be photographed. Negritos refused to climb trees on demand or to have their feet measured. Unlike other athletic competitors at the World's Fair, Anthropology Days participants were not offered cash prizes, so many indigenous people just said no. Others declined the invitation because they did not understand the rules for these totally foreign sports. Organizers tried to persuade potential participants by bringing them to witness Olympic trials so they could learn the rules by watching athletes in action. After watching swimming trials, there were no takers, aside from the Samal Moros. It didn't help that the rules were never explicitly explained—organizers opted not to hop the language hurdles. Further, indigenous athletes were not allowed to practice. The game was rigged; some Native Americans, like the Arapahos and Wichitas, departed en masse instead of playing along with the racial experiment.[121]

McGee and Sullivan were undeterred—they had theories to prove. Heats for running events were arranged, one for each individual group. As Sullivan reported, there were heats for "Africans, Moros (Philippines), Patagonians, and the Ainu (Japanese), Cocopa (Mexican), and Sioux Indian tribes."[122] A St. Louis University professor explained the rules in English and without interpreters. The goal was to collect the fastest person from each group and place each one in the final. Sullivan was to compare their times with those of his prized athletes from the United States and Northern Europe. But cultural differences wrecked the master plan. Instead of plunging through the finish-line ribbon, indigenous runners would wait for their colleagues or duck under the tape. As Parezo notes, "Cooperation was more important than 'victory'... waiting for friends was a sign of graciousness and a symbol of respect in many cultures."[123] To Sullivan, these breaches of the rules were unforgiveable; rule-breakers were unceremoniously disqualified.

Even by the standards of the day, many found the Anthropology Days absurd and shameful. Stephen Simms, of the Field Museum in Chicago, was taken aback by the charade of racism masquerading as scientific method.[124] McGee himself initially downplayed the results of Anthropology Days over concerns that not enough data were obtained. Such quibbles did not faze Sullivan, who made capacious generalizations about the "utter lack of athletic ability on the part of the savages."[125] He compared indigenous participants to Olympic medal-winners like track star Ray Ewry and pronounced that the comparison "proves conclusively that the savage is not the natural athlete we have been led to believe."[126]

Parezo demonstrates how such conclusions carried wide-ranging ramifications: "To Sullivan the Anthropology Days proved that his opinions about sports as a medium for shaping the moral and cognitive development of young people were correct but that Native peoples were intellectually, socially, cognitively, and morally inferior by nature." As such, "they were not as good prospects for assimilation as European immigrants."[127] McGee apparently agreed. In his final report on Anthropology Days he asserted "the lesson" of their Special Olympics was that "primitive men are far inferior to modern Caucasians in both physical and mental development."[128] Sullivan concurred: "The whole meeting proves conclusively that the savage has been a very much overrated man from an athletic point of view."[129]

Although Sullivan deemed his "Special Olympics" a "brilliant success," Coubertin did not agree. He called Anthropology Days "a mistake," "inhuman," and "flawed"[130] and feared that they marked the "beginnings of exotic athleticism" that were "hardly flattering."[131] Although the Anthropology Days were "the only original feature offered by the program," they were "a particularly embarrassing one."[132] Other commentators agreed. Writing more than a quarter-century later, Hugh Harlan declared that featuring athletes "from various backwards nations" created "confusion and mis-direction," a "sad spectacle" that meant the "St. Louis games could not be anything except a failure as far as an international sport festival is concerned."[133]

Some of the racialist assumptions that underpinned the Anthropology Days arguably persist today. Historian Mark Dyreson writes, "The contemplation of racial and national difference remains a central feature of Olympic sport in the twenty-first century. Rather than discrediting scientific and popular measurements of the 'physical value' of human populations, Anthropology Days embedded that practice in modern discourse."[134] The episode also helps us better understand modern-day indigenous resistance to the Olympics, a theme I will take up later.

Despite the religious rhetoric that pervades Coubertin's writings, Sigmund Loland asserts, "we can characterize Olympism as a secular, vitalistic 'humanism of the muscles'."[135] At the 1904 Games in St. Louis "humanism" was scarce. But the Olympics could also provide a platform for athletes to challenge colonialism, if through the lever of nationalism. That is what happened at the 1906 intercalary Games in Athens.

Olympian Dissent in 1906

After the debacle in St. Louis, the Olympics verged on imminent fizzle. Coubertin's control of the Olympics was slipping, and it wasn't entirely clear who was running the show.

According to the Baron's original vision, the Games would rotate through the major cities of the world, touching down every four years in a new location to spread the Olympic gospel. But Greek boosters and their German allies had other plans, which they hatched at the 1901 IOC meeting in Paris. They proposed holding the Olympics every two years, alternating between Athens and "other large cities of the civilized countries."[136] This would ensure that the Olympics landed in the Greek capital every four years, beginning in 1906.

Coubertin's grip on the Games was far from ironclad. Many Olympics boosters in Greece saw him as a trespasser stealing their historical birthright. The American James Sullivan undermined his authority at every opportunity. The IOC was wracked with internal turbulence as members threatened to defect.[137] Under these circumstances, Coubertin grudgingly pledged the IOC's support for the 1906 Athens Olympics, which eventually became known as the "intercalary" Games.[138] However, the Baron refused to attend the 1906 Games, and later did everything he could to undercut their historical importance, stopping just short of plugging his ears with his index fingers and ululating, la-la-la-la-la, whenever someone broached the topic.[139]

The 1906 Games opened with a grand procession of the aristocracy. More than 60,000 raucous spectators watched the arrival of a carriage chock full of royalty, including King George of Greece, his sister Queen Alexandra of Great Britain, King Edward VII of Britain, Queen Olga of Greece, the Prince of Wales and his spouse, Princess Mary. The royal box seats were packed with delegates from various European courts as well as members of the Greek royal family, including the Duke and Duchess of Sparta.[140] Sullivan, then US commissioner to the Olympics, described the scene: "Flags were waved in a frantic manner. The fringe of soldiers around the top row of seats stood saluting, the naval officers stood back of the throne in salute. The cheers grew louder and louder—not only the people in the Stadium were cheering, but all Athens was cheering."[141]

But the most memorable moment from the 1906 Olympics was not the regal cavalcade at the opening ceremony but the audacious act of dissent carried out by the son of an Irish shipbuilder: track athlete Peter O'Connor. O'Connor was not only one of the most accomplished Irish tracksters in history, but also an ardent Irish nationalist who abhorred the idea of having to compete as a British athlete. The English Amateur Athletics Association (AAA) tried to induce O'Connor and his fellow Irishman Con Leahy to compete for Great Britain at the Athens Games. At 34, O'Connor was nearing the twilight of a successful career, but the British felt he and Leahy were capable of boosting their medal tally. However, O'Connor and Leahy were determined to go out in a blaze of Irish green competing for the small Olympic contingent from Ireland heading to the Games.[142]

O'Connor traveled to Athens with Con Leahy and two other Irish athletes, John Daly and John McGough. Everyday Irish men and women keen to see Ireland represented at the Olympics had raised money for the athletes' passage to Athens. In correspondence with Olympic officials, the Irish athletes had made it clear they wished to represent Ireland.

But to their great dismay, upon their arrival they learned—by reading souvenir programs, no less—that they were listed with the British delegation.[143] The 1906 Athens Games were the first in which athletes had to be affiliated with a National Olympic Committee (NOC) to compete. Ireland was still governed from Westminster at the time and had not yet formed an NOC.[144] O'Connor—a working-class clerk for a Waterford solicitor—wrote an appeal and submitted it to the Olympic organizers. He was summarily denied.[145] But, as O'Connor's granddaughter Rosemarie O'Connor Quinn told me: "He was a fiery man. He was not a man to be crossing."[146]

For the first time ever the Olympics held an opening ceremony that resembled the flag-waving parades of today's Games. At this first "March of Nations" the Irish athletes offered a foretaste of the protests to come, sporting bright green blazers embossed with golden shamrocks on the left breast and ornate golden braids along the cuffs and collars.[147] They also donned identical green caps emblazoned with a shamrock. The athletes lagged behind the rest of the British contingent, conspicuously distancing themselves from the pack and ignoring the English AAA's demand that they feature Union Jacks on their sport coats.[148]

The plot thickened once the athletics competition finally began. In the long jump, O'Connor alleged that Olympic official Matthew Halpin—who doubled as event judge and the manager of the US squad—engaged in biased officiating. According to O'Connor and others at the scene, Halpin allowed US long jumper Myer Prinstein to leapfrog ahead in the jumping order, thereby allowing him to run on a smoother, faster track. Halpin also called O'Connor for fouls on two of his jumps.[149] O'Connor later railed to the *Limerick Leader*: "I was enraged … If my wife had not been present looking on at this contest, which restrained me, I would have beaten Halpin to a pulp as I was half insane over the injustice."[150] On the spot, O'Connor submitted a written appeal, but he was gaining a reputation as a troublemaker and was again denied. He was forced to settle for the silver.[151]

O'Connor was determined to have the last word on the matter. During the medal ceremony, when the Union Jack was hoisted up the flagpole in honor of his silver-medal performance, O'Connor scampered over to the pole and swiftly shimmied up it. He unfurled a large green flag bearing a golden harp and the words *Erin Go Bragh*, or Ireland Forever. Below, his teammate Con Leahy waved a similar flag and fended off the Greek police, giving O'Connor more time atop the pole.[152] O'Connor later reminisced: "When I climbed a pole about 20 feet in height and remained aloft for some time, waving my large flag and Con waving his from the ground underneath the pole, it caused a great sensation ... I was an accomplished gymnast in my youth and my active climbing of the post excited the spectators who had observed my violent protest to Halpin being sole judge and declaring my best jumps foul."[153] O'Connor's great grandson Mark Quinn later wrote, "The Irishman's points might well be accredited to Great Britain, but the flying of the Irish flag left none in doubt as to where O'Connor's true allegiances lay."[154] Quinn told me: "Events dictated that he become political. To not become political would be to submit to British authority."[155] As Rosemarie O'Connor Quinn put it, "Over 800 years of repression and dominance of a colonial power certainly inspired Peter O'Connor to pull down the British flag."[156]

Not everyone championed this act of dissent. After describing the incident, the *Daily Mail* noted, "The question of the flags was the subject of considerable comment both in the Stadium and in the city, the Irishmen's attitude being universally disapproved."[157] More broadly, O'Connor and Leahy were a vital precursor for future acts of athlete activism at the Olympic Games. They also showed how nationalism could be used as a political lever against colonial oppression in the context of sport.

Although Olympic officials were displeased with O'Connor's act of political dissent, they did not expel him from the Games. He went on the win gold in the "hop, step, and jump" event, known today as the triple jump. When Leahy won a gold medal in the high jump he repeated his flag-waving protest, this time from the ground.[158] In 1956 O'Connor remarked, "The British failed miserably in their efforts to annex any credit for the Irish successes and the flag incident received wide publicity in the world's press and turned the spotlight very much on the Irish political situation at a period when very few dared to raise a protest against the British domination of our country."[159] Athletes were in the vanguard of political dissent.

There is disagreement among Olympic mavens over whether the 1906 intercalary Games qualify as an official Olympics. In the late 1940s, an IOC commission directed by future IOC president Avery Brundage decided that the 1906 Athens Games were not an actual Olympics, but a bevy of Olympic historians disagree. One scholar has gone as far as to say that those Games "may be the most important Olympic Games of the modern era—they saved the Olympic Movement."[160] After all, in the aftermath of St. Louis, the Games were reeling.

The striking success of US athletes in Athens—especially in track and field events where they were dominant—lent credence to the Americans' "scientific" training regimen. They were a hit off the field too. Their fawning deference to and enthusiastic fraternizing with the Greek aristocracy ingratiated them with their hosts. After defeating O'Connor in the long jump under dubious circumstances, Prinstein wrote a letter to his fiancée describing a wild night of partying with the Greek king where they slugged down champagne, raided the royal cigar stash, attended "a millionaire's villa and dance," and behaved "like wild Indians."[161] Even the *New York Times* covered the "gala dinner" given by the king to commemorate "these never-to-be-forgotten days."[162]

The 1906 Athens "intercalary" Olympics brought numerous innovations that remain with us today. As mentioned earlier, these Games had an opening ceremony with roughly 900 athletes parading behind twenty-two national flags. NOCs played a newfound role. During the Games, many athletes lived in the Zappeion, a de facto Olympic Village (although one the US team found unsatisfactory, moving quarters partway through the competition). And the Olympic organizing committee published for the first time ever an official list of participants and results, setting a trend for what became common practice as Official Reports at subsequent Olympic Games.[163] Despite these strides, political instability in and around Greece made hosting another "intercalated" Olympics in Athens unviable. After the 1906 Games the region was wracked with conflict, and the Greek government, strapped by the costs and consequences of war, lacked resources.[164] These and other factors made the four-year rotation of the Olympics the norm.

The Games Find Their Footing

When Mt. Vesuvius erupted in 1906, forcing the 1908 Games to be relocated from Rome to London, Lord Desborough stepped in to help. An Olympic fencing medalist and IOC titan from Britain, Desborough announced that the Games "shall be carried out by private enterprise, and without help of any sort from the government, a distinction which other nations do not share."[165] This subtle allusion to disgruntlement in Rome, where locals had protested the high costs of hosting the Games, points to a lasting question in Olympic history: Who should pay the five-ring tab?[166] Despite Desborough's assurances, the Baron once again had to attach the Olympics to a World's Fair, the Franco-British Exhibition, "for budgetary reasons."[167] But Lord Desborough's support was part of a pivot, transforming the IOC from what was essentially a paper-tiger front group, to one that took a much bigger role in organizing the Olympic Games.[168]

The London Olympics would turn out to be a mixed success, but one thing about them is undeniable: they ran thick with monarchic entitlement. Bowing to the whims of privilege, the marathon began on the lawns of Windsor Castle, per the request of King Edward and Queen Alexandra, who wanted their grandchildren to see the start of the race without having to leave the cozy confines of their property. The race concluded in front of the Royal Box in the stadium. This put the marathon distance at 26 miles, 385 yards, which has remained the official length ever since.[169]

The Games were marked by strident nationalism, much of it coming from the Americans who traveled across the Atlantic to compete with their former colonizers. US Olympic officials were displeased with the lodging the team was assigned in London, perceiving it as a slight, and decided to stay in Brighton instead.[170] The American flag was not flown at the opening ceremonies, furthering tensions, so the US flag bearer returned the favor by opting not to dip the flag in deference to the British monarchy in attendance. Irish-American athletes, meanwhile, bristled at Britain's rejection of Irish independence. US Olympics officials including James E. Sullivan complained about the officiating, an objection European observers dismissed as American hyper-competitiveness.[171] British royalty were offended by the Americans' behavior, and Coubertin agreed, noting the American athletes' "barbaric shouts that resounded through the stadium." As for Sullivan, "he shared his team's frenzy and did nothing to try to calm them down."[172]

Sullivan lived up to his reputation as a cutthroat competitor, working hard behind the scenes to declare ineligible the Canadian Tom Longboat—an Onondaga runner from the Six Nations of the Grand River First Nation in Ontario—who was favored to win the marathon. Longboat was ultimately declared an amateur and allowed to participate, but for many, the American's efforts to exclude him left a sour taste.[173] Such fractiousness prompted the *New York Times* to report, "Thoughtful men in England have serious doubts ... as to whether the Olympian games serve any good purpose, while theoretically they are supposed to foster international friendship." A prime outcome of the 1908 Games was "to create international dissensions and kindle animosities."[174] Meanwhile, feminist activists like Emmeline Pankhurst used the Olympics as a platform for suffrage, vowing to interrupt the Games if organizers refused to allow women to participate. They used guerrilla tactics like shoveling up golf courses and leaving behind messages like "No Votes, No Golf."[175]

While the 1908 Games in London were a mixed picture, many historians identify the 1912 Games in Stockholm as the Olympics that established them as a top-tier international event.[176] Coubertin described the contrast between the two: "Whereas in London the life of the huge metropolis had not been influenced by the invasion of Olympism, the whole of Stockholm was impregnated by it."[177] Sullivan concurred. Upon his return to the United States after Stockholm, he beamed, "I have never seen a better managed set of sports since I've been in the Games."[178] The Olympics were becoming more advanced technologically and organizationally. To preempt allegations of bias, officials from international sports federations served as judges rather than local coordinators.[179] Swedish officials set the standard for record keeping, deploying electric timers and finish-line photographic technology for greater precision. The "Pentathlon of the Muses" was born, with prizes handed out for literature, architecture, and the arts.[180] Stockholm was where Coubertin won gold for his pseudonymous poem "Ode to Sport."

Jim Thorpe was arguably the biggest superstar of the Games. He was a Native American from Oklahoma, born to a father of Sac and Fox and Irish descent and a mother who was Potawatomie and French. Thorpe was a dazzling multi-sport athlete who starred in football, baseball, and track and field.[181] In 1912 he achieved the remarkable feat of winning both the pentathlon and the decathlon. Among his competitors in these two events was a young Avery Brundage, the future president of the IOC. Brundage noted in his personal papers that the "1912 Games were the first that were really properly organized."[182] But Brundage himself did not have his act together. He actually dropped out of the pentathlon when he knew he was out of contention rather than completing all the events, a decision that shamed him decades later. According to his biographer, "Thorpe's shadow was to haunt Brundage the rest of his life."[183]

In a front-page story, the *New York Times* anointed Thorpe—whom the paper had once called "the Redskin from Carlisle"—the "finest all-around athlete in the world." King Gustav V of Sweden concurred, telling Thorpe, "Sir, you are the greatest athlete in the world." Sullivan deemed Thorpe "the real hero of the Olympics." When Thorpe was announced as champion of the pentathlon, the *New York Times* reported: "There was a great burst of cheers, led by the King. The immense crowd cheered itself hoarse, renewing its efforts a few moments later when Thorpe reappeared to receive a valuable silver model of a Viking ship presented by the Emperor of Russia to the winner of the decathlon."[184] Thorpe kindled pride in Native Americans and non-Natives alike.

Nevertheless, the Games weren't pure bliss. Despite Coubertin's pleas for internationalism, the Olympics once again stirred intense nationalist sentiments that bubbled up throughout the festival. Media coverage encouraged a nationalist frame by regularly tallying up the number of medals and points secured by each country.[185] And inevitably, global politics intruded. Olympians from Finland were anything but pleased by having to participate under the Russian flag. They marched with their own flag at the opening ceremonies, aggravating the Russians.

One year after the Games, Thorpe was stripped of his medals for having broken the amateur code—in 1909 and 1910 he received a small sum of money ($60 a month) for playing semiprofessional baseball.[186] Coubertin actually opposed taking away the medals but was outvoted by his fellow IOC members.[187] In response, Coubertin wrote an Olympic oath, steeped in the principles of amateurism, that athletes would be required to swear by. "Beside its wonderful moral value," wrote the Baron, "the athlete's oath is proving to be the only practical means to put an end to this intolerable state of affairs," by which he meant "disguised professionalism."[188] The oath was first used at the 1920 Olympics in Antwerp.[189]

A campaign to get Thorpe's medals restored emerged, and persisted for years. Thorpe's old rival, Avery Brundage, became ensnared in the controversy as a member of the IOC and eventually as its president. Brundage was barraged with letters from a range of individuals and groups—from the Carlisle Jaycees to the US Senate Committee on Post Office and Civil Service—asking him to return Thorpe's medals. Florida congressman James A. Haley pointed to French skiers whose commercial connections violated the spirit of amateurism but were still allowed to compete. The Committee for Fair Play for Jim Thorpe sent a telegram imploring him to restore the medals since "Thorpe is an ailing and aging man and return of the medals will bring happiness to a great athlete in the twilight of his career." A private citizen, H. T. Cooke, wrote, "I am hoping there will be a reconsideration of this ruling before the old Redskin passes on to the Happy Hunting Ground" since "it would be favorably received by the general public."[190] Senator A. S. "Mike" Monroney of Oklahoma reasoned, "I seriously doubt that all of the money that Jim Thorpe earned in his professional career as an athlete measures up to the money that 'amateurs' are paid today to play college football, basketball, baseball, run track, or participate in other events, which in many cases qualify them for participation in the Olympic Games."[191]

However, through the years Brundage remained unmoved, performing mental gymnastics of Olympian proportions to justify his continued refusal to restore Thorpe's medals. He informed Senator Monroney that Thorpe's medals been redistributed to other athletes and that, in any case, Thorpe's "outstanding record as an athlete in competition remains, and actual possession of the medals would add little to it."[192] He wrote to the sportswriter Grantland Rice, "I doubt if the men who received Thorpe's medals would give them up"; moreover, the medals were handed out by the Swedish Organizing Committee and "I am very doubtful that they would have any interest in the subject."[193] He told H. T. Cooke that "Olympic Games medals have no particular intrinsic value, since only silver gilt medals are given to the winner." He then concluded dismissively, "This matter was reviewed by the 1951 Amateur Athletic Union Convention with 300 delegates from all over the United States and it was decided that nothing could be done."[194]

But something could be done and eventually was. In 1982, at the behest of USOC president William Simon, the IOC voted to return Thorpe's gold medals. In a ceremony in early 1983, Juan Antonio Samaranch presented Thorpe's children with replacement gold medals as well as replica silver medals for each of them.[195]

It would be conjecture to attribute Brundage's obstinacy to personal resentment at losing to Thorpe in Stockholm. After all, in one letter he wrote, "Jim Thorpe was one of the greatest athletes of all time, we were on the same Olympic team and I was subsequently American all-around champion, so that I naturally have a very friendly feeling toward him and would be happy to please him if it could be done."[196] In another letter he suggested, "Everyone has great sympathy for Thorpe," so "instead of wasting time and energy on a couple of medals, whose intrinsic value is probably not more than $3.00 or $4.00 each, that you take up a cash collection for him, to which I and many others will be happy to contribute."[197] More likely Brundage's opposition to restoring the medals emerged from his dogmatic commitment to amateurism, which for him was "an abstract, fixed quality that does not alter or change from day to day."[198] In the years ahead, Brundage's "fixed" version of amateurism would be challenged and ultimately overturned.

But the early years of the Games are all about the Baron Pierre de Coubertin. Thanks to his indefatigable vim, the Olympics were destined to be more than just a footnote on the page of history. He had a flair for the symbolic and a knack for the spectacular that lasted to the very end. In his will, he left clear instructions to slice his heart from his chest after he died and entomb it in Olympia. His wish was granted on March 26, 1938, when his heart was ceremoniously ensconced in a marble stele meters from the ancient stadium.[199] Still Coubertin's vision for the Games abounded with contradictions —peace and good will, bound up with sexism, racism, and class privilege. In response, sports-minded feminists and leftists would soon organize viable, vibrant alternatives.

2

Alternatives to the Olympics

"Will war someday shatter the Olympic framework?" Baron Pierre de Coubertin wondered in 1913. He answered his own question with plenty of bombast: "Olympism did not reappear within the context of modern civilization in order to play a local or temporary role. The mission entrusted to it is universal and timeless. It is ambitious. It requires all space and time."[1] The following summer, however, Archduke Ferdinand was assassinated, setting off a sequence of events that careened into World War I. Coubertin enlisted in the French military despite his advancing age (he was in his early 50s) and was assigned to the country's propaganda service. Because the Baron believed the IOC should not be "led by a soldier," he temporarily handed over the reins to his trusted colleague Baron Godefroy de Blonay.[2] Once the war broke out, the IOC moved its headquarters from Paris to Lausanne, in neutral Switzerland.

World War I forced the cancellation of the Sixth Olympiad, which had been scheduled to culminate in 1916 at Berlin. But the Baron proved correct when he maintained that when it came to the Olympic Games, "war can merely delay, not stop, its advancement."[3] Sure enough, the Olympics returned after the Great War, to Antwerp in 1920. Having survived German invasion during the war, Belgian organizers played politics, declining to invite Germany and its wartime allies Austria and Hungary; the IOC looked the other way.[4] Germany wouldn't return to the Olympic fold until 1928. Russia was also absent in 1920 because of its recent revolution and the fighting that ensued.

For the first time, Coubertin's five-ring Olympic flag flew overhead.[5] The flag proved popular with athletes—so popular that many pilfered them as souvenirs. Coubertin wrote, "Unfortunately, the Police were on guard: arrests, trials, consular interventions, followed."[6] Another first: athletes took a symbolic oath, pledging allegiance to the Olympic spirit. Coubertin and the IOC oversaw the proceedings from their headquarters in Switzerland.[7]

Antwerp organizers had a mere year to prepare for the Olympics. As a consequence, many facilities, like the main stadium, were only partly built, and interest from everyday Belgians was minimal. Coubertin tried to deflect criticism, chalking it up to "a crotchety journalist" here and "a professional spoilsport" there. He insisted that the Games were "held with a mastery, a perfection, and a dignity matched by the strenuous and persevering efforts of its organizers."[8]

Perhaps unsurprisingly, nationalism flared up at the Games. After a hard-fought water polo match between England and Belgium, the crowd booed and hissed the British national anthem. The heckling continued as the monarchs in attendance filed out of the arena. British Olympic officials lodged a complaint for what they described as a "national insult," urging further exploration of the matter.[9] Media accounts routinely adopted a nationalistic frame, echoing the prevailing spirit.[10] American athletes hitched a ride to the Games aboard military vessels. Upon their return home, they complained bitterly of "the treatment they received at the hands of foreigners" in the Olympic city. Some athletes claimed that conditions in Antwerp were so terrible that they almost opted to withdraw entirely from the Games. They alleged Belgians "displayed the greatest hostility to the competing Americans and created feelings which greatly hampered the work of the men."[11]

"Men" was the operative word. The Antwerp Games highlighted the lopsided gender relations that were typical of sports of the era. Twenty-two female athletes had taken part in the 1900 Olympics, and by Antwerp that number had climbed to sixty-three. But as a percentage of overall Olympic participants, this translated to a minuscule upward blip from 2.2 percent to 2.4 percent over the twenty-year period.[12] Women's participation had essentially flatlined. They were still not allowed to participate in track and field at the Antwerp Games. For that they would have to wait until the 1928 Amsterdam Olympics.

In the early 1900s a worldwide women's movement was demanding political inclusion, with some success. In 1906, Finland granted women full voting rights, followed in subsequent years by Norway, Denmark, Iceland, Armenia, Estonia, Latvia, Lithuania, Russia, Ukraine, Uruguay, Austria, Germany, Poland, Russia, the United Kingdom, Belgium, Georgia, and Luxembourg. The United States passed the Nineteenth Amendment to its Constitution in 1920, granting women full voting rights in that country. The times were changing, but they weren't changing the Baron. Behind the scenes, some IOC members were quietly moving to expand women's participation, but Coubertin was implacable, angling for the continued marginalization of women's sports. After the 1912 Stockholm Games, he and many of his IOC colleagues believed "an Olympiad with females would be impractical, uninteresting, unaesthetic and improper."[13] Other members of the Olympic family who wished to keep the lineage patrilineal included the Americans James Sullivan and Avery Brundage. But as we shall see, many condemned the exclusion of women.

The 1924 Olympics were awarded to Paris as a shout-out to Coubertin for his decades of dedication to the Olympic cause. The Baron had announced he would retire as IOC president after the Games, perhaps in part to ensure that the Olympics ended up in France, but perhaps also to fend off accusations of an "Olympic monarchy."[14] Coubertin had sent a letter to his IOC brethren notifying them of his impending resignation following the 1924 Games and urging them to award the Olympics to Paris. "At this moment when the reviver of the Olympic Games judges his personal task to be nearly at an end," he wrote, "no one will deny that he is entitled to ask that a special gesture should be made in favor of his native city, Paris." The IOC granted this "special gesture," completing what Coubertin dubbed in his memoirs "a masterly coup d'etat!"[15]

But politics jeopardized his "masterly coup." In 1923 the French government sent troops into Germany to enforce war reparations, raising the specter of another armed conflict. Moreover, in what was becoming a regular headache for the IOC, elected officials in the host city challenged the use of public funds on the Olympics. In March 1922, the Paris City Council voted to contribute only 1 million francs to the Games instead of the expected 10 million. But the Chamber of Deputies eventually came through with the funds, ensuring Coubertin's dream.[16] Still, the Baron wasn't taking any chances. With the possibility of war, European economic collapse, or simple underfunding endangering the Paris Games, he had quietly forged a back-up plan with organizers in Los Angeles who were eager to debut as hosts of the Games. While the backdoor plan to transfer the Games to LA didn't become necessary, it did lay the groundwork for the city to secure the 1932 Olympics. In any case, the Paris council's fiscal concerns were well merited—the Games wound up saddling the city with debt. And once again, the Olympics dissuaded tourists who otherwise would have visited Paris to spend their money, an example of what economists came to call the "stayaway factor."[17]

Political friction tarnished Coubertin's swan song. The French, like their counterparts in Antwerp, did not extend an invitation to Germany.[18] The British Olympic Association insisted on an "empire plan"; rather than enter alphabetically during the opening ceremony, Great Britain would walk in first, followed by its "Dominion teams" from countries like

Canada, Australia, and New Zealand.[19] During a rugby match between France and the United States, the Americans were drowned in boos; two US fans were roughed up in the stands.[20] After a contentious fencing match between a Frenchman and an athlete from Italy, the Italian squad stalked off chanting the Fascist anthem. Against this backdrop, the IOC argued against calculating standings based on a point system in an effort to minimize jingoism. Nevertheless, a whole host of entities—from journalists to sports lovers—devised point systems and then argued over which one was most just.[21] All this led the *New York Times* to report that the Games "have left in the minds of not a few of the contending teams and with the public a feeling of irritation and distaste."[22] Ever the optimist, the Baron acknowledged the "irreparable repercussions" of the funding battles prior to the Games, before extolling "the universal good humour of the athletes" and the steady progression of Olympic spirit. "From Stockholm to Antwerp, from Antwerp to Paris, its encouraging action continued," he wrote.[23] Perhaps most significantly, the 1924 Olympics brought the first incarnation of what eventually became the Winter Games, as the IOC gathered athletes to compete in Chamonix, France, ahead of the Summer Games in Paris.[24]

For Coubertin, the Olympics were a religion. Fortunately for him, there were enough disciples to carry on the five-ring gospel. In 1925, at its meetings in Prague, the IOC replaced the retiring Baron with a Count—more precisely Count Henri Baillet-Latour of Belgium. More arbiter than firebrand, Baillet-Latour had long been a member of the IOC, serving competently on various committees. Most observers saw Baillet-Latour's selection as staying the Coubertin course.[25] But one place where the Count differed was his grudging willingness to allow the increased participation of women at the Games.[26]

The 1928 Olympics in Amsterdam—the first without Coubertin at the helm—doubled the number of female participants: almost 300 women took part in the Games, thanks largely to the inclusion of a small slate of women's track and field events. However, citing medical "evidence," the IOC ruled after the Amsterdam Games that the 800-meter run was too dangerous. In Amsterdam, after completing the race, a number of competitors fell to the turf to regain their strength. Anti-feminists pounced at the opportunity, arguing that women were too frail to run such distances, and quite remarkably their views won out. Women were not allowed to compete in the 800-meter run until the 1960 Olympics in Rome. Still, in 1928 women comprised about 10 percent of all Olympic athletes. Germany was also allowed through the Olympic gates for the first time since World War I. The Amsterdam Olympiad continued the trend started in Paris four years earlier of including all sports played on snow or ice in a separate Winter Olympics, this time at St. Moritz, Switzerland. The Summer Games featured an Olympic flame for the first time, thanks to architect Jan Wils, who designed a cauldron for the Amsterdam stadium. On the commercial front, Coca-Cola became an Olympics sponsor, a relationship that has lasted through the present day.[27]

Amsterdam was nearly derailed as host when the Dutch Parliament rejected public funding for the Olympics, partly because of fiscal considerations but also because many parliamentarians felt holding sports competitions on Sundays would desecrate the Sabbath. The Dutch Olympic Committee, forced to conjure an end run, found financing through a hefty loan from the Municipal Council of Amsterdam: some 5 million guilders (about $2 million at the time). The Dutch East Indies also kicked in a substantial sum, backed by a group of wealthy Dutch bankers. Nevertheless, the center of gravity for Olympic funding was shifting toward the state.[28]

The Amsterdam Games was the five-ring farewell for one of the most successful Olympians ever, Paavo Nurmi of Finland. Nicknamed the Flying Finn, Nurmi won nine gold medals and three silvers over three Olympic Games in 1920,

1924, and 1928. Nurmi was a long-distance specialist who excelled in the 1,500-meter, 5,000-meter, and 10,000-meter runs. The working-class runner who was famous for training with a stopwatch in hand might have won more medals, had the International Amateur Athletic Federation (IAAF) not deemed him ineligible ahead of the 1932 Olympics for allegedly accepting money to compete. Athletics honchos, including Avery Brundage, ruled that Nurmi had sacrified his amateur status on the altar of cash-compensated professionalism.[29] The battle over amateurism had flared up once again.

Women's Games

The Olympics echoed the gender and class structures of the time, but marginalization sparked an innovative response. In the 1920s, dissident athletes teamed up in solidarity with sympathetic supporters to organize alternative athletic competitions rooted in principles of equality.

To challenge IOC sexism, women and their allies organized alternative games, a vital yet largely forgotten act of political dissent. Everywhere women looked, the Olympic cards were stacked against them. The IOC, as led by Coubertin, opposed women's full participation, as the minutes of the 1914 IOC general session made clear: "No women to participate in track and field, but as before—allowed to participate in fencing and swimming."[30] Discrimination was baked into the master plans.

Enter Alice Milliat, a French athlete and activist whose bold actions scythed a path for women's participation in the Games. After the exclusion of women from track and field in Antwerp, Milliat founded the Fédération Sportive Féminine Internationale (FSFI) on October 31, 1921. At its first meeting, the group voted to establish a Women's Olympics as an alternative to the male-centric Games. In total four Women's Games were staged, in 1922 (Paris), 1926 (Gothenburg, Sweden), 1930 (Prague), and 1934 (London), with participants coming mostly from North America, Western Europe, and Japan. Milliat and the FSFI found a way into the Olympic structure, thanks to a highly placed, grudging ally, J. Sigfrid Edström of Sweden. In 1912 Edström, a longtime Olympic movement booster, founded the International Amateur Athletic Federation to govern Olympic track and field, with Coubertin's blessing. In 1922, following the successful Women's Games, Edström and his colleagues brought the FSFI under the umbrella of the IAAF. This opened a path for women's participation in the Olympics, but the price to the FSFI was forfeiting a certain degree of autonomy to the IAAF. As part of that price, the FSFI had to rename its event the Women's World Games to avoid mentioning "Olympics," a foretaste of the hypervigilant defense of branding to come.[31]

The first Women's Olympics in 1922 were largely a success. More than 20,000 people attended the single day of competition at Paris's Stade Pershing, where athletes from five countries (Britain, Czechoslovakia, France, Switzerland, and the United States) competed in eleven events, more than twice as many as the IOC would include when it finally allowed more women's track and field events in 1928. Newspapers of the day reported favorably, if somewhat backhandedly, on the strides women were making in sports. According to the *New York Times*, 1922 "was notable for the development of women athletes in all branches of competitions *fitting to their sex*. Remarkable progress was made by them, and almost overnight, they assumed a place of great prominence in the world of athletics." No longer were "girl athletes ... a decided novelty," but "capable of impressive performances."[32]

Four years later at Gothenburg, the now renamed Women's World Games were also a one-day affair, although with athletes from eight countries. In 1930, Prague played host to a three-day gathering featuring more than 200 top-flight female athletes from seventeen countries. Media coverage was typical of its day, if belittling by present-day standards. In an article titled "Girls Go to Prague," one newspaper reported, "Nine girls from Vancouver B.C., young, athletic and socially prominent, accompanied by a chaperone, are on their way to Czechoslovakia."[33] Nevertheless, the event drew considerable public interest, with more than 15,000 spectators. The fourth Women's World Games were held in London in 1934, with nineteen participating countries. Organizers added basketball to the slate of track and field events.[34]

In a way, the FSFI was undercut by its own success. By 1936 the group had increased membership from five to thirty countries and had secured allies in the IAAF, but, Mary H. Leigh and Thérèse M. Bonin argue, "no matter how determined they were and no matter how good their arguments were, women could not get very far without the support and alliance of the male sport establishment."[35] The IAAF had incrementally taken more and more control of women's track and field and absorbed it into the Olympic schedule.

In a last-ditch effort to maintain control of women's sports, the FSFI asserted that unless the IOC offered a full roster of events to women and afforded them a measure of representation at the IOC itself, they would cease participating in track and field events. Edström wrote Avery Brundage, then the top Olympic official in the US: "Madame Milliat had sent a letter asking that all Women's Sport be omitted from the Olympic Games, as she wished to have separate Olympic games for women. The proposition was rejected."[36] In another letter he fumed: "I suppose you know that Mme Milliat's federation has caused us so much trouble that we certainly have no interest at all to support it. We should like the whole thing to disappear from the surface of the earth."[37] In 1936 the FSFI folded, after serving great purpose.

One result of the FSFI's activism was to induce the IAAF to include a handful of women's track and field events at the 1928

Amsterdam Olympics as an experimental trial (the discus, the running high jump, 100-meter dash, 800-meter run, and the four by 100-meter relay).[38] Despite being disappointed with the limited number of events, the FSFI voted to approve the offer, although female athletes from Britain showed their disapproval by boycotting the Games. Meanwhile, traditionalists chafed at the inclusion of women. The minutes of the IOC Executive Committee reported: "A harsh discussion between Edström and [Reginald J.] Kentish took place as the former points out that the IAAF absolutely wishes to have the 4 women-events on the program. Kentish points out that in most countries the masculin [sic] and feminine sports are separated and he thinks that such a decision will not be very popular."[39]

Edström and the IAAF eventually won out, with more and more women's track and field events staged at the Games. Still, men debated which sports were appropriate for women. Sometimes, those who wished to limit the range of sports positioned themselves as progressive advocates of women's athletics. For instance, Dr. Frederick Rand Rogers, the director of the Department of Health and Physical Education for the State of New York, adopted the approach of "more, rather than less, but of the right kind." Cloaking paternalism and sexism in the respectable garb of science, Rogers argued for "less strenuous" sports for women, and opposed women's participation in the 1932 Olympics.[40]

Alice Milliat and her colleagues used a classic inside-outside recipe for political change. They worked inside the corridors of power with IAAF and IOC power brokers while creating a viable alternative outside the IOC's orbit—the Women's Olympics. Their relentless pressure on the men who controlled the Olympics paid off in an early breakthrough for women in sport.

But an uphill battle still lay ahead. Many sports administrators were skeptical of women's sports, including Brundage.

While embroiled in a 1932 controversy over whether the athlete extraordinaire Mildred "Babe" Didrikson was an amateur or a professional, he remarked: "You know, the ancient Greeks kept women out of their athletic games. They wouldn't even let them on the sidelines. I'm not so sure but they were right." Didrikson had been suspended by the Amateur Athletic Union (AAU) for alleged professionalism because she had appeared in an advertisement for milk. This was enough for Brundage to advocate suspension, although Didrikson was later reinstated.[41] At the time Brundage was head of the Amateur Athletic Union, so his opinions carried weight. In 1949, as IOC vice president, he wrote: "I think it is quite well known that I am lukewarm on most of the [Olympic] events for women for a number of reasons which I will not bother to expound because I probably will be outvoted anyway. I think women's events should be confined to those appropriate for women: swimming, tennis, figure skating and fencing but certainly not shot putting."[42]

In 1957, Brundage still clung to these beliefs. In a circular letter to members of the IOC he wrote, "Many still believe that events for women should be eliminated from the Games, but this group is now a minority. There is still, however, a well grounded protest against events which are not truly feminine, like putting a shot, or those too strenuous for most of the opposite sex, such as distance runs."[43] These opinions were very much in tune with those emerging from the IOC. The General Session minutes from the April 1953 meeting in Mexico City read—under the heading of "Reducing the number of athletes and officials"—that "women not to be excluded from the Games, but only participation in 'suitable' sports."[44] Some within the IOC claimed that limiting women's sports was a way to cut costs in the face of an emerging concern with "gigantism." They argued that the Olympics were becoming too big and unwieldy—and that slicing women's sports could slim down the Games.

Sometimes the mainstream press could be even more extreme. In 1953, Arthur Daley wrote in the *New York Times* that he would entertain the idea of eliminating women from the Olympics entirely. "There's just nothing feminine or enchanting about a girl with beads of perspiration on her alabaster brow, the result of grotesque contortions in events totally unsuited to female architecture," he wrote. "It's probably boorish to say it," he conceded, "but any self-respecting schoolboy can achieve superior performances to a woman champion." Boorish indeed, but Daley wasn't finished: "The Greeks knew exactly what they were doing when they invented the Olympics ... Not only did they bar the damsels from competing but they wouldn't even admit them as spectators." He cautioned: "Don't get me wrong, please. Women are wonderful. But when those delightful creatures begin to toss the discus or put the shot—well, it does something to a guy. And it ain't love, Buster."[45]

Such commentary from prominent journalists notwithstanding, more and more women were participating in the Games, and from countries that did not necessarily have strong Olympic histories. The Soviet Union helped jump-start participation of female athletes in the 1950s as the athletic arena became a proxy for international tension. Soviet involvement would also play a role in the emergence and maintenance of another alternative to the IOC's Games: the Workers' Olympiads.

Workers of the World, Exert!

In 1928 the Baron wrote, "I have been delighted to see labor organizations embrace the Olympic ideal." He may have been subconsciously tipping his hat to the working-class athletes who were organizing a vibrant alternative to the Olympics.[46] The International Workers' Olympiads heralded a fresh ethos that blended sport with solidarity, socialism, cooperation, and working-class tradition.[47] More about healthy lifestyles and class opportunity than hyper-competition and elites, the Workers' Games pushed back against the nationalism plaguing the established Olympics; they were meant to circumvent prejudice and jingoism while undermining the growing fixation on record-breaking performances by superstar athletes. People of all races, ethnicities, and genders were welcome to take part. Organized primarily by European socialists, the Workers' Olympiads took place in 1925 (Frankfurt), 1931 (Vienna), and 1937 (Antwerp), before World War II put an end to the experiment. Labor activists also staged Winter Workers' Olympiads in those years, in Germany, Austria, and Czechoslovakia.

In 1936 another socialist-inspired alternative to the Olympics was scheduled, the People's Olympiad in Barcelona, but it was canceled by the July outbreak of the Spanish Civil War. Nevertheless, a June letter of invitation from the Olimpíada Popular de Barcelona to the Amateur Athletic Union in the US captures the spirit of the Workers' Games movement: "The object of the Peoples' Olympiad is to unite in friendly competition the sportsmen of all countries, regardless of race, and thus to give a practical demonstration of the true Olympic spirit—the fraternity of races and peoples." The letter continued, "In the struggle against fascism the broad masses of all countries must stand shoulder to shoulder, and Popular Sport is a valuable medium through which they may demonstrate their international solidarity."[48] Implicit in this invitation was the recognition that sport was no mere opium of the masses, but rather a powerful lever for political consciousness.

In the interwar years, the International Workers' Olympiads were an important part of the labor movement.[49] Thanks to the restrictive definition of amateurism enforced by the IOC, many workers were simply ineligible for the Games. But workers' sports clubs—some with roots stretching back to the

1890s—provided laborers and their families an outlet for physical engagement in numerous countries from Czechoslovakia to Canada. In contrast to the ingrained elitism of the IOC, these sports clubs championed the democratization of sport, encouraging all to take part regardless of skill level or class background.[50] In 1920, trade unionists founded the Socialist Worker Sports International (SWSI), also called the Lucerne Worker Sports International, or LSI, because the congress took place in Lucerne, Switzerland. The SWSI assumed a prime leadership role in organizing the Workers' Olympiads.[51]

The first Workers' Olympiad was staged at Frankfurt in 1925. The four-day affair featured 150,000 participants from nineteen countries. Unlike the "bourgeois Olympics" in Antwerp (1920) and Paris (1924), where the defeated nations from World War I (Germany and Austria) were not invited, the Workers' Games welcomed all comers. And if one wanted to compete in a sport, participating in the cultural festival was mandatory. So participants played their sports, but they also sang and acted. The opening ceremony featured a 1,200-person choir. Later, 60,000 people staged a performance called "Worker Struggle for the Earth." The opening and awards ceremonies replaced national flags with red flags and national anthems with "The Internationale." The motto for these Games was "no more war." The Olympiad was largely considered a success, although it suffered from the sectarianism that plagued wider relations on the left; disagreements between the SWSI and the communist Red Sport International (RSI) led to the exclusion of the latter. Worker sport organizations were forced to choose one side or the other.[52] As William Murray notes, "Both bodies ran their own sports meetings, often dedicated, like their stadiums, to heroes from the socialist past, but they neither competed with nor against each other."[53]

The second Workers' Olympiad took place at Vienna in 1931. Approximately 80,000 worker-athletes from twenty-three nations participated. To boost attendance, organizers dovetailed the Games with the Socialist and Labour International's fourth congress. The Games featured a separate festival of sport for kids, as well as art shows and running and swimming events for the masses. Some 65,000 people attended the final match of the soccer tournament, while 12,000 went to the cycling finals and 3,000 went to the water polo title match. On the final day of the Games, a crowd estimated at 250,000 watched a "festive march" consisting of approximately 100,000 athletes.[54] The socialist government in Vienna built a new stadium for the Olympiad, complete with an athletic field, bike track, and swimming pool, at a cost of $1 million. Locker rooms were constructed to accommodate the thousands of athletes who took part.[55] According to Robert Wheeler, the Vienna Olympiad "was in many ways the high point of the workers' sports movement," and "compared favorably or better with the 1932 Olympics in Lake Placid and Los Angeles."[56]

In 1936 the Republican government in Spain planned a People's Olympiad as a counterpoint to the 1936 Berlin Olympics, or "Nazi Games." The Comitè Català Pro-Esport Popular led the planning with the intention of creating a hybrid Games for worker athletes as well as IOC-sanctioned athletes who wished to boycott the Berlin Games for political reasons. The organizers set up a three-tier system for participants: elite athletes, almost-elite athletes, and recreational athletes from worker sport clubs. Funding came from the Spanish central government, the Catalan autonomous government, Barcelona City Hall, and the Popular Front government in France. Numerous art exhibitions were scheduled. The Catalan writer Josep Maria de Sagarra supplied the lyrics for the *Olimpíada Popular* hymn, and the German musician Hans Eisler wrote the orchestration. Unlike the IOC, People's Olympiad organizers allowed for the participation of athletes from Algeria and Morocco, despite their colonial status, and afforded nation status to Catalonia, Euskadi (Basque country), and Galicia. A contingent of Canadians planned to attend, as did Palestinian athletes and worker-athletes from the US. But all these plans were scuttled. On July 19, 1936, the day of the opening ceremony, Fascist forces led by Francisco Franco carried out a coup that foiled the Olimpíada Popular. Some athletes fought fascists in the streets. Others fled to safer havens.[57]

Although the People's Olympiad was canceled, the third International Workers' Olympiad was succesfully staged the following year at Antwerp. Approximately 27,000 worker-athletes participated from seventeen countries. Some 50,000 people attended events in the stadium on the final day of the Games, and 200,000 made the final march through the city. At these Games, RSI athletes were allowed to participate as a united front against the ascendance of fascism in Europe. This labor solidarity—the Popular Front—was notable, and unique in the history of the Workers' Olympiad. Although the sport festival did not live up to Barcelona's ambitiously planned grandeur, it remained a significant accomplishment given the challenging period in which it was staged.[58] The next International Workers' Olympiad was scheduled for 1943 in Helsinki, but World War II prevented it from becoming reality.

Despite their success, the Workers' Olympiads were largely marginalized by the mainstream media of the time, limiting their reach to the wider public. The fracture between socialists and communists also hampered their effectiveness. Within the Games, there was also a certain amount of tension between the commitment to break athletic records and the commitment to non-competitive mass participation; many worker-athletes who strove for record-breaking achievement were labeled "bourgeois" by their colleagues.[59] James Riordan argues that overt politics may have undercut the political value of the Workers' Games: "Many worker sport leaders failed to understand that a sport organization might be more politically effective by being less explicitly political."[60]

Like the Women's Olympiads, the alternative Workers' Olympiads definitely had an impact on the IOC's power brokers. The Avery Brundage archive contains brochures about the 1936 Barcelona People's Olympiad as well as an invitation to the Amateur Athletic Union to come take part in those Games.[61] Such terminology raised the IOC's concerns that the organizers of the alternative Games were infringing on the Olympic brand. The IOC Executive Committee minutes from 1925 note: "The miss-use [*sic*] of the word 'olympic' was growing rapidly and among organization[s] using it were the 'Olympic Games for Women', 'The Worker's Olympic Games', 'Student's Olympic Games'. Members from these organizations were present and told that the word 'olympic' was the property of the IOC and could not be used."[62] More recently, however, the Olimpíada Popular has been reincorporated into official Olympic history; the Olympic Museum in Barcelona features posters from the alternative competition and a brief description of the organizers' goals.

The Olympics Pivot

Meanwhile, the "bourgeois Olympics" pressed on. The 1932 Olympics in Los Angeles brought a number of features that embedded themselves in Olympic tradition. The Los Angeles Games inspired the Baron to panegyric; he raved that crowds attending the opening ceremonies "had never before seen such a spectacle. They seem to have been greatly impressed by it, and the organizers, for their part, seem to have achieved the maximum of the desirable Olympic eurythmia on this solemn occasion." The Games were "a glorious apotheosis on the shores of the Pacific Ocean."[63]

Ahead of the Los Angeles Olympics, Avery Brundage, then head of the American Olympic Committee, wrote to President Herbert Hoover asking him to offer remarks during the Games' opening broadcast. "Knowing your great interest in health-ful recreation and sport," he wrote, "we are certain that you will not refuse unless there is conflict with your other engage-ments." The window Brundage offered President Hoover was relatively slim: "Any time at your convenience between five and eight o'clock in the afternoon of October first, will be sat-isfactory."[64] Besides Brundage's self-assurance, the specificity of the request revealed the burgeoning prestige and confidence enjoyed by the Olympic movement at that point, thirty-six years after the modern revival of the Games. Although President Hoover declined Brundage's request, he sent Vice President Charles Curtis in his stead. In front of 105,000 spectators—at that time the biggest crowd to attend an opening ceremony in the history of the Games—Curtis declared the Olympics officially open. It took Los Angeles only three days to surpass the total number of five-ring fans in Amsterdam. The Games were attended by some of Hollywood's biggest stars, including Charlie Chaplin, Marlene Dietrich, Douglas Fairbanks, Mary Pickford, and Will Rogers.[65]

According to the Olympics scholar Alan Tomlinson, the 1932 Games signaled "a markedly political intensification of the event."[66] They were being put on during the Great Depression, and organizers took care not to stage the Games in a lavish manner while the world writhed in economic pain. Organizers made prudent use of existing buildings and struc-tures. They downplayed the incipient commercialism of the Olympics while at the same time embracing it. The Official Report claimed that "not a single note of commercialism was allowed to permeate the consummation" of Olympism, but organizers quietly lined up sponsorship and service-provision deals.[67] Such commercial pacts eventually became an integral part of the political-economic architecture of the Games.

Yet commercial contributions were meager compared to the enormous public funding that underwrote the Games. In 1927 the California legislature passed the California Tenth

Olympiad Bond Act, which supplied $1 million to the Olympic cause, and the measure was ratified in a public referendum by a one-million-vote majority. But in 1929 the US was rocked by the stock market crash that triggered the Great Depression. Activists took to the streets to protest spending money on the Olympic spectacle while everyday Californians were suffering. Demonstrators in Sacramento raised protest placards reading "Groceries Not Games! Olympics Are Outrageous!" Feeling the political heat, California governor James Rolph remarked, "These Games are an impossible venture. What do they want, riots?" Still, Rolph did not push to cancel the Games—he had a political career to consider, and local business heavyweights were in the Olympic corner. Jittery citizens were assured that hosting the Games would bring jobs and tourism to the city—a trope that would become standard-issue Olympic rhetoric.

In retrospect there's little evidence that the Games buoyed the local economy. But thanks to thrift, sponsorship, high attendance, and a spike in interest from Hollywood, the Olympics earned a profit of $150,000, most of which was plunged into servicing the debt on the $1 million bond and reimbursing the city and county for the facilities they anted up for the Games.[68] The city paid a quieter price when the bond market wavered on public works projects, stoking a crisis that culminated in a recall election for the mayor. The *New York Times* proclaimed that "the public is thoroughly 'fed up' on these experiments in political economy."[69] Such "experiments"—where the costs of the Olympics are socialized, with the public taking on the bulk of the risk—ultimately became the go-to move for funding the Games.

In the words of the Official Report, the Olympics survived "the depths of a dark abyss of world depression."[70] For the first time, organizers built a formal Olympic Village where visiting athletes stayed during the competition, although female athletes were segregated at the nearby Chapman Park Hotel.[71]

The medal ceremonies and three-tiered platform we see today made their first appearance. Organizers also condensed the Games' duration, limiting competition days to sixteen, a tradition that has essentially continued through to the present. The shortened calendar helped focus media and public attention. Organizers enabled the media in other ways. They set up a "Press Department" in December 1929, long before the Games began, to do the work of a modern sports information office. When the Olympics arrived two and a half years later, more than 900 journalists from around the world were on hand to cover them, and the Press Office was well seasoned in its job of helping them.

Coubertin still criticized the news media's coverage, decrying "a press campaign with bitterness of tone and an unfairness of intent equaled only by the self-interested calculation that inspired it."[72] But social science content analysis demonstrates that media coverage actually presented a neutral or positive portrayal of the Games.[73] The "lizards" Coubertin claimed were bad-mouthing Olympism, "proclaiming its imminent or more gradual collapse," were more phantom than opera.[74] In fact, Olympic press officials managed the commercial media effectively, shaping the message to the organizers' advantage.

Time magazine assessed the Games as "a gorgeous, unprecedented success."[75] The Los Angeles organizing committee was even tossed into the mix for the Nobel Peace Prize.[76] Mildred "Babe" Didrikson raised the bar for women's athletics, dazzling the assembled throngs with remarkable Olympic feats. Although she qualified for all five individual track and field events, Olympic power brokers only allowed her to compete in three. Didrikson won the 80-meter hurdles and the javelin, setting world records along the way. She also won silver in the high jump. On the flip side, after Luigi Beccali won the 1,500-meter race, he speared a fascist salute skyward as the Italian national anthem played during the award ceremony. This act was mentioned in the press, but only in passing and without analysis of its political import.[77] Such scant attention to the politics of the Games would not be possible four years later.

Nazi Games

The Olympics were initially of little interest to Adolf Hitler. When the 1936 Games were awarded to Berlin in 1931, a centrist, democratic coalition held power in Germany. Even in 1932, Hitler was referring to the modern Olympics as "a plot against the Aryan race by Freemasons and Jews."[78] But propaganda minister Josef Goebbels convinced him that the Games were a prime opportunity to bathe the swastika in the Olympic glow on the world stage. Although in *Mein Kampf* Hitler praised boxing for the "steel-like versatility" it instilled, the Führer was no fan of sports.[79] But after becoming chancellor in January 1933, Hitler supported the Olympics, even plowing significant state funds into the event.[80] Hitler and Goebbels became intent on using the Olympics to demonstrate German superiority.

Hitler's belief in the racial supremacy of the so-called Aryan race clashed intrinsically with the doctrine of inclusiveness in the IOC's official charter. The year before the Berlin Olympics and the Winter Games in Garmisch-Partenkirchen, Germany had passed the Nuremburg Laws, formalizing policies that marginalized Jews. The IOC took a middle path. When Baillet-Latour saw anti-Semitic signage peppering the German landscape he complained vehemently to Hitler, threatening to cancel the Games. The Führer relented, ordering the signs' removal.[81] In Avery Brundage's personal notes, he wrote, "Baillet-Latour said to Hitler 'You keep your law, I keep my Games.'"[82]

Opposition to the Nazis' racist policies emerged in the United States in 1933, when the Amateur Athletic Union voted to boycott the Games unless anti-Jewish discrimination was reversed in Germany.[83] The AAU vote did not influence the group that mattered, the American Olympic Committee, which decided to participate in the Games. The decision was made after the committee chief, Avery Brundage, made a "personal investigation" into the matter and received a pledge from the German government not to discriminate against Jewish athletes.[84] Nevertheless, the push to boycott the Games continued from a variety of sources, including students at Columbia College, various religious groups, and the Committee on Fair Play in Sports, a liberal organization formed specifically to oppose American participation at Berlin.[85] To be sure, the United States had its own deep-seated problems with racism, but the 1936 Olympics provided a chance to point the finger away from home. In a March 1935 Gallup poll, 43 percent of respondents favored a boycott.[86]

Brundage's "personal investigation" largely entailed listening to and then believing German officials. The more Brundage publicly explained his reasoning, the more flimsy it appeared. He told the *New York Times*: "Germany has nothing whatsoever to do with the management of the games. The Germans provide the facilities and make preliminary arrangements, but that is all." The Olympics, he argued, was "under the sole jurisdiction" of the IOC. Plus, he added: "The fact that no Jews have been named so far to compete for Germany doesn't necessarily mean that they have been discriminated against on that score. In forty years of Olympic history, I doubt if the number of Jewish athletes competing from all nations totaled 1 per cent of all those in the games. In fact I believe one-half of 1 per cent would be a high percentage."[87] Behind the scenes, he was more direct about his feelings. When Edström wrote Brundage to complain that "all the Jews in the whole world are attacking us,"[88] Brundage responded with an accusatory screed:

The situation on this side of the Atlantic has become extremely complicated. As you no doubt know, half of the Jewish population of the United States is centered in New York City. The New York newspapers which are largely controlled by Jews, devote a very considerable percentage of their news columns to the situation in Germany. The articles are 99% anti-Nazi. As a matter of fact, this applies to the American press generally. As a result, probably 90% of the populace is anti-Nazi. The Jews have been clever enough to realize the publicity value of sport and are making every effort to involve the American Olympic Committee. Boycotts have been started by the Jews which have aroused the citizens of German extraction to reprisals. Jews with communistic and socialistic antecedents have been particularly active, and the result is that the same sort of class hatred which exists in Germany and which every sane man deplores, is being aroused in the United States.[89]

Brundage's biographer asserts that Brundage "continued obstinately to see a conspiracy of Jews and Communists" and that he was blinded by his anti-Semitism.[90]

Edström had his own issues. In response to Brundage he wrote: "As regards the Jewish population in Germany, there are strong anti-Jewish tendencies, as you know. This is owing to the fact that the Jews have taken a too prominent position in certain branches of German life and have—as the Jews very often do when they got in the majority—misused their positions. This is the main reason of the Arian [*sic*] movement in Germany." Lest anyone mistake him for an anti-Semite, Edström pointed out, "I have, myself, Jews in my service. You met Mr. Eliash, yourself. I saw him the other day in Berlin and he was satisfied and happy. I have heard that the treatment of the Jews in Germany is better during the last months."[91] Previously Edström noted, "When I last visited Berlin I was assured ... that there are several Jewish athletes on the preparatory team for the German participation in the Olympic Games."[92] After his epistolary exchange with Edström, Brundage traveled to Germany. There he drank wine from a historic goblet that previously had only been presented to German leaders like Bismarck and Hitler.[93]

The deference Brundage and his IOC counterparts showed the Nazis allowed them to manufacture an Olympic experience that would place them in a positive light. A German sports official, Carl Diem, came up with the Olympic torch relay, a tradition that would become a staple of the Games. The Berlin Games were the first in which a flame lighted at Mount Olympus wended its way to the host city's main stadium, where it ignited the Olympic cauldron. The relay chimed with Nazi propaganda identifying German Aryans as the true and worthy heirs of the ancient Greeks. The route from Olympia to Berlin also allowed Hitler to swing Nazi propaganda though central and southeastern Europe, key areas of future Nazi ambitions. During the final days of the relay, those chosen by the regime to carry the torch through Germany were exclusively blond and blue-eyed, perfect exemplars of the Nazis' Aryan "master race."[94] The torch relay, which Coubertin called "gallant and utterly successful," was a Nazi creation that seamlessly became part of Olympic tradition.[95] Another innovation had sticking power; the Berlin Games, for the first time ever, provided live TV coverage of the Olympics, as seventy-two hours were telecast to public viewing booths in Berlin and Potsdam.[96] Also, the opening ceremony for the 1936 Games in Berlin featured the finale of Beethoven's Ninth Symphony, "Ode to Joy," a favorite of Coubertin. After Berlin 1936 it was woven into many subsequent Olympic ceremonies, from the closing ceremony at the Mexico City Games of 1968 to the 1980 Moscow Olympics to the Cultural Olympiad at the London 2012 Summer Games.[97]

To keep up the right appearances, the Nazi regime gave Berlin a makeover that scrubbed away blatantly anti-Semitic advertising and signage. The notorious Nazi newspaper *Der*

Stürmer was not sold on the streets during the Olympics. Moreover, Goebbels instructed the German press that "the racial aspect must not be remarked upon in the reporting" on the Games.[98] The press obeyed and put its usual racism and chauvinism on hiatus. Jazz, which was previously maligned as an immoral force, was allowed in nightclubs.[99] But the swastika was ubiquitous, often hanging on banners next to the Olympic flag.[100] Hitler himself took full advantage. *Time* magazine reported, "Most conspicuous in the gigantic crowds, mostly composed of provincial Germans, who stared at all these doings, was Realmleader Adolf Hitler. Suddenly become an omnivorous sports enthusiast, Herr Hitler hardly missed a day's attendance."[101]

Hitler loomed large in the Olympic stadium, but US track star Jesse Owens ruled the athletics oval, winning four gold medals. Owens, the son of an African-American Alabama sharecropper who moved his family north to Cleveland, Ohio, in search of opportunity, was the indisputable superstar of the Berlin Games. He dominated in the 100-meter race, setting a world record. He also smashed the Olympic records in the 200-meter run and the long jump. And he ran a leg in the 400-meter relay team that set a world record. Shirley Povich noted in the *Washington Post* that Owens's success had stark political implications: "Hilter declared Aryan supremacy by decree, but Jesse Owens is proving him liar by degrees." Owens was more conciliatory, and his focus was on political relations at home. In an open letter to the *Pittsburgh Courier* he wrote, "I am a proud that I am an American. I see the sun breaking through the clouds when I realize that millions of Americans will recognize now that what I and the boys of my race are trying to do is attempted for the glory of our country and our countrymen." He concluded, "Maybe more people will now realize that the Negro is trying to do his full part as an American citizen." But in general, Owens was partial to the bromide that politics and sports competitions shouldn't mix.[102]

Yet, Owens's fourth gold medal, as part of the 400-meter relay squad, sparked political controversy as much as racial reconciliation. In a last-minute coaching decision, Owens and fellow sprinter Ralph Metcalfe were inserted into the relay team, replacing two Jewish athletes, Marty Glickman and Sam Stoller, who had been training expressly for the event and who were expected to win gold. Glickman openly chalked up the eleventh-hour rebuff to anti-Semitism, pointing a finger not only at the track coaches but at Avery Brundage, too. The athlete claimed they did not wish to make the German hosts uncomfortable by having to witness two Jews standing triumphant on the medal stand. Stoller was so distraught that he vowed to quit track altogether.[103]

The grandeur of the Games was captured and magnified by Leni Riefenstahl's iconic *Olympia*. The film prominently featured Jesse Owens, despite Goebbels's demands that Riefenstahl leave footage of Owens on the cutting room floor.[104] Riefenstahl, famous for her pro-Nazi propaganda film *Triumph of the Will*, was enraptured by Owens, noting in her memoir that he was "the athletic phenomenon of the Games."[105] Hitler may have told Riefenstahl that he "was not very interested" in the Olympics and would "rather stay away," but he largely supported her artistic autonomy with *Olympia*, sometimes shielding her from the cretinous Goebbels and his thuggish attempts to thwart the film. Riefenstahl had also secured special permission from the IOC to film the Games. She used groundbreaking film techniques to produce a cinematic masterpiece that, in her words, aimed to "combine the Olympic idea with the most important Olympic contests." Owens apparently approved. When the filmmaker and the athlete reunited in Munich at the 1972 Games, the meeting was "deeply emotional," full of hugs, kisses, and near tears, according to Riefenstahl.[106] *Olympia* also had an admirer in Avery Brundage. When theaters in the US refused to publicly screen the film, he went ballistic, fuming to one German journalist that "unfortunately the theaters and moving picture companies are almost all owned by Jews."[107]

At the 1936 Berlin Olympics, Owens received friendly greetings from everyday Germans as well as German Olympic officials—Jeremy Schaap goes as far as to assert that the Germans in attendance "embraced him as if he were one of its blond, blue-eyed Teutons."[108] But the Gestapo secretly tailed him and his fellow African American athletes to ensure they didn't have *too much* contact with Germans. Of particular concern to the German secret police was African Americans' interaction with German women. During the Games, police cited more than fifty German women for approaching the foreigners "in an unseemly manner."[109] Meanwhile, back at home, Southern newspapers minimized the athletic feats of Owens and other African Americans—the *Atlanta Constitution* failed to run a single photo of Owens or his black teammates. In fact, Owens resented President Franklin Delano Roosevelt, who never sent him a note of congratulations, more than Hitler. Owens called Hitler "a man of dignity." Later, when campaigning for Republican candidate Alf Landon in the 1936 US presidential election against Roosevelt, part of Owens' stump speech mentioned that "Hitler didn't snub me—it was our president who snubbed me. The president didn't even send me a telegram."[110]

In the wake of the Games, American athletes were expected to travel through Europe competing in various exhibitions. Meanwhile, big-money offers came pouring in to Owens from the United States. Part way through the tour he decided to ditch the exhibition circuit and head home to cash in. He had the full-throated support of his college coach, Larry Snyder, who helped him to Olympic glory in Berlin. With the possibility of Owens earning $100,000, Snyder said, "Jesse has a chance to make more money now than he may earn the rest of his life through ordinary channels." He added, "I cannot conscientiously advise Owens not to seize what may be the chance of his lifetime." The AAU, headed by Brundage, promptly suspended Owens, prompting the athlete to lash out at the organization, calling it "one of the great rackets of the world" and accusing it of "trying to run the Olympics on strictly business lines." He added, "Somebody's making money somewhere" and that the AAU was "trying to grab all they can" while athletes couldn't even afford souvenirs. Coach Snyder said the athletes were being treated "like cattle." He was blunt: "You wouldn't ask the poorest show troupe to work the way these boys worked immediately after the games—all without a cent of spending money with which to brighten an otherwise drab picture."[111]

Unfortunately for Owens, the lucrative offers to capitalize on his Olympic glory evaporated upon his return to the United States. Most of the overtures were mere publicity ploys. Owens tried to make a living off his notoriety, starting an unsuccessful dry-cleaning chain before ultimately declaring personal bankruptcy in 1939. Later he became owner of a Negro League baseball team in Portland, Oregon—the Portland Rosebuds—which only lasted a year. He even resorted to racing horses. He reportedly stated, "People said it was degrading for an Olympic champion to run against a horse, but what was I supposed to do? ... I had four gold medals, but you can't eat four gold medals." Eventually Owens became a successful motivational speaker, but achieving financial stability was a long road. Although Owens struggled to cash in, memorabilia collectors did not—in 2013 one of Owens's gold medals from 1936 was auctioned off for $1.47 million to a Los Angeles billionaire investor.[112]

At the close of the Berlin Games, Coubertin hailed them as "powerful and diverse," and said, "I thank the German people and their leader for what they have just accomplished."[113] Most commentators also hailed the Games as a success. In an article titled "Olympics Leave Glow of Pride in the Reich," the *New York Times* asserted that the Games contributed nothing less than "the undoubted improvement of world relations and general amiability." The newspaper also reported that visitors left the Olympics with the impression that "this is a nation happy and prosperous almost beyond belief; that Hitler is one of the greatest, if not the greatest, political leaders in the world today, and that Germans themselves are a much maligned, hospitable, wholly peaceful people who deserve the best the world can give them."[114] Brundage echoed such high praise: "No country since ancient Greece has displayed a more truly national public interest in the Olympic spirit in general than you find in Germany." He added: "We can learn much from Germany. We, too, if we wish to preserve our institutions, must stamp out communism. We, too, must take steps to arrest the decline of patriotism."[115] So much for staying out of politics. In his personal notes, he even wrote: "An intelligent, beneficent dictatorship is the most efficient form of government. Observe what happened in Germany for six or seven years in the 1930's."[116]

Brundage's key role in the Berlin Games catapulted him into a position in the IOC, where he continued to extol the virtues of separating politics and sport. In a talk he gave in Munich he explained: "The enemies of Hitler, and there were many, decided to try to spite him by boycotting and spoiling the Games. We could not tolerate such a use of the Games as a political weapon. This battle centered in the U.S.A., where I was President of the NOC [National Olympic Committee], and we led the successful struggle to save them. I was often called a Fascist and a Nazi but I have also been called on other occasions a Communist or a racist or a capitalist, which has left me, as you can see, unaffected."[117] In another speech titled "The Wondrous Flame of the Olympics" he said that the Olympic movement "should be like a protective antitoxin neutralizing the infections of future wars. It is not natural for humans to wish to fight those whom they know as friends, those whom they have found to be good sports on the field of honor."[118] Brundage's lofty words proved untrue as the world plunged into war. The thirteenth Olympiad scheduled for Tokyo and moved to Helsinki was canceled, as were the 1944 Olympics that were tentatively scheduled for London.

Cold War Inklings

In 1948 the Olympics emerged from the ashes of war, returning to London for a second time. The Winter Games were held in St. Moritz, site of the 1928 Games. Edström, a longtime IOC insider, had taken over the IOC presidency after Baillet-Latour suffered a heart attack and died in 1942. Edström was determined to get the Games back on track, and according to the Official Report for the 1948 Olympics, the robust Swede and his colleagues faced "a herculean task," especially with regard to the Summer Games.[119] Europe was devastated by war. Resources were thin. London was still cratered from aerial bombing, and the detritus of war littered the city. Shortages in food and housing wracked the city's residents, and rationing for basic staples was still in effect. Cash-strapped British officials saw the Games as a chance to gain hard currency from tourist expenditures and ticket sales, but accommodation for athletes was makeshift and many of them brought their own food from home. As such, the 1948 Games became known as the "Austerity Olympics."

The Games were officially awarded to London in 1946, so Olympic officials had little time to prepare. Organizers also had to fight against what Janie Hampton describes as "defeatism of the press," as critics charged that the Games were misspending public money while regular Londoners suffered. *The Times of London* questioned whether the city and the country had the gumption to pull it off: "With only a few weeks left there is little evidence that Britain is grasping this opportunity."[120] In a *New York Times* opinion piece, Dudley Carew wrote of the Olympics as "money-spinning gladiatorial shows which usurp the honorable title of sport." He argued that the Games encouraged facile, false generalizations about nations and their inhabitants based on their exploits on the field, which only exacerbated stereotyping and nationalism. He concluded, "The Olympic Games are a financial proposition, and when money comes tinkling in at the turnstiles, the spirit of true sport has a way of flying out the window."[121]

Others revived a charge from the 1908 London Games, that American hyper-competitiveness led to an "unpleasant atmosphere" that in turn led to an "argument over the success of the Olympic games as a builder of international good will."[122] Arthur Daley of the *New York Times* telegraphed his later musings on the female athlete, airing his displeasure over the increased participation of women at London. The Greeks excluded women from the ancient Olympics, he argued, but spectators have "long suffered from watching female footracers and hardware heavers burlesque a noble sport. They just haven't the correct architecture for it. So why run counter to the obvious wishes of Mother Nature?"[123]

On the broadcasting front, for the first time ever a national television network—the British Broadcasting Corporation—consented to pay an organizing committee for the right to broadcast the Games. Amid the austerity, the IOC moved to tighten its grip on Olympic symbology. At the London Games, the IOC made itself the exclusive proprietor of the Olympic symbol of five interlocking rings as well as the long-used motto "Citius, Altius, Fortius."[124]

One conspicuously absent participant was the Soviet Union. This would change in 1952 when Helsinki hosted the Summer Games, starting a process whereby the USSR would become a major Olympic player. The coming decades would see an absence of direct war between the world's biggest military powers; instead, that rivalry played out in proxy wars across the Third World and in bitter competition in Olympic sport.

3

Cold War Games

The Games of the Cold War era may well have best approx-
imated Orwell's sport-induced "orgies of hatred," with
chauvinistic spittle spraying in every direction.[1] Although revolutionary Russia had ditched the Olympics as "bourgeois,"
by the 1940s the Soviet Union wanted back in. The 1952
Helsinki Games marked the return of the Soviets to the five-
ring fold for the first time since Lenin's revolution. During the
Cold War, the Olympics emerged as a prominent venue for
rival systems to assert their superiority. As one journalist put
it years later, "Our nukes are fueled by better steroids than
your nukes."[2] The Games became a platform for the press to
assess who was winning the wider war. The "Free World" or
the Communists? Capitalism or socialism?

The IOC admitted the USSR to its hallowed body in May
1951. Within the IOC, this meant that Olympism trumped
anti-communism. Even Avery Brundage supported Russian
reentry, though he privately opined that "communism can
never succeed over a long period of time because of the human
desire for freedom."[3] Meanwhile, the Soviets hailed their reintegration into the Olympic fold as further evidence that the
USSR was a major player on the world stage. American political culture was plenty primed for the rivalry. Commenting on
the anti-Soviet hysteria that swept the US after World War II,
Allen Ginsberg wrote in his classic poem "America": "Them
Russians them Russians and them Chinamen. And them
Russians. The Russia wants to eat us alive. The Russia's power
mad. She wants to take our cars from our garages."[4] For many

sports buffs in the United States, them Russians also wanted to snatch Olympic medals off American necks.

Soviet inclusion undeniably ramped up the quality of Olympic competition. In women's track and field events at the 1952 Helsinki Summer Games, Olympic records were set in every event but the high jump. In men's track and field, twenty-one Olympic records and three world records were eclipsed.[5] Concomitantly, the Helsinki Games became a surrogate battle for superpower supremacy. The news media and national-level Olympic officials obsessively tracked point totals, often deploying different systems that yielded divergent results. One *New York Times* headline captured the zeitgeist: "Russians Hail Olympic 'Victory' But Fail to Substantiate Claim: Pravda Cites 'World Superiority' of Soviet Athletes in Helsinki Games Without Providing Tabulation of Points."[6] Competition overshadowed good will. The USSR refused to allow the Olympic torch relay to pass through Soviet territory. Athletes from the Eastern and Western blocs stayed in separate Olympic villages in Helsinki; a large portrait of Stalin was erected outside the Eastern bloc's athlete village. The amateur status of athletes from behind the Iron Curtain was questioned. Meanwhile, Helsinki organizers sold and monitored the rights to providing services at the Games to various businesses. Eighteen firms—including Coca-Cola, Nestle, and Omega—provided "in-kind" donations as commercialism continued to creep into the Olympics.[7] In this era, "sport was a weapon of international affairs," as historian Christopher Hill notes, but it was also becoming a more significant arrow in capitalism's quiver.[8]

The Brundage Era

At the Helsinki Games, Avery Brundage was elected president of the IOC, defeating Lord David Burghley of Britain by a margin of 30–17. The *New York Times* reported that the bulk of the aristocrat's support came from "Iron Curtain countries," proving that the Olympics make for strange bedfellows.[9] When Edström handed him the keys to his Lausanne office later that year, Brundage made a comment he'd utter thousands of times thenceforth: the Olympics should stay out of politics and "must not be used by any individual groups or nations for their own selfish purposes."[10] In a classic formulation of this belief he wrote, "We *actively combat* the introduction of politics into the Olympic movement and are adamant against the use of the Olympic Games as a tool or as a weapon by any organization."[11] A close look at Brundage's ideals, biases, and foibles shows how much the Olympics have evolved since his heyday.

Brundage was known for what *Life* magazine called "a dictatorial temperament."[12] In *The Official History of the Olympic Games and the IOC*, David Miller, an Olympic true believer, writes:

> Avery Brundage was despotic, a moral bulldozer, fanatical defender of de Coubertin's legacy, loyal to close friends (who were few and occasionally undeserving), prominent engineer/building contractor and self-made millionaire, champion of public virtue and philandering husband. His presidency ... varied in style between that of godparent and bully, so it was unsurprising that his nickname was 'Slavery Bondage.' He was the best and occasionally the worst friend that the Olympic Movement could have, for his obsessive commitment to the past, to traditional sporting ideals of the nineteenth century and what he perceived as de Coubertin's philosophy, blinded him to the changes of an evolving society, almost all of which operated at a financial level out of sight and far below his acquired standard of living.[13]

Indeed, Brundage often seemed ferociously out of touch. He once told *Life* magazine that in all his decades in sport he had "never known or heard of a single athlete who was too poor to participate in the Olympic Games."[14] Yet he was not born into privilege. Brundage grew up working class before making his fortune in the construction industry. To the Olympics he brought an ambitious agenda focused on taming excessive nationalism. "In primitive countries spectators want their man to win; in more sophisticated circles they want the best man to win," he wrote.[15] Brundage also aimed to enforce amateurism and rein in "gigantism"—the Games' evolution into a sprawling, difficult-to-manage extravaganza.

Critics of Brundage abounded. But he also had his grudging admirers. Fellow IOC member Richard Pound described him as charitably as anyone. "Brundage held the Olympic movement together, almost by the sheer force of his personality, during the difficult postwar period when it could easily have split apart," Pound wrote.[16] The Olympic scholar Robert K. Barney adds, "Few could have been equal to the task of steering the Olympic schooner through such turbulent waters during the 1950s, 1960s, and early 1970s, but Brundage proved to be a capable captain."[17]

The "capable captain" often found himself embroiled in controversy, but his belief in the Olympics was unsinkable. For Brundage, the Games were "the most important social force in the world. The word OLYMPIC is the magic word."[18] Sport could succeed where other undertakings broke up on the shoals of politics. At a 1966 IOC meeting in Rome, he said: "Despite the Cold War, the Games thrive and attract more followers. The Olympic Movement appears as a ray of sunshine through clouds of racial animosity, religious bigotry, and political chicanery."[19] Brundage believed in the myth that the Olympics were apolitical; so, with politics supposedly sidelined, there was almost nothing sport couldn't achieve. The Olympics were "an oasis in an over-charged and over-heated world"[20] and sport was "one of the most potent influences in American life … a most wholesome sign of the times."[21]

Giving short shrift to love, he called sport "the only universal language."[22]

Sometimes Brundage's passion for and deep belief in the power of sports blinded him to wider realities. In late 1933, as the Great Depression kicked into high gear, Brundage wrote a letter to President Franklin Delano Roosevelt:

> It would seem to be most appropriate at this time for you to address the American Olympic Association ... After all, the N.R.A. and other governmental agencies which you have created, are for nothing more than the extension of the code of good sportsmanship, deviation from which is not tolerated by the people in their sports and games, to commerce and industry. When the people demand the same spirit of fair play in business which they insist on in sport, most of our troubles will be over. There is an opportunity here to make a telling point under the most favorable auspices.

He signed off with, "Trusting that you will be able to find time among your multitudinous duties to be our guest, I am."[23] Two weeks later the president's assistant secretary responded that FDR would not be able to find time: "The pressure at the White House has been so great that even a tentative engagement for a future date is impossible at this time, and I would suggest that you defer your request in that respect until conditions are somewhat easier."[24] Against the backdrop of the Great Depression, Brundage's demands were politically tone-deaf, if not monomaniacal.

In many ways, Brundage continued what Coubertin started. The Olympic historian Otto Schantz viewed him as "the guardian of the grail of Coubertin's Olympic ideal." Coubertin was his "spiritual father."[25] Indeed, both Coubertin and Brundage imbued the Games with the sanctity of religion. In his personal notes, Brundage referred to the Olympics as "a solemn semi-religious rite."[26] They shared a belief that, as Brundage put it, "true culture is built by physical as well as mental training."[27] They also shared a concern for amateurism, but while Coubertin's views on the topic evolved, Brundage's ossified into dogma. Brundage's biographer Allen Guttmann dubs him "the apostle of amateurism"[28] but for Brundage, amateurism was "a thing of the spirit and is not easily understood."[29] Writing about the topic seemed to induce in him a penchant for hyperbole. He argued that the misuse of athletes for commercial purposes "could be considered a violation of the rights of man."[30] He also wrote: "When colleges pay boys for playing football, they destroy many illusions: the spirit of loyalty, the satisfaction that comes from successful play, the fun of it, the amateur spirit. It is like killing Santa Claus."[31]

When not mixing homicide and holidays, Brundage was busy distrusting the influence of commercialism on the Games. "Freedom from commercial and political interference is essential if the Games are to continue,"[32] he wrote. He urged all to "strive to keep the Games clean, pure and honest, and free from politics and dollar signs."[33]

He asked, "Why should amateur sport leaders spend their own time and money arranging competitions so that professional promoters can make a fortune exploiting the athletes that are developed[?]"[34] Professionalism was, for Brundage, indicative of the "rabid materialism" he hoped to prevent from besmirching his beloved Games.[35] In short, he believed "commercial intrusion" in the Games was an "insidious thing."[36] Yet his fervor often clouded his judgment. He attributed the success of the Olympics entirely to "the fact that it is amateur and free from political or commercial influence," and, he warned, "*abandonment of these principles will sound the death knell of the Games.*"[37] Despite his zealous disdain for athletes and "professional promoters" who wished to profit from sport, he could not prevent the IOC from gradually becoming a more commercial entity during his twenty-year tenure.

Brundage made grand claims about the democratization of sport and the spreading of democratic ideals through sport.

The Olympics, where the best athlete won regardless of social or national background, constituted a "high level of democracy … found in few other lines of endeavor."[38] He argued, "Sport flourishes particularly in democratic America because, after all, sport is a great democratic institution."[39]

However, Brundage was adamantly against practicing democracy within the IOC. At an IOC meeting in 1968, he commented, "The International Olympic Committee may be undemocratic, but its structure, with all its members free and independent, and pledged to the Olympic Movement first rather than to their country or to their sport, has enabled it to organize the Games with progressively greater and greater success."[40] He also championed the IOC's antidemocratic process of anointing new members, claiming it safeguarded the movement from politics: "To allow countries to select their representatives on the Committee would be fatal. Political considerations would soon control and all the good work of the last sixty years would be destroyed."[41] This opened the group to criticism that it was a safe haven for aristocratic privilege. One Olympic historian declared that Brundage managed the IOC "like a secret society, the selection of members determined by a coterie of upper-class gentlemen and various counts, princes, and marquesses, the last dying vestiges of European royalty."[42]

Brundage frequently jotted down notes on politics, which he kept in his personal files. He wished to expunge politics from the Games—especially when people pressed political agendas that clashed with his ostensibly apolitical ideals. But his own views, as expressed in his personal writings, often veered toward the zany and reactionary.

In his personal notes Brundage raged against the social safety net as supporting the undeserving. Offering a particularly brutish version of social Darwinism, he wrote:

Social security and other socialist measures give support to the lazy, the worthless, and the shiftless. Society thus destroys itself by interferring [*sic*] with nature's laws, which eliminates those who are unwilling to take care of themselves. It is the same with medication, which extends the life of the unhealthy and eventually destroys virile society. We are doing the same with our tax laws, where we penalize the successful and handicap the strong and intelligent. In this manner, countries have grown soft and been overwhelmed by the so-called more primitive countries which follow the rules of nature.[43]

This led him to the conclusion that "the whole philosophy of Social Security is wrong" and that "our system will never be a success unless those who have no responsibilities *are not permitted to vote*." The disenfranchisement of the marginalized was only one of his panaceas; compulsory labor was another: "We take care of the lazy and shiftless instead of forcing them to work."[44] These "leeches" attached themselves to the state and as a consequence "bleed it to death."[45]

Brundage had no patience for elected leaders in the United States. "Professional politicians never want a competent candidate that they cannot control because half of them would lose their jobs," he wrote. "Politics is their racket and most of them could not succeed in other more legitimate pursuits, so we are bound to be continually condemned to mediocre government, or even worse." Not a particularly controversial sentiment, but his solution for the problem was typically oligarchical. He believed "good rulers have to be drafted" rather than show ambition for public office. "Most politicians want to get something for themselves and not to give something to the country."[46] As mentioned above, in short, he opined, "we are ruled by the stupid and incompetent."[47]

Brundage had a conspicuous amount of admiration for dictators. In his personal notes he wrote: "An intelligent, beneficent dictatorship is the most efficient form of government.

Observe what happened in Germany for six or seven years in the 1930's."[48] Writing in 1955, he concluded: "Germany in the 1930's had a plan which brought it from almost bankruptcy to be the most powerful country in the world in a half dozen years. Other countries with dictators have accomplished the same thing in a smaller way."[49] Despite his vehement anti-communism, he even looked to the Soviet Union for political inspiration, writing admiringly that political matters were streamlined and efficient in the USSR: "There are no political parties, so that expense is eliminated. There are no strikes, no labor troubles—so, there is a tremendous saving."[50]

For Brundage, Russia was in some ways personal. After being beaten by Jim Thorpe at the Stockholm Games of 1912, he competed in St. Petersburg, where, thanks to challenging conditions like tarps spread over hard turf instead of sand pits for the jumping events, he broke his wrist. A Russian doctor deemed it merely a sprain, and Brundage winced onward. *Life* reported, "He could neither dress himself nor feed himself until several months after his return to America."[51] Whether or not that experience colored his later opinions on Russia, Brundage became both an anti-communist and an admirer of Stalin's iron grip, and, ultimately, an advocate for the Soviet Union's reintegration into the Olympic fold.

"Crooked unions" were another target of his ire, as we might expect from a conservative Republican and self-made business tycoon. He wrote: "The advance of unionism in the ranks of labor has carried with it several tendencies. Since all workmen are of equal rank and receive equal pay there is a tendency to do as little as possible. Output shrinks to that of less efficient workers."[52] He believed "unions controlled by gangs" imperiled democracy.[53] They gave the enemy a chance to scoff: "The Communists laugh at us struggling with the crooked unions ... They do not permit things of this kind and say it demonstrates the weakness of our system."[54]

The media fared little better than unions in Brundage's eyes. "We feed our young people on TV and newspaper crime and then wonder why we have juvenile delinquency," he wrote. Thanks to "the undue power of the Press" politicians had an incentive to take short cuts in the name of getting media attention.[55] He believed "the journalists, the cinema and the counting house have, willy-nilly, taken possession of the Games."[56]

Brundage monitored the press, copying and distributing articles he could thread into his dogmatic tapestry. When a journalist from the *Marquette Tribune* penned a positive article on the Olympics, Brundage wrote him a personal letter thanking him for "presenting the Olympic philosophy so well."[57] After the Nazi Olympics, Harold Lord Varney published a piece in the *American Mercury* titled "The Red Road to War," which explained the behind-the-scenes international politics at those Games. Brundage was delighted by the article and wrote a personal letter of praise to Varney. Varney responded in kind, commiserating that "anti-Fascism has become an extremely profitable racket in America." Brundage bought numerous copies of the piece, sending them to friends and acquaintances such as the meat magnate Oscar Mayer. In one letter critical of the press, he wrote, "If all newspaper publishers knew the true situation perhaps the noxious flood of insidious and traitorous propaganda, which is inundating our country, might not be given so much publicity."[58]

Boycotts and Dustups

The cultural theorist Stuart Hall pinpointed 1956 as a vital "conjuncture" for "the 'first' New Left" because of two key events: the British and French incursion into the Suez Canal zone and the USSR's brutal repression of the Hungarian revolution. Hall wrote that this one-two wallop laid bare the political violence undergirding both Western imperial aggression and Stalinism. These "boundary-marking experiences" not only "symbolized the break-up of the political Ice Age"; they also paved a path for the emergence of a vibrant New Left.[59]

The year 1956 was also crucial for the Olympics. For the first time ever, the IOC staged the Games in the Southern Hemisphere, highlighting, among other things, that the idea of "Summer" and "Winter" Olympics arose entirely from a Northern perspective. Melbourne, Australia, hosted the Summer Games in November and December, having edged out Buenos Aires for the right.

Participation in the Melbourne Olympics was undercut by the same two international acts of aggression that gave rise to the New Left. Egypt boycotted the Games over the Suez situation and was joined by Iraq and Lebanon.[60] The Netherlands and Spain boycotted the Olympics over the Soviets' incursion against Hungary. The president of the Dutch Olympic Committee asked: "How can sports prevail over what has happened in Hungary? How would we like it if our people had been atrociously murdered, and someone said that sports should prevail?"[61] The Swiss joined the boycott, even though the IOC was based in Lausanne.

Meanwhile, the IOC tried to convince the world that the Games should persevere in the face of political events. "Every civilized person recoils in horror at the savage slaughter in Hungary, but that is no reason for destroying the nucleus of international cooperation," Brundage said. "In an imperfect world, if participation in sports is to be stopped every time the politicians violate the laws of humanity, there will never be any international contests."[62] As it happened, the "laws of humanity" were pretty well violated in the swimming pool when Hungary squared off against the Soviet Union in water polo. Hungarian fans packed the natatorium and heckled the Soviet athletes, and as *Sports Illustrated* reported, "the ball was all but disregarded as fighting broke out all over the pool. Like barracudas, the contestants flailed at one another underwater, sending up whirlpooled proof of titanic struggles beneath."[63] The water ran red with blood, after a Hungarian player was apparently punched late in the match. Hungary emerged from the pool victorious and went on to win gold. Rather than return home, forty-five Hungarian athletes applied for political asylum in the West.[64]

The People's Republic of China also withdrew from the Melbourne Games as part of its continued fight with the IOC over the recognition of Taiwan. The dispute dated to 1949, when the Chinese Communists ascended to power and the Nationalists fled to Taipei. In the aftermath of the Chinese revolution, the Soviet Union, seizing the chance to solidify a budding Cold War alliance, shepherded Beijing toward the 1952 Helsinki Games. Bumbling through its own internal strife, the IOC ended up issuing invitations to both Beijing and Taipei— on the day before the Helsinki Games commenced—thereby giving rise to the "two China" Olympic problem. Taiwan miscalculated and opted not to attend, which created space for the People's Republic of China (PRC). The PRC swooped right in, with those in the highest echelons of power—Mao Zedong, Liu Shaoqi, and Zhou Enlai—personally approving the move. The PRC's Olympic delegation arrived in Helsinki a mere day before the closing ceremony, so only one athlete, a swimmer, competed. But China participated in cultural programming, and its flag flew alongside those of the other Olympic participants, a real symbolic coup.[65] Not everyone in the IOC was happy about China's participation. In a pungent response to a critic, Brundage revealed: "I did everything in my power to prevent them from taking part. Unfortunately, I had only one vote and because many others present did not feel the same way I was out-voted."[66]

The "two-China question" dogged the IOC as both Beijing and Taipei aggressively pressed for the other's exclusion from the "Olympic family." The PRC actually sent an Olympic squad to Melbourne in 1956, but the Taiwanese team had already arrived, decamped at the Olympic Village, and hoisted its flag. When the IOC refused to expel Taiwan, the PRC vamoosed in protest. Under the influence of the PRC, IOC member Dong Shouyi sent a scathing resignation letter to Brundage in 1958, calling him "a faithful menial of the U.S. imperialists bent on serving their plot of creating 'two Chinas'."[67]

But Beijing's decision to vacate the Olympic movement and snipe from the sidelines did not mean that the IOC could sidestep the battle over who represented China. IOC members from the Soviet Union had long argued that allowing Nationalists to identify as the Chinese National Olympic Committee was a farce, since they did not oversee sport in mainland China. The IOC went along, requesting that Taipei come up with a name change, even though Brundage was, as the historian Xu Guoqi notes, "obviously pro-Taiwan."[68]

In response to the IOC's compromise measure, critics went ballistic. Detractors described the name change as a de facto expulsion of Nationalist China from the Olympic movement. Brundage was deluged with letters condemning the decision. The president of Wheaton College argued that the IOC "had nothing to gain by bowing to communists and insulting freedom-loving people." Atlanta mayor William Hartsfield wrote to "add my protest to the exclusion of Free China from the Olympic Games." Retired brigadier general Eugene S. Bibb concluded that "you and your weak, stupid colleagues on your foul committee succumbed to the chicanery and blackmail of this evil, Godless communist conspiracy to enslave the world!" Private citizen Jasper Crane of Wilmington, Delaware, concurred: "Any recognition of Communist China by the Olympic Committee would provide definite assistance to the Communist programme of world conquest."[69]

Even President Dwight D. Eisenhower weighed in, pointing out that numerous countries referred to the Nationalists as the "Republic of China." He then stabbed at Brundage's heart, saying, "Frankly, it seems to me that the Olympic Committee has gotten into politics rather than merely into international athletics."[70] The State Department twisted the dagger, publicly accusing the IOC of "a clear act of political discrimination" that was "a manifest injustice."[71] A *New York Times* editorial dubbed the IOC's decision "cowardly, evasive and shameful." The newspaper continued, "Now, under the open leadership of Moscow, the Communists have cracked the whip and forced the committee to carry out their political aims." The newspaper found its target: a marked-up copy of the editorial can be found in Brundage's personal files.[72] An IOC official, Otto Mayer, responded to a critic: "You have been badly informed by the American press, which got very excited on the Chinese problem ... I am far from being a communist, but we in the I.O.C., have in our rules a mention which says that we assemble the Youth of the World, should they be from one side or the other. WE DON'T MAKE POLITICS."[73]

Such claims rang hollow at the 1960 Rome Olympics, where the athletes chosen by Nationalist sports authorities had to participate under the label "Taiwan" rather than "China." Senator Thomas Hennings of Missouri joined the ranks of American officials pressuring Brundage to ditch the "Taiwan" designation, but to no avail.[74] Displeased with the situation, Chiang Kai-shek orchestrated a high-profile protest at the opening ceremony. When athletes from Taiwan entered the stadium, the head of the delegation unfurled a hand-painted sign that read "Under Protest."[75] Of course, the IOC was livid. But the organization wasn't able to loosen the politico-linguistic Gordian knot until Brundage retired and Lord Michael Killanin took over as IOC president.

At the 1976 Summer Games in Montreal, the plot thickened when the Canadian government, which operated under a policy that recognized the mainland government as China, refused to allow Taiwan to participate if the word "China"

appeared in its name. Taiwan rejected this stricture, withdraw-
ing from the Games the day before the opening ceremony.
At the tail end of the 1970s, mainland China reentered the
Olympic fold as the Chinese Olympic Committee, and Taiwan
was re-labeled the Chinese Taipei Olympic Committee.[76]

Forces Forcing Change: GANEFO

Although China wasn't participating in the Olympics, it also
wasn't sitting quietly on the sidelines of international sport.
It joined up with Indonesian president Sukarno and others
to create an alternative to the Olympics: Games of the New
Emerging Forces (GANEFO). The organization arose out of
a squabble. Indonesia was slated to host the fourth Asian
Games in 1962, but for political reasons it did not offer invitations to two Asian Games Federation members: Taiwan and
Israel. This displeased the IOC, which threatened to withdraw recognition of the Games and to suspend the Indonesian
National Olympic Committee. Indonesia didn't bend; the IOC
responded by suspending it for violating the Olympic Charter.
Indonesia, in turn, set up GANEFO.

In announcing the Games, Sukarno used language that must
have made Brundage livid: "Sports cannot be separated from
politics. Therefore, let us now work for a sports association on
the basis of politics. We do not want to put on any masks; let
us create a sports association on the basis of the new emerging forces."[77] Sukarno further asserted: "The International
Olympic Games have proved to be openly an imperialistic
tool ... Now let's frankly say, sports have something to do
with politics. Indonesia proposes now to mix sports with politics, and let us now establish the Games of the New Emerging
Forces, the GANEFO ... against the Old Established Order."[78]
Sukarno's anti-imperial, anti-colonial rhetoric played well in
many African, Asian, and Latin American countries. The IOC

viewed GANEFO as a challenge to its authority, as well as a threat to its effort to bring countries from the Global South into the Olympic movement. The month before GANEFO, the IOC cautioned athletes that taking part in the Games might result in their being banned from Olympic competition.

Nevertheless, Sukarno and his allies pressed ahead. In November 1963, more than 2,200 athletes from forty-eight countries participated in GANEFO. Competitors convened at Jakarta from Argentina, Brazil, Cambodia, Cuba, Guinea, Iraq, Japan, Mali, Morocco, North Korea, North Vietnam, Pakistan, Saudi Arabia, Somalia, Yugoslavia, and elsewhere. Palestinian athletes participated for "Arab Palestine." Since GANEFO was for "emerging forces," progressive athletes from "old established order" countries like Belgium, Finland, France, Italy, and the Netherlands also participated—making for a gathering that recalled the Workers' Olympiads of old. China, which was especially keen for the games to succeed, paid transport costs for all participating teams. Sukarno assumed the title of founder and honorary president of GANEFO, and used the games as a political bullhorn for a vision that connected with the ideals of the nascent Non-Aligned Movement.[79] He stated, "We will crush the old established order through unity among the newly emerging forces."[80]

While Western journalists derided GANEFO as a "snafu" and "the most completely disorganized sports event of which history has any record," most participants—and the huge crowds that gathered to watch—viewed it as an enormous success.[81] China used GANEFO as a way to compete in international athletics outside the purview of the IOC. The Soviet Union helped bankroll venue construction, but, in light of IOC threats to ban GANEFO participants from competing in the Olympics, suggested making it a youth event. (In the end, the USSR opted to send athletes to participate who would not qualify for the 1964 Olympics.) Chinese athletes flourished at GANEFO, winning more medals than any other country.

The Soviet Union's second-tier squad took second, followed by Indonesia.[82] Everyone walked away with a booklet called "Indonesia and the International Olympic Committee," which laid out Sukarno's grievances against the IOC and how "the 'old established forces,' whose interests run parallel with those of the old group of Brundage in the I.O.C." should be challenged.[83] GANEFO was a not-to-be-missed propaganda opportunity. On the one-year anniversary of the games Sukarno crowed, "Go to hell with the I.O.C. We of the New Emerging Forces are having a new sports grouping—GANEFO."[84]

But, like the alternative Games that preceded it, this "new sports grouping" didn't last long. Organizers planned GANEFO II to take place in Cairo in 1967, but the financial burden of staging the competition, along with Sukarno's overthrow by Suharto in 1966, sapped the energy from the movement. GANEFO II was never to be.[85] But the Games of the New Emerging Forces demonstrated that the Olympics—and sport more generally—are eminently political. Alternative models for organizing sport along political lines were indeed possible.

Apartheid, Activism, and the Games

The Olympic historian Allen Guttmann labels the early 1960s "the era of (relative) good feelings" for the Games.[86] Yet the good feelings were certainly besmirched by the animosity over the role of apartheid South Africa in the Olympics. For years the IOC had exhibited a willful gullibility when it came to South Africa. The IOC chose to take South African sports officials at their word that they would not exclude athletes from their Olympic teams based on race, despite abundant evidence to the contrary.

For the IOC, handcuffed by its ostensible doctrine of ignoring politics, South Africa was a nettlesome topic. In March

1964, as the Tokyo Games approached, Brundage wrote testily in a letter to Australian IOC member Hugh Weir, "Our South African problem is almost impossible to separate from the political question, with which we are not concerned."[87] Not surprisingly, Brundage had long argued to keep South Africa in the Olympic family, despite the country's overtly racist laws. He reasoned that the South African National Olympic Committee (SANOC) should not be held responsible for the wider policies of the government. But his colleagues within the IOC had other ideas. In light of the apartheid policies that had permeated South African sport itself, they voted to withdraw South Africa's invitation to the 1964 Tokyo Games.[88] Later, SANOC was also excluded from the 1968 Olympics at Mexico City, after thirty-nine countries—the thirty-two nations in the African Supreme Council for Sports as well as Cuba, Iraq, Malaysia, Pakistan, Saudi Arabia, Somalia, and Syria—promised to boycott the Games if South Africa were readmitted.[89] In 1970, the IOC officially expelled South Africa from the Olympic Movement.

Meanwhile, a general boycott of South Africa was gaining momentum across the globe. In 1964, after the Tokyo Games but before he picked up that year's Nobel Peace Prize, Dr. Martin Luther King spoke in London against the "bloodbath" brought on by apartheid. Presaging the divestiture movement, he said, "If the United Kingdom and the United States decided tomorrow morning not to buy South African goods, not to buy South African gold, to put an embargo on oil, if our investors and capitalists would withdraw their support for that racial tyranny that we find there, then apartheid would be brought to an end."[90]

Dissidents in South Africa zeroed in on the importance of the Olympic Games to the struggle against apartheid. In 1958, the poet-activist Dennis Brutus helped found the South African Sports Association (SASA). Comprising 60,000 members of all races, the group worked with Nelson Mandela, author Alan Paton, and human-rights organizer Patrick Duncan. The group helped keep South Africa out of the 1962 Commonwealth Games. Even though SASA was arguably the most powerful sports organization in South Africa, it lacked formal standing in the eyes of the IOC. Therefore, the group decided in 1962 to strategically rename itself the South African Non-Racial Olympic Committee (SANROC), just one letter off from SANOC. Initially there was resistance to the name change from within the African National Congress, but Mandela and Walter Sisulu persuaded the ANC to go along.[91] Brundage was apoplectic. In 1967, he contended that the IOC would not confer with SANROC unless it removed the term "Olympic" from its name. Technically speaking, SANROC accommodated the IOC, inserting "Open" for "Olympic." However, through the 1970s its stationery still read, "South Africa Non-Racial Olympic Committee."

Dennis Brutus, the president of SANROC, used the anti-discrimination principles enshrined in the Olympic Charter to argue that the organization was merely trying to slide South Africa into compliance with IOC policies and principles. Brutus later recalled: "Many friends would say, 'Why are you being so pedantic? Why are you sticking within the Charter?' The answer was simple; any argument that was not based on the Charter was thrown out by the IOC because the white, largely Anglophone members were not interested in expelling South Africa."[92] The idea was to implore the IOC and the international sports federations to live up to their own stated principles. The stratagem proved effective. Giulio Onesti, president of the Italian Olympic Committee, argued in a circular letter to IOC members, "If for reasons beyond my comprehension, it is desired at all costs to admit the South African NOC to the [1968] Games, it only remains to modify the text ... of our Charter, allowing the fact of racial discrimination."[93] The views of the president of the Italian Olympic Committee carried the day.

Prime Minister Jan de Klerk and the Afrikaaner-led government dug in, refusing to reform the system of separate "controlling associations" for each racial group, with the proviso that "white associations would control the code, send representatives to the world federation, and assist the development of black associations." De Klerk flatly stated that "racially mixed teams would not represent South Africa," and that "sports officials would not invite racially mixed teams from abroad to play in the Republic."[94] The apartheid government had doubled down.

Meanwhile, the South African government placed banning orders on Brutus, whose mixed-race heritage made him "Coloured" under apartheid regulations. The banning orders imposed in 1961 prohibited him from writing, and further orders passed in 1963 prohibited him from belonging to any organization or meeting with more than two people.[95] Police also quashed his plans to meet with a former Swiss sports administrator in South Africa. Later, when Brutus tried to travel to Germany to meet IOC officials, Portuguese authorities in Mozambique took him into custody and handed him over to South African officials. Back in Johannesburg, Brutus tried to escape and was shot on the street by South African security. He was left to bleed for an hour before a "Coloured" ambulance took him to a hospital, where his life was saved. All the while, members of the IOC and South African sport officials chastised SANROC for blending politics and sports, and detractors labeled the group "communist." SANROC went underground in 1965, emerging in 1966 outside South Africa. After serving nearly two years in prison, Brutus fled the country for London.[96]

Once in the UK, Brutus, along with fellow activists Sam Ramsamy, Reg Hlongwane, and Chris de Broglio, continued to use Olympic sports as a lever for political equality. They urged sympathetic national governments to join a boycott of the 1968 Games, even though Avery Brundage insisted that "the word 'boycott' is a political word not used in Olympic circles."[97] Brutus traveled to Canada and the United States, where he spoke to the House Foreign Affairs Sub-Committee as well as the UN Special Committee on Apartheid.[98] For years, SANROC bombarded IOC officials with letters challenging apartheid and demanding to be regarded as a National Olympic Committee. In one letter to the 1976 Montreal Organizing Committee, Sam Ramsamy informed organizers that SANROC would be sending delegates to Montreal and requested "the usual courtesies which will facilitate our entry into the Olympic Village and other venues where the meetings will be held."[99] SANROC also pressured regional sports officials, insisting they not host teams from apartheid South Africa. In a letter to the lead organizer of the Commonwealth Games, Brutus wrote, "It is my duty to advise you that SANROC is prepared to campaign vigorously for Commonwealth countries to decline to participate in the Games this year, if a team from South Africa is touring Britain at the same time." He urged organizers "to use whatever pressures are available" to avoid taking the "wrongheaded and unwise" path.[100] IOC President Lord Killanin—the Irishman who took over for Brundage in 1972—even circulated SANROC letters and informational materials to Olympic officials.[101]

SANROC worked with anti-apartheid groups worldwide. The former Canadian Olympian Bruce Kidd, at the time an untenured professor at the University of Toronto, wrote to Harry Kerrison, the head of the Canadian Track and Field Association, to dispute sending athletes to compete in a track meet in South Africa. Kidd contended, "Very few of our members would like to see our national champions lend their support to the repressive system" of apartheid. "And yet that's exactly what happens when they compete under the contrived conditions of the South African Games." He promised, "I am not prepared to leave it at writing one letter" and followed through, putting consistent pressure on Canadian officials to align their rhetoric and their actions.[102]

The boycott push paid off. South Africa's invitations to the 1964 Tokyo Olympics and the 1968 Mexico City Games were withdrawn. When Brundage announced the Mexico City decision to the press, he reportedly had tears in his eyes.[103] Brundage wrote in a cable to IOC members, "In view of all the information on the international climate received by the executive board ... It is unanimously of the opinion that it would be most unwise for a South African team to participate" in Mexico City.[104] SANROC had played a vital role in creating the climate that severely limited Brundage's range of choices, as did the dozens of countries that vowed to boycott the Games if South Africa was re-admitted to compete. After South Africa's expulsion from the Olympic movement, it lurched around the sports wilderness until the fall of apartheid allowed it to return to the Olympics in 1992 at Barcelona.[105] SANROC's efforts to undercut the racist sports structure in South Africa and to use sport to raise larger political questions were a success.

1968 Olympics in Mexico City

Anti-apartheid activism created momentum for a historic act of dissent on a related but separate issue. At the 1968 Summer Games in Mexico City, the African American track stars Tommie Smith and John Carlos stood in their socks on the medal stand and thrust their black-glove-clad fists toward the sky as they bowed their heads while the US national anthem played. They were protesting the poverty and racism that plagued the United States and the wider world. Their shoe-less feet and black socks symbolized poverty. Their black gloves signified black pride. Carlos's open jacket represented his working-class roots. Carlos later wrote: "We decided that we would wear black gloves to represent strength and unity. We would have beads hanging from our neck, which would represent the history of lynching. We wouldn't wear shoes to symbolize the poverty that still plagued so much of black America. On the medal stand, all we would wear on our feet would be black socks."[106] As Tommie Smith later explained, "The totality of our effort was the regaining of our black dignity."[107] Carlos told me they took action "to set a standard. To have a society show its best face. To bring attention to the plight of people who were less fortunate. To wake up the consciousness of those who had let their conscience go dormant. And to encourage people to stand for what's right as opposed to standing for nothing."[108] Both men pinned human-rights buttons on their track jackets. The silver medalist, Peter Norman of Australia, sported a button in solidarity.

Radical politics were thrumming around the globe as the Olympics took the stage in Mexico City, and so was the violent reaction of the state. Only a few weeks prior at Tlatelolco Plaza in the host city, security forces massacred scores, perhaps hundreds of protesters, a measure of how far Mexican authorities were willing to go to maintain order. The Tlatelolco Plaza demonstrators were protesting the allocation of vast funds for the Olympics while social programs went unfunded. Brundage took stock of the turbulent times and told the opening session of the IOC, "We live today in an uneasy and even rebellious world, a world marked by injustice, aggression, demonstrations, disorder, turmoil, violence and war, against which all civilized persons rebel, but this is no reason to destroy the nucleus of international cooperation and goodwill we have created in the Olympic Movement." Trying to distance the Olympic movement from the radical politics of the moment, he added, "You don't find hippies, yippies or beatniks on sports grounds."[109]

But there were principled activist-athletes on the playing fields of 1968. Smith and Carlos were not lone renegades; they were part of a political movement rooted in athletic achievement. In the United States, Harry Edwards, a sociologist and political organizer, had helped found the Olympic Project for Human Rights (OPHR) in 1967. At a press conference in December of that year, the group unveiled six demands, which it listed as following:

1. Restoration of Muhammad Ali's title and right to box in this country.
2. Removal of the anti-Semitic and anti-black personality Avery Brundage from his post as Chairman of the International Olympic Committee.
3. Curtailment of participation of all-white teams and individuals from the Union of South Africa and Southern Rhodesia in all United States Olympic Athletic events.
4. The addition of at least two black coaches to the men's track and field coaching staff appointed to coach the 1968 United States Olympic team.
5. The appointment of at least two black people to policy-making positions on the United States Olympic Committee.
6. The complete desegregation of the bigot-dominated and racist New York Athletic Club.[110]

The IOC president and the injustices emanating from South Africa sat in the center of OPHR's sites, evidence of the group's global vision. Tommie Smith stressed in his autobiography that the OPHR's name highlighted "human rights, not civil rights—nothing to do with the Panthers or Black Power—all humanity, even those who denied us ours."[111] Yet improving the lives of black people was a central goal. Writing retrospectively, Edwards identified OPHR's key aims: "to stage an international protest of the persistent and systematic violation of black people's human rights in the United States" and "to expose America's historical exploitation of black athletes as political propaganda tools in both the national and international arenas."[112]

To press toward these goals, the OPHR threatened to orchestrate a boycott of the 1968 Games. In April, to combat apartheid, sixty-five US athletes signed on to a list that supported a boycott if South Africa were allowed to participate. Numerous prominent athletes signed, including Arthur Ashe, Wilt Chamberlain, Jim Bouton, Len Wilkins, Oscar Robertson, Jackie Robinson, and Ruben Amaro. The track stars John Carlos and Lee Evans also joined.[113] A few months earlier, Jackie Robinson led a group of famous athletes, including Tommie Smith, Dave Bing, Bob Gibson and K. C. Jones, pushing for South Africa to be banned from the Games.[114] Months of activist campaigning—often led by athletes themselves—built up to Smith and Carlos's act of defiance. Movements created space for the athletes' iconic moment.

Meanwhile, the powerful were becoming nervous. In July 1968, Vincent X. Flaherty, a Los Angeles sports journalist, wrote Brundage a letter that promised to craft a critical article on the boycott threat. Flaherty asked: "Why can't the Negro athletes sign now as to their intentions? Why can't recalitrants [*sic*] be barred now so as to avoid any possible disgraceful demonstrations[?]" Ditching even the pretense of journalistic objectivity, he also suggested ignoring OPHR figure Harry Edwards: "I think this man Edward's [*sic*] name should be kept out of print, and I also think the IOC should take a definitive action." He added, "I think you will agree this sort of thing has no place in the Olympics as a whole, nor does it have any right to be foisted upon the host country."[115] Indeed the IOC president agreed. In less than two weeks Brundage responded: "The action of Edwards is directed against the people of the United States ... It is unfortunate that so much publicity is given to these people." He continued, "The Olympic Games have given the negro an opportunity to display his talents on a completely equal basis, and it is outrageous that they should be used for political purposes."[116] This interaction underlines what sociologist Ben Carrington calls "the fear of the black athlete" as rooted in "the projection of white masculinist fantasies of domination [and] control." The powerful were squirming.[117]

The sports media establishment tended to agree with the Brundage line, urging the athletes to shut up and play. Once Smith and Carlos took their stand on the medal stand, many commentators became outright hostile. Arthur Daley of the *New York Times* wrote, "Smith and Carlos brought their world smack into the Olympic Games, where it did not belong, and created a shattering situation that shook this international sports carnival to its very core. They were also divisive."[118] Brent Musburger, writing for the *Chicago American*, railed against the "black-skinned storm troopers" he deemed "unimaginative blokes." He fumed: "One gets a little tired of having the United States run down by athletes who are enjoying themselves at the expense of their country. Protesting and working constructively against racism in the United States is one thing, but airing one's dirty clothing before the entire world during a fun-and-games tournament was no more than a juvenile gesture by a couple of athletes who should have known better."[119] The *New York Times* found division within the US squad. The gold-medal-winning boxer George Foreman, who dismissed their efforts, told the paper: "That's for college kids. They live in another world."[120]

Brundage was livid with Smith and Carlos. He pressured the US Olympic Committee to suspend the athletes from the team and dismiss them from the Olympic Village. The USOC obliged, releasing a statement that read in part, "The United States Olympic Committee expresses its profound regrets to the International Olympic Committee, to the Mexican Organizing Committee and to the people of Mexico for the discourtesy displayed by two members of its team in departing from tradition during a victory ceremony at the Olympic Stadium on October 16th." The USOC labeled their act "untypical exhibitionism" that "violates the basic standards of sportsmanship and good manners." Pivoting to threat, it then noted, "A repetition of such incidents by other members of the US team can only be considered a willful disregard of Olympic principles that would warrant the severest penalties."[121] This threat was echoed by the IOC official Lord David Burghley—also known as the Marquess of Exeter—who said: "I will not countenance such actions again. I'll refuse to hold a victory ceremony if any such attempt is made again."[122]

Brundage received a trailer load of mail regarding the Smith and Carlos affair and how he handled it. Many defended the act of dissent. One letter writer told Brundage, "A wonderful week of sportsmanship has been spoiled for me by the punishment of the young American athletes," and added, "these young men understood that justice and brotherhood are the only gold medal worth having, and they had the courage to stand up and say so."[123] Another alluded to South Africa's exclusion from the Games and asked: "Yet two Negro athletes were expelled for 'mixing politics and athletics.' How hypocritical can you get?!"[124] One critic from Los Angeles slammed "the senseless, idiotic, racist reaction of our Olympic Committee." He concluded that Carlos and Smith "will be greeted as black power heroes by an incensed black America, more convinced than ever that white America has nothing but hatred for the black man." He closed by promising to send a $25 check to the Urban League "in the hopes that they can achieve brotherhood in the world, since you have so badly failed."[125]

Numerous people writing Brundage specified that they were white before accusing the International Olympic Committee of undermining "one of the United States' most cherished traditions, the right to speak out"[126] and taking action that was "disgusting, uncalled for, narrow-minded, and indicative of your prejudice."[127] Many called the suspension of Smith and Carlos "unduly harsh treatment for their quiet and dignified act of protest against conditions in their country. They were not protesting the Olympic Committee, or the games, or Mexico, or any other country."[128] Telegrams flooded in from around the world from groups like the Athletex Welfare Association of Nigeria and the Southern Christian Leadership Conference (SCLC). Jesse Jackson wrote a telegram directly to Tommie Smith congratulating him for his courageous act, stating, "You may have been on the wrong side of the Olympic Committee, but on the right side of history." He issued Smith an open invitation to come speak at the SCLC's breadbasket community meetings, expenses paid.[129]

Many, however, weighed in to chastise Carlos and Smith and offer support to Brundage. Racism sometimes showed through, as in a letter from Omaha, Nebraska, that read:

> The actions of the two Negroes, Smith and Carlos, was a national disgrace. I hope you stick to your decision to keep them off the team. Some others should be booted off, too. Our State Dept. should take action on such traitors, but for political expediency they won't. The white man owes the Negro nothing. Let some of them return to the stone age delights of tribal Africa. In all time the Negro race is the only race to have contributed nothing toward civilization. They do excell [sic] in motor co-ordination.[130]

Brundage often took the time to respond to letter writers who supported the dismissal of Smith and Carlos. Frequently he wrote, "Good manners and sportsmanship are more important than athletic ability." Among the other sentiments he expressed: "We do not propose to permit demonstrations of any kind at the Olympic Games"[131]; "The boys were sent home, but they should not have been there in the first place"[132]; "As a matter of fact people of that kind should not have been on the Olympic team at all. This was not a school boy prank as some seem to think ... it left international repercussions very harmful to our country"[133]; "You are exactly right and your views have been supported by all true United States citizens. The action of these negroes was an insult to the Mexican hosts and a disgrace to the United States."[134]

After the Games, Brundage bristled over the possible inclusion of Smith and Carlos in the official Olympic film. In a letter to the chair of the Mexico City Organizing Committee, Brundage railed about "the rumors that have reached my ears about the use of pictures of the nasty demonstration against the United States flag by negroes in the official film of the Games of the XIX Olympiad." He went on to argue, "It had nothing to do with sport, it was a shameful abuse of hospitality and it has no more place in the record of the Games than the gunfire at Tlaltelolco." He reiterated his point by concluding, "With the hope that this objectionable feature will be eliminated, I am."[135] In a separate letter, Mexican IOC member José de J. Clark wrote, "To beg you that said scene be omitted from the official film of the Olympic Games."[136] The Mexico City Olympic organizers wrote back with a compromise: excluding the protest by Smith and Carlos in the version of the film sent to the official IOC archive and to NOCs, but keeping it in the copies that would shown commercially.[137] Brundage's biographer notes: "Brundage was clearly unable in this instance to apply the aesthetic criteria that he relied upon in his eloquent defense of Leni Riefenstahl's film of the 1936 games. The Nazi salute and the swastika were part of the *Gesamtkunstwerk* of the Olympic ceremony, but the black-power salute and the black berets were somehow 'political'."[138]

Both Carlos and Smith paid a high price for their actions. They received a steady stream of threats on their lives. They were pilloried in the press. Jobs were scarce. They lost marriages to the stress. Carlos and Smith's own relationship strained as friction mounted between them. Peter Norman, who stood with them in solidarity on the medal stand, was treated like a pariah in Australia. Despite posting times that would qualify him for the 1972 Games, he was cut from the Australia squad. When Sydney hosted the 2000 Olympics, Norman was not officially acknowledged.

Yet Smith, Carlos, and Norman never backtracked, and

history has vindicated them. Even President Barack Obama publicly praised Carlos and Smith. "To signify in that Olympics that there was more work to do, to acknowledge the injustices that were still taking place, I think that was a breakthrough moment in an overall push to move this country towards a more equal and more just society," he said, "I think that what they did was in the best tradition of American protest."[139] This is an example of the common tendency to revere activists the further they recede in the rearview mirror of history. The entire episode also highlights, as the sociologist Douglas Hartmann puts it, "the thrill of victory and the agony of activism," and helps us understand why more Olympic athletes don't use their high-profile athletic stage to engage politics.[140]

The athlete-activism did not end with Carlos and Smith. Vera Caslavska, the most successful Czech gymnast in the history of the Olympics, also took a political stand on the medal stand. Two months before the Mexico City Games commenced, the Soviet Union led an invasion of Czechoslovakia in order to crush the "Prague Spring," inklings of democracy—or at least moves toward less surveillance and repression—that aimed to loosen the Soviet stranglehold on the country. The Czechoslovak National Olympic Committee nearly opted to withdraw from the 1968 Games, as the incursion made training nearly impossible for athletes and major transatlantic airlines were not flying out of Prague. Less than a month before the Games' opening ceremony, Czechoslovakia decided to press ahead and send its 100-strong team to Mexico City.[141]

Caslavska had already established herself as a top-flight gymnast, winning three gold medals and a silver at the Tokyo 1964 Olympics. She had also shown herself to be an athlete willing to speak out, signing onto the *Manifesto of 2,000 Words* in April 1968, which protested Soviet hegemony in Czechoslovakia. Four months later, the Soviets invaded and Caslavska fled into hiding where she trained in suboptimal, stressful conditions. But with the Soviet-led assault as a political backdrop, Caslavska shined in Mexico City, winning four more gold medals and two silvers. In the process, she beat out archrival Soviet gymnasts, to the ecstatic cheers of local spectators, and not simply because she selected the "Mexican Hat Dance" as the accompaniment for her final floor performance. Only days after Carlos and Smith thrust their fists skyward, Caslavska made her own political statement on the medal stand, if a more subtle one, dipping her head in silent protest during the Russian national anthem. Caslavska was clearly motivated by politics. "I am a Czechoslovak citizen," she later said. "We all tried harder to win in Mexico because it would turn the eyes of the world on our unfortunate country."[142] She paid a price for her principles. The Soviet-compliant government in Prague forbade her from traveling abroad or from competing in gymnastics. But years later, with another significant shift in the political winds and the rise of Vaclav Havel, Caslavska would become the head of the Czech National Olympic Committee as well as the eighth woman coopted as a member of the IOC.

1972 Olympics

The 1972 Olympics at Munich are known first and foremost for the terrorist attack that occurred partway through the Games. On September 5, 1972, armed members of a Palestinian militant group calling itself Black September snuck into the Olympic Village and kidnapped eleven Israeli coaches and athletes, killing two of them. This eventually led to a gun battle in which all nine remaining Israelis, five Palestinian militants, and one German police officer were killed on the airport tarmac as the militants and their hostages prepared to board a plane.

Brundage was faced with a vexing situation. What should be done in the aftermath of a mass killing? As in 1968, when

Mexican security forces gunned down innocent protesters shortly before the Summer Olympics commenced, he decided to press ahead with the Games. In a swiftly prepared response he announced:

> Every civilized person recoils in horror at the barberous [*sic*] criminal intrusion of terrorists into peaceful Olympic precincts. We mourn our Isreal [*sic*] friends victims of this brutal assault. The Olympic flag and all the flags of the world fly at halfmast. Sadly, in this imperfect world, the greater and more important the Olympic Games become, the more they are open to commercial, political, and now criminal pressure. The Games of the XX Olympiad have been subjected to two savage attacks. We lost the Rhodesian battle against naked political blackmail. We have only the strength of a great ideal. I am sure that the public will agree that we cannot allow a handful of terrorists to destroy this nucleus of international cooperation and good will we have in the Olympic Movement. The Games must go on and we must continue our efforts to keep them clean, pure and honest and try to extend the sportsmanship of the athletic field into other areas. We declare today a day of mourning and will continue all the events one day later than originally scheduled.[143]

Brundage took flak for his decision to proceed with sport. A *New York Times* editorial blasted the IOC, asking: "Are medals and commercial contracts more important than human lives? That question rises inevitably in the wake of the incomprehensible decision to continue the 1972 Olympic Games." The paper went on to assert, "Perhaps the whole concept of the Olympics needs re-examination."[144] Others lashed out at his clumsy inclusion of Rhodesia in his statement on the terrorist attack and killings. Rhodesia had been excluded by a majority of IOC members through processes marked out by the Olympic Charter. The outcry, led by African nations, forced an apology from Brundage—sort of. He issued a press statement that read in its entirety: "As President of the International Olympic Committee we regret any misinterpretation of the remarks made during the solemn memorial services in the stadium yesterday. There was not the slightest intention of linking the Rhodesia question which was purely a matter of sport with an act of terrorism universally condemned."[145] Brundage's response demonstrated his intransigence and his tendency to blame others and their "misinterpretations" of his remarks.

But Brundage got his wish and the Games went on, and in an atmosphere thick with politics. The dissident spirit of 1968 still pulsed in 1972, when the Games moved to Munich. In the early 1990s John Carlos observed: "The '68 Olympics are *alive*. The juice, the fire of '68, that scared a lot of people. All of us were such strong personalities, and *that* scared people. It scared government and business, everybody. It *still* scares them."[146] The American track stars Vincent Matthews and Wayne Collett, Olympic teammates of Smith and Carlos in 1968, caused a stir when they accepted their gold and silver medals for the 400-meter dash in a deliberately nonchalant fashion that many perceived as insolent. Mindful that conditions for African Americans hadn't much improved since the last Games, Matthews and Collett lounged as the national anthem played, swirling their medals around their fingers and stroking their chins. The *New York Times* described the athletes' "indifference and disrespect" as provoking "spectators' wrath" in Munich.[147]

The IOC expressed its own wrath by banning the two athletes from the rest of the Munich Games and from all future Olympic competitions, even though the athletes made no overt political gestures. Matthews said, "We came up with no protest in mind, but the crowd had protest in mind when we left. If people call our talking on the stand a protest, well, some people can watch 'Alice in Wonderland' and get pornography out of it." Collett added, "My actions mirror the attitude of white America toward blacks. They treat us in a casual manner as long as we don't embarrass them."[148] Brundage had no patience for such explanations. He scolded the USOC: "The whole world saw the disgusting display of your two athletes, when they received their gold and silver medals for the 400 M event yesterday. This is the second time the U.S.O.C. has permitted such occurrences on the athletic field."[149]

The discussion of the athletes' actions in the IOC Executive Committee minutes, a record not normally known for emotion-packed prose, was severe. Under the heading of "Bad behaviour," the IOC chided: "The two black athletes Matthews and Collett had acted disgracefully during the victory ceremony of the 400 m event. It had been a disgrace for the USA. The USOC-officials agreed fully in the complaint of the IAAF and it had been decided to send the two athletes back to USA immediately. Later this had been changed as such action would only make heroes of them." Under "Decisions" the minutes read, "The two athletes eliminated from taking part in any future Olympic competitions" and "the USOC to be cautioned about future competitors."[150] These lifetime bans exceeded the penalties leveled against Smith and Carlos. The Executive Committee minutes made no mention of the USOC enlisting Jesse Owens to talk to Matthews, Collett, and others the day after their controversial medal stand actions. Owens implored the athletes to apologize, promising employment for them after the Games. The athletes rebuffed Owens, much as Carlos, Smith, and other athletes from the 1968 Games did when the star of the 1936 Olympics asked them to tone down their politics.[151] Meanwhile, many in the US drew inspiration from Matthews and Collett, with Black Panther Party artist Emory Douglas commemorating their actions in the organization's newspaper.

In an op-ed Matthews wrote for the *New York Times*, he pointed out that as he climbed the medal stand the "Rhodesian question and the Arab-Israeli affair" had been flitting through his mind.[152] By the "Rhodesian question" he meant the ongoing controversy over the IOC's exclusion of the southern African country because of the racist sports policies of its white minority government. After the IOC banned Rhodesia from the 1968 Games, it initially opted to reinstate the country for the 1972 Munich Olympics. However, after pressure mounted from American and African athletes the IOC backpedaled, disinviting Rhodesia only days before the Games began. "The Arab-Israeli affair" was shorthand for the terrorist attack that marred the Games.

The terrorist attack in Munich was a pivotal point in Olympic history. Ever since, terrorism has been a major concern, and host cities have ramped up security measures to prevent attacks. This has proved controversial, however, as those same security forces can also be used to quash or discourage political activism. Additionally, many argue that increased security unduly militarizes public space in the name of a two-and-a-half-week sports extravaganza.

The 1972 Munich Games also brought the first official Olympic mascot, a multicolored dachshund called Waldi.[153] The Games were also the last for President Brundage, the IOC's longtime resident bulldog. His twenty-year reign came to a close, but he went out the door kicking. According to the IOC Executive Committee minutes, he "deplored the way the Games were exploited" for commercial purposes.[154] He viewed Waldi as emblematic of a creeping commercialization, even though it was quaint compared to the corporate cornucopia that was to follow. Lord Killanin took over at the conclusion of the Games. Brundage died in May 1975; one suggested epitaph for his headstone was "For once, he gave in."[155] A new era of Olympic history was coming, and the 1976 Olympiad was its kickoff.

4

Commercialization of the Olympics

Today the Olympic Games are an enormous sports, media, and marketing juggernaut, a top-tier athletic festival awash in corporate cash. The IOC sits at the center, oscillating Janus-faced between multinational conglomerate and global institution. To understand how we got to this point we need to start with the 1976 Summer and Winter Olympics.

Even before the attack in Munich, the Olympics were in trouble. Activists in Colorado were strategizing to scuttle the 1976 Winter Games, which the IOC had chosen to stage in Denver. "It's going to be a great thing for Colorado," the state's governor, John Love, promised after winning the bid in 1970. The president of Denver's Chamber of Commerce vowed the Games would have a "great economic impact" and enthused, "It makes us look like we're alive and we're recognized worldwide as a major city."[1] But environmental activists in Colorado had other ideas. Organizations like the Rocky Mountain Center on Environment and Protect Our Mountain Environment deluged IOC officials with letters imploring them to relocate the Olympics because of the ecological degradation they said the Games would cause. They teamed up with critics of government spending to force a state bond referendum in which Coloradans voted to reject funding for the Olympics.[2] The IOC had no choice but to go to Plan B: moving the Games to Innsbruck, Austria. Denver became the first city to spurn the Olympics after the IOC selected it as host. Here, sport most definitely became a locus of political resistance.

Meanwhile, Montreal was preparing to host the 1976 Summer Games. In early 1973, Roger Rousseau, the head of the Montreal organizing committee, vowed that the Games would be "self-financing, without adding in any way to the Canadian taxpayers' burden, without any special subsidy of any type whatsoever," provided that the federal government allowed him to access national lottery funds and jumpstart a commemorative coins and postage stamps program. Jean Drapeau, the charismatic mayor of Montreal, echoed Rousseau's optimism, assuring journalists that the Montreal Olympics would be "self-financing." But when Drapeau said, "You should hear before long some debate about how the surplus will be spent," the reporters in the room erupted in laughter. The mayor doubled down: "I know you laugh now ... but ... it won't be very long before some argument is started throughout Canada to find out how the surplus will be spent."[3] Oh, how wrong he turned out to be. The Games ran up a debt of $1.5 billion that wasn't paid off until 2006, thirty years after IOC officials had helicoptered away from the province of Quebec.[4] These two money-draining episodes paved a superhighway toward the commercialization of the Games, as Olympic power brokers recognized the need to change their game plan.

Dissent in Denver

In 1970, one month before the IOC awarded the 1976 Winter Olympics to Denver, the Mile-High City's mayor, William J. McNichols Jr., was high on Olympism. He wrote to the IOC, "Those of us in Denver, young and old, are enthusiastic at the prospect of having the honor of welcoming the Olympic family to Denver in 1976."[5] In a cover letter accompanying Denver's candidature file, the mayor poured it on thick: "May you continue to be blessed with the wisdom and foresight necessary for the furtherance of the Olympic ideal."[6] Most of Colorado's political class rallied behind the Games, as did the Denver Chamber of Commerce, the Colorado Association of Commerce and Industry, the Rotary Club of Denver, and numerous other community groups. Various Kiwanis clubs and Optimist societies signed on. The University of Denver's board of trustees passed a resolution endorsing the Games and the University of Colorado, Boulder, offered support.[7]

But not everyone shared the enthusiasm. Concerned by the possibility of escalating costs, a tax hike, potential environmental damage, and runaway development, an array of organizations gathered under the umbrella group Citizens for Colorado's Future. "Don't Californicate Colorado!" became a popular slogan.[8]

Activists barraged the IOC with letters urging the relocation of the Games. The escalating price tag was a prime point of concern. While Denver organizers originally assured the public that the Olympics would cost $14 million and remain within the Denver area, projected costs climbed to $35 million, with plans to spread venues deep into the Rocky Mountains.[9] Critics raised the issue of opportunity costs. One local resident suggested that rather than spending public money on Olympic venue building, funds could be spent on "the purchasing of food, medicine, and education for those unfortunate people throughout the world." He argued, "It is my opinion that dollars spent in this manner will certainly benefit mankind far greater than a new ski jump in Evergreen, Colorado." Another proposed to the IOC that the Games should be held in the same location every four years: "Would it not be sensible to encourage a permanent base for the Games and not tear up country after country for new sites?"[10]

Critics also slammed the Denver Organizing Committee for lacking transparency and for ignoring citizen input. The communications director from Citizens for Colorado's Future maintained that the local organizing committee "has to date shown itself to be insensitive to citizen opinion, undemocratic and secretive in its operations, and careless to the point of negligence in its management." Another critic accused organizers of proliferating "blatant misinformation" about the Games and their impact.[11] The president of the Mountain Area Planning Council wrote a scathing letter to Brundage, chastising the Denver Organizing Committee's "flagrant disregard" for its environmental commitments and asserting the council was "unequivocally opposed" to siting any competitions in the front-range mountains of Jefferson County.[12] Brundage's papers contain four folders full of letters from concerned Coloradans.

Elected officials also weighed in. The Aspen City Council wrote to protest the Denver Organizing Committee's unwillingness to meet with them to discuss site selection. After numerous requests for consultation and information, Denver 1976 organizers had "not even seen fit to have a meeting with the city council." A petition signed by 1,500 Aspen residents prompted the Aspen city council to request the IOC that the resort town be excluded from hosting alpine ski events.[13] Richard Lamm, the Colorado House of Representatives assistant minority leader, wrote Brundage expressing opposition to the Games based on fiscal concerns. "Colorado, painfully, cannot afford to host the 1976 Olympics," he wrote. "We are a small state, already on the verge of taxpayer revolt. We cannot afford to do justice to our schools, to our institutions, to our many other pressing needs now; and as we become aware of the vast financial commitment to host the 1976 Olympics we see increasingly that we do not have the will or the tax base to afford the 1976 Olympics."[14] In a letter to Canadian IOC member James Worrall, Lamm argued, "The debate over the ability of our small state to properly host the Games is tearing us apart and dividing our people. Candidates of both parties are lining up to run on the anti-Olympics platform." He wrote, "I urge you to remove the Games from Colorado. It would be to the benefit of both Colorado and the Olympics."[15]

The letters had an impact in the upper echelons of the Olympic movement. In May 1972, Brundage wrote a memo cataloging activist grievances and detailing the number of critical telephone calls he had received.[16] IOC member and future president Lord Killanin sent a packet of critical letters to US Olympics official Clifford Buck and exclaimed: "I fear these political, social and technical problems in Colorado are not helping the Olympic Movement! The letters seem reasonable and not cranky!"[17]

Yet there also was some underestimation of the protesters. At an IOC meeting in September 1971, Brundage asked Robert Pringle, the president of the Denver Organizing Committee, about "some unfortunate publicity that appeared in the press" on anti-Olympics protesters and Pringle scoffed at "any chance of success" for the activists.[18] In early 1972, Pringle wrote Brundage to alert him that "some of the environmental leaders in Colorado are again attempting to show opposition." He dismissed the fightback as merely "a nuisance."[19]

At an IOC meeting one attendee asserted that anti-Olympics petitions "were, more often than not, signed by 'crack-pots' and groups of school children encouraged to sign just to fill out the protest."[20] Later the IOC Executive Committee miscalculated when it dubbed the protesters "ridiculous" and incapable of gathering the signatures required for a referendum on public funding of the Games. IOC officials believed that even though activists had forced a referendum, two-thirds of the population would support holding the Games in Denver.[21] But the referendum concerned officials, who feared that "it would not be good for athletes to come to a city where everybody was hostile to them." Denver organizers dismissed the concern, making the distinction between opposing the Olympics and opposing funding the Olympics. As the referendum date approached, Lord Killanin chided Denver organizers for minimizing protesters as mere "cranks."[22]

Protesters generally stayed within the boundaries of legal

tactics, although activists occasionally veered into sabotage. According to one media account, "Somebody even burned down the steep-slope ski jump that towers above town" in Steamboat Springs, "scribbling anti-Olympic obscenities on the charred remains."[23]

In the run-up to the November 1972 referendum, pro-Olympics forces enjoyed significant advantages. They poured more than $175,000 into a marketing campaign, received endorsements from prominent Olympians, and were helped by a compliant press. As *Sports Illustrated* put it at the time, Olympic supporters "trotted out that old pro-Olympian Jesse Owens and flooded the state with entreaties to 'light the torch now,' meanwhile receiving sustenance from the *Denver Post*, which in the campaign's final days devoted up to five times more news space to Olympic boosters than to critics."[24] Activists, by comparison, ran a modest campaign. Citizens for Colorado's Future spent less than $24,000 during its entire existence, and most of those funds were raised through five-to-ten-dollar donations. The group's media budget barely topped $2,000. Yet the activists won handily at the ballot box with 60 percent of the final vote. Afterwards, the chairman of the Denver Organizing Committee conceded defeat: "The voters made their position clear ... they don't want the Olympics."[25] USOC president Clifford Buck wrote the newly minted IOC president, Lord Killanin, with the official version of the bad news: "The city of Denver and State of Colorado have no choice but to withdraw the invitation extended to the IOC for the holding of the 1976 Olympic Winter Games at Denver."[26]

By subverting the funding, Colorado activists and their allies successfully rebuffed the Games, forcing the IOC to relocate the 1976 Winter Olympics to Innsbruck. *Sports Illustrated* concluded that the activist campaign and referendum in Colorado "was not a vote against the Olympics per se, nor a vote against sport. But it was a vote against sporting facilities that cost taxpayers millions of dollars" and in

favor of "essential conservation attitudes in the area concerned."[27] Activism in Denver helped shift the tectonic plates
of Olympism. So would the debacle of Montreal.

Men, Babies, and Boycotts

Late in 1972, Canadian IOC member James Worrall sought
to assuage concerns about Olympic "gigantism." "The success
of Montreal in staging the Games on a more modest scale of
costs is important to Canada, but also could save the life of the
Olympics," he said.[28] Montreal's mayor, Jean Drapeau, also
forecast a modest Games: "The Olympics should not come
as an astronomical enterprise. We promise that in Canada,
in Montreal, we will present the Games in the true spirit of
Olympism, very humble, with simplicity and dignity."[29] In a
statement that would later come back to haunt him, Drapeau
claimed, "The Montreal Olympics can no more have a deficit,
than a man can have a baby."[30]

In the early days of organizing the Games Drapeau said the
Olympics could be staged for $125 million. Later he admit-
ted to the Canadian writer Jack Ludwig: "That was not an
estimate. In 1970 we had no specific plans for any type of
installation. One hundred and twenty-five million dollars was
—how shall I put it?—*a budgetary envelope*."[31] Later in
1970, the "budgetary envelope" ballooned to a guessti-
mate of $310 million. When Drapeau first pitched the IOC
he hadn't secured federal financial support. For its part, the
federal government in Ottawa favored the idea of staging the
1976 Winter Olympics in Vancouver, since the Winter Games
were cheaper and Canadian athletes excelled at winter sports.
Liberal prime minister Pierre Trudeau held Drapeau in suspicion, given Drapeau's support of right-wing ideologies and
alignment with the conservative forces within Québécois
nationalism.

By 1973, the Quebec provincial government said it would act as a fiscal backstop for the Games. The federal government followed suit, chipping in funds from an Olympic lottery as well as a commemorative stamp and coin scheme. But the fiscal foot-shuffling severely hampered planning. The blueprints for the extravagant Olympic Stadium, designed by the French celebrity architect Roger Taillibert, weren't finished until September 1974. By January 1975 Drapeau was insisting Montreal could host the Games for $583 million and still break even. Meanwhile the Montreal Organizing Committee was predicting that costs would exceed that amount by another $60 million.[32] Even with the promise of federal support, by September 1975 Drapeau had to resort to evasive language. "Recently you have heard a wrong word—a deficit of $250 million that the Games would leave," he said. "This is not a deficit. This is a gap."[33]

The Montreal Games ended up costing $1.5 billion, making them the most expensive Olympics to that point, and saddling Canadians with a debt that would take them three decades to pay. The Stade Olympique—which wasn't fully completed until years after the Games—earned the derisive moniker "the Big Owe."[34] And, if that weren't enough, two years after Montreal finally retired its debt, a man had a baby: Thomas Beatie, a transgender man from Bend, Oregon, gave birth to a healthy baby girl in July 2008.[35]

Olympic VIPs always put a happy face on the progress of Games preparations, and Montreal was no exception. But behind the scenes they were in panic mode about spiraling costs and negative publicity. IOC members and Canadian Olympic Association (COA) officials grilled the Comité Organizateur des Jeux Olympiques (COJO), firing off a stream of fretful missives. In 1972, with Games funding in the air, IOC official James Worrall wrote in a private letter, "I am concerned about progress in Montreal, but certainly do not wish to make any public statements that will be misinterpreted." He complained of mounting costs and increasingly negative public perceptions. He mentioned "Drapeau's originally-announced figure of $120 million," which had become a public talking point. "I never was sure where he got this figure," he wrote, "but it certainly is being held up to ridicule at this time."[36] In another letter, Worrall agonized that the ever-escalating costs were becoming an open target for media mockery. He complained about critical articles appearing in the *Toronto Sun* before demanding that "COJO must take steps as quickly as possible to prevent this kind of snowballing effect from continuing."[37] When boosters in Vancouver suggested bidding on the 1980 Games, Worrall replied with exasperation, "I think we have enough of a problem in Montreal at the moment."[38] In January 1975, then COA secretary and future IOC member Richard Pound wrote Rousseau with a long list of concerns. He closed his letter by noting the stakes: a sub-par Games would be "a national catastrophe."[39] No pressure or anything.

For certain parties the Montreal Games were a moneymaker. One commentator observed, "Enormous profits were reaped by banks, entrepreneurs, developers, construction companies and advertising agencies."[40] The 1976 Games brought a leap in Olympic sponsorship. When the federal government refused to cover the Olympics' fiscal deficit, Montreal organizers went full-on corporate, teaming with commercial "sponsors" and "official suppliers." Coca-Cola bathed in the Olympic glow, contributing $1.3 million and all the soda athletes could quaff. Adidas paid $500,000 to outfit ushers and other Olympic personnel. Cadbury Schweppes provided free chocolate and grape juice to Olympians. Tetley's proffered the tea. Molson Breweries became an "official sponsor." Olympic officials justified their newfound commercialism as "consistent with the spirit of the Olympics," arguing that the Games were "a competitive challenge, not only for athletes but for a vast supporting infrastructure of equipment, materials and supplies."[41] The idea that corporations had a vital role to play in the "Olympic family" would intensify and become baked into the Olympic mix during the following decade. But Montreal and its money woes paved the way.

Bruce Kidd, the onetime Canadian Olympian turned Olympic critic, reveled in the "joyous 15 days of breathtaking performances and moving personal encounters" that the Montreal Games provided. "For two weeks," he wrote, "all the contradictions seemed to stand still."[42] The fourteen-year-old Romanian gymnast Nadia Comaneci became the first ever to score a perfect ten at an Olympics en route to becoming the youngest all-around champion in the history of the Games. The Nicolae Ceausescu regime converted her success into a propaganda opportunity.[43] Representing West Germany, future IOC president Thomas Bach won gold in fencing. In 2015 he returned to Montreal as an "honorary citizen" to collect a key to the city.[44] And US decathlete Bruce (now Caitlyn) Jenner won gold, becoming the proverbial "world's greatest athlete" after years of selling insurance part-time while then wife Chrystie worked full-time as a flight attendant for United Airlines.[45] The New York Times wrote, "After his record-breaking victory in the Olympic decathlon today, he probably can be anything he wants."[46] The paper's confidence in the Olympian was justified: in July 2015, Jenner took the enormously significant step of publicizing her gender transition, speaking openly about her transgender identity.[47]

Despite these athletic feats, Montreal was also wracked with dissension. The "two-China problem" reared its head again when the Canadian government's one-China policy aggravated the Taiwanese, who were not allowed to have the word "China" appear on any of their Olympic paraphernalia. Unable to compete under its flag, name, or national anthem, Taiwan withdrew on the eve of the Games. IOC member Reginald Alexander of Kenya was so livid that he proposed banning Canadian prime minister Trudeau and his fellow

Liberal Party colleagues from all Olympic venues and social events.[48]

There would be more controversy. After the government of New Zealand condoned sending a rugby team to play in South Africa, the Supreme Council for Sports in Africa took action. Athletes and sports administrators demanded that the IOC ban Kiwi athletes from the Games, or at the very least, either publicly object to the decision to hold a rugby tour in South Africa or pressure the New Zealand prime minister to call the squad home. Jean-Claude Ganga, a boycott leader from the Congo Republic, said: "Just deploring apartheid isn't enough. When the crocodile is hitting you, it's crying at the same time. You need acts and action, not only declarations."[49] But the IOC steadfastly refused to get involved. To protest apartheid, approximately thirty countries—mostly African nations plus Guyana, Iraq, and Sri Lanka—ended up plucking their athletes from the Olympic Village and sending them home.[50] The *New York Times* asserted that because of the boycott, "the solidarity and quality of the Olympics have been severely eroded. And the five rings, corresponding to the five sections of the world, are no longer completely entwined."[51]

The boycotts continued in 1980. Less than a month after the Soviet Union invaded Afghanistan in December 1979, US president Jimmy Carter presented the USSR with an ultimatum: withdraw troops or the US would boycott the 1980 Moscow Summer Olympics. The House of Representatives and Senate overwhelmingly passed pro-boycott resolutions. Carter pressured allies to support the boycott. He dispatched the boxing great Mohammad Ali to Kenya, Liberia, Nigeria, Senegal, and Tanzania to persuade African leaders to boycott. The crowds chanted "Ali, Ali, Ali" everywhere he went, but the Greatest got not-so-great results from the leaders. Kenyan president Daniel Arap Moi hopped on the boycott bandwagon, as did Liberian president William Tolbert and

President Léopold Sédar Senghor of Senegal, a sports-and-politics-don't mix zealot—Senegal had been one of the very few African countries to participate at Montreal. Meanwhile, Nigerian president Alhaji Shehu Shagari and President Julius Nyerere of Tanzania refused to meet with Ali. At a meeting with a Tanzanian government minister, Ali was handed a note bearing the stinging accusation that he was Carter's stooge.[52]

The Moscow boycott debate went on hiatus during the 1980 Winter Games in Lake Placid, New York, where the US hockey team upset the Soviets in what became known as the Miracle on Ice en route to the gold. President Carter wrote in his memoir: "I was hoping this victory and the gold medal were an omen of better days ahead. But that was not to be."[53] Indeed. In the wake of the Winter Games, the Carter administration turned up the heat on the US Olympic Committee, intimating it might lose its tax-exempt status and federal financial assistance if it didn't get in line. The USOC buckled, voting in April 1980 to support Carter's stance on boycotting the Summer Games in Moscow. IOC president Lord Killanin watched the USOC debate on TV from Dublin. He later wrote that he "found the national emotionalism embarrassing." The US-led boycott was joined by more than sixty other countries, including Canada, West Germany, Japan, Kenya, Israel, Saudi Arabia, and Chile, then ruled by Augusto Pinochet. Margaret Thatcher publicly supported a boycott but the British Olympic Committee defied the Iron Lady and her Conservatives in the House of Commons, sending athletes to Moscow.[54]

Because of the boycott, many athletes' Olympic dreams were crushed. US swimmer Glenn Mills, who qualified to compete in Moscow, did not make the squad the next time around. He told me, "The path over the next decade or so was where the real hurt came in. The 'did not compete' asterisk that typically accompanied our names in any media guide became our burden. It came with a sense of shame, and demanded justification that we really did do what we set out to do."[55] The boycott inadvertently bestowed second-class status on numerous top-flight athletes.

Before Carter's decision to boycott, Soviet Olympic officials were orchestrating a capitalist-style bidding war for television rights to the Moscow Games. During the Montreal Games, the Soviet cruise ship Aleksandr Pushkin anchored in the St. Lawrence River, where Moscow Olympic honchos hosted a heaping feast. As one journalist put it: "The decks were awash with gallons of Stolichnaya vodka and Armenian cognac. The tables groaned beneath platters of cracked lobster, sliced sturgeon, caviar. The event was purely social, even jolly." The Olympics were once again spawning strange bedfellows. On one side stood network executives from ABC, CBS, and NBC, the one-percenters of their time. *Sports Illustrated* reported: "They came from stately Manhattan skyscrapers, quick-witted, supersophisticated salesmen given to Gucci shoes and manicured hands." They were there to negotiate with "a battery of grim Russian bureaucrats—burly, pallid fellows, some former peasants with hands still hard from years of labor in the fields of Mother Russia." But the Soviets held the five-ring trump card, and the television executives were not only keen to cover the Games but also give a glimpse of life behind the Iron Curtain to an American audience. Quixotically, Moscow started the bidding at $210 million in cash, but that gambit never gained traction. NBC eventually won the rights to broadcast the Moscow Olympics for $85 million. But the US decision to boycott rendered all the hobnobbing and negotiating moot—NBC opted not to televise the Games. The network's insurance policy with Lloyd's of London helped cover its losses.[56]

Television rights were becoming integral to the Olympic money machine. The earliest, experimental version of television coverage emerged at the 1936 Olympics in Germany. But after Melbourne organizers charged for the TV rights to

the 1956 Games, subsequent Organizing Committees realized broadcasting fees could be extremely profitable, even
though many IOC members would have just as soon avoided
the discussion.[57] Ahead of the 1960 Games at Rome, anti-
fascists revamped monuments to Mussolini, chiseling away
inscriptions praising Il Duce.[58] While they were scrubbing out
political history, the IOC was fortifying its future through
television rights, earning nearly $1.2 million for the TV rights
to the Rome Games.[59] At the 1964 Tokyo Summer Olympics
television revenues climbed to $1.6 million.[60] It was becoming
clear that "the transformation of the IOC into a corporate
entity was under way—and television money, more than any
other factor, provided the impetus for this change."[61] But even
with the spike in television revenues, after Denver, Montreal,
and the string of high-profile boycotts, the Olympics were
on their back foot. In the roiling seas of uncertainty, hyper-
commercialism would become the Olympics' rudder.

LA '84, Samaranch, and the Olympic Partners Program

In 1969, Ronald Reagan, then the governor of California,
wrote Avery Brundage to inform him that "California is desir-
ous of hosting the 1976 Olympic Games in the beautiful city
of Los Angeles ... so we can, again, have the nations of the
world join hands in friendship and peace and in true sportsmanship."[62] Yet only three years earlier, Edmund Brown,
Reagan's predecessor, had written Brundage to offer "my own
personal observation that a magnificent locale for the 1976
Summer Games would be Florence, Italy ... Florence and the
Olympics would make a fitting combination."[63] These conflict-
ing messages would finally be resolved in 1978, when the IOC
selected the City of Angels to host the 1984 Summer Games.

In truth, the IOC had no choice. There were only two serious
candidates—Los Angeles and Tehran—and the Iranian capital

dropped out before the final vote. But Californians were not keen to get hoodwinked, and Mayor Tom Bradley was not eager to become another Drapeau. He assured jittery citizens that public money would not be used. The Los Angeles City Council lent its support to the Olympics on the condition that it assumed no fiscal responsibility. In 1979, voters amended the Los Angeles city charter to limit public funds for the Games to a $5 million hotel tax and an Olympic ticket tax.[64] This maneuver clashed with Rule 4 in the Olympic Charter, which held host cities liable for any Games-induced debt. To prevent a standoff, the USOC took the unprecedented step of teaming up with the LA Organizing Committee, a private corporation, to share financial responsibility for the Games. The IOC grudgingly waived Rule 4.[65]

If this was the perfect storm for privatization, Peter Ueberroth stood placidly in the storm's eye. Ueberroth was a well-connected LA businessman who eagerly took the helm at the Los Angeles Olympic Organizing Committee. For the first time in Olympic history a private group, rather than the city itself, would organize the Games. Reagan was now president of the United States, and Ueberroth was gung-ho to inject the Games with a dose of Reaganomics. Privatization was paramount. A cavalcade of corporate partners would "let the market decide." Under Ueberroth's guidance, the 1984 LA Games became the first full-throttle, corporate, capitalist Olympics. He wrote in his autobiography: "From the beginning people said private enterprise would not step forward. But from the beginning I said, doomsayers be damned. The Olympics was the perfect vehicle to join the public and private sectors in partnership." The Games, he added, provided "an opportunity for private enterprise to enhance itself and show what is good about mankind."[66] Ueberroth was dogwhistling the neoliberal notion that public–private partnerships were done to benefit private enterprise. The public was to be a pedestal for private capital's ascendance.

Ueberroth was well aware of the previous Olympic fiascos. An Angeleno himself, he wrote, "I didn't want my tax dollars wasted in Los Angeles in the same way as was done in Montreal."[67] He also wanted to avoid another Moscow Games, which he estimated cost $5 billion.[68] Instead, he vowed to run the Olympics for only $500 million. Unlike Drapeau, Ueberroth did not suffer from an edifice complex. He trimmed costs by using buildings and structures that were already constructed, including the LA Coliseum, which was built for the 1932 Games. He convinced private partners like Atlantic Richfield Company, McDonald's, and the parent corporation of 7-Eleven convenience stores to refurbish the Coliseum and construct the swimming pool and velodrome. He brokered a record $225 million TV deal with ABC. He cut deals to funnel the local hotel tax and Olympic ticket tax into a trust fund that would give the city $19.3 million, $15 million of which was used to pay the LA Police Department for Olympic security at venues, the athletes' village, and transportation for the "Olympic family." *Sports Illustrated* crowned him "the prince of the private sector" and a "miser with the Midas touch." Even the decision by the USSR and its satellite allies in Eastern Europe to boycott the Games didn't stanch the plaudits flowing in the direction of the Olympic "prince."[69]

Ueberroth's corporate organizing committee took responsibility for cost overruns. Members of the committee believed that the privatized nature of the Games "made them a powerful instrument to demonstrate the validity of the American free enterprise system."[70] But even the barons of privatization quietly reaped public subsidy. Public services arrived gratis, as did an enormous flock of unpaid volunteers who did much of the grunt work. The federal government contributed to security for the Games. Transportation networks were already extant, as was the publicly funded communications structure.[71] In the end, the Los Angeles Olympics reaped a profit of about $215 million.[72] Some 40 percent of these profits went to the USOC for their efforts to rescue the bid from near withdrawal, while 20 percent went to US national governing bodies for Olympic sports and 40 percent went to the organizing committee's Amateur Athletic Foundation in order to promote local sports.[73]

Avery Brundage once said: "Business is business and sport is sport. It is impossible to mix them."[74] Ueberroth and his allies punctured this fiction. As the sport sociologist Alan Tomlinson notes, the 1984 Games were "the pivotal moment when the Olympics were steered down a path toward their Disneyfication," and not just because they transpired in LA.[75]

A key element of this "Disneyfication" was the corralling of big corporate sponsors. At the Montreal Games a patchwork of more than 600 smaller sponsors supplied funding.[76] Ueberroth and his fellow organizers limited the number of official sponsors and required them to kick in a minimum of $4 million in cash or in-kind goods. Thirty-five corporations enlisted, creating a veritable Who's Who of 1980s corporate power: American Express, Anheuser-Busch, AT&T, Atari, General Motors, Coca-Cola, Converse, Levi Strauss, McDonald's, Mars, Motorola, Sanyo, United Airlines, Westinghouse, and Xerox. The list of sixty-four "official suppliers" featured household names like Adidas, Panasonic, Rawlings Sporting Goods, and Toshiba. A licensee program gave sixty-five additional companies exclusive use of the five-ring logo for their advertising and souvenirs.[77] Organizers teamed up with the US Customs Service to make sure unlicensed products were not allowed in the country.[78]

None of this would have been possible were it not for Ueberroth's ally at the top of the IOC pyramid: Juan Antonio Samaranch. Elected in 1980 to replace Lord Killanin as president of the IOC, Samaranch argued that the IOC "can only concur with the position taken by the LAOOC to deal in the open marketplace in order to obtain the most favorable agreements possible."[79]

Ueberroth's biographer calls the entrepreneur's Olympic tenure a "totalitarian utopia."[80] Samaranch could certainly identify with the "totalitarian" part. He was a former Franco functionary who took on a number of leadership roles for the Falangists—from fascist parliamentarian to sports minister —over the course of nearly four decades. Samaranch regarded himself as "one hundred per cent Francoist" up to the dictator's death.[81] For years Samaranch courted Brundage with letters that heaped praise on the IOC president for his sagacity and prudence. The men shared a right-wing vision. Once Samaranch had ascended to the IOC presidency he realized the Olympic movement needed to diversify its revenue streams so it wasn't so reliant on television-rights money. As the Canadian Richard Pound put it, "The economic model of the Olympic movement at the time he became president was a prescription for disaster."[82] Too many companies were free-loading off the Games, basking in the five-ring glow without forking over nine-figure fees.

With this in mind, Samaranch established the Commission for New Sources of Financing in 1983. Two years later, after the splashy LA Games, he teamed up with Horst Dassler of Adidas to jump-start "The Olympic Programme" (TOP), which later became "The Olympic Partner Programme," or the "Worldwide Partner Program" of today. The idea was that a selective group of corporate mega-sponsors would contribute sizable sums in exchange for exclusive use of the Olympic symbol, which would be fiercely guarded from unauthorized use. Host city organizing committees could secure additional sources of sponsorship revenue, but only if those local deals didn't encroach on the worldwide partners' commercial turf. The TOP program formalized the tight relationship between big business and the Olympics, foreshadowing what the investigative journalist Andrew Jennings describes as a "multi-billion dollar exercise in global marketing locked up and ring-fenced by sabre-toothed attorneys."[83]

TOP launched at the 1988 Seoul Summer Olympics and the 1988 Winter Games in Calgary. TOP I (1985–1988) brought nine corporate sponsors together, raising $95 million. Although the Official Report for the Seoul Olympics in 1988 downplays the role of the TOP program, merely stating, "The joint marketing program was the first of its kind ever tried in Olympic history," TOP was on the scene to stay.[84] TOP II (1989–1992) raised $175 million from twelve sponsors. TOP III (1993–1996) generated more than $300 million from ten sponsors.[85] TOP IV (1997–2000) brought in $579 million, including $276 million of in-kind goods and services. TOP V (2001–2004) raised the intake to $663 million despite the scandals that plagued the IOC and its host-city selection process. Top VI (2005–2008) generated in the neighborhood of $866 million.[86] And TOP VII (2009–2012) raked in a record $950 million from eleven corporate sources: Coca-Cola, Atos, GE, Omega, P&G, Visa, Acer, Dow, McDonald's, Panasonic, and Samsung. On average these firms each paid $100 million (£61 million).[87] And this doesn't count the other "tiers" of sponsorship, which include the likes of Adidas, BP, Cadbury, EDF, Lloyd's TSB, and UPS.[88] TOP VIII for the 2013–2016 period includes many familiar corporate faces: Coca-Cola, Atos, Dow, GE, McDonald's, Omega, Panasonic, P&G, Samsung, and Visa.[89] They'll collectively chip in about $1 billion.[90] In March 2015, the IOC signed Toyota to a whopping $835 million sponsorship deal running through 2024. By creating a new "mobility category" for Worldwide Olympic Partners, the IOC pulled a power move that undercut the ability of local organizing committees to sign sponsorship contracts with automobile companies.[91]

For many, all this corporate cash put the Games on a slippery slope toward "the prostituting of the bidding process for Olympic festivals."[92] But when it came to diversifying the IOC's revenue sources, the TOP program worked wonders. In the early 1970s, 98 percent of the Olympic movement's revenue came from auctioning television rights.[93] TOP changed this. Today only about half of the IOC's revenue comes from granting television rights, while corporate sponsorship makes up 45 percent and ticket sales only 5 percent.[94]

Hyping the "Barcelona Model"

In 1986, the IOC voted to stagger the Summer and Winter Olympics at two-year intervals, beginning with the 1994 Winter Games. This would maximize revenues from advertisers, corporate sponsors, and television rights. Samaranch also finagled the 1992 Summer Games for Barcelona, closing the nearly forty-year circle from his days as a Barcelona city councilman and member of the Spanish Olympic Committee under Franco to bringing the Games home to a post-Franco Spain. He arranged victory for Barcelona by cleverly scheduling the 1992 Winter Games vote before the 1992 Summer Games vote. Engineering the '92 Winter Games for Albertville, France made Paris, Barcelona's main rival for the Summer Games, less appealing.[95]

Many consider the Barcelona Games the pinnacle of Olympism. Not even the "ugly American" theme, which coursed through media coverage of the Games, could dampen the mood. The American "Dream Team" basketballer Charles Barkley elbowed an Angolan player in a game the US won, 116 to 48, and asked, "How did I know he didn't have a spear?" Later, all twelve Dream Teamers unzipped their Reebok-sponsored Team USA jackets during the medal ceremonies to conceal the corporate logo in order to protect the interests of six players under contract with Nike. Barkley and Michael Jordan—two of the Nike athletes—even pinned American flags over their shoulders to cover the archrival's insignia. Jordan said, "I'm a person who feels that whatever you believe in, you stand up for it."[96] Apparently, Jordan believed in the People's Republic of Nike. Nevertheless, as the Olympics wrapped up, the *Guardian* hailed Barcelona as "the very best Games in memory, possibly ever, certainly since they became global fandangos."[97] The *New York Times* gushed, "The athletes never had a chance. No matter how well they jumped and ran and rowed, they could never dominate these Summer Games. The city won the Games."[98]

Scholars have largely agreed that "the city won the Games" because Barcelona city officials converted the Olympics into a chance to revamp and redevelop significant swaths of the city center and seafront. The Poblenou industrial area in downtown Barcelona was rebuilt as an Olympic Village to be converted later into housing, the airport was revamped, extensive ring roads around town were built, and the polluted river system that sliced through Barcelona to the Mediterranean Sea was remediated. The Barcelona Olympics were part of a long-term urban redevelopment first formulated in 1976, a full decade before the IOC selected the city as host. By that time, twenty-seven of the thirty-seven sports facilities eventually put to Olympic use had already been constructed, while another five were in the process of being built. As the economist Andrew Zimbalist notes, "the games were put at the service of a preexisting plan, rather than the typical pattern of the city development plan being put at the service of the games."[99] This became known as the "Barcelona Model," the paragon of Olympic urbanism and a template for future hosts.

The Games cost $11.5 billion, the bulk going toward infrastructure and Olympic facilities. One-third (32.7 percent) of these costs were covered by the private sector while two-thirds (67.3 percent) came through public financing. Only 2 percent of Games costs came from the city of Barcelona.[100] Unemployment decreased, the construction industry boomed, and to the delight of developers the housing market enjoyed an upward turn.[101] After the Games, Barcelona leapfrogged up the list of most-visited tourist destinations in Europe.

Barcelona organizers also created the Cultural Olympiad program, reviving Baron de Coubertin's wish "to reunite the Muscles and the Mind."[102] The Cultural Olympiad stretched over four years, commencing right after the 1988 Olympics in Seoul. This included annual Autumn Festivals with theater, dance, music, outdoor shows, exhibitions, and an Olympic Arts Festival.[103] After Barcelona, each Summer Olympiad adopted the four-year format. The Baron surely would have approved. Overall, the positive effect of hosting was "far more intense and sustained than that of other host cities," one economist observed.[104]

Zimbalist notes that four particular conditions helped move Barcelona toward fiscal success: (1) the unusually large chunk of the Olympic pie paid for by the private sector; (2) an opportune macroeconomic situation in a country ripe for stimulus spending; (3) Spain's entrance into the European Economic Community (now the European Union), which jump-started trade, tourism, and investment; and (4) Barcelona was a relatively hidden gem of a city that had untapped room for growth. He writes, "While many prospective host cities would like to believe they can emulate Barcelona, few would be able to bring together the special features that characterized Barcelona in the 1980s."[105]

However, the "Barcelona model" has some notable downsides. The Barcelona bid egregiously lowballed the costs, initially attaching a $667 million price tag to the Games; after winning the bid, costs ballooned above $11 billion.[106] Funds spent on the four principal Olympic sites spiked twenty-nine times higher than the original estimate.[107] This is an extreme example of a tactic used by bidding cities: underestimating costs in order to rally public support. Once the Games are granted, costs inevitably rise.

The Games also intensified gentrification, with the Geneva-based Centre on Housing Rights and Evictions (COHRE) finding, "The Olympic Games served to reinforce and exacerbate the consequences of the privatisation of a basic need such as housing."[108] The availability of public housing nosedived while rents spiked by 145 percent and housing prices jumped 139 percent. Gentrification contributed to a 250 percent cost-of-living increase in Barcelona in the six years leading up to the Olympics.[109] Cultural and class diversity suffered. As the urban geographer Francesc Muñoz notes, "Ongoing processes like gentrification and the 'brandification' of urban space go hand in hand in reinforcing the lack of diversity of many urban areas in the city."[110] When it came to Games-related housing policy, the benefits skewed in favor of Barcelona's affluent.

The construction of the Olympic Village crystallized these dynamics. The village was a $1.9 billion public-private partnership that was a boon for speculators. It accelerated gentrification in a working-class area of the city. Much of the employment created by construction projects consisted of temporary jobs ("contratos eventuales").[111] To be sure, in and around the Olympic Village, public spaces were revamped for the better, but construction companies and property owners were the prime beneficiaries of the Olympics-driven fix-up.[112] In the eyes of Olympic planners, the city's poor and marginalized amounted to little more than collateral damage. Also, as is common with Olympic planning, transparency was lacking. COHRE noted, "Despite the wide scope of this urban regeneration *no participative processes were anticipated in the Olympic candidature, and no specific protocols or commissions were set up in relation to forced evictions or the possible impact of the Olympic Games on access to housing.*"[113] Again, the IOC stayed silent on these matters, claiming them beyond their purview. So the "Barcelona Model" was much more of a mixed bag than it is often portrayed by full-throated boosters of the Olympics.

Atlanta's "Coca-Cola Olympics"

When Atlanta organizers unveiled the mascot for the 1996 Summer Games, the press openly ridiculed the mystery creature. The appropriately named "Whatizit" was an amorphous, computer-animated, bluish blob. Readers of USA Today dubbed the mascot "Bubba the Blue Slug" and "a sperm with legs." The New York Times called it "a soap bubble with a thyroid condition." NBC sportscaster Bob Costas said the mascot was "a genetic experiment gone horribly, ghastly wrong" while the creator of The Simpsons, Matt Groening, surmised it emerged from "a bad marriage of the Pillsbury doughboy and the ugliest California Raisin."[114] Renaming the critter "Izzy" couldn't prevent it from being labeled "unquestionably the most despised of all Olympic mascots" by the Vancouver Sun.[115]

Enigmatic mascots were the least of Atlanta's problems. Organizers opted to go the low-budget route, aiming to replicate the largely privatized LA Games of 1984. The Atlanta Committee for the Olympic Games (ACOG) financed the Olympics for $2.2 billion and walked off with a small financial surplus, though the urban studies scholar John R. Short points out that "this ignores the approximately $2 billion spent by public authorities including $996 million in federal government investment, $226 million in state funds, and $857 million in local funds."[116] While some economists pointed to a modest uptick in employment in counties close to the Olympic action, finer-grained analysis found minimal evidence of significant economic impact, let alone long-term legacy; positive employment effects occurred only during the Olympics, and solely in three sectors: (1) retail, (2) accommodation and food, and (3) arts, entertainment, and recreation.[117] Researchers concluded, "The employment effects seem too small and too concentrated sectorally and locally to justify public funding from general sources at the state level."[118] Although everyday

Atlantans did not experience an economic windfall, ACOG president Billy Payne raked in a salary of more than $669,000, making him the highest-paid head of a nonprofit in the United States.[119]

Another clear beneficiary was Coca-Cola, the Atlanta-based behemoth that had sponsored the Olympics since the 1928 Amsterdam Games. With the 1996 Games occurring on the centennial of the Olympic revival in Greece, Athens was a sentimental favorite, but many murmured that Atlanta only beat out the Greek capital because of the Coca-Cola factor. Coke's influence was "the real thing." Indeed, Coca-Cola pumped more than half a billion dollars into marketing and sponsorship, funding the Olympic Torch relay, building a $20 million Coke theme park in downtown Atlanta, and providing nearly 1,000 volunteers at Olympic venues.[120]

Atlanta organizers originally believed they could auction US television broadcasting rights for $600 million and that $550 million would be "low." However, feeling the budgetary pinch, they hastily sold off these rights to NBC for only $456 million.[121] That forced ACOG to bolster commercialization to make up the gap. It sold cut-rate sponsorships to corporations, charging $10 million to $20 million to numerous companies. A torrent of corporate logos gave the Games a tawdry tinge. Journalists compared Centennial Olympic Park to "a corporate trade show," while Payne weakly defended the consumerist parade as not mere advertising, but "sponsor footprints" that featured newfangled "state-of-the-art technology."[122] Meanwhile, Andrew Young—civil-rights icon, former Atlanta mayor, and Payne's co-chair at ACOG—publicly announced that the Olympics had "divine potential." At another point he asked, "Could it be that Atlanta could play some special role in the plan of God?" In his memoir he reckoned that the Games were part of "God's plan for Atlanta."[123] Young talked God, but the true believers—and major beneficiaries—walked corporate.

Coca-Cola's land grab to create space for its very own theme park was representative of the real estate deals that marked the Atlanta Games. Fulton County Commissioner Martin King, the oldest son of the Atlanta-born civil rights icon of the same name, railed against a sweetheart Olympic Stadium deal that Atlanta organizers delivered to private parties, including the Ted Turner–owned Atlanta Braves baseball team:

> We really have two Atlantas. One for the rich and prosperous and another for the poor and downtrodden. One group who can afford the luxuries that Atlanta has to offer. The other who can barely make it through the month … The way I see it, the stadium deal is a one-sided deal. Not only does it place an unknown liability on the taxpayers of this county and city, but it allows the rich to get richer … This is on top of the fact that the last stadium displaced many members of the same community, with little or no positive effect on the lives of the people who still live in the impacted neighborhoods.

King concluded, "Greed, exclusivity and elitism have become the symbols of Atlanta's Olympic movement—all things that my father fought against—and they are all reflected in the deal proposed before us, the rich and affluent on one side, the poor and hopeless on the other side."[124] Corporate-sponsor exclusivity was assured by a municipal sign ordinance meant to dissuade ambush marketers. Within the measure, a special concession allowed Olympic sponsors to erect massive ten-story-tall billboards around town. Coke carried out the necessary "political arm-twisting" behind the scenes to win the exemption.[125] The Games quickly became known as "the Coca-Cola Olympics" or "les Jeux Cocacolympiques."

In the lead-up to the Games, gentrification ran rampant, with rents near the Olympic Park skyrocketing. One particularly imperious property manager, Intown Properties, aimed to cash in on inflated prices during the Olympic period by telling tenants they either had to vacate or pay $3,000 per month. Public housing was demolished to make way for the Games, including Techwood Homes, the country's first federally subsidized public housing project. The New Deal–era development was bulldozed in 1995. Techwood and Clark Howell Homes were replaced by the Olympic Village. The urban planning scholar Charles Rutheiser remarked ironically that self-appointed Atlanta Olympic barons proceeded with "a truly remarkable sense of amnesia as to the relatively free play of market forces that had creatively destroyed downtown."[126] Another scholar described the process of purging the poor as "from Techwood Flats to Techwood Flattened," with the main beneficiaries being Georgia Tech University and a particular carbonated-beverage company.[127] An *Atlanta Journal and Constitution* editorial found the positive in the housing project's demolition and intensified identification with the corporate, asserting that "an area known for blight amid progress can begin to feel a part of the progressiveness of Georgia Tech and Coca-Cola."[128]

Meanwhile, the homeless were not meant to feel at home. According to advocates for the homeless, in 1995 and 1996 alone more than 9,000 homeless people were arrested, often without probable cause, as part of a social cleansing program that got the attention of federal authorities, who ultimately issued a cease-and-desist order.[129] Some homeless and poor people were even issued one-way bus tickets to Alabama and Florida.[130] According to the Center on Housing Rights and Evictions, "The demonizing of poor and homeless Atlantans by the moneyed power elite did not begin with the Olympics, but hosting the 1996 Summer Olympic Games gave that practice the adrenaline it needed to become the city's prevailing, even blatant, public policy."[131] Socially excluded groups like the homeless and working poor were swept aside.

The Atlanta Olympics sparked a spate of additional controversies. Organizers located a number of prominent events —such as tennis, cycling, and archery—at Stone Mountain

Park, where earlier in the century the Ku Klux Klan infamously staged its rebirth. The park contains a massive Confederate memorial carved into the mountain, featuring Jefferson Davis, Stonewall Jackson, and Robert E. Lee.[132] (Even the Klan was dissatisfied with the Games. In late 1995 it protested in Atlanta with signs reading "Olympukes Go Home."[133]) By 2014 the Stone Mountain Tennis Center sat abandoned and fenced off, an empty shrine to false five-ring legacies. Foragers have scavenged the salvageable copper wiring and metal piping.[134]

Tragedy struck the Games when a bomb blast ripped through Centennial Olympic Park, killing one person and wounding more than one hundred others. Initially authorities accused an Olympic Park security guard, Richard Jewell, of carrying out the attack. Later it emerged that the bomb was planted by an anti-abortion zealot, Eric Robert Rudolph. He said he wanted to "confound, anger and embarrass" the government for its legalization of abortion. He added that the Olympics foisted the "despicable ideals" of "global socialism" on the public.[135] It was the second time that the Olympics became a target for terrorism. At the closing ceremony, IOC president Samaranch said, "No act of terrorism has ever destroyed the Olympic movement, and none ever will." Yet Samaranch couldn't bring himself to call these the "greatest Games ever," as he had done in Barcelona four years prior— he merely proclaimed the Atlanta Games "exceptional." In a final flourish of pomp, he conferred an Olympic Order medallion on Billy Payne.[136]

Atlanta also provided a foretaste of the feast of corruption to come. Three years after the Games concluded, the US House Commerce Subcommittee on Oversight and Investigation revealed that Atlanta bid jockeys had lavished gifts on IOC members in hopes of garnering their votes. ACOG violated spending limits nearly forty times. Andrew Young anted up a Georgia Tech University scholarship to the daughter of a Nigerian IOC member. A Hungarian IOC member's daughter was offered a college scholarship to attend the University of Georgia. Presents for IOC members from Cuba and Libya breached the US trade embargos against those countries. Atlanta's bid committee surveilled IOC members, creating dossiers that outlined their exploitable proclivities. One entry read: "Likes pretty women. Likes to talk about Nigeria and going on safari." Another stated: "Does accept gifts. His wife is influential with him. Gift for his wife may be useful." A third asserted: "Lives in a palace. Did accept two ladies from Barcelona."[137]

Many Shades of Olympic Green

The 1992 Winter Games in Albertville, France, were an unmitigated environmental disaster spread over 1,000 square miles. Local organizers disfigured the mountain landscape in order to carve out Olympic-standard ski runs. Overflowing sewer systems glugged into pristine streams. The debacle generated negative press, and the IOC was keen to clean up its act.[138] In the lead-up to the 2000 Sydney Olympics, the IOC increasingly embraced the rhetoric of ecology. For Olympic honchos, green was the new green: claiming the mantle of environmental sustainability meant positive public relations, and big bucks as well.

The IOC was influenced by the 1992 Earth Summit in Rio de Janeiro, where sustainable development was front and center. The Rio Declaration prescribed a principle still relevant today: "Where there are threats of serious or irreversible damage, lack of full scientific certainty shall not be used as a reason for postponing cost-effective measures to prevent environmental degradation."[139] The United Nations Environment Programme issued "Agenda 21," its plan for sustainable capitalist development.

The IOC rode the zeitgeist. In 1993, IOC member Richard Pound suggested the group reduce paper consumption and "encourage environmentally-responsible behaviour and actions around the world," which he viewed as "a responsibility as well as an opportunity."[140] In 1994, the IOC declared that the environment was "an essential component of Olympism."[141] By 1995, it even added a rule to the Olympic Charter asserting that the Games "are held in conditions which demonstrate a responsible concern for environmental issues."[142] The IOC also launched a Sport and Environment Commission. In 1999 it initiated its own Agenda 21, whereby Olympic partners would "integrate sustainable development into their policies and activities" and "encourage all individuals ... to behave in such a way as to ensure that their sporting activities and their lifestyles play a part in sustainable development."[143] Ultimately, the IOC enshrined this precept as the third pillar of Olympism, alongside sport and culture.[144]

As a result, claiming to be "the greenest Games ever" has become obligatory. But not everyone is convinced. Janice Forsyth, then director of the International Centre for Olympic Studies at Western University in London, Ontario, argued in 2011, "Agenda 21 thus far appears like a watered-down statement of environmental concern that shifts the focus of attention to special interest groups without actually requiring the industry to do something meaningfully concrete."[145] The urban geographer and mega-event critic Christopher Gaffney notes that gestures toward sustainability are simply "inadequate to deal with the fundamental problem that the events themselves generate."[146] Two sociologists, Graeme Hayes and John Horne, agree; the Olympics, they argue, are "a fundamentally unsustainable event."[147] John Karamichas of Queens University, Belfast, surveyed the history of IOC-style environmentalism and concluded that "no causality was identified between Olympic Games hosting and improvements in the EM [ecological modernization] capacity of the host nation."[148] In other words, assertions of Olympic sustainability are hocuspocus, a harbinger of hooey.

To be sure, "sustainability" is a notoriously slushy term, a big-business buzzword. All too often, sustainability rhetoric is a prettified scrim obscuring capitalism's incessant rapacity. The Olympic Movement's newfound greenspeak more often resembles tickbox ecology than consequential environmentalism. When the IOC's Sport and Environment Commission publishes reports "with the support of Shell International," it veers toward greenwashing—doing the bare minimum to claim green esteem.[149]

IOC-style conservationism made its splashy debut at the 2000 Sydney Games. Organizers insisted that environmental progress "was one of the shining achievements" of the Olympics, "a hallmark of Sydney's Games."[150] Sydney officials revamped a ramshackle industrial zone, the Homebush area, into a sparkly social space. Boosters underlined a slate of environmental measures: improved waterways, tree planting, the installation of solar power in the Olympic Village, species and water conservation, and recycling.[151] Yet the environmental clean-up was carried out on the public dime; the "polluter pays" principle did not apply. Still, Olympic officials trumpeted their environmentalism, and Sydney organizers patted themselves on the back for partnering with Greenpeace and Green Games Watch 2000, a coalition of environmental watchdog groups.[152] Sydney launched an Olympic tradition whereby organizers claim theirs "the greenest Games to date."

The Olympic Movement's green cred was dented when the Sydney Organizing Committee decided to stage the beach volleyball competition at Bondi Beach, an ecologically sensitive spot along the Pacific Ocean. Hosting beach volleyball meant building a 10,000-seat temporary stadium that would cut off beach access for everyday people. But corporate behemoths were calling the shots. NBC forked over $600 million for the Games' television rights, and it demanded that beach volleyball take place at Bondi Beach because of the telegenic backdrop.[153]

When construction on the temporary stadium began, activists from Bondi Olympic Watch buried themselves up to the neck in sand to thwart bulldozers from getting to work.[154] Even though they staged the event in a festive style, protesters were met by heavily armed security forces. One witness described "three Blackhawk helicopters, two police launches, fifteen mounted police officers, and one hundred and fifty SWAT team police on foot."[155] With the Olympics only three months away, the pro-Games press pounced. One op-ed in Sydney's *Daily Telegraph*—"Sun, Sand and Angry Hippies"—branded activists "a bunch of septuagenarians, leftover hippies and the odd goateed youth," many of whom were "squawking about police brutality."[156] Other media accounts derided protesters as scant in number.[157] The protesters couldn't stop the juggernaut: Olympic volleyball took place on Bondi Beach.

"Social sustainability" in all its nebulousness was another buzzword at Sydney. Games supporters hoped that hosting the Olympics would foster reconciliation between Australia's Aboriginal population and their historical oppressors in the majority culture. The Aboriginal track star Cathy Freeman was selected by organizers to light the Olympic cauldron at the opening ceremony. But Freeman was no quisling. Two months before the Games began she pilloried Australian prime minister John Howard for his refusal to apologize for the "stolen generations" of Aboriginal people—including her own grandmother—who were brutally snatched from their culture. She also vowed to carry both the Aboriginal and Australian flags if she were to win at Sydney, a breach of IOC protocol.[158]

Indeed, after Freeman triumphed in the 400-meter run, she entwined the two flags as she took her victory lap. The mainstream press lauded her achievement. According to the *Sydney Morning Herald*, Freeman was "running not just for herself, or for her nation's sporting glory, but for Aboriginal Australia, for a reconciled Australia."[159] *USA Today* reported in an article titled "Freeman Lights Up Games: Aboriginal Star Runs to Glory for Her People, All Australians" that "the country fairly vibrated with joy."[160] The official history of the Olympics proclaims, "Freeman was not just running one lap but acting as a symbol, for her country and indeed for the world," before adding awkwardly, "The soul of Australia had been momentarily condensed into the figure of this one Aborigine: until this moment, a lesser Australian."[161] For many, Freeman's success allowed for convenient amnesia, a free pass to glide over centuries of indigenous repression and discrimination.

While boosters crammed Freeman's actions into the slot of palatable multicultural atonement—defanging her trenchant critique along the way—letters to the editor in Australian newspapers told a different, more troubling story. One argued, "Let us keep politics, and particularly 'politically correct' politics, out of the Olympics and our society in general." Another pondered, "I thought that sport and politics within the Olympics were separate issues ... to have Cathy Freeman light the cauldron ... was a sad, sad ending to a great event." Another viewed Freeman's opening-ceremony role as "the single most racist act in our entire history." Multiple letter writers argued that the selection of Freeman to light the cauldron was strategically designed to defuse activism that Aboriginal groups were planning. One described Freeman's choice as "an obvious and blatant suck up to these people in an attempt to get them to tone down their protests." Another wrote it was all a "political gesture of pacification, bordering on obsequiousness, in pandering to the minority who have selfishly threatened to disrupt this once-in-a-lifetime ceremony."[162]

But the predominant narrative coming from Olympic boosters was that Freeman's participation at the Games—and her gold-medal performance in the 400-meter run—helped atone for the nation's colonial past, an example of "social sustainability." Not everyone agreed, however. Forsyth, the Olympic scholar who is also a member of the Fisher River Cree First

Nation, told me: "The word 'social' is so hard to define and pin down in Olympic discourse. It means anything and everything that the IOC and National Olympic Committees [NOCs] can use to convince the public the Games are a good and necessary feature in our lives." She added, "The IOC and the NOCs are very skilled and practiced at adapting to and co-opting broader societal concerns that 'we'—including the public, informed observers, and organized resistance movements—have about the role of the Games in our lives." Forsyth concluded, "But in looking at what happens to the most marginalized people when a city hosts the Games, we can see where 'social' priorities really are focused, which is often on reproducing wealth and consumption in a city."[163]

The Sydney Games may have evoked feelings of goodwill and reconciliation, but they left a $1.7 billion debt in their wake, an unwanted legacy for the taxpaying public that would undercut the ability of the state to assist the marginalized populations Forsyth mentioned.[164] Even so, at the Games' closing ceremony, Samaranch even reprised his "best Olympics ever" routine, stating that Sydney 2000 "could not have been better." He said, "I am proud and happy to proclaim that you have presented to the world the best Olympic Games ever."[165]

But in the months before the Games, a former Australian auditor general condemned the Sydney bid committee for violating the $200 limit on gift-giving to IOC members. Sydney bid officials also breached the rules by treating Danish and Irish IOC members and their families to the French Open and Wimbledon tennis tournaments.[166] Journalists also uncovered that back in 1993, when Sydney bidders were trying to woo key IOC members from Africa, the Australian Olympic Committee channeled millions toward a training center for African athletes. Beginning in 1994, aspiring Olympians from eleven African countries earned $9,000 per year. Just before the IOC vote on the 2000 host, Australian Olympic official John Coates also funneled $70,000 to two IOC members: one from Kenya and the other from Uganda. At the next day's voting, Sydney eked out a 45–43 victory over Beijing, with the support of numerous African IOC delegates.[167]

Scandal in Salt Lake City

The shady shenanigans on the road to Sydney were trifling compared to the sleaze-slopped superhighway to Salt Lake City. In bidding for the 1998 Winter Games, Salt Lake City lost out to Nagano, Japan, even though it had assembled a much stronger technical bid. Nagano lavished an average of $22,000 on more than sixty IOC members whose votes they desired. Details are scarce since the Nagano bid committee shredded all its records after the Games.[168] In response, Salt Lake City bid doctors started files on individual IOC barons and corralled the cash necessary to coddle them. They found out quickly that IOC members were raring to suckle.

In November 1998, local news media in Utah revealed bribery and corruption on a scope that was breathtaking. A special US Senate commission found some 1,375 separate expenditures totaling nearly $3 million that were designed to sway individual IOC members, and which didn't even include swanky in-kind inducements.[169] Congolese IOC member Jean-Claude Ganga hauled in more than $250,000 worth of gifts and freebies. Ganga made six separate visits to Salt Lake City where, courtesy of the bid committee, his mother-in-law got a knee replacement, his wife underwent cosmetic surgery, and he himself was treated for hepatitis. The Salt Lake City bid leader Tom Welch even formed a business partnership with Ganga that purchased land in Ogden, Utah, and quickly flipped it for a $60,000 profit. The Salt Lake City bid committee funneled more than $111,000 to the son of Swaziland IOC member David Sibandze. The committee also ran a full-blown scholarship program for IOC family members. The daughter of Cameroonian IOC member René Essomba scored free tuition and living expenses to the tune of $108,000 at American University in Washington, DC. Salt Lake City organizers spent hundreds of thousands on middlemen whose job it was to persuade IOC members to vote for the bid. When IOC voters made site visits to Utah they were showered with largesse: free shotguns, skis, clothing, video games, hunting trips, shopping sprees, tickets to NBA basketball games, and even a $524 violin. Salt Lake City bidders also doled out cold, hard cash.[170]

The revelations prompted the IOC to move swiftly to contain the damage. It hired Hill & Knowlton, the high-powered PR firm that previously worked damage control for the Bhopal gas disaster, Three Mile Island, and the Gulf War.[171] The IOC also suspended six members, who were eventually expelled. Four additional members resigned. Even non-tarnished IOC higher-ups avoided traveling to the US in order to sidestep the FBI. For its part, the Salt Lake City Olympic Committee fired Vice President David Johnson. The committee president, Frank Joklik, resigned in January 1999. Tom Welch, who was neck deep in bribery allegations, resigned after pleading no contest to spousal-abuse charges, though he quietly continued to work behind the scenes as a consultant.[172]

The Salt Lake City team desperately needed a symbolic facelift. Enter Mitt Romney. At first the venture capitalist, devout Mormon, and graduate of Brigham Young University encountered friction with Rocky Anderson, the freshly elected, progressive mayor of Salt Lake City who had won partly because he expressed concern about the city getting stuck with the Olympic tab. When Anderson raised the idea of creating independent income streams for the city that were separate from the official IOC corporate sponsorships, IOC marketing official Michael Payne threatened to sue the city government for breach of contract. Anderson relented, joining forces with Romney to make the most of the situation.[173] Anderson later beamed, "Mitt did an absolutely fantastic job."[174] Payne, an Olympic true believer, wrote of Romney, "He understood the true power of the Olympic brand and the symbolism of the rings, and their ability to inspire."[175]

The Salt Lake City Winter Olympics were the first Games staged after the attacks of 9/11. Olympic organizers requested $4 billion in government funds, although in the end, taxpayers kicked in $1.5 billion, around $335 million of it for security. Still, this total was 1.5 times the amount that the United States Treasury spent on all seven previous US Olympics combined.[176] A security force of 12,000 policed the Games, replete with biometric surveillance technologies, riot gear, and paint-pellet weapons for dispersing crowds. Even before the attacks of 9/11, the Salt Lake City Organizing Committee was planning on cordoning off special areas where protesters could demonstrate if they secured permits. With the backing of both Anderson and Romney, these protest pens were rebranded "public forum zones." Two weeks before the Games commenced, the city council passed an ordinance that forbade demonstrators from donning masks in public during the Olympics. Undeterred, activists did wind up staging scatter-shot protests in parks, streets, and protest zones on a range of issues, from environmental concerns to animal rights to the misuse of taxpayer funds on lavish Games rather than local problems.[177] Local Olympic organizers claimed a profit of $56 million, which they did not put toward the social issues that animated political activists. Instead, they divided the money among the IOC, USOC, and a foundation that would maintain Olympic venues.[178]

In response to the Salt Lake bid scandal, the IOC formed a new Ethics Commission composed of four IOC members and five outsiders. However, it is a relatively toothless group that is hardly independent; it reports to the IOC Executive Board, which has the final word.[179] Samaranch also spearheaded the IOC 2000 Commission, which made fifty recommendations, all of them summarily approved by the IOC. The reforms ran the gamut from milquetoast to mundane. They included imposing an age limit—seventy—on new members (while members over the limit were grandfathered in) and requiring a smidgen more fiscal transparency. The biggest change was the elimination of site visits to Olympic candidate cities, one of the very few reforms that generated resistance within the IOC.[180] Through it all, Samaranch remained at the helm, despite the fact that he had been in power during all the bribery and corruption. In fact, Samaranch had long been privately touting himself and the IOC for the Nobel Peace Prize, and the Salt Lake City scandal did nothing to deter him. (In response to the scandal he elevated Henry Kissinger, a previous winner of the Nobel Peace Prize, to an honorary position on the IOC board in 2000.[181]) But Samaranch never won the prize. Instead, he was named honorary life president of the IOC, a title he cherished until his death in 2010.

5

The Celebration Capitalism Era

If modern sport is "capitalism at play," as the historian Tony Collins has noted, then the Olympic Games are particularly instructive for mapping the terrain of capitalism. Collins has written that nineteenth-century sport "was not merely co-terminous with the expansion of capitalism but an integral part of that expansion, not only in economic organization but also in ideological meaning."[1] So it is with the Olympic Games in the late twentieth and early twenty-first centuries. An economic juggernaut, the Olympics do not merely symbolize or reflect capitalism; they actively produce it.

In this century, the Olympics have taken the form of what I call "celebration capitalism," a political-economic formation marked by lopsided public–private partnerships that favor private entities while dumping risk on the taxpayer. The normal rules of politics are temporarily suspended in the name of a media-trumpeted, hyper-commercial spectacle, all safeguarded by beefed-up security forces responsible for preventing terrorism, corralling political dissent, and protecting the festivities.[2] Celebration capitalism is an upbeat shakedown, trickle-up economics with wrenching human costs.

Celebration capitalism is not standard-issue neoliberalism marked by privatization, deregulation, fiscal austerity, and the abrogation of the state's responsibility for economic planning, ownership, and most social provision. "Neoliberalism," the geographer and social scientist David Harvey rightly notes, "has become hegemonic as a mode of discourse" with its mantra of "letting the market decide" masquerading as common sense. However, the Olympics of the twenty-first century remind us that capitalism is a nimble shapeshifter and that a gap can emerge between neoliberal word and political-economic deed. The specific formation of celebration capitalism spotlights what Harvey calls "divergences from the template of neoliberal theory."[3] Celebration capitalism cannot be reduced to "actually existing neoliberalism": geographically specific, context-dependent paths of neoliberalization known for their "perplexingly amorphous" ways.[4] Something qualitatively different is going on.

Some contend that recent Olympic history indicates a "neoliberalisation of the Games."[5] To be sure, the modern Olympics radiate neoliberal capitalism in several ways. As we have seen, the Games have become decidedly more commercialized as private capital has taken on a higher profile with corporate sponsorship. Also, private security firms have occasionally assumed a prominent role in policing the Games. Yet the public routinely pays for and meticulously regulates a large majority of Olympic costs, and corporate sponsors hold a privileged position for future pacts—the free market does not decide. Rather than deregulation, we see a stringent regime of rules and regulations emanating from the IOC and unilaterally forced on the host city. The geographer Mike Raco dubs this "a utopian top-down model of contractual management" where public actors are prime movers.[6] In sum, the principles and policies of neoliberalism, as relevant as they are in some respects, do not fully explain the political economics of the Olympics. Instead, the Olympics Games are the quintessential example of "celebration capitalism," a capitalist formation that in many ways slices against the neoliberal grain and more resembles "regulatory capitalism"[7] marked by "state-led privatization" and "public-private hybridities."[8] In academic circles, neoliberalism has become the catch-all explanation for nearly all social processes.[9] Celebration capitalism is meant to be a friendly corrective to that analytically promiscuous tendency.

Celebration Capitalism

In *The Shock Doctrine: The Rise of Disaster Capitalism*, Naomi Klein clarifies how neoliberal capitalists capitalize on catastrophe by exploiting social stress and trauma. Disasters—wars, hurricanes, military coups d'état, terrorist violence, and severe economic downturns—spark collective states of shock that soften up the populace to the point where it is willing to concede to aggressive elites what it would otherwise ardently defend. In the aftermath of disaster, while the population is reeling, well-positioned corporations and their collaborators in government orchestrate neoliberal policies rooted in privatization and deregulation. Free-market proponents thus take advantage of social instability. As Klein puts it, they offer "the promise of a quick and magical cure—however illusory."[10] While Klein notes that privatization can often "be paid for with public money," her primary contention is that "the ultimate goal" of the corporations at the center of disaster capitalism is to normalize the privatization of the public sphere, to convert government responsibilities into corporate functions in the "perpetual quest for clean sheets and blank slates upon which to build model states."[11] In case after case—as in New Orleans in the aftermath of Hurricane Katrina, when the city's school system was largely privatized—her theory rings true. The investigative journalist Antony Loewenstein has pushed the thesis further, examining how "disaster capitalism" plays out in other places around the world—from Pakistan to Papua New Guinea—but also in the privatized prison and detention industries in Britain and the United States. The methods may vary depending on context, but time and again, "the strategy is the same: exaggerate a threat, man-made or natural, and let loose unaccountable private-sector contractors to exploit it." The plausible "end-point of this process" of "predatory capitalism," he argues, is "the privatization of the natural world itself."[12]

Capitalism has proved to be an effective economic chameleon, changing colors dexterously in the face of social, political, and economic obstacles. John Lauermann and Mark Davidson write, "Capitalism is neither uniform nor consistent, and consequently, responding to crisis within it will necessitate a diverse range of initiatives."[13] Indeed, capitalism has exhibited divergent forms in different moments in history and appeared in different formations in a single instant: Anna Tsing calls this "the heterogeneity of capitalism at every moment in time."[14] Such is the case with disaster capitalism and celebration capitalism. Together these forms of "actually existing capitalism" (not "actually existing neoliberalism") can harmonize into a potent combination, with celebration capitalism clearing a path for disaster capitalism, and vice versa—a devastating one-two punch. While the predominant economic current may flow thick with neoliberalism, it also contains distinctly non-neoliberal elements. Examining the Olympics in the twenty-first century helps underscore the dynamics of celebration capitalism that cut against neoliberal trends.

Both disaster capitalism and celebration capitalism occur in states of exception: catastrophe and exuberance respectively. In *State of Exception*, Giorgio Agamben explained how an exceptional political moment can lead to a blizzard of judicial and extrajudicial measures deployed by the powerful to maintain their advantage. Meanwhile, political rights are quashed as the state flexes its sovereignty, creating what Agamben called "a lasting practice of government."[15] As such, the state of exception creates political space for repressive techniques of government that can, in turn, become normalized. Agamben argued that the state of exception is a space where "above all *the very distinction between public and private* ... is deactivated."[16] Both disaster capitalism and celebration capitalism convert the state of exception into an exceptional opportunity, carving paths for opportunistic politicians and their economic allies. While Klein and Loewenstein highlight how the state of exception can be brought about by disaster, it can also be brought about by unique celebrations where, rather than a frenzy of dread, the public rejoices in a jamboree of sport and spectacle.

The Olympics are an elite-driven affair with scant opportunity for meaningful public participation. Olympic elites insulate themselves from civil society, which Graeme Hayes and John Horne assert has "rarely been factored into the definition of the Games or Games projects. The role of civic organizations and publics is one of implementation and support, not one of definition and decision."[17] Both disaster capitalism and celebration capitalism undercut democracy. However, while disaster capitalism leads to the weakening of the state and the installation of neoliberal policies, celebration capitalism deploys state actors as strategic partners, putting forth public–private partnerships—rather than full-on privatization—as the dominant mode of economic transaction. While some lump public–private partnerships under the rubric of neoliberalism, not all public–private partnerships are created equal.[18] Accountability, risk, and input can vary wildly and yet still be called public–private partnerships. In the context of the Olympics, these public–private partnerships are egregiously lopsided: the public pays more, thereby taking on more of the risk. And the IOC plays a unique role in unilaterally imposing strictures on Games organizers, rendering neoliberalism's deregulation a myth.[19]

Celebration capitalism is disaster capitalism's affable cousin. It thrives on social euphoria, not collective shock. While this century has already seen whipsaw economic undulations and the Great Recession, there have also been moments of celebration, at least from the perspective of profit-seeking capitalists. The Olympics are one such global celebration that with metronomic regularity enraptures people regardless of political stripe or social class. Olympic-style celebration capitalism does not "fight for the advancement of pure capitalism" as with disaster capitalism;[20] rather, it proffers the feel-good rhetoric of public–private partnership, whereby the state isn't abolished or eviscerated, but leveraged as a font of private profit. In a happy-faced bait-and-switch, the taxpaying public shoulders the risk while private groups scoop up the rewards. As the Vancouver-based activist Am Johal told me, "The Olympics are a corporate franchise that you buy with public money."[21] This is the inimical spirit of celebration capitalism.

Like "neoliberalism," the term "public–private partnership" is an example of definitional legerdemain. The urban planning scholar Faranak Miraftab contends that public–private partnerships can be a "market-enabling strategy" rooted in deceptively fuzzy terminology.[22] For instance, the term "private sector" can mean many things, from local small businesses to multinational behemoths. And all too often the failure to distinguish "dodges the question of vested interests by large private sector industries." Boosters promise small-business success but more often play their corporate trump cards. She argues, "All such loose terminology is not innocent, because it permits the interests of the strongest partners to be served under the guise of serving the weak."[23] These partnerships might look shiny on the surface, but often "further dispossess the poor from their locally mobilized resources."[24] And public-private partnerships related to Olympic ventures are so complicated that a legion of lawyers are required, thereby boxing out smaller companies from the competition for contracts.[25]

Olympic Economics

Olympics boosters routinely rely on misdirection. They proffer economic impact studies, typically designed by economic consultants who predict economic success. The finance and tourism scholar John Crompton notes: "Most economic impact studies are commissioned to legitimize a political position rather than to search for economic truth. Often, this results in the use of mischievous procedures that produce large numbers that study sponsors seek to support a predetermined position." He also points to economic impact studies' questionable deployment of "multipliers," or secondary spending that enters from outside and reverberates through an economy.[26] The economist Victor Matheson agrees, adding that multipliers "can easily be manipulated to yield inflated results."[27] Much of what is counted as local gains winds up in the pockets of multinational corporations based elsewhere.[28]

Furthermore, academic economists have found that the modern-day Olympics suffer from a stay-away factor and a tourism displacement effect. Visitors who would otherwise holiday at the Olympic city change their plans to avoid crowds and inflated prices.[29] Economic impact statements also show a tendency to underestimate the role of the "substitution effect": when people attend the Olympics, they do not spend their money in their own communities, thereby shifting their expenditures from one geographical area to another.[30] Academic sports economists have come to the general conclusion that hosting the Olympics does not generate the benefits that economic impact studies promise. After reviewing the major studies on the modern-day economic impact of the Olympics and soccer World Cup, Andrew Zimbalist concluded, "In sixteen cases, the games were found to have no statistically significant effect on employment or income, in seven cases a modest positive effect on income or short-run employment was found, and in three cases a negative effect on income was found."[31]

Staging the Olympics gives host governments an incentive to bail out projects when they go wrong, avoiding embarrassment under the global media spotlight. This allows private companies to surrender fiscal responsibility in the pinch, leaving the taxpaying public to pay the tab. David Whitson and Donald Macintosh assert that the predominant pattern is that "the games lose large amounts of public money and add to public sector debt." They continue: "Public sector debt will repay itself, according to the standard official rhetoric, in private sector opportunities and ultimately in economic growth that will benefit the whole community. Investment in the games is thus framed as a particular form of public assistance to private accumulation, a postindustrial variant of traditional subsidies to industry."[32] As such, public financing of the Games sets the table for private capital to capitalize on the revamped city. These dynamics are the economic crux of celebration capitalism.

Surveillance and Security

A final key dimension to celebration capitalism is the rise of security and surveillance to protect the sports spectacle. Local and national policing forces use the Olympics like their own private cash machine, multiplying and militarizing their weapon stocks. In the twenty-first century, the Olympics are the biggest peacetime operation most host cities will ever experience. While the Games justify the creation of a security structure designed to thwart terrorism, that very same structure can also be deployed to suppress or intimidate acts of political dissent. Terrorism and political protest are often conflated in official rhetoric by blurring the two into "threats" or "risks" to the Olympics. At London 2012, for example, when Chris Allison, Scotland Yard's assistant commissioner and the national coordinator of Olympic security, briefed the London Assembly in late 2011 on policing costs for the Olympic and Paralympic Games, he singled out "four key risks to the Games": terrorism, protest, organized crime, and natural disasters.[33] The role of security officials is to prevent this mishmash of "key risks" from marring the celebration.

The security and surveillance industries as well as local police forces are some of the biggest beneficiaries of celebration capitalism. While securitization thrives under neoliberalism and disaster capitalism, with celebration capitalism the state security apparatus—more than private policing ventures—experiences a sharp boost in its capacities. A recent exception is the world's largest private security firm, G4S, which was entrusted to supply more than 10,000 bag-checkers and other personnel for London 2012 venues, as stipulated in its £284 million ($458 million) contract. However, just before the Games commenced, G4S announced it would be unable to supply the trained security personnel, and British troops were called in to make up for the shortfall.[34] This highlights a trend under celebration capitalism: the public bails out private entities when they flop under pressure.

It's vital to highlight that celebration capitalism and disaster capitalism are complementary. Celebration capitalism, with its ample public spending, can scythe a way for disaster capitalism to follow, creating political space for the argument that there is no choice but to institute austerity in line with neoliberalism. Claiming fiscal emergency, governments can launch austerity programming and cuts to social spending. Dave Zirin maintains that in this way, sports mega-events can be "neoliberal Trojan horses" or "a shock doctrine of sports."[35] The inverse is also possible: the harrowing perils of pure-grade neoliberalism can leave the general public craving the happier inducements of social celebration. In short, celebration capitalism and disaster capitalism can act as a formidable political-economic one-two punch.

Greek Mythology: The 2004 Olympics in Athens

The 2004 Athens Olympics mark a pivotal moment in the history of celebration capitalism and the Games. When

Athens was awarded the 2004 Summer Olympics, Greek organizers assured the IOC a balanced budget of $1.6 billion. Boosters escalated public expectations by assuring a swirl of economic benefits that would lift Greece to the pinnacle of the Eurozone. Yet the *New York Times* noted that still-to-be-built Olympic venues would be "financed with public money" and that Greek prime minister Costas Simitis "has guaranteed that the Government will make up any shortfall." But quite remarkably, the newspaper reckoned, "a deficit seems unlikely now."[36] Reality quickly set in. The Games ending up costing Greece $16 billion.[37] Athens was total celebration capitalism, with the Greek government supplying around 85 percent of this whopping sum and sinking into calamitous debt in the Games' wake.[38]

Part of the reason for the monstrous discrepancy—from $1.6 billion to $16 billion—is a willful conflation of operating costs with overall costs. The IOC and host-city organizing committees begin by touting the smaller operating budget while neglecting to mention overall costs. That leaves out the bulk of budget-busting expenditures: venue construction, infrastructure development, and security. Such mendacity makes the Games appear cheaper than they actually are. Narrowing discussions of the budget to operating costs allowed the Athens 2004 Official Report to claim that the "final financial result" was a surplus of more than €7 million.[39] This was not, of course, the "final financial result" for everyday Greeks, for whom, according to the *Financial Times*, "the economic benefits never materialized."[40] Athens organizers aspired to bring in 105,000 foreign tourists per night during the Olympic period, but merely achieved 14,000.[41] The Games were an economic flop.

On the bright side, the Olympics sparked a much-needed upgrade of the city's infrastructure and telecommunications and transportation networks. The Athens Metro was revamped, as were railway connections between Athens and its periphery and the international airport.[42] But Athens organizers lacked a legacy plan. A decade after the Games, a majority of the Olympic stadiums and venues are in squalid abandonment. The beach volleyball arena is now a field of weeds. A fountain in the Olympic Village sits bone-dry and splotched with graffiti. The Aquatic Center looks like a post-modern Greek ruin.[43] Mark Perryman notes: "Twenty-one out of twenty-two of the stadiums, arenas, sports halls and swimming pools built for the Games are either derelict, in a state of disrepair, boarded up or unable to find a buyer and underused. As the Beijing Games opened four years later Athens faced a bill estimated at £500 million [$784 million] simply to maintain this ghost town of Olympian extrava-gance."[44] In short, Athens left a legacy of white elephants scarfing down scarce public funds simply to keep them from crumbling while the IOC helicoptered off to its next desti-nation. The best use for the stadiums may well have been when the government used them to shelter homeless people during bouts of cold weather or when, in October 2015, they were used to house migrants and refugees from Afghanistan and Syria.[45]

Arguing that the 2004 Games caused Greece's financial crisis is an overstatement, but it is fair to view the astronomi-cal costs of the Athens Olympics as a contributing factor in Greece's economic nightmare. The overinflated hope sparked by the Games contributed to the Euro bubble that, when it popped, exacerbated Greece's economic woes.[46] To be sure, the claim in the Official Report that "because of the Games, Greece is a more economically vibrant nation" is pure fiction.[47]

Athens hosted the first Summer Games staged after the attacks of 9/11. Greece spent around $1.5 billion on security measures—nearly $143,000 per athlete—an increase of more than 700 percent over the previous Summer Games.[48] The IOC also took out a multimillion-dollar insurance policy against the possible cancellation of the 2004 Games, an Olympic first.[49]

The Greek security apparatus jumped at the once-in-a-generation opportunity to add another layer to the surveillance state. Police officials in Athens created what the security critic Minas Samatas calls an "Olympic super-panopticon" made up of a welter of instruments, from surveillance cameras to vehicle-tracking devices to satellites. The US-based government contractor SAIC set up the C4I centralized security system (Command, Control, Communication, Computer and Integration) to make sense of all the surveillance data. The system was originally designed for military use, with SAIC a major partner to the Central Intelligence Agency (CIA). Their "super-panopticon" made Athens "the testing ground of the latest antiterrorist surveillance technology."[50]

Olympics-goers could be forgiven for thinking they had mistakenly arrived at a military hardware convention. According to Samatas:

The military security umbrella was activated on July 27, 2004, just before the Olympic Games were to start. Hundreds of CCTV cameras swept the main avenues and squares of Athens, whereas three police helicopters and a zeppelin, equipped with more surveillance cameras, hovered overhead. The helicopters and the zeppelin were flying almost around the clock throughout the games. Dozens of new PAC 3 (Patriot Advanced Capability) missiles were armed and in position at three locations around the capital, including the Tatoi Military Base near the athletes' Olympic Village, to provide a defense umbrella over Athens. Security forces also received 11 state-of-the-art surveillance vans that received and monitored images from around the city. The coast guard positioned six of them around the port of Piraeus, where seven luxury cruise ships were used as hotels during the Games. Authorities also got two mobile truck screening systems capable of locating explosives, weapons, or drugs in trucks and other large cargo vehicles. They screened all vehicles bound for any Olympic venue during the games and the Paralympics. The mobile units screened more than 2,000 lorries throughout the games. By the August 13 opening ceremony, authorities had installed thousands of CCTV cameras and deployed all over Greece more than 70,000 military and security staff on patrol.[51]

The arsenal also included thirty-nine explosives detection devices, 4,205 automatic vehicle locators, and numerous chemical and radiological detection systems.[52] To help with intelligence and training, the Greek government assembled an Olympics Advisory Security Team that included Australia, France, Germany, Israel, Spain, the United Kingdom, and the United States. Europol, the CIA, and NATO went on patrol in Athens.[53] All told, it amounted to the biggest, priciest peacetime operation ever, up to that time.[54]

And yet even this wasn't enough to reassure the US government. Thanks to WikiLeaks, we know that the George W. Bush administration took extra measures to safeguard US Olympic athletes. Although the "Greeks are extremely sensitive about their national sovereignty," the State Department Bureau of Diplomatic Security provided more than 100 security agents to protect the American squad.[55] In the end, the US government spent $35 million on Games security, with the State Department, Defense Department, Justice Department, the Department of Homeland Security, the Department of Energy, and the Defense Intelligence Agency all taking part.[56]

Many Greek security officials viewed the new security architecture as a long-term venture. Former Minister of Public Order George Floridis wrote: "This great expenditure is not concerned only with the duration of the Olympics. It is an investment for the future." He continued, "The special training, technical know-how, and ultramodern equipment will turn the Hellenic Police into one of the best and most professional in the world, for the benefit of the Greek people."[57] In other words, the military-grade technologies acquired during the Olympic state of exception would be bricked into worka-day policing after the Games. Officials from the Ministry of Public Order also aimed to export its newfound expertise, founding a "Center for Security Studies" to share its know-how with future Olympic host cities. One of its first clients was China, host of the 2008 Beijing Olympics.[58]

The Cha-Ching in Beijing: Handcuffs and Money

In 2001 the IOC chose Beijing to host the 2008 Summer Olympics, prompting boosters to claim that China would open up to enhanced civil liberties and political freedom. Wang Wei, a Beijing bid committee official, said, "We are confident that, with the Games coming to China, not only are they going to promote the economy, but also enhance all the social sectors, including education, medical care and human rights."[59] The IOC's then president, Jacques Rogge, said, "It is clear that the staging of the Olympic Games will do a lot for the improve-ment of human rights and social relations in China."[60] Even the human-rights champion Nicholas Kristof argued that the Beijing Games created "a new lever ... to try to win better behavior from China."[61]

It would not turn out that way. In the lead-up to Beijing 2008, Liu Xiaobo, a prominent dissident and winner of the 2010 Nobel Peace Prize, dubbed China "a hot wok of boiling nationalism" primed for repression.[62] Amnesty International pointed out that the Chinese government actually escalated its crackdown on dissent by targeting activists, reserving especially draconian measures for protesters challenging human rights violations and displacement related to the Games.[63] Sophie Richardson of Human Rights Watch argued that the Olympics set back the clock on political freedom in China. "Not a single world leader who attended the Games or members of the IOC seized the opportunity to challenge the Chinese government's behavior in any meaningful way," she observed. "Will anyone wonder, after the Games are over, why the Chinese government remains intransigent about human rights?"[64]

Behind the convenient smokescreen of terrorism prevention, the Chinese government spent billions to retool its repressive apparatus.[65] It installed a $6 billion closed-circuit television system. To track Games-goers, it embedded Radio Frequency Identification (RFID) tags in tickets. Some 300,000 surveillance cameras—many equipped with facial- and license-plate-recognition software—winked across Beijing's urban terrain.[66] In addition, Olympic organizers recruited more than 600,000 volunteers to reconnoiter foreign visitors and fellow Chinese alike, reporting suspicious activity to the authorities. Local government in Beijing created a Capital Civilization Office to dissuade people from perpetrating minor acts like littering, spitting, or hurling insults at sports opponents.[67] All this sent an unequivocal message to anyone even dreaming of dissent. As a former chief of criminal intelligence for the Hong Kong police commented, "I don't know of an intelligence-gathering operation in the world that, when given a new toy, doesn't use it."[68]

The Chinese state tiptoed across a political tightrope, enlisting the assistance of Western governments and multinational corporations for security assistance while not surrendering control. Beijing organizers collaborated with security officials from a dozen countries, including Canada, France, Germany, Greece, Israel, Japan, Russia, South Korea, and the United States. Beijing created a Security Command Center to coordinate these international players and harmonize their efforts with those of the Chinese national army, navy, air force, and municipal police.[69]

Olympic officials forged strong relationships with private information-system firms like Cisco, Dell, Honeywell, Hewlett-Packard, and IBM. They established relations with the European Aeronautic Defence and Space Company, JVC,

Nokia-Siemens, Panasonic, Philips, and United Technologies. Their efforts were supplemented by private Chinese firms like Golden Vision, Nine Vatech Technology Company, and Tsinghua Tongfang.[70]

US companies also had to maneuver to avoid violating a law that forbid exports to China destined for law enforcement purposes. The statute, passed after Chinese security forces killed hundreds of protesters at Tiananmen Square, contained a convenient loophole: security systems with industrial applications were legal. Thus, with the Commerce Department's blessing, GE and IBM were allowed to sell their high-tech surveillance systems.[71] Capitalism trumped geopolitics.

Chinese officials made it clear that protests related to the Olympics would not be tolerated. To appease critics—including those within the IOC—Beijing Olympic officials created three "special zones" where people could gather to demonstrate. However, to inhabit these official protest areas, activists had to apply for a permit from the Public Security Bureau, supplying personal information as part of the application. The Bureau could reject permit applications if the proposed protests would "harm national, social and collective interests or public order." Under these fuzzy criteria, all seventy-seven permit applications were summarily denied. The protest zones were political traps devised to ensnare activists more than safety valves for dissent. Numerous protesters who applied for permits were detained and arrested. Two elderly women—aged seventy-seven and seventy-nine—who requested protest permits were instead handed one-year sentences of "re-education through labor." This sentence—imprisonment without charge followed by forced labor—was a common form of suppression during the Olympiad. During the Games themselves, the "special zones" sat empty. But Beijing Olympic officials could claim they had tried to facilitate political dissent.[72]

In China, eight is a lucky number. The opening ceremony of the Beijing Games commenced at 8 p.m. on August 8,

2008—the eighth hour of the eighth day of the eighth month of the eighth year. But the Games were anything but lucky for the 1.5 million people who were displaced from their homes, according to the Centre on Housing Rights and Evictions, to make way for the Olympics. Deploying dubious administrative measures, the government vacuumed up 8,400 acres for the Games, in the process dispossessing everyday people, often without proper consultation or compensation.[73] Activists who challenged the eviction process were handed one-year "re-education through labor" sentences.[74] COHRE noted that Olympic organizers "have been responsible for destroying affordable rental housing stock, and authorities have used tactics of harassment, repression, imprisonment, and even violence against residents and activists."[75] One Beijing resident, after being evicted from his home and receiving meager compensation, told the *Washington Post*, "Chinese people do support the Olympics, but we also need reasonable compensation." He added: "The government always blames outsiders for politicizing the Olympics, but domestically they make the Olympics a political issue. We don't believe that our houses were torn down for the Olympics. The real purpose is moneymaking."[76]

Indeed, moneymaking was motivating many. The Olympic marketing maestro Michael Payne gushed about how the Beijing Games would "usher in a new era in global commerce and relations" as well as "the renaissance of the Olympic Movement itself."[77] Capitalists salivated at the opportunity Beijing 2008 presented. China's massive—and in some ways captive—market beckoned. The question was whether capitalism and authoritarianism could forge a happy marriage. The answer appeared to be yes. Multinational corporations were certainly willing to give it a try, furnishing lavish "donations" to the Beijing bid committee and organizing committee in hopes of currying favor. Coca-Cola reportedly paid $1 billion for sponsorship rights in Beijing.[78]

The Chinese characters for "Coca-Cola" translate to "Delicious Happiness." But the IOC Marketing Media Guide for Beijing 2008 vowed to spread "delicious happiness" to all its corporate partners. For starters, sponsorship brought "association with the rings—one of the most widely recognised symbols in the world." Beyond that, the IOC enthused: "The Olympic Movement also provides unparalleled returns on an investment for sponsors. The Olympic Games provide a global marketing platform, based on ideals and values, providing excellent opportunities for a company's sales, showcasing, internal rewards, and community outreach programmes. Sponsors are also able to develop marketing programmes with various members of the Olympic Movement including the IOC, the NOCs, and the Organising Committees."[79] The Beijing Organizing Committee covered every angle. In 2002 it hired Morrison & Foerster LLP as international legal counsel. It also worked with Hill & Knowlton on communications strategy.[80] The US-based law firm Akin Gump Strauss Hauer & Feld LLP teamed up with Publicis consultants to deal with brand management and crisis control before and during the Games. They carried out oppositional research, focusing on NGOs that might criticize human rights violations.[81]

The Chinese state shoveled money into the Games. During the bid process, Beijing boosters estimated overall costs at $14 billion.[82] But after Beijing won the Games in 2001, costs ballooned to $30 billion. In the end, the five-ring price tag was more than $40 billion, dwarfing the enormous bill from Athens.[83] The airport was revamped at the cost of nearly $2 billion, while to the tune of $7 billion, the urban terrain was ribboned with ring roads, highways, a subway, and light rail.[84] Billions were spent on Olympic venues like the Bird's Nest Stadium, the Watercube aquatic center, and the Wukesong Cultural and Sport Center, which doubled as both a basketball arena and a shopping mall.

Many of the Olympic venues are now hulking white

elephants. The Bird's Nest is essentially an empty nest. In February the year after the Beijing Games, the stadium had only one event on its schedule, Puccini's opera *Turandot*, which coincided with the one-year anniversary of the Olympics opening ceremony. Today the Bird's Nest sporadically holds concerts and sports exhibitions, but mostly it is a tourist attraction that costs $10 million per year to maintain.[85] Ai Weiwei, the architect who helped design the Bird's Nest, eventually criticized the Olympic enterprise, expressing regret for his participation and calling the Games an "empty event" for elites.[86] Tourism actually declined in China during the year of the Games, decreasing nearly 7 percent from 2007.[87]

Both domestic and international media were discouraged from reporting such inconvenient truths. Two years before the opening ceremony, the Central Propaganda Department gave the Chinese media precise instructions on what to cover and what was forbidden. Reporters Without Borders found that Chinese journalists who flouted the edict were placed under house arrest or kicked out of China for the Olympic period. The *Sydney Morning Herald* even revealed that Chinese officials had issued a twenty-one-point decree delineating what was permissible to report. Hot-button topics like Tibet, Falun Gong, and food safety were off limits. Journalists were also ordered to disregard the three barren official protest zones and refrain from criticizing the opening ceremony. In 2008 China ranked 167th of 173 countries on Reporters Without Borders's Press Freedom Index. In 2014 the country dropped to 175th out of 180 countries, raising serious questions about the Olympics' capacity to stimulate democracy.[88]

Beijing officials also placed strictures on the international press. The Committee to Protect Journalists issued a scathing report in June 2008, accusing Chinese authorities of reneging on their promise to allow freedom of the press for the Olympiad. The group also placed blame on the IOC, asserting it had "been remiss in confronting Beijing on its unfulfilled promises."[89] The American sportswriter Thomas Boswell described "an unknowably complex and security-conscious control structure" that monitored the media. He wrote that in his decades writing for the *Washington Post*, "this is the first event I've covered at which I was certain that the main point of the exercise was to co-opt the Western media, including NBC, with a splendidly pretty, sparsely attended, completely controlled sports event inside a quasi-military compound. We had little alternative but to be a conduit for happy-Olympics, progressive-China propaganda."[90]

Some of the propaganda had a distinctively green hue. The *Beijing Review* assured the world that by the opening ceremony Beijing would be "boasting of fresh air, a beautiful environment and sound ecology to attain the goal of 'green Olympics'."[91] To its credit, the government constructed numerous wastewater treatment plants, built multiple public transportation lines, increased vehicle emission standards, and pioneered water conservation measures. Before the Games, Chinese officials also relocated around 200 polluting industries and issued environmental impact statements for Olympic construction projects.[92] The month before the Olympics began, Beijing took drastic measures to improve air quality, shuttering factories, forcing power plants to employ alternative fuels, placing cars on an every-other-day schedule, and banning around 300,000 heavy-polluting vehicles from Beijing. Thanks to fortunate weather conditions—low temperatures and consistent rainfall (some of which was induced through cloud seeding)—these policies helped reduce pollutants during the Olympic Games, with harmful concentrates of carbon monoxide, sulfur dioxide, nitrous oxide, black carbon, and benzene decreasing significantly.[93] This led to higher birth weights for babies born to mothers pregnant during the Beijing Games.[94] However, these policies were rescinded at the end of September, once the Games were over, and some pollutant levels returned to their previous levels.[95] Beijing's green measures turned out to be an environmental Potemkin village—an example of celebration capitalism written in Chinese characters.

Vancouver 2010: "No Olympics on Stolen Native Land"

As the 2010 Winter Olympics in Vancouver approached, a local artist, Jesse Corcoran, created a mural featuring the five Olympic rings encircling four frowny faces and one smiley face. The work was installed outside the Crying Room Gallery on East Cordova Street. Corcoran said at the time, "The oppressive nature of the Games is what I wanted to capture and how the majority is suffering for the minority."[96] His installation, and the imbroglio that followed, distilled the "oppressive nature" of the Olympic state of exception.

In the twenty-first century, Olympic host-city contracts dictate that localities harmonize their laws with IOC rules. To achieve that, the City of Vancouver passed a "2010 Winter Games By-law," an ordinance that prohibited posters, placards, and banners that were not "celebratory," although it was legal to hoist "a sign that celebrates the 2010 Winter Games, and creates or enhances a festive environment and atmosphere." The ordinance criminalized anti-Olympics signs and provided officials with the right to remove them, even if that meant confiscating them on private property.[97]

Corcoran's mural attracted the attention of local police who insisted he remove it, as it violated the sign bylaw. The response from activists, civil libertarians, and artists was fierce, and it forced the city to backpedal. City officials argued that the mural was actually removed because of an anti-graffiti bylaw. Ultimately the city relented, and the piece was reinstalled. Activists and the British Columbia Civil Liberties Association (BCCLA) teamed up and pushed back with a legal challenge that helped defang the ordinance. Nevertheless, in line with the IOC's "Clean Venue Guidelines," the revamped ordinance still outlawed signs that undermined the logos of Olympic corporate sponsors.[98] Sponsorship had its privileges.

The Vancouver Winter Olympics were marked by vigorous activist fightback, as civil libertarians, indigenous dissidents, anti-poverty advocates, environmentalists, artists, and anarchists teamed up in a city with a long history of direct-action protest. While the *Vancouver Sun* derided protesters as "whiners and grumble-bunnies" who couldn't "hold their tongues even on a special occasion" so Canadians could "relax and cheer on the home team," anti-Olympics activists offered spirited, sweeping criticism: The Olympics were taking place on unceded indigenous (Coast Salish) land; taxpayer money was being squandered on a sports mega-event instead of indispensable social services for those in need; civil liberties were being crushed underfoot by militarized security forces.[99]

Campaigners emerged in Vancouver in 2002—one year before the city was granted the Games by the IOC—and built momentum right through the Olympics. Activists helped to force a non-binding referendum in February 2003 on whether the city should continue to seek the Olympics. The pro-Olympics side won easily with 64 percent of the vote, assisted by spending 140 times more than the anti-Olympic side.[100] The result helped seal Vancouver's bid, which was chosen by the IOC in July. But the referendum campaign provided a vital precedent for future demonstrators to leverage public conversation around the Games. Today, public referendums are a key tactic in resistance to the Olympics. Plebiscites have torpedoed bids in Germany, Poland, Sweden, and Switzerland in recent years.

The groundswell of dissent in Vancouver included groups like the No Games 2010 Coalition, which ran a long-term public education project to demystify Olympic discourse. Poets hosted action-inducing programming at the VIVO Media Arts

Centre. The NGO Impact on Community Coalition staged panels and seminars that deepened public debate. More militant groups with direct-action experience like No One Is Illegal and the Anti-Poverty Committee provided more radical analysis. Religious, environmental, and indigenous groups got on board, including Streams of Justice, Native Youth Movement, the Power of Women Group, Van.Act!, and No 2010 Olympics on Stolen Native Land. The Olympic Resistance Network (ORN) formed in Spring 2008 and pulled in people from all these groups. ORN's decentralized, anti-authoritarian approach helped build a strong alliance grounded in principles of consensus-style democracy and mutual aid. Local universities canceled classes during the Games, creating an infusion of young people with more free time for hitting the streets. On the eve of the Games, I sat down with David Eby, then the executive director of the British Columbia Civil Liberties Association. He told me, "There is a real unanimity of purpose around NGOs in Vancouver as a result of the Olympics." He described the activist atmosphere as "cooperative and reinforcing."[101] Resistance took the form of a two-track fightback, with one wing working inside the institutional corridors of power and another applying pressure from the outside through direct action and public displays of solidarity.

One major grievance revolved around the cost of the Games. Once again, Olympic boosters grossly underestimated costs, pegging the overall price tag of the Games at $1 billion. But by January 2010, on the eve of the Games, costs had soared to $6 billion. Once the post-Games Olympic hangover wore off, estimates were a sobering $8 billion to $10 billion. Through taxes, each resident of the city donated nearly $1,000 to bankroll the two-and-a-half-week party.[102] The economic collapse of 2008 was untimely for Olympic organizers, but they were already in the habit of lowballing costs and shifting fiscal responsibility onto the backs of taxpayers. The funding structure of the Games was nominally a public-private partnership, but various levels of the Canadian government were on the hook when the going got rough.

The most egregious instance of the Canadian public being forced to backstop private ineptitude was the construction of the Olympic Village. The Olympic Village was supposed to be the crown jewel of Olympic development and a rainmaker for the city. In reality, the project became a debacle that hemorrhaged public funds. Millennium, the private developer that won the bid to build the Olympic Village, lost its financial backing while the Village was only half built, and the city responded with a $100 million bailout. The *Globe and Mail* columnist Gary Mason called the episode "one of the biggest financial losses in the City of Vancouver's history." Olympic organizers had initially promised that 20 percent of all units would be converted into non-market housing for low-income people. But once taxpayers took on responsibility for the cost of construction, which ballooned to $875 million a full year before the Games began, the city needed to recoup what it could from condominium sales, scuttling the promise of low-income housing.[103]

This was especially galling given that in the year of the Olympics, one think tank found Vancouver to be the least affordable of nearly 300 cities it examined. Vancouver's median household income was $58,200 while the median house price in Vancouver was nearly ten times that: $540,900.[104] The gap between great wealth and dire poverty was especially stark in Vancouver's Downtown Eastside neighborhood, a gritty eight-by-fifteen-block area that is Canada's poorest postal code outside Aboriginal reserves. Nevertheless, Vancouver's place in the silver-toned terrain of global capitalism fits Andy Merrifield's description of a modern-day cosmopolitan city like a spandex speedskating suit: "Cities themselves have become exchange values, lucre in situ, jostling with other exchange values (cities) nearby, competing with their neighbors to hustle some action."[105] Local developers and real estate barons had

Baron Pierre de Coubertin on the Croisette in Cannes. Date unknown.

MR. P. O'CONNOR, THE WORLD'S LONG-JUMP CHAMPION.

Peter O'Connor in his specially made Ireland jacket for the 1906 Olympics

Alice Milliat at the 1928 Olympics in Amsterdam with the jury and International Refereeing Committee during the track and field events. The IOC's Sigfrid Edström sits second from the right.

Count Henri de Baillet-Latour, Avery Brundage, and Sigfrid Edström (left to right). The three Olympic power brokers meet in the United States, 1936.

Photo of Jim Thorpe at the
1912 Olympics in Stockholm

The US 400-Meter Relay Team at 1936 Olympics in Berlin. Jesse Owens,
Ralph Metcalfe, Foy Draper, and Frank Wykoff (left to right) won gold
at "Hitler's Games." The last-minute inclusion of Owens and Metcalfe
stirred controversy, as it meant two Jewish athletes, Marty Glickman
and Sam Stoller, were left off the squad.

Avery Brundage during a meeting with international sport federations in 1972

Taiwan athletes unfurling a banner at the Rome 1960 Olympics opening ceremonies

An Emory Douglas drawing inspired by the US Olympic medal winners Vincent Matthews and Wayne Collett, September 1972

Another Emory Douglas drawing, this one highlighting Olympics-induced police repression, August 1976

Future IOC president Juan Antonio Samaranch (center, front row) making the fascist salute at a ceremony marking the anniversary of the Spanish Civil War. Barcelona, July 18, 1974.

Former Olympic Village for the Athens 2004 Games in ruins, August 2012

© Martin Slavin

Police on duty in front of corporate sponsor logos at the Olympic Park construction site in London before the 2012 Summer Games

© Pete Fussey

British Army on patrol at the London Olympics, July 30, 2012

Olimpíadas para Quem? (Olympics for Whom?). Anti-Olympics protesters take to the streets in Rio de Janeiro, August 2015.

"OLIM(PIADA)" graffiti at Vila Autódromo favela in Rio. The word for joke ("piada") is embedded in the word "Olimpíada" (Olympics). The white fence separates the favela from Olympic construction.

hustled themselves the Olympic Games. They were abetted by politicians of all stripes, including Vancouver mayor Gregor Robertson, a New Democratic Party-style liberal and the co-founder of the Happy Planet organic juice company. When it came to the Olympics, Robertson drank the Kool-Aid.

Over-the-top security measures also taxed the Vancouver Olympic budget. The initial security cost was pegged at a laughable $175 million. Eventually it catapulted to more than $1 billion, as opportunistic Canadian authorities used the Olympics to jack up the state's Kevlar-per-capita quotient. Gord Hill, an indigenous activist from the Kwakwaka'wakw Nation, described the process to me as "police extortion from the ruling class."[106]

Vancouver's special blend of celebratory militarism included more than 1,000 surveillance cameras pegged to posts across the city. Military-grade helicopters and CF-18 Hornet fighter jets patrolled from above. Below, police with semi-automatic weapons strolled through Olympic space and patrolled anti-Olympic demonstrations. Security officials acquired a Medium Range Acoustic Device, or MRAD; deployed by American forces in Iraq, the device uses focused high-decibel sound for what is billed as non-lethal crowd control. However, after pressure from activists and civil libertarians, authorities were forced to disable its weapons function, essentially transforming it into an exorbitant bullhorn.[107] Activists were well aware that the military-style equipment for today's state of exception could become the quotidian instruments of tomorrow's everyday policing.

The Olympics triggered the formation of the Vancouver Integrated Security Unit (VISU), an assemblage headed by the Royal Canadian Mounted Police (RCMP) and composed of more than 20 policing agencies. VISU had a distinctive military sheen, with 4,500 to 5,000 military personnel involved, surpassing the 2,900 that were stationed in Afghanistan at the time. One-fifth of the entire country's policing power saturated

Vancouver for the Olympic moment, including 6,000 officers from almost 120 different police departments. The Vancouver Police Department provided another 1,300 men and women. In total, more than 17,000 security officials descended on the city, including people from the RCMP, the Canadian Security Intelligence Service, the Department of National Defence, city police forces, and almost 5,000 private security agents. The Canadian Border Services Agency circulated its officers in the Downtown Eastside, demanding proof of citizenship from residents and acting as de facto immigration police. VISU teamed up with their cross-border colleagues from the FBI and the Department of Homeland Security, which organized an "Olympics Coordination Center" in nearby Bellingham, Washington.[108]

VISU moved aggressively to infiltrate protest groups. Speaking at the Vancouver International Security Conference, Jamie Graham, the police chief of Victoria, BC, revealed that a police informant had worked his way into dissident circles, becoming a bus driver who transported activists to a protest of the Olympic torch relay. Police harassment and intimidation were commonplace. Activists told me that virtually everyone involved in the Olympic Resistance Network was visited by VISU, whether at home, at work, or on the street. Beginning in June 2009, VISU harassed the renowned Vancouver Olympics critic Christopher Shaw. Sometimes officials held a copy of his book—*Five Ring Circus: Myths and Realities of the Olympic Games*—and said they found "disturbing information" that they wanted to discuss with him. By the time the Olympic year rolled around these visits occurred almost daily. VISU also questioned Shaw's friends, girlfriend, and ex-wife. On the eve of the G8/G20 summit in Toronto, which took place four months after the Vancouver Games, VISU even tried to flip him into becoming an informant, a proposition he refused.[109]

Indigenous peoples—First Nations, Inuit, and Métis— played a vital role in challenging the Vancouver Games.

Relatively recent history had more than a little to do with it. During the closing ceremonies of the 1976 Summer Olympics in Montreal, nine First Nations, agreed to participate in an official commemoration ceremony, in which 200 native representatives were joined by 250 non-indigenous dancers sporting costumes and paint to pass themselves off as First Nations people. According to the Montreal Games' Official Report, the "sumptuous procession" was "made even more exciting by the play of lights and the theatrical music based on André Mathieu's *Danse sauvage*." The First Nations scholar Janice Forsyth concluded, "In the end, non-Aboriginal performers dressed and painted to look like 'Indians' led the Aboriginal participants through their own commemoration."[110]

In 2010, some indigenous groups were once again willing to work with the IOC, participating in opening and closing ceremonies. But this time, for the first time ever, the IOC recognized Aboriginal people as official host partners. In advance of the Olympics, four First Nations from British Columbia—the Lil'wat, Musqueam, Squamish and Tsleil-Waututh—created the Four Host First Nations to host and assist with the Games. The three official mascots were also First Nations–inspired: Miga, a mythical sea bear; Quatchi, a sasquatch; and Sumi, an animal spirit.[111] Although Aboriginal people played a more prominent role than in any previous Olympics and were not being outrageously typecast and imitated as at Montreal, they made up only a tiny slice of the Olympic workforce. In 2006–2007 Aboriginal people comprised 1.2 percent of workers in the Vancouver Organizing Committee. Between 2007 and 2009 this increased slightly—to 3 percent—before inexplicably dipping back down to 1 percent in 2009–2010.[112] The indigenous studies scholar Christine O'Bonsawin from the Abenaki Nation at Odanak told me that promises to indigenous peoples "fell far short in providing resources that would appropriately support impoverished and disadvantaged indigenous groups throughout British Columbia. Olympic commitments that were intended to be truly anti-colonial or decolonizing in nature would have provided long-term support structures and systems, rather than short-term and shortsighted financial payoffs, as was the case with the 2010 Olympics."[113]

Thanks to the hard work of activists, the specter of dispossession haunted the Vancouver Olympics. The indigenous intellectual Taiaiake Alfred notes that due to the relative dearth of treaty relations, British Columbia "remains in a perpetual colonialism-resistance dynamic." The IOC's decision to stage the Games on unceded Coast Salish territory put a spotlight on this dynamic and led to "No Olympics on Stolen Native Land" becoming a predominant anti-Olympic slogan. Eighty of the 203 indigenous bands in British Columbia refused to participate. This is remarkable in light of ubiquitous pro-Olympic propaganda promising economic gain.[114] O'Bonsawin points out, "The inclusion of colonial narratives has tacitly been enshrined in the Olympic formula," creating storylines that set indigenous peoples in historical stone, "thereby removing them in time and space from present-day realities."[115] Indigenous anti-Olympics activists took to the streets to remind all that athletes were skiing the slopes and hitting the halfpipes on unceded Aboriginal land.

Indigenous elders played a key role at one of the biggest direct actions of the Games: the creation of the Olympic Tent Village. On February 15, 2010, a few days following the official opening ceremonies, demonstrators challenging the twin processes of gentrification and homelessness criminalization descended on 58 W. Hastings Street, where they took control of the space owned by developer Concord Pacific and leased to VANOC for use as a parking lot during the Olympics. The site was strategic: the lot was a highly visible location where inequality is indelibly inscribed in the social landscape. Concord Pacific had a permit in hand to develop high-priced condominiums on the plot. More than one hundred tents were eventually pitched there. Harsha Walia, who was at the center of tent city organizing, told me the action demonstrated that "there's an increasing willingness to engage in more creative tactics ... that break the ritual of protest."[116]

Upon entering the Olympic Tent Village, one saw a sacred fire tended by aboriginal elders. Another community fire burned in the back of the lot, with music and workshops filling the area. Food Not Bombs provided victuals. Activists from Streams of Justice (a Christian social-justice group) and Van. Act! (an outgrowth of the University of British Columbia's Students for a Democratic Society) helped with logistics. A security crew prevented unwanted outsiders, like the news media, from entering the camp and helped assuage tensions that arose inside the village; at one point two suspected police infiltrators were ejected. Leadership emerged organically from the vital organizing efforts of the Power of Women Group, a collection of Downtown Eastside residents—many of them Aboriginal elders—with deep roots in the neighborhood and widespread respect within activist circles. Individuals from this group, along with Dave Diewert of Streams of Justice and Harsha Walia of No One Is Illegal, served as media spokespeople. Every day or so community meetings helped set and enforce camp protocols and create work schedules.[117]

The Olympic Tent Village led to unique social interactions, where university students could intermingle with people from the streets, the professoriat with the subproletariat, rich exchanges that would not have happened with more traditional forms of protest. The original plan was to run the tent village for five days, but because of the overwhelmingly positive energy, the action was extended beyond the end of the Olympics. Numerous activists I spoke with stressed that the Olympic Tent Village was not merely a symbolic act but a material victory too. Because of the action, approximately eighty-five people secured housing through the City of Vancouver and the provincial agency BC Housing.[118] The action was also a vital precursor to Occupy Vancouver, which sprung up the following year.

Another concrete advance that Vancouver activists achieved was the cultivation of the Vancouver Media Co-op (VMC). Headed by Franklin López and Dawn Paley and composed of numerous citizen journalists, the VMC provided the public with up-to-date information, politically driven art, and all the news that's unfit to print in the corporate media. The VMC mobilized alternative versions of the Olympics, filing stories from the streets of Vancouver and creating space for independent journalists to post their blow-by-blow documentary work. The VMC produced two segments for *Democracy Now!*, the leading community media outfit in the United States, thanks to López's previous connection as a producer for the show. After the *Democracy Now!* host Amy Goodman and two of her colleagues were detained and questioned at the US-Canada border in November 2009 on their way to Vancouver, the show's producers were alerted that something unique was going on. Suspicious that she intended to speak out against the Olympics at a lecture planned for the Vancouver Public Library, border guards rifled through her personal effects and grilled her about the subjects she would cover in her talk and whether one of them was the Winter Olympics.[119]

VMC journalists were skeptical of the efficacy of social media like Twitter and Facebook, dubbing them the "social media mafia." As López told me, it "pushes the model of corporate social media as an alternative media, which it really isn't. A lot of it is ad-driven and event-driven." VMC journalists were aware of what Mark Andrejevic calls the "digital enclosure," whereby we create an interactive, online field in which all of our actions—and transactions—generate a slew of revealing information about ourselves that can facilitate state surveillance.[120] VMC journalists' critique of social media also dovetailed with Jodi Dean's conception of "communicative capitalism," which reframes the social-media surge as ersatz political participation: "Communicative capitalism captures our political interventions, formatting them as contributions to its circuits of affect and entertainment—*we feel political, involved, like contributors who really matter.*" She adds, "The intense circulation of content in communicative capitalism occludes the antagonism necessary for politics, multiplying antagonism into myriad minor issues and events."[121] Although many anti-Olympics activists employed social media to get the word out about events (for instance, through Facebook's "events" function), it was striking how many activists told me they slid offline and into the streets for the Olympic moment. For them, keyboard activism could supplement boots-to-pavement protest, but it shouldn't supplant it.

In Vancouver, the prospect of using mainstream media to deepen the Olympic debate was not particularly promising. Both Canwest—which owns the *Vancouver Sun* and the *Vancouver Province* newspapers—and the *Globe and Mail* were official sponsors, or "print media suppliers," of the Games.[122] Still, activists did not write off the mainstream press. They often appeared as sources, providing quotations informing the public why they were demonstrating. They also placed op-eds in newspapers that made the anti-Olympics argument. The VMC's Dawn Paley referred to the mainstream media as "SQUM," or status-quo media, but was quick to point out that "mainstream media are very relevant because they set the agenda."[123] Social media could help generate numbers at protests and circulate information, but in terms of reaching a general audience, the mainstream media still mattered. As with many dichotomies that were exploded in Vancouver, the mainstream media–alternative media conundrum was not an either-or but a both-both.

For some, the Vancouver Olympics are remembered as a major athletic success for the home country. Canada's "Own the Podium" campaign—whereby the country ramped up its sports funding for five years prior to the Games in order to win as many gold, silver, and bronze medals as possible—was successful, helping Canada haul in twenty-six medals, including fourteen gold. But others will remember the Games for the spirited dissent they engendered. As Harsha Walia told me: "The Olympics provided a foundation for a much-longer-term analysis and debate and vision of our terrain of struggle. It was pivotal for bringing the local terrain of struggle to a national and international scale." And the VMC was a vital Olympic legacy, if one not planned by Olympic organizers. According to Gord Hill, "The VMC reenergized and raised the standard of the radical alternative media structures that we have in this country."[124]

The London 2012 "Schmoozathon"

In early 2012, WikiLeaks released a trove of more than five million internal emails from Stratfor Global Intelligence, a Texas-based private intelligence firm with clients like Goldman Sachs, Lockheed Martin, and the Department of Homeland Security.[125] The "Global Intelligence Files" revealed that Coca-Cola, a Stratfor client and "Worldwide Olympic Partner," was fretting that animal-rights activists from People for the Ethical Treatment of Animals might cause havoc at the 2010 Vancouver Games.[126] With the London 2012 Summer Olympics on the horizon, Dow Chemical requested that Stratfor track activism around the 1984 Union Carbide gas disaster in Bhopal, India. In 1999 Dow had acquired Union Carbide and vehemently insisted it wasn't responsible for the catastrophe that had killed thousands and sickened many more. Dow, another "Worldwide Olympics Partner," had doled out $100 million to the IOC. It also created an $11 million decorative wrap that was strapped to the Olympic Stadium. Stratfor maintained a Bhopal activism file for Dow, which included entries on protesters from the Bhopal Medical

Appeal, a group piggybacking off the Olympics to draw attention to Dow. Activists from Games Monitor, a London-based anti-Olympics group, were also ensnared in the "digital enclosure" of Stratfor's surveillance of online activist planning.[127]

While anti-Olympics dissent in Vancouver trended toward brass-knuckle seriousness and boots-to-pavement mobilization, activists in London tended to go with the celebratory grain, relying on spoof and wit. This strategy was a response to heavy-handed police actions before the Games. Jess Worth of the UK Tar Sands Network and the Reclaim Shakespeare Company told me, "Given the police crackdown that there already has been and will continue to be in the run-up to the Olympics, I think as activists we're having to be quite creative as to how and where and when we do our interventions … through subvertising, culture jamming, greenwash-exposing."[128] Most of this activism in London took place before the Olympics, with only a few actions carried out during the Games.

The Counter Olympics Network (CON) was the activist hub, organizing de facto spokescouncil planning meetings for diverse groups, with each organization sending a representative or two to coordinate actions. Games Monitor and Our Olympics focused their energy online, transmitting information about protests and the historical underbelly of the Olympics. Occupy London and Youth Fight for Jobs held events contrasting government austerity with five-ring lavishness. The groups Save Leyton Marsh and No to Greenwich Olympic Equestrian Events (NOGOE) confronted Olympic organizers' aggressive seizure of public space. The Defend the Right to Protest campaign zeroed in on civil-liberties issues, as did the Newham Monitoring Project, which started a Community Legal Observer program that trained dozens of local people in strategies and protocols for cop-watching. Kerry-anne Mendoza of Our Olympics described activism as a "rainbow coalition of discontent."[129] London mayor Boris

Johnson responded to this "rainbow coalition" by writing: "Oh come off it, everybody—enough whimpering ... Cut out the whining. And as for you whingers, put a sock in it, fast. We are about to stage the greatest show on earth in the greatest city on earth."[130]

When the Olympics come to town, all that is partisan melts into air. Johnson's Tories were joined by the Labour Party and Liberal Democrats who were more than keen to create a tri-partisan, five-ring lovefest. When the American candidate for president and former Salt Lake City Olympic executive Mitt Romney suggested that London might not be ready to stage the Games, he was savaged from all sides. Romney once wrote that he was "mystified by those who say the Games have become too commercial."[131] But activists in London were not afflicted with such bafflement, leveraging corporate privilege and greed into humor-laced protests.

In London 250 miles of VIP driving lanes were set up to transport IOC members, athletes, medics, and, of course, corporate sponsors. Everyday people were barred from what critics dubbed "Zil lanes" in honor of Soviet-era fast lanes exclusively for Politburo honchos.[132] To great public outcry, corporate sponsors snapped up one of every ten slots in the Olympic torch relay, which was ostensibly meant to honor community leaders and well-known Britons, and were given nearly 10 percent of all sports-event tickets. This came to light when sponsors couldn't even be bothered to show up, leaving conspicuous patches of empty seats, to the chagrin of every-day people who had been denied tickets to sold-out events.[133] A smorgasbord of capitalist hobnobbing took place, leading Mayor Johnson to call the Olympics "a gigantic schmooza-thon." In a report published ahead of the Games, Moody's investor services delineated who would benefit from Johnson's "schmoozathon": "Moody's expects that corporate sponsors will benefit most from the Games." After all, the 2012 Summer Games were "a huge marketing opportunity for corporates."[134]

And London political elites were keen to lend the "corporates" a hand. They united to alter British law to bring it into sync with IOC dictates. The Olympic Charter's Rule 50 states, "The IOC Executive Board determines the principles and conditions under which any form of advertising or other publicity may be authorised." To harmonize local law with this IOC rule, elected officials passed the London Olympic Games and Paralympic Games Act of 2006, which defined trademark infringement stringently, listing specific words that couldn't be used in close proximity "in relation to goods or services." Linking together two of the words "games," "Two Thousand and Twelve," "2012," or "twenty twelve" meant breaking the law. So did combining any of those four words with this seven-word list: "gold," "silver," "bronze," "London," "medals," "sponsor," or "summer."[135]

The London 2012 Olympic Delivery Authority, a public body, took seriously its brand policing on behalf of private companies. It strong-armed one café into removing from its menu a "flaming torch breakfast baguette." It forced a flower shop to disassemble a decorative, tissue-paper window display in the shape of the Olympic rings. Even Michael Payne deemed enforcement overzealous, calling it a major "own goal" that went "too far."[136] Nevertheless, London Olympic head Lord Sebastian Coe explained to the BBC: "It is very important to remember that actually by protecting these brands, by protecting the companies that have actually put money into the Games, we're also protecting the taxpayer. Because if we don't reach these targets, then actually the taxpayer is the guarantor of last resort."[137] The idea that brand policing actually protected British taxpayers was a crystalline articulation of celebration capitalism's core: the public will bail out private companies when the going gets rough.

Corporations forked over £1.4 billion ($2.25 billion) in sponsorship fees. Eleven "Worldwide Olympic Partners"—Acer, Atos, Coca-Cola, Dow, GE, McDonald's, Omega, P & G,

Panasonic, Samsung, and Visa—kicked in around £700 million ($1.1 billion), with each firm furnishing about £63 million ($100 million). Lower-tier corporate partners provided £700 million more in cash, goods, and services, with "London 2012 Olympic Partners"—Adidas BMW, BP, British Airlines, BT, EDF, Lloyds TSB—giving £40 million ($64 million) each. "London 2012 Olympic Supporters"—Adecco, ArcelorMittal, Cadbury, Cisco, Deloitte, Thomas Cook, and UPS—each contributed another £20 million ($32 million). "London 2012 Olympic Providers and Suppliers" like Eurostar, G4S, GlaxoSmithKline, Heineken UK, Holiday Inn, Rio Tinto, and Ticketmaster provided approximately £10 million ($16 million) apiece, much of it in goods and services.[138] This seems like a lot of money, but it covered only about 12 percent of the overall cost of the London Games, if one accepts the £11.4 billion price tag that was bruited about in the press. Taxpayers were on the hook for most of the remaining 88 percent.

When it came to corporate deference, activists weren't inclined to go as soft as the politically conservative Lord Coe. They argued that corporate scoundrels were becoming Olympic sponsors to engage in what Dave Zirin calls "corporate sin washing"—using the Games to nuzzle up to consumers so they'll forgive them their trespasses.[139] Activists zeroed their attention on Olympic sponsors with dubious records. When London 2012 officials created a "sustainability partner" sponsorship program that included BP, BMW, BT, Cisco, EDF Energy, and GE, activists from the Greenwash Gold campaign and the Reclaim Shakespeare Company went on the attack. Turns out there were no standards for becoming a "sustainability partner." It was entirely a pay-to-play game.[140]

The Greenwash Gold campaign linked three activist groups —Bhopal Medical Appeal, London Mining Network, and UK Tar Sands Network—to focus on fake green sponsors. Activists produced snappy micro cartoon films on BP, Dow, and Rio Tinto, and requested people to vote on who deserved the gold medal for greenwashing. With the Deepwater Horizon oil disaster in the Gulf Coast fresh in mind, activists made BP a prime target. Campaigners focused on Rio Tinto, the mining company supplying the metals for the Olympic medals, for polluting communities from Quebec to West Papua. On April 16, 2012, activists staged an event at Amnesty International where they screened the three videos, following them with testimonial panels of people from around the world—from Bhopal to Utah, from Mongolia to Mississippi—who were affected by these firms' environmental malfeasances.[141]

A week before the Games' opening ceremony, Greenwash Gold activists hit Trafalgar Square to award the gold, silver, and bronze for corporate greenwashing, as determined by online voting. Once faux representatives from Rio Tinto, BP, and Dow climbed the makeshift medal stand, they were doused with lime-green custard. Police swooped in and arrested seven participants on suspicion of criminal damage for littering the public square. The "Custard 7" was born. No one from the group was ever charged with a crime, but their bail conditions restricted their movement, preventing them from entering places like Trafalgar Square, Wimbledon, Wembley Football Stadium, Horseguards Parade, Hyde Park, and Lord's Cricket Ground because "it is feared that" the individual "will attend these sites to commit further offences due to the fact that they are being used for Olympic venues."[142] In September, after the Olympics and Paralympics concluded, British officials dropped the case, but the bail conditions had succeeded in keeping them away from Olympic-related venues. Arresting activists on questionable grounds without leveling formal charges was a common police tactic to temporarily demobilize dissent.

As a sponsor of the Royal Shakespeare Company, which ran programming as part of the London 2012 Cultural Olympiad, BP attracted additional activist attention. The Reclaim Shakespeare Company (RSC) described itself as "anarcho-thespians" who were "brought together by a shared love of the Bard and a loathing of badly behaved oil companies," as RSC participant Danny Chivers wrote in *London Late*, the alternative newspaper published during the Games.[143] The RSC blended comedy, creativity, and pluck in a series of direct actions designed to strip BP of its credibility in theater circles. Each guerrilla performance was tailored to the play that followed, as activists crafted their interventions with a dash of Shakespearean panache.

The first intervention came on William Shakespeare's 448th birthday in April 2012 at the Royal Shakespeare Theater in Stratford-Upon-Avon, where guerrilla actors stormed the stage before the show. Dressed in Shakespearean garb, Richard Howlett delivered a soliloquy that tweaked the Bard's verbiage for activist purposes: "What country, friends, is this? / Where the words of our most prized poet / Can be bought to beautify a patron / So unnatural as British Petroleum?" Howlett punctuated his monologue with a plea: "Let us break their staff that would bewitch us! Out damned logo!" He then ripped the BP logo from the back of the program, encouraging others to join him. The Reclaim Shakespeare Company's debut performance was met with both bemusement and applause, with many in the crowd tearing out their BP logos. Reclaim Shakespeare went with the celebratory flow, punching the target at an angle, implicitly following the words of poet Emily Dickinson: "Tell all the Truth but tell it slant." Chivers told me: "It's important that we don't set ourselves up as the anti-fun opposition. And it helps for engaging activists—people have joined us because they think it looks like fun." Howlett added, "Getting the audience to laugh at BP is a great thing."[144]

Comedy was vital to another activist group at work during the Olympic moment: the Space Hijackers. The London-based activists are self-proclaimed "anarchitects" who since 1999 have been engaging in humor-based subversion. Composed of numerous "agents," they orchestrate rollicking frolics designed to put the "fun" in "fundamentally opposed to capitalism" while blurring the lines between politics, art, and activism. Agent Maxwell explained: "For us, it's about how public space is increasingly heavily securitized and a lot of that has to do with the privatization of public space ... It's about trying to reclaim space that has been taken over by powerful interests for the benefit of a wealthy minority, and we try to challenge who that space is being taken from and given to. We're trying to re-imagine what you can do in the space."[145] When I sat down with a group of Space Hijackers one hot summer afternoon to discuss their strategies and tactics, Agent Monstris said: "We're all frustrated cosmonauts or astronauts" interested in "physical space, virtual space, mental space, political space, sexual space. The idea is to turn it on its head and to look at things in a very different way that will engage people. Because when you start talking about 'the politics of public and private space,' most people will turn off and start falling asleep."[146]

In spring 2012 the group declared itself "the Official Protesters of the London 2012 Olympic Games" by starting a web page and changing its Twitter avatar. After Olympic organizers complained, Twitter swiftly responded, writing, "We have received reports from the trademark holder, London Organising Committee of the Olympic Games and Paralympic Games Ltd [LOCOG], that your account, @spacehijackers, is using a trademark in a way that could be confusing or misleading with regard to a brand affiliation. Your account has been temporarily suspended due to violation of our trademark policy."[147] The crackdown sparked an online firestorm that eventually led to the reinstatement of their account. Tongue in cheek, the Space Hijackers released a statement: "Eventually after tense negotiations Twitter allowed us access back to our account, along with the hundreds of new followers that we had gained. We would like to thank Locog and the IOC for this Official Recognition and look forward to working with them to facilitate further protest in the future."[148] Meanwhile they hatched plans to catapult chips into Olympic venues to undermine McDonald's brand-protected french-fry lockdown.

Space Hijackers also received communications from the Metropolitan Police asking them to reveal their protest plans so that the Met could facilitate the demonstrations. The group ignored the requests. Two weeks before the Games, they headed to the site of the Olympic stadium and Westfield shopping mall where they measured the range of their megaphone, simulated evasion of security officials, and assessed would-be materials for barricade-building and projectile-hurling. On their web site they reported, "As Official Protesters we wanted to ensure that provisions had been made not only to facilitate our protests, but also that any non-brand-compliant protesters would be safely removed from the area."[149] They were harassed by mall police, but used humor to deflect their inquiries.

Other activists went online to challenge the fact that the Olympics turned parts of London into a de facto tax haven where Games sponsors won temporary exemptions from the UK Corporation Tax and UK Income Tax. Foreign nationals who "carry out an official function or work for a London 2012 Partner"—including sponsors, athletes, journalists, and IOC officials—were not charged income tax, which translated to more than £600 million in foregone tax revenues.[150] This led to perhaps the most successful activist challenge at London 2012: the UK-based group 38 Degrees organized an online campaign designed to compel companies to forgo their tax breaks, and after thousands of netizens signed an online petition, fourteen prominent Olympic sponsors agreed to waive their tax-free status: Acer, Adidas, Atos, BMW, Coca-Cola, Dow, EDF Energy, GE, McDonald's, Omega, P & G, Panasonic, Samsung, and Visa.[151]

Some athletes also challenged Olympic norms. Rule 40 in the Olympic Charter prevents athletes from advertising their personal corporate sponsors if they are not also official Olympic partners. The rule reads: "Except as permitted by the IOC Executive Board, no competitor, coach, trainer or official who participates in the Olympic Games may allow his person, name, picture or sports performances to be used for advertising purposes during the Olympic Games."[152] This was done to prevent ambush marketing. The rule, which was in effect for about a month during the Olympic period, drew the wrath of the American track superstar Sanya Richards-Ross, who said: "People see the Olympic Games, when athletes are at their best but they don't see the three or four years before when many of my peers are struggling to stay in the sport. The majority of track and field athletes don't have sponsors. In the sport, a lot of my peers have second and third jobs to be able to do this. We understand that the IOC is protecting its sponsors but we want to have a voice as well."[153] On Twitter, Olympic track athletes like Dawn Harper, Nick Symmonds, and Jamie Nieto used the hashtag #wedemandchange or #rule40.[154] To be sure, this was no John Carlos/Tommie Smith moment, but it highlighted the fact that athletes are workers and that not all athletic careers are created equal: monetarily there's a big difference between the basketball player LeBron James and the middle-distance runner Nick Symmonds.

Damien Hooper, a 20-year-old Aboriginal boxer from Australia, came closer to the Carlos/Smith spirit when he entered the ring for his match against the American boxer Marcus Browne wearing a T-shirt bearing the Aboriginal flag. Technically this violated Rule 50 of the Olympic Charter: "No kind of demonstration or political, religious or racial propaganda is permitted in any Olympic sites, venues or other areas."[155] The Australian Olympic Committee publicly scolded Hooper, but the IOC chose not to impose a penalty. Hooper defended himself: "I'm Aboriginal, representing my culture, not only my country but my people as well. I'm very proud and that's what I wanted to do and I'm happy I did it.

I was just thinking about my family and what mattered to me. It made my whole performance a lot better."[156] He also agreed to not wear the shirt in subsequent bouts.

As with previous Games, security officials used the Olympics to employ new capabilities. In 2007 the *Telegraph* revealed a leaked memo titled "No. 10 Policy Working Group on Security, Crime and Justice, Technological Advances," that stated, "Increasing [public] support could be possible through the piloting of certain approaches in high-profile ways such as the London Olympics."[157]

The Olympics militarized London's public sphere. The Ministry of Defence placed Starstreak and Rapier surface-to-air missiles in the city, even ratcheting them to the roofs of residential apartment buildings. London's airspace was patrolled by Typhoon fighter jets and Puma helicopters, replete with trained snipers who had the green light to use lethal force.[158] The Royal Navy docked the amphibious assault ship HMS Ocean on the River Thames.[159] The Metropolitan Police acquired more than 10,000 plastic bullets and set up mobile stations to facilitate swift deployments and bookings.[160] The BBC reported that Olympic security had acquired a Long Range Acoustic Device (LRAD), big brother to the MRAD purchased for Vancouver 2010.[161] As mentioned above, after G4S belly flopped on its responsibilities, more than 18,000 military personnel policed venues, affording the Games a strikingly military flavor. Another 17,000 police were also on hand. Three months before the Olympics began Scotland Yard organized "dispersal zones" where police could bar those they deemed to be engaging in anti-social behavior.[162] These zones remained in place for three full months after the Games ended. Estelle du Boulay of the Newham Monitoring Project civil liberties group told me that in the state of exception created by the Olympics, local police were "rolling out more draconian measures and more attempts to increase the power of the police." She noted that in the year before the Olympics "we've seen a different kind of policing, a harder form of policing against our communities, and just a far greater police presence on the ground. It's been quite an intimidating presence."[163]

And all this was expensive. London's bid claimed the Games would cost around £2.37 billion ($3.8 billion), but costs spiked to at least £11.4 billion (or $18 billion). Critics like Julian Cheyne of Games Monitor calculated costs at £13 billion ($21 billion), and a Sky Sports investigation that included public transport upgrade costs skyrocketed the price tag to £24 billion ($38 billion).[164] This should not have come as a surprise. Only a year and a half after securing the 2012 Games, the House of Commons Media, Culture, and Sport Committee reported that "*it was always likely that these would escalate over time.*"[165]

It didn't help matters that once again the Olympic Village developers needed a taxpayer bailout. Originally envisioned as a £1 billion showpiece of London 2012's urban regeneration plan, the Olympic Village project was entrusted to Australian developer Lend Lease. The deal reeked of cronyism, with David Higgins, the chief executive of the Olympic Delivery Authority until February 2011, previously Lend Lease's managing director and group chief executive. The 2008 economic collapse and related credit crunch led Lend Lease to abandon the project, leaving the British government holding the bag. In Spring 2009, Olympic organizers openly admitted that the Village would be "fully nationalized."[166] In August 2011 the Village was sold at a taxpayer loss of £275 million to the Qatari ruling family's property firm. Bizarrely, Culture Secretary Jeremy Hunt championed the transaction as a "fantastic deal that will give taxpayers a great return and shows how we are securing a legacy from London's Games."[167]

The London Games, however, were hardly a moneymaking proposition, as government officials had long known. After a clear-eyed analysis of Olympic economics, a 2002 report from the UK government's Department for Media, Culture and Sport stated, "The quantifiable evidence to support each of the perceived benefits for mega-events is weak." The report went on to conclude, "The message is not: 'don't invest in mega events'; it is rather: 'be clear that *they appear to be more about celebration than economic returns*'."[168]

"Swindler's Paradise": The Sochi 2014 Winter Games

When the IOC awarded Sochi the Olympics, a headline in the *Melbourne Herald Sun* declared, "Russia Wins 2014 Cold War." Alexander Zhukov, Russia's deputy prime minister, boasted that hosting the Olympics would not only burnish Russia's reputation on the global stage, but also "accelerate positive change in our young democracy."[169] It quickly became apparent that colossal funding would be required; in a political and business climate rife with corruption, this was a recipe for graft. And as the Olympic juggernaut rolled over the toes of various political, environmental, and social groups, the coercive capacity of the Russian state would require retooling to quietly quash dissent before the global media spotlight arrived. In President Vladimir Putin, Sochi 2014 had a fervent champion who was more than willing to both wring the requisite funds from cash-rich oligarchs and ratchet up state control. Putin was key to securing the Sochi Games in the first place, winning over IOC voters with a mélange of machismo and mettle. Once Sochi was picked to host, Putin played an active role in sculpting the spectacle.[170]

Once again, Olympic cost overruns would run rampant. An Oxford University study found that between 1960 and 2012 every single Olympic Games ran over budget. In real terms, the average cost overrun was 179 percent, a far higher rate than other mega-projects such as dam construction and infrastructure development.[171] The Sochi Olympics supersized this tradition, racking up $51 billion in spending, more than all previous Winter Games combined.[172] At one point, Sochi 2014 was the biggest construction site in world; in a city of 400,000 people, almost 100,000 were working 24–7 to develop Games infrastructure. This included the extreme exploitation of migrant workers from places like Armenia, Ukraine, and Uzbekistan.[173]

Thanks to the neoliberal bacchanalia in the 1990s orchestrated by Russian president Boris Yeltsin, opportunistic oligarchs had amassed enormous fortunes. These economic titans converted Yeltsin's privatization schemes into what one economist dubbed a legalized "swindler's paradise" and "an exercise in plunder instead of an equitable denationalization."[174] Under Putin, corruption continued in a revised fashion. Putin dialed back Yeltsin's neoliberal strategies a few notches, assigning the state a more prominent role, sometimes by renationalizing successful corporations.[175] The scholar Martin Müller describes "the regulatory arrangement of the Sochi Olympics" as a "model of state dirigisme that accords primacy to the national state." Very much in tune with the tenets of celebration capitalism, he adds, "In Sochi the national state coordinates the preparation process and directs the investment for the Olympics, reining in the autonomy of the private sector."[176] While private investment in the Games appeared significant on the surface, with oligarchs like Oleg Deripaska (head of Rusal, an aluminum firm), Vladimir Potanin (chief of the metals company Norilsk Nickel), and Vladimir Yakunin (Russian Railways president) donating millions to the cause, in reality the state was backstopping the effort. In essence, Putin allowed the oligarchs to keep their billions on the condition they dole out millions to finance the Games.[177] No mere rubes with rubles, the oligarchs went along with Putin's master plan. The Russian business daily *Vedomosti* reported that in March 2014, they were rewarded for their compliance. At a private awards ceremony, numerous oligarchs, including Deripaska, Potanin, and Yakunin, were given medals of honor by the state for their support of the Sochi Games.[178]

In this atmosphere of intimidation and favoritism, corruption reigned. Ahead of the Games, the opposition figures Leonid Martynyuk and Boris Nemtsov asserted that around $30 billion had been siphoned off through egregious "kickbacks and embezzlement" in a "monstrous scam" mostly carried out by Putin's allies.[179] Nemtsov said in 2013 that "the Olympics are being built almost entirely at the taxpayers' expense. Moreover, at the end of last year, the authorities officially announced that almost all the Olympic facilities without exception have been built at a loss and will never pay for themselves."[180] In February 2015 Nemtsov was shot four times in the back as he walked across a bridge in central Moscow near the Kremlin. His daughter contended Putin was "politically responsible" for his assassination.[181]

Nemtsov and Martynyuk were right about the intense corruption. Olympic costs skyrocketed thanks to schemes whereby employers fabricated workers in order to receive state funds, kickbacks related to state contracts, overbilling for construction costs, and transferring Olympic money out of the country instead of toward five-ring projects. The creation of Olimpstroy, a state corporation established to organize pre-Games preparations, smoothed the path for gobsmacking corruption. The Russian government assigned Olimpstroy special legal status that shielded it from public scrutiny.[182]

The Sochi 2014 bid committee assured IOC members that Russia was "a representative democracy" that "provides all Russians with the right to pursue their interests through free democratic elections, freedom of expression, and a balance of power in a climate of social, political and economic stability."[183] Human rights groups were not fooled. As Sochi prepared to host the Olympics, Human Rights Watch disclosed:

> The Russian government has unleashed a crackdown on civil society unprecedented in the country's post-Soviet history. The authorities have introduced a series of restrictive laws, harassed, intimidated, and in several cases imprisoned political activists, interfered in the work of nongovernmental organizations (NGOs), and sought to cast government critics as clandestine enemies, thereby threatening the viability of Russia's civil society.[184]

The Putin-approved "restricted laws" included one that required NGOs engaging in "political activity" and receiving funds from outside Russia to register as "foreign agents," a term rippling with negative connotations from the Soviet era. The law defined "political activity" in extremely broad fashion: any time an NGO "participates (including through financing) in organizing and implementing political actions aimed at influencing decision-making by state bodies intended to change state policy pursued by them, as well as in the shaping of public opinion for the aforementioned purposes." Groups that failed to sign on to the government's special registry for "foreign agents" would have their assets frozen and be vulnerable to administrative and criminal sanctions. Failure to comply could lead to fines of up to approximately $1,000 (30,000 rubles) for individuals and almost $10,000 (300,000 rubles) for groups.[185] At the behest of the Federal Security Service, the Duma also approved legislation with a broad, imprecise definition of "high treason." Civil libertarians voiced concern that it could be applied to any Russian—especially political activists—who worked with foreign groups.[186] In March 2013 Russian security forces ratcheted up the intimidation, carrying out unannounced inspections of hundreds of NGO headquarters.[187] Prominent activists were targeted, often accused of orchestrating "extremist" actions. In July 2013, the prominent left opposition leader Alexei Navalny was handed a five-year sentence in a prison camp on what the *Guardian* described as "a demonstrably sham charge." In the end, a Russian court suspended his sentence but upheld a questionable conviction for theft.[188]

Six months before the Games, Putin issued a decree banning all non-Olympic "gatherings, rallies, demonstrations, marches and pickets" in Sochi between January 7 and March 21, thus creating a one-month protest-free buffer on either side of the Games. Russian authorities eventually backpedaled, vowing to establish "protest zones," with the closest one in Khosta, a village more than seven miles from the nearest Olympic site. Not a single significant protest was staged in Khosta, where the protest zone was tucked under a highway overpass.[189] Political activists and NGOs were sent an unmistakable message: protest at your own peril.

In summer 2013, Russia also passed legislation outlawing propaganda of "non-traditional" sexual relations to minors, which was understood to be a law aimed at intimidating gays, lesbians, and trans people in general.[190] Violators of the law were subject to significant fines—$1,500 for individuals and $30,000 for organizations—while foreigners could be deported. Many people pointed out that the law was incongruent with Principle 6 of the Olympic Charter, which read, "Any form of discrimination with regard to a country or a person on grounds of race, religion, politics, gender or otherwise is incompatible with belonging to the Olympic Movement."[191]

The law galvanized a strong international response. Activist groups like Athlete Ally and All Out pushed the IOC to live up to its own charter. Others pressed for an Olympic boycott. The English actor Stephen Fry penned an open letter to the IOC and Prime Minister David Cameron, arguing, "An absolute ban on the Russian Winter Olympics of 2014 in Sochi is simply essential." He suggested the IOC should "stage them elsewhere in Utah, Lillehammer, anywhere you like. At all costs, Putin cannot be seen to have the approval of the civilised world." Fry compared the 2014 Sochi Games to the

1936 Olympics in Nazi Germany. He argued that Putin was "making scapegoats of gay people, just as Hitler did Jews," and called for the UK to boycott the Games.[192]

President Barack Obama made a strong statement when he named two out lesbians—Caitlin Cahow and Billie Jean King—to his official Olympic delegation.[193] A third member of Obama's delegation, the figure-skating champion Brian Boitano, came out of the closet two days after Obama selected him. King was forced to stay at home when her mother fell ill, but Boitano and Cahow were outspoken in Russia. Upon arriving in Sochi, Boitano said: "We feel very strongly [about] tolerance and diversity. And that's why we're here. Everyone knows why we're here. We've made it obvious and quite public as to why Caitlin [Cahow] and I are supporting the delegation and are here. I think Russians know that and I think Americans know that and we're proud to come from a country who supports tolerance and diversity and we stand strong." Cahow, an Olympic medal winner in ice hockey, spoke directly to the Russian LGBTQ community: "If there's one person sitting out there watching me on television and realizing that there's someone like them out there and there is the opportunity that one day you may feel safe and you may feel like you can live your life, that's what I want to be able to do."[194]

Feeling the pressure, the IOC made a concession, allowing athletes to speak their minds at press conferences. This allowance inadvertently placed a spotlight on Rule 50 of the Olympic Charter that forbid athletes from bringing politics into the Olympic arena.[195] At the same time this safety valve afforded athletes space to speak out without fearing reprimand of the variety John Carlos and Tommie Smith experienced in 1968 when they were kicked out of the Olympic Village. On the eve of the Sochi Games, Carlos told Dave Zirin and me: "If I was an athlete today, I wouldn't be concerned about anything other than what's right. You need to follow your conscience, follow your heart, follow your wisdom, and follow your education as to what the plight is. If you feel like you must do something, the only thing you will regret is doing nothing."[196]

Numerous athletes accepted Carlos's challenge to "follow your conscience." When the media breached the topic of the anti-gay law, US skier Bode Miller commented: "I think it's so embarrassing that there's countries and people who are that ignorant ... As a human being, I think it's embarrassing." He also targeted Rule 50 when he said, "Politics in sports and athletics are always intertwined even though people try to keep them separate." He added, "Asking an athlete to go somewhere and compete and be a representative of a philosophy and all that different crap that goes along with it and then tell them they can't express their views is pretty hypocritical and unfair."[197] Australian snowboarder Belle Brockhoff vowed to publicly rubbish the law. US snowboarder Hannah Teter described the law as "very inhumane" and hinted at Sochi activism, even if that meant breaking rules against dissent. "That's what snowboarders do: we break rules," she said. Brian Burke, the director of player personnel for the Sochi-bound US men's hockey team, dubbed the anti-gay law "repugnant." Burke said: "Olympians, when you pack your skates, pack a rainbow pin. When you practice your Russian, learn how to say, 'I am pro-gay'."[198] Fifty-two Olympic athletes, past and present, signed an open letter to repeal anti-gay laws. The Sochi-bound Australian four-man bobsled team signed on, as did Canadian biathlete Rosanna Crawford and US snowboarder Seth Wescott. They were joined by athletes like Martina Navratilova, Megan Rapinoe, Robbie Rogers, and Nick Symmonds.[199]

During the actual Olympics a handful of athletes carried out low-profile dissent. When Avery Brundage said, "You don't find hippies, yippies or beatniks on sports grounds,"[200] he obviously had never seen snowboarding. Early in the Sochi Games, Russian slopestyle snowboarder Alexey Sobolev zipped down the hill on a board featuring a female sporting a balaclava and wielding a knife, a bold homage to the high-profile feminist punk-rock performance-art collective Pussy Riot. (In early 2012 Pussy Riot entered a Moscow cathedral and carried out a confrontational "punk prayer" performance. Three members—Maria Alyokhina, Nadezhda Tolokonnikova, and Yekaterina Samutsevich—were given two-year prison sentences on charges of hooliganism but Samutsevich was given a suspended sentence in October 2012 and Alyokhina and Tolokonnikova were released from prison in 2013 on the eve of the Games.) At the end of his heat, Sobolev flopped onto the snow, posing astride his snowboard. Asked whether his action should be construed as a gesture of solidarity with Pussy Riot, he replied cryptically, "Anything is possible."[201] The day after Sobolev's cheeky homage, Dutch slopestyle snowboarder Cheryl Maas shoved a rainbow glove—complete with a golden-horned unicorn—toward the television camera after a preliminary run. This was the first open challenge of the anti-LGBTQ law at Sochi. Prior to the Games, Maas, a married lesbian, had slammed the IOC for choosing to stage the Olympics in Russia.[202]

A few days later US cross-country skier Andrew Newell spearheaded an effort to raise awareness of climate change. He was one of 105 Olympic athletes who signed an open letter prodding world leaders to "recognize climate change by reducing emissions, embracing clean energy and preparing a commitment to a global agreement at the UN Framework Convention on Climate Change in Paris 2015." Signatories came from Australia, Canada, Estonia, France, Germany, Italy, Norway, Sweden, Switzerland, and the United States. In response *Investor's Business Daily* ran an editorial titled "In the Olympic Spirit, Shut Up and Ski" that criticized Newell and fellow Olympians for "their poor judgment and naiveté" in proliferating "junk science." The publication implored Newell and his colleagues to "suppress their urges to hector the rest of us and express themselves through their athletic performances. We like our Olympics politics-free."[203] Vladimir Putin, a high-profile climate-change denier who wanted to keep overt politics to a minimum, couldn't have said it better himself.

As the Sochi Olympics proceeded, political turmoil engulfed Ukraine. Before the Games had concluded, skirmishes in the streets of Kiev led to dozens of deaths and injuries. Ukrainian president Viktor Yanukovich fled the country the day before the Games concluded. By early March a convoy of Russian troops had arrived in Crimea and Crimea's local parliament voted to join Russia. On March 7, the first day of the Sochi Paralympic Games, rallies in Russia encouraged the people of Crimea to join Russia. On March 16, the closing day of the Paralympics, the people of Crimea voted to do just that. All this effectively shredded the Olympic Truce.

The roots of the Olympic Truce stretch back to ninth-century B.C. Greece, where a temporary halt to fighting allowed safe passage to the Games in Olympia. In 1993, the United Nations teamed up with the IOC to reinstate the tradition so as encourage a truce in the war-torn city of Sarajevo, host of the 1984 Winter Games. Since then, the UN General Assembly has routinely adopted a resolution to respect the Olympic Truce.[204] But the Olympic Truce is sort of like a unicorn bought with a bucket of Bitcoin. Believing in it doesn't make it real. Numerous countries have flouted the truce. The US is a prime culprit, failing to curtail the wars and occupations in Afghanistan or Iraq during the Olympics. During the 2008 Beijing Summer Games, Russia and Georgia continued their violent skirmish over South Ossetia.[205]

Russia's aggression inspired Ukrainian skier Bogdana Matsotska to depart Sochi in order to join in solidarity with protesters. The athlete's coach and father posted on Facebook, "In solidarity with the fighters on the barricades ... and as a protest against the criminal actions made towards the protesters, the irresponsibility of the president and his lackey government, we refuse further performance at the Olympic Games in Sochi 2014." At a press conference, the Ukrainian gold-medal-winning biathlon athlete Olena Pidhrushna requested that reporters offer a moment of silence out of respect for the political turbulence in Ukraine. The assembled reporters complied.[206]

Non-athlete activists also protested during the Games. Partway through the Olympics, ten members of Pussy Riot—including the recently freed Alyokhina and Tolokonnikova—were detained by security officials on the peculiar suspicion of stealing a woman's handbag from a hotel, but the charges were dropped. When they carried out a guerrilla performance in Sochi—in part to capture footage for their new political video "Putin Will Teach You to Love the Motherland"—they were attacked by horsewhip-wielding Cossacks. Police officials in street clothes sprayed a mace-like irritant in the activists' faces. All this was captured on camera for the world to see. Dmitry Kozak, a deputy prime minister in charge of Olympic preparations, blamed Pussy Riot for carrying out a "hooligan act," asserting: "The girls came here specifically to provoke this conflict. They had been searching for it for some time and finally they had this conflict with local inhabitants."[207]

The news media paid attention when Doku Umarov, a high-profile Chechen rebel, implored his fellow militants to "do their utmost to derail" the Olympics, which he viewed as "satanic dances on the bones of our ancestors."[208] But peaceful dissidents also protested what they saw as Olympic festivities transpiring on blood-soaked land. The Sochi Games occurred some 150 years after the forced removal of the Adyghe people, or Circassians, from the Black Sea littoral by Tsar Alexander II, an event that scholar Matthew Light describes as a "violent ethnic cleansing of the indigenous inhabitants." He notes that "many Circassian activists today would use the term 'genocide'."[209] The downhill ski slope in the Krasnaya Polyana mountain area is the site of a brutal nineteenth-century battle in which the Russians violently pacified the local population; Krasnaya Polyana translates to "red meadow," so named for the bloodstained fields left in the battle's aftermath.[210] Dana Wojokh, a New Jersey–based Circassian, asked me: "Would you have an Olympics in Darfur? Would you have an Olympics in Auschwitz? No, so why Sochi?"[211]

Wojokh teamed up with fellow Circassians to start the activist group No Sochi 2014. Zack Barsik, an active member of the group, told me, "For 150 years, Circassians around the world always wanted their rights to be heard and their grievances to be addressed, and once Sochi popped up, it crystallized into the perfect platform for Circassians to try to bring to the world the plight that we've been experiencing."[212] Between 2008 and 2014 No Sochi 2014 carried out more than one hundred demonstrations, from Istanbul to Israel, from Germany to Jordan, and from New York to the Caucasus. On May 21, 2012, the anniversary of Circassian surrender to Tsarist forces in 1864, No Sochi 2014 mobilized a worldwide day of action in cities like Brussels, Istanbul, and New York in an effort to raise awareness of the Circassian plight.[213] A few months later, No Sochi 2014 took its show on the road to London, where it convened at the Albert Memorial in Kensington Gardens, directly in front of the Sochi House, the official Sochi 2014 Winter Olympics hotspot where for £30 ($45) one could revel in the pro-Putin version of the upcoming Games. Just outside, No Sochi 2014 activists in traditional Circassian clothing presented an alternative narrative that included the genocide of the Circassian people. Blending anti-Olympics chants and Circassian history, they presented their case to passersby and members of the international media.[214]

In Russia during the Games, Circassian activists organized demonstrations in Nalchik and Maykop, cities in the same region as Sochi. Russian police rounded up protestors and arrested the leader Asker Sokht. Afterwards across

Russia, many Circassians, intimidated, did not want to speak out for fear of government reprisal.[215] No Sochi 2014 held solidarity demonstrations across the diaspora. On the night of the Sochi 2014 opening ceremony, more than 200 activists descended on Times Square. "We had to have a physical protest," said Wojokh. Barsik added: "Everyone was in solidarity: Georgians, Armenians, Polish, Ukrainians, Estonians, Lithuanians, Latvians. Anyone who had previous experience with Russian imperialism and occupation supported us."[216] The No Sochi 2014 web site was hacked as the Olympics got underway, but activists pressed ahead with their message. As Wojokh noted, the Olympics were "the perfect platform for us to talk about the issues that are facing the Circassian world: issues of repatriation, issues of our identity crisis as Circassians in diaspora and even in the homelands, the rights that we do not even have in the homeland, and the assimilation we are facing with the loss of our language, the loss of our culture by living in diaspora and elsewhere."[217]

Nine months after the Sochi Olympics concluded, International Ski Federation president Gian-Franco Kasper, an IOC member, openly criticized Sochi's "luxury and gigantism." "Do you really need Buckingham Palace as your start for bobsled?" he quipped. "A lot of cities and countries feel they can no longer afford the Olympics after this $51 billion price tag in Sochi. This is not a good sign."[218] The era of celebration capitalism puffed up the Olympics into an exorbitant spectacle that left debt, displacement, and repression in its wake. Everyday people across the globe were waking up to the Games' grisly underbelly. Even the most enthusiastic proponents had to acknowledge that the Olympics had skidded into crisis.

6

The 2016 Rio Summer Olympics and the Path Ahead

When Jacques Rogge announced that the IOC had picked Rio de Janeiro to host the 2016 Summer Olympics, the Brazilian contingent, including President Luiz Inácio Lula da Silva and the soccer legend Pelé, leaped joyfully into the air, fists pumping like pistons. Lula threw a Brazilian flag over his shoulders like a superhero cape and exclaimed: "Today is the most emotional day in my life, the most exciting day of my life. I've never felt more pride in Brazil. Now, we are going to show the world we can be a great country." Lula even laid an unsolicited smooch on the forehead of a visibly glum Juan Antonio Samaranch, the IOC member and son of the former IOC president of the same name, who had been cheerleading for the Madrid bid. Meanwhile, elated residents in Rio— cariocas—flooded onto Copacabana Beach to celebrate.[1]

Rio beat out Chicago, Madrid, and Tokyo in the 2009 voting, despite persistent lobbying from the Spanish and Japanese prime ministers and a direct plea from Barack Obama, who made a special trip to address IOC members in Copenhagen where the vote was staged. Rio's raucous response broke with the IOC's stiff-jawed protocol, but Rogge said of Rio's presentation, "There was absolutely no flaw in the bid."[2] Brazil was on a roll. A November 2009 issue of The Economist featured on its cover the iconic Cristo Redentor statue blasting off like a rocket from Cape Canaveral. The magazine noted that Brazil used to be "a country with a growth rate as skimpy as its swimsuits," but that the Olympics marked its "entrance onto the world stage."[3] This generic media trope, portraying

Rio's Olympic victory as proof that Brazil had finally arrived on the global stage, was a meaningless confection that helped justify profligate Olympic bidding. For some—especially the ridiculously anthropomorphized "market"—Rio's winning bid helped shed the perception that Brazil was a geopolitical welterweight, marking the rise of the BRIC nations as Olympic titans. Rio was to be a coming-out party.

Brazilians had good reason to be a bit defensive. In 1982 US president Ronald Reagan traveled to Brazil and toasted President João Baptista Figueiredo and "the people of Bolivia."[4] By winning the right to host both the World Cup and the Olympics, Lula and his supporters hoped to bury those memories of the "great communicator" deep in the historical dirt. Lula's hands-on involvement was symbolic of the comprehensive sandpapering of his radical political edge. The former head of a steelworkers' union, he helped found the Workers Party (or PT, Partido dos Trabalhadores) in 1980, cobbling together a coalition of trade union members, environmentalists, liberation theologists, and socialists. In sweeping into office Lula demanded a rupture from capitalism, but once ensconced in power he offered market-friendly assurances and reforms that would slake the political thirst of any pro-capitalist.

On one hand, Lula established federal programs like the Bolsa Família (Family Purse), which transferred cash directly to the neediest Brazilians, and Minha Casa, Minha Vida (My Home, My Life), a housing program that extended low interest rates to low-income people. These programs unequivocally assisted the poorest of the poor. But on the other hand, Lula did not challenge Brazil's entrenched oligarchy. He helped fashion Brazil into what Dave Zirin dubs "the neoliberal darling of international capital and its media organs."[5] Lula actually accelerated neoliberal financialization and export-stoked growth. As the president embarked on his second term, Francisco de Oliveira wrote in *New Left Review* that "Lula seems to have entirely lost his way," promoting "the constant bombardment of neoliberal privatization, deregulation and attacks on rights."[6] Traditional corruption flourished during his presidency, as evidenced by the *mensalão* vote-buying scandal and the enormous Petrobras kickback scheme—known as *Lava Jato* (Car Wash)—that undercut the Workers Party's legitimacy. With his full embrace of the Olympics, Lula once again talked transformation but walked neoliberal.

Rio's Olympic bid book promised not only the *Cidade Maravilhosa*'s breathtaking natural beauty and its ability to "excite and inspire television audiences, young and old"; it also noted that putting the first South American Olympics in the city would give the IOC a gateway for "brand enhancing initiatives" to reach burgeoning audiences on an under-tapped continent.[7] The bid vowed to stage "Games that will open new markets and encourage other countries to share the [Olympic] dream."[8] The bid also claimed that the Games would "help continue the ongoing growth of the Brazilian economy."[9] And it outlined an array of infrastructural upgrades: improved water quality, shiny sports venues, a thorough revamp of the port area, and transportation improvements like the Bus Rapid Transit system (BRT).

Rio's bid touted its experience staging the 2007 Pan American Games as a template for the 2016 Olympics. Bidders promised to make thrifty use of existing venues from the Pan Ams. But Rio's Pan American Games were a curious model to tout. Initially slated to cost $250 million, the event's price tag skyrocketed to $2 billion, making it the most expensive Pan American Games in history (a mark eventually eclipsed by Toronto in 2015). The Estádio Olímpico João Havelange cost $192 million alone, six times the initial estimate. The stadium was forced to close only six years later because of dangerous structural weaknesses, leaving Rio without a working stadium while the historic Maracanã was being revamped for the World Cup.[10]

The 2007 Pan Am Games brought a host of broken promises. Under the pressure of tight deadlines, ambitious assurances about public transport upgrades and boosts for social programs went out the window. Instead, Pan Am organizers bolstered security and created militarized enclaves where the sports competitions took place. The Brazilian geographer Gilmar Mascarenhas and his colleagues concluded:

> For the 2007 Pan American Games, a First World "city" was built parallel to the "normal" Rio de Janeiro. People who had enough money could pass through the walls guarded by National Force patrols and x-rays to enter a completely different world. These people had access to a clean and colorful entertainment district. They were treated to highly organized services and information. Those without enough money had to follow it on TV. When, outside of the Games, people go to watch a soccer match they will not get access to the walled services, but suffer the repression of local military police.[11]

Many *cariocas* suspected that Rio 2016 would provide a supersized version of the disastrous Pan Ams, where sport barons converted public money into privatized pleasure, rammed plans down the public's gullet, and used deadlines to renege on grand promises that had justified hosting the spectacle in the first place. As the Brazilian journalist Juca Kfouri put it: "What worries me is that the Olympics are in the hands of those who committed the debacle that was the Pan American Games in Rio de Janeiro. I have no reason to believe that it will be different. And we should remember that we spent almost 10 times more public money than it was anticipated." He noted that despite the steep hike in costs, "the Bay of Guanabara was not depolluted, as had been promised, the Rodrigo de Freitas lagoon was not depolluted, the metro linking the Pan American Village to the Galeão Airport was not built."[12] These locations would be in the spotlight once again when Rio 2016 rolled around.

Rio 2016 Olympic bidders pegged overall costs at $11 billion, although the *Guardian*'s Simon Jenkins put the bill at $15 billion, the urban geographer Christopher Gaffney projected it to reach $16.5 billion, and the economist Andrew Zimbalist estimates the final tally will vault closer to $20 billion.[13] But Brazil was on a hot streak, having just landed the 2014 soccer World Cup, a huge psychological boost for Lula and for the entire country. Even the critic Kfouri said, "It is absolutely right for Brazil to organize a World Soccer Cup, by all Brazil means to world soccer."[14] While Brazil has struggled to consistently win Olympic medals—its best showing was in 2012, when it won seventeen (three gold, five silver, and nine bronze)—soccer, or *futebol*, has long been king. In popular culture, soccer holds a special place alongside music and religion, a vital component of Brazilian national identity. Yet Mascarenhas points out that soccer was also a key element in "a process of territorial conquest ... of colonization."[15] With Swiss-based FIFA at the helm, the World Cup resurrected the colonial specter.

With the World Cup (Copa do Mundo) on the docket, anything seemed possible. However, a year before the Copa do Mundo began, the political winds shifted. On June 6, 2013, less than two weeks before the Confederations Cup—a tune-up tournament for World Cup hosts that occurs about a year before the big event—protesters from the Movimento Passe Livre (Movement for Free Passes) organized demonstrations in São Paulo over the imminent rise in public transport fares. A mixture of Global Justice Movement activists, anarchists, and Workers Party veterans, the group struck a social nerve. When the Military Police responded with indiscriminant viciousness, their attacks attracted sympathetic attention from a wider swath of the population. Thousands of protesters multiplied into hundreds of thousands across more than 350 cities and towns, expanding the scope of critique far beyond transportation costs.[16]

Juliana Barbassa describes the protests as "the growing pains of a middle-income country with a middle class that had awakened to the reality that they paid taxes, they voted, and they wanted what was their due: decent services and elected officials who represented their interests."[17] Add to this a "precariat" of mostly younger workers who had entered the formal workforce during Lula's reign (2003–11), but who labored under unstable conditions where pay was meager and job security close to nil, and you get what André Singer called "a crossover of classes."[18] The 2013 Confederations Cup became a political petri dish for dissent.

Many protests focused on FIFA as the plutocratic puppet-master pulling the World Cup strings. Demonstrators demanded FIFA-quality schools and hospitals on par with the FIFA-standard stadiums. FIFA played the perfect villain, after a series of damning revelations exposing the world governing body for soccer as inhabiting a land of caviar and stretch limousines, the 1 percent of the global 1 percent, the apple of Thomas Piketty's ire. For a nonprofit organization, FIFA sure was a profitable one: the Zurich-based group would rake in $4.5 billion from the Brazil World Cup alone.[19] As protests rippled across Brazil, Romário, the soccer phenom turned congressman, said that FIFA was "the real president of Brazil" and that the group was "taking the piss with our money, with the public's money, it's a lack of respect, a lack of scruples."[20]

The Brazil World Cup was an archetypal case study in celebration capitalism. Thanks to a sport-induced state of exception, World Cup host cities were exempted from Brazil's Law of Fiscal Responsibility, which sought to corral reckless deficit spending. Although FIFA only required eight stadiums, Brazil built twelve, spreading the patronage while increasing the cost. Since many of the stadiums were built in cities without teams that could fill the stands in the wake of the mega-event, a herd of white elephants was born. Protesters found it especially galling that vast sums of public money—$15 billion to

$20 billion—were being shunted toward luxury soccer stadiums that would become privatized enclaves they'd never be able to access. As Gaffney put it, "these new stadiums have consolidated the privileges of the elite at the expense of everyone else." He added, "The 2014 World Cup became a smokescreen for Brazil's violent dystopia even as it exacerbated the stark economic and social inequalities that define this country of 200 million."[21] In considering whether the 2014 Brazil World Cup was worth it, Jorge Castañeda wrote: "For the rest of the world, it was a great big party on someone else's dime. Brazilian taxpayers footed the exorbitant bill."[22] Every time Lula's successor, Dilma Rousseff, appeared on screen during the Cup, she was roundly booed. So was Sepp Blatter, the tone-deaf president of FIFA who would soon find himself embroiled in a vast racketeering scandal being prosecuted by law enforcement agencies in the United States and Switzerland.

The World Cup and Olympics signaled wider changes, together forming what Orlando Santos Junior, urban planning professor at the Federal University of Rio de Janeiro, called a "privileged moment" for imposing a happy-faced version of creative destruction on Brazil. "These two sports mega-events constitute expressions of urban projects that restructure the host cities, and the dissemination and adoption of a new pattern of neoliberal governance," he wrote.[23] While not neoliberal phenomena in themselves, the sports galas functioned as a two-headed battering ram for neoliberalism. They relied heavily on a law passed in 2004 that baked public–private partnerships into the country's financial future. The law codified two types of public–private partnerships: the "sponsored concession" (*concessão patrocinada*), linked to managing public services, and the "administrative concession" (*concessão administrativa*), or contracts to provide services to the government.[24] In short, celebration capitalism scythed the path for normalizing neoliberalism in Brazil.

In many ways, the World Cup was a foretaste of what was to come with the Olympics. The Brazil squad marched toward the World Cup final until its gruesome 7–1 semifinal loss to a merciless German team that ultimately claimed the Jules Rimet trophy as world champion. For Brazil, *o jogo bonito*— the beautiful game—was all of a sudden not so *bonito*. Neither was Rio 2016 organizers' progress on the Olympics. While the country wallowed in the *seleção*'s drubbing, construction projects for the Rio Games lagged behind schedule, as Brazil's Ministry for Labor halted construction work at two Olympic venues over health and safety concerns.[25] Experienced IOC officials slid into freak-out mode. IOC vice president John Coates announced that preparations in Rio were "the worst that I've experienced," causing the IOC to "become very concerned. They are not ready in many, many ways."[26] But by spring 2015, the IOC was sounding much more relaxed, with the Brazilian federal auditor reporting that construction only lagged behind by a month.[27]

To be sure, the Olympics are a much more complicated endeavor than the World Cup. Rio 2016 features more than 10,000 athletes from 205 countries, whereas the Brazil World Cup involved 736 soccer players from thirty-two nations. Given the difference in those figures, we shouldn't be surprised at Andrew Zimbalist's assertion that "whatever deficiencies cropped up in hosting the 2014 World Cup, they appear to be magnified severalfold for the 2016 Summer Games."[28] In fact, Eduardo Paes, the blue-jeans-wearing, English-speaking, beer-quaffing mayor of Rio, agreed. "The World Cup compared to the Olympics is kind of easy; the Olympics is very complicated," he said. "I've been spending much more time on Olympics than the World Cup."[29] A year before the Games, Paes confessed, "Of course I am worried."[30] The mayor has a lot to worry about. He has hinted at pursuing higher political office, and his political fate may well be tied to the Games.

"Transformation Games"

Momentary pangs of doubt aside, Paes has been an enthusiastic ambassador for Rio 2016. He often refers to them as the "transformation Games," and has even argued they'll make a larger positive impact on the city than the 1992 Games did for Barcelona, becoming the "benchmark" for the Olympic legacy. "I want to do better than Barcelona did," he said, "and I think the city is moving that way because of the Olympics." He claimed that Olympic organizers had actually delivered more infrastructure projects than pledged in the bid.[31]

Perhaps "transformation" was the title of an Olympic memo of the day with the instructions "just add a dash of hyperbole and stir." Carlos Nuzman, president of the Rio Organizing Committee and a participant in volleyball at the 1964 Olympics in Tokyo, said Rio would bring the "greatest transformation" in the history of the Games.[32] Nawal El Moutawakel, the IOC member leading the coordination commission in Rio, proclaimed, "I think Rio and Brazil will experience a full transformation of the city."[33] However, in a poll of *O Dia* readers taken a year before the Olympics opened, 69 percent believed the Games would *not* leave a legacy for everyday *cariocas*.[34] Mayor Paes inadvertently encouraged such skepticism when he said that despite promises to clean up Rio's polluted waterways, the environmental goal was not likely to be met. "It is indeed a wasted opportunity," he noted. "As a Rio resident, I think it's a shame."[35] Overall, though, Rio boosters raised sky-high expectations, claims that boomeranged back to bedevil them.

Staging a so-called "transformation Games" would, of course, require money. Thanks to recent high-priced Games in Beijing and Sochi, *The Economist* could write without irony that "compared with other recent Olympic games, Rio's look cheap. Brazil reckons it will cost 37.7 billion reais ($12.5 billion)."[36] Notwithstanding the fact that $12.5 billion was a low-end estimate, optimism for a "low-cost" Games was soured by a capitalist downturn that sent Brazil plunging toward its worst recession in a quarter century. In September 2015, Standard & Poor's downgraded Brazil's debt to "junk" status. Still, boosters pointed to articles trumpeting the idea that taxpayer money comprised only 43 percent of overall Games costs.[37]

The idea that the public was on the fiscal hook for less than half of overall Games costs is extremely misleading. It fails to tally tax exemptions, financing with markedly reduced interest rates, and the brazen transfer of real estate assets, sometimes through violent displacement. One study by Brazilian tax officials found that tax exemptions for the Olympics would be around four times higher than the World Cup, where tax breaks amounted to about $250 million.[38] Rio 2016 organizers and their allies in government enticed the participation of private developers with sweetheart deals backed by government funds. Once again, when it came to Olympic funding, the state was a fiscal backstop, assuming risk while teeing up windfalls for private players. Orlando Santos Junior summed up the fiscal sleight of hand as an "alchemy" concocted by the mayor's office that is "distorted because of the absence of key information."[39]

Beyond this, the Rio Olympics rely on an army of volunteer labor. The 70,000 unpaid volunteers at the Games will save some $100 million, and that's if volunteers were merely paid minimum wage. Moreover, volunteers get free meals and transportation only on days they work. They must pay their own way to Rio and find their own accommodations in the *Cidade Maravilhosa*, which is also marvelously expensive. When pressed about the issue, Christophe Dubi, the Olympic Games executive director, replied, "It is about the spirit of volunteerism."[40]

This sort of fiscal hoodwinkery has led Gaffney to argue, "The flaccid Olympic mantras, superstar pedestal climbers, stadiums, and legacy promises are mere distractions from the realpolitik of urban development." The Olympics are all about real estate.[41] As Stephen Wade of the Associated Press asked: "Why would anyone spend billions if the Games were simply a sports event? In Rio, why would Mayor Eduardo Paes be so intimately involved—be seen by the IOC as the most important person on the ground in Brazil—if this is only a sports championship?"[42]

Rio's brand of fiscal chicanery crystallized in the construction of the Olympic Village, a brazen transfer of public wealth into private pockets. At the center of the heist sat Carlos Carvalho, the Brazilian real estate baron whose firm Carvalho Hosken took responsibility for building the Olympic Village, alongside Odebrecht, the scandal-wracked contractor embroiled in the Petrobras bribery imbroglio. Rio's Olympic bid innocuously posits: "Carvalho Hosken, acting as land owner and developer, will assume responsibility for the construction of the Olympic and Paralympic Village. Carvalho Hosken has already entered into a cooperative and collaborative development relationship with Rio 2016." The plan was to have Rio 2016 rent the Olympic Village—thirty-one high-rise buildings—from Carvalho at a capped cost of around $19 million.[43]

But the bid fails to note that Carvalho stands to make astronomical profits from the Games by converting the Olympic Village into more than 3,600 unapologetically high-priced condos called Ilha Pura (Pure Island). All this was done on the back of a 2.3 billion real loan from the Brazilian bank Caixa. Meanwhile, Carvalho and another developer in Barra da Tijuca donated more than a million reais to Eduardo Paes's election campaign. Geophysically speaking, *Ilha Pura* isn't even an actual island. Rather, it's a social island where class is the password. Sounding like Montgomery Burns of *Simpsons* fame, Carvalho claimed he wanted to create "a city of the elite, of good taste ... For this reason, it needed to be noble housing, not housing for the poor." But in a way, "the poor" had a role to play. A year before the Games, Brazilian news media revealed that construction workers at the Olympic Village were laboring under slave-like conditions, inhabiting living quarters teeming with rats and cockroaches. Carvalho's role in building the Olympic Village and Olympic Stadium helped make him the thirteenth richest person in Brazil, with a net worth of $4.2 billion.[44]

Riffing off the proverb "God is Brazilian," the Rio-based writer Luiz Alfredo Garcia-Roza notes of the *Cidade Maravilhosa*, "If the world had been created by God, he had used his best material and all his inspiration to create that landscape."[45] Television broadcasters salivated over Rio's idyllic landscapes, with beaches as backdrop and the iconic Cristo Redentor hovering above. Plus, Rio sits only one time zone ahead of the US East Coast, bestowing on NBC the first live, prime-time Olympics since the 1996 Atlanta Games. "Prime time is still the mothership for us," an executive producer of NBC's Olympics coverage said. He described the Rio Games as "an embarrassment of riches" for the network. Another NBC sports exec said, "We expect the games in Rio to be the biggest ever."[46] Much was at stake for NBC. After forking over $4.4 billion to cover the 2014 through the 2020 Olympics, the network paid a whopping $7.65 billion for the Games stretching from 2022 through 2032. A select group of IOC and NBC bigwigs christened the deal at an exclusive dinner with veal, wild mushrooms, and self-congratulatory backslapping at the Lausanne Palace luxury hotel.[47]

Not everyone in Brazil was feeling quite so giddy. At anti-government protests across the country in August 2015, some right-wing demonstrators connected corruption under President Dilma Rousseff, the onetime revolutionary and daughter of a Bulgarian communist, to misspending on the Olympics. One demonstrator said: "I am against the Olympic Games. We must take [care] of ourselves, the economy, and everyday life. Everything is wrong with this government."[48] Protests were igniting on all sides of the political spectrum. The United Movement of Street Vendors rallied against the repression of *camelôs*, or street vendors, who were being cleared from the streets by the Municipal Guard. Bearing banners with the slogan *Olimpíadas Para Quem?* (Olympics for Whom?), they protested to challenge the suppression of the informal sector, an unmistakable trend in mega-event hosting.[49]

Groups that were active in the 2013 Confederations Cup protests were also girding for an anti-Olympics fight. The Comitê Popular da Copa e das Olimpíadas (Popular Committee of the World Cup and Olympics) organized chapters in the twelve cities hosting World Cup soccer matches. In a way, the Comitê branch in Rio de Janeiro was political progeny of the Comitê Social do Pan, a group that rose up to challenge the injustices magnified by the 2007 Pan American Games. The Comitê in Rio brought together political organizers with academics, neighborhood associations with NGOs. They engaged in consensus-based organizing around the negative effects of sports mega-events, writing research-driven dossiers, hosting public debates, and taking to the streets. The Comitês Populares were instrumental in stoking protest around the World Cup and recalibrated their sights on the Rio Olympics.

In late September 2015 I attended the Comitê's launch of a dossier documenting the harmful impacts of Rio 2016 within a larger social-justice framework around the right to the city. The event took place at the Union of Professional Journalists in front of a packed house. After watching a few short, snappy videos on a range of issues—from the displacement of local fishermen to the struggle of local activist groups to fend off aggressive privatization—we heard a range of speakers, including activists, community leaders, and academics. Solange Chagas, a leader from the Maracanã neighborhood, site of the Games' opening ceremony, described the ironic demolition of a local athletic arena—the Estádio de Atletismo Célio de Barros—to make way for sports mega-events. The destruction of the facility left the community bereft of a place to exercise. "Rio will host the Olympics and we have no place to train," she said. "For me, the Olympics was the worst thing that has happened. We are punished." After the presentations, numerous attendees took to the microphone to deliver passionate testimonies against all the money being spent on a lavish party for the rich while many residents of Rio lacked basic services.

Demian Castro, a longtime member of the Comitê, was another speaker at the launch. When I asked him a few days before the event why he opposed the Olympics, he offered a nuanced critique reminiscent of other activists from previous host cities. "I am not opposed directly to the Olympic Games, because I love sports," he said. "The criticism of the Games is their commercial logic and especially how they strengthen neoliberal urbanism in the host city." In Rio, he said, "the Olympics strengthens a business model favoring mainly property developers, landowners, and construction. The result is a more exclusive city, marked by violent removal processes and evictions, increased segregation, displacement of the poorest people to outlying areas, and an exponential spike in the cost of living."[50] At the dossier launch he added, "The social legacy of the Olympics could be a social apartheid."

Santos Junior, a Comitê member, told me that the public launch of the dossier served many purposes: to spotlight social rights violations caused or exacerbated by the Games; to amplify the demands of affected groups; to sensitize people to the neoliberal project creeping in behind the Olympics; and to ramp up pressure on public bodies with the purview to make amends. His list represents a set of activist goals that could resonate across Olympic sites.[51]

Repression and Displacement

When Rio de Janeiro applied for the 2004 and 2012 Olympics, it lost out partly because of perceived shortfalls in providing security. With that in mind, when Lula went to Copenhagen in 2009 to pitch Rio's Olympic bid, he was accompanied by Captain Pricilla Azevedo, a commander of the Pacification Police Units (or UPPs, Unidades de Polícia Pacificadora), a program designed to quell violence in favelas.[52] Begun in 2008, the UPP program was a concerted shift in direction. UPPs essentially stormed favelas to root out *traficantes*, circumvent highly corrupt police units, and establish dominance on the *morros*, the hills upon which many favelas are built. In short, it is an internal colonization program designed to make favelas more legible to the state. UPP personnel are not only heavily armed, but also trained in community relations and human rights. The program has been effective, sometimes creating a conveyor belt for much-needed social services within favela communities.[53] Gaffney writes, "There is no question that UPP has improved security and quality of life in the communities in which the program operates." However, the process inherently militarizes public space, often "substituting one form of martial law with another" and can reinforce the stark divide between favela dwellers and the rest of Rio. It has also jacked up real estate values in favelas occupied by UPPs, exacerbating the displacement of longtime favela residents.[54] Thirty-nine of the first forty UPP incursions were carried out in Olympic zones identified in Rio's original bid.[55]

All this comes with a hefty price tag. Beginning with the 2007 Pan Am Games and running through the 2016 Olympics, Rio de Janeiro has spent around $6 billion reais in public funds on security for sports mega-events. UPP costs add another R$1 billion per year.[56] The Brazilian Defense Ministry reported purchasing Black Hawk helicopters for use at the World Cup as well as A-29 Super Tucano aircraft suited for aerial surveillance and counterinsurgency—high-tech weapons that would be available for the Olympics.[57] The Rio 2016 organizing committee even hired former New York mayor Rudy Giuliani's security firm, Giuliani Security and Safety, as a consultant to provide advice on technology and weaponry.[58]

In a way, the use-value of militarized spectacle was moot. The wider significance of the ostentatious policing power in the lead-up to Rio 2016 is its exchange-value: the symbolic transformation of Rio into a business-friendly metropolis smack in the center of the circuit board of capital. The idea, as Mascarenhas notes, is to exude the "image of a competitive city, disciplined, healthy, vigorous and enterprising, ready to compete successfully ... to attract private investment."[59] One group of Brazil-linked academics argued that with this process, the *perception* of safety—"*the sale of the sense of security*"—is a baseline requirement.[60] Spectacle in the service of capital. Propping up Giuliani behind the press conference podium to prattle on about security threats fits this plan like skin-tight spandex.

An in-your-face security presence was always part of the Rio 2016 plan. According to the bid, the Brazilian Defense Forces are integral, making "a significant contribution to Games security planning and operations. The Army will have a key venue security role in the Deodoro Zone, and the Air Force and Navy will provide airspace control and protection and maritime security for Games venues." In addition the bid stated that the Army would "be an important part of the counterterrorism plan for the Games."[61]

In July 2015, Olympic security honcho Andrei Augusto Rodrigues announced that Rio 2016 would deploy 85,000 personnel to police the Games, more than doubling the number at London 2012. "There has never been anything like this in the country," he said.[62] The security force includes 1,500 personnel whose sole focus is anti-terrorism, even though Rio's Olympic bid stated that "Brazil has no history of any significant international or domestic terrorist activity and Brazilian authorities have not identified any terrorism threats to the 2016 Games in Brazil."[63] In other words, the Olympics and its gigantism made Rio a terrorism target.

All this is troubling in the eyes of human rights proponents. The historian Bryan McCann writes that in Rio de Janeiro, the end of the military dictatorship in 1985 did not lead to a wholly peaceful path. In fact, "the police became far more homicidal under democracy than they had been under dictatorship."[64] A report on police repression issued by Amnesty International a year before the Games revealed that Brazil's military police had carried out 1,500 killings in the previous five years. Amnesty deemed many of the deaths "extrajudicial executions" occurring through excessive force or after the victim was injured or had surrendered. Furthermore, between 2010 and 2013, 79 percent of the victims were *cariocas* of color (51 percent brown and 28 percent black) and 75 percent were young (between fifteen and twenty-nine years old).[65]

Protesters have extra reason for concern, since the original Rio bid openly conflates activism with terrorism. In a section titled "Activist/Terrorist Risks" the bidders asserted, "The risk to the Games from protest action and domestic terrorism is low." The bid specifically identified "issue motivated groups" that are "concerned with indigenous rights, environmental or anti-globalization issues." (Incidentally, this was the only mention of indigenous peoples in the entire Olympic bid.) Although most of these groups' protest actions are both legal and nonviolent, Brazilian security officials "are putting in place comprehensive civil order plans" and "establishing designated protest areas."[66]

Historically, Rio favelas have long been the site of state repression. With the Olympics on the way, these communities also became vulnerable to displacement. A study from the Rio-based think tank Instituto Igarapé estimated that the Olympics could displace 100,000 people.[67] Theresa Williamson, the founder of Catalytic Communities, a Rio-based advocacy NGO that has been working tirelessly on human-rights and displacement issues in favelas since 2000, told me: "The biggest problems with the Olympics are growing inequality, the death of culture, and the marketization of the city. They're all related in one big process."[68] The favelas were a crucible for these dynamics. Real estate prices were skyrocketing even as Brazil slid into recession. In the eyes of developers, favelas were poorly placed eyesores thwarting monster profits.

Favela dwellers in Vila Autódromo, a small working-class neighborhood along the Jacarepaguá lagoon on the edge of Barra da Tijuca, found themselves in front of the Olympic steamroller. The favela stood in the way of access roads for the Olympic Park. Originally a fishing village founded in the 1960s, Vila Autódromo has long been treated like a barrier to progress. But residents have thrown down their anchor and girded for a fight. As the metropolis stretched west in the 1990s, developers and their allies in government—including a young deputy mayor of Barra da Tijuca by the name of Eduardo Paes—alleged that the favela caused environmental and aesthetic damage and required demolition. "Vila Autódromo is a symbol in so many ways," Williamson said. "It's a symbol for activists because of its resistance. It's a symbol for the city, and how determined the elite are to keep the status quo in terms of inequality."[69]

Fighting through the judiciary, residents won a concession in 1998 that granted them the right to stay for ninety-nine years. But the city government was not deterred. It played the sustainability card, claiming the favela was located in an environmentally sensitive area. And it used the Olympics as a handy justification for offering residents payments to leave and relocating them in social housing elsewhere. Favela residents teamed with urban planners from two Brazilian universities to create a People's Plan that would preserve the neighborhood while investing in social programs that would enliven it.

The Plano Popular da Vila Autódromo included new streets, a revamped sewer system, and a shiny medical facility and childcare center. All this was reckoned to cost about 13.5 million reais ($4.4 million), while the government instead spent seven times that amount—96 million reais, or $32 million—to evict and relocate residents. The Plano Popular was even selected from 170 community projects in Rio to win the Deutsche Bank Urban Age Award. Rather than hand residents a high-profile public victory, Mayor Paes canceled the awards ceremony. He also ignored the People's Plan. One Vila Autódromo resident told the *Guardian*, "The Olympics is spitting in our face."[70]

A year before the Rio Games, 90 percent of the families had left Vila Autódromo. But around fifty families refused to budge, creating a stand-off. On a rainy Saturday in September 2015 I visited Vila Autódromo with Theresa Williamson of Catalytic Communities and the Rio-based writer Julia Michaels. We walked through the favela, passing rubbled homes in the center of the favela and along the waterfront on the Jacarepaguá lagoon. Anti-Games graffiti adorned the walls dividing the community from the Olympic construction site. One read, *As Olimpíadias Passam A Justiça Fica Suja!* (The Olympics Pass and Justice Remains Dirty!). Another was a play on Giuliani's zero-tolerance policing policy, imported from New York and selectively used against street vendors and the poor: *Choque de Ordem no Parque Olímpico, Justice Socioespacial* (Shock of Order on the Olympic Park, Sociospatial Justice). Creativity abounded, with one panel reading "OLIM(PIADA)," the Portuguese word for joke (*piada*) nestled within a word for Olympics. Another read *Paes Sem Amor!!!* (Paes Without Love!!!), a tweak of the phrase *Paz e Amor* (Peace and Love). One still-standing two-story house had two phrases scrawled in spray paint across its front: *Quero ficar / Vamos lutar!!!* (I want to stay / We will fight!!!) and *Não Deixe a Vila Morrer!* (Don't let Vila die!).

We met with Heloisa Helena Costa Berto, a resolute holdout at Vila Autódromo. An Afro-Brazilian woman who practices Candomblé religion, she exuded calm strength and tenacity. As we dodged enormous puddles on the road to her home nestled along the shore of the lagoon she told us about her protracted plight, a roller coaster of negotiations with Rio officials marked by psychological mind games. She said she had even received death threats. "Because when you are talking about land," she told us, "people are willing to kill." City negotiators persistently pressured her to sign a lowball offer and undermined her plans to resettle in the small section of the community that would be allowed to stand after the Games. She suspected religious discrimination; racism was another possibility. Under the stress of the situation, her health deteriorated. But despite the grim, omnipresent strain of Olympics-induced precariousness, life bloomed around her home. The sacred herbs and trees she uses for ceremonies flamed green around the yard. Dogs bustled about the property. Two kittens huddled in a suitcase.[71]

In a 2012 TED Talk, Paes said: "Favelas are not always a problem. Favelas can sometimes really be a solution, if you deal with them, if you put public policy inside of favelas." One such "public policy" was Morar Carioca, an ambitious and concertedly participatory favela upgrade program. Paes touted the program as a way to bring basic infrastructure to favela dwellers: paved roads, sewer systems, reliable water, and improved electricity lines. In 2010, Paes assured the public that, thanks to "Olympic inspiration," the Morar Carioca program would be a lasting social legacy of the Games. In the TED Talk he vowed to have all favelas "completely urbanized" by 2020.[72] Yet the president of the Brazilian Institute of Architects, which oversaw contracting for Morar Carioca, accused the Paes administration of allowing the program to wither away after 2013 and of voiding the contracts with architecture firms without justification.[73] In May 2014, Paes contradicted the architects, claiming that Morar Carioca was ongoing. However, he also made a political U-turn, maintaining that the program had absolutely nothing to do with Olympic legacy.[74] "There are so many broken promises" related to the Olympics, Williamson told me. "The one that bites the most from the perspective of our work is Morar Carioca. Essentially it was used as an electioneering tool to get votes in 2012," and that was about it.

Greenwash Gold

Rio's Olympic bid zealously made the requisite ecological pronouncements, promising to "accelerate the implementation, and in some cases the initiation, of major sustainability projects, including those related to environmentally sensitive sites, air quality and waterways."[75] A critical discourse analysis of the Rio 2016 bid books found that while "security" was the word most often deployed, "environment" (along with derivatives like "environmental") was a close second. The "sustainability" buzzword was also common, appearing three times as often as "education" and eleven times as often as "citizen."[76] But a gaping chasm emerged between lofty words and actual deeds. Time and time again, reality failed to measure up to rhetoric, putting Rio 2016 on track to become the most greenwashed Games ever.

The Rio bidders promised to plant 24 million trees by 2016 to offset carbon emissions. In 2012, the Environment Secretary for the State of Rio de Janeiro upped the ante, vowing to deliver 34 million trees for the Games. But by 2014, the official "Rio 2016 Sustainability Report" conspicuously failed to mention any progress on the tree-planting front. Nevertheless, the PR wheels continued to spin. Rio organizers launched an "Embrace Sustainability" program, with Dow—the notorious chemical firm and "official chemistry company of the Olympic

Games"—the first member of the corporate club. Rio 2016 Sustainability General Manager Tania Braga also showed up at the 2015 Sustainable Brands summit in Rio to boast of the Games' supposed green cred. However, in May 2015, environmental officials revealed that only 5.5 million saplings had been planted. Rio 2016 was on track to plant 8.1 million trees by the time of the Games, less than a quarter of the revised promise.[77]

The Rio bid promised that the Olympic "excitement will be contagious" for *cariocas*, tourists, and the global media audience alike.[78] But by 2015, it appeared the water might actually be more contagious than the Games. In April 2015, thirty-seven tons of fish mysteriously floated dead to the surface of Lagoa Rodrigo de Freitas in central Rio, site of Olympic canoeing and rowing events. The enormous die-off followed a similar calamity in February 2015, when scores of dead fish were found in Guanabara Bay, the Olympic sailing venue.[79] One Brazilian sailor told the *New York Times* he encountered human corpses four times in Guanabara Bay. Another said, "It can get really disgusting, with dog carcasses in some places and the water turning brown from sewage contamination."[80] UNESCO had named Rio de Janeiro a World Heritage Site in 2012, but the metropolis's waterways were starting to look more like some sort of warped prophecy from the Old Testament.

Then, about a year before the Olympics opened, the Associated Press released a groundbreaking investigative report that revealed every single Olympic water venue was unsafe for boating or swimming. The waters percolated with human sewage that transmitted "dangerously high levels of viruses and bacteria." This threatened the health of Olympic athletes and everyday *cariocas*, who could experience "explosive diarrhea, violent vomiting, respiratory trouble and other illnesses." Merely ingesting three teaspoons of the polluted water gave a person a 99 percent chance of infection by virus (although that does not automatically mean that person would fall ill). Contracting hepatitis A was a distinct possibility. Ivan Bulaja, a coach of the Austrian sailing team, said, "This is by far the worst water quality we've ever seen in our sailing careers."[81]

The IOC's response was to argue that bacterial rather than viral testing would be sufficient. Nawal El Moutawakel, head of the IOC's coordination commission for Rio 2016, was asked whether she'd be willing to swim in the polluted waters to prove they were safe. She shrugged off the idea with a chuckle. "We will dive together," she said, gesturing toward other Olympic officials. Dubi, the Olympic executive director, went further, taking partial credit for the AP investigation's impact. "Thanks to the Games, the level of awareness regarding the bay has been raised to unprecedented levels, which is a good thing," he said. Dubi's comment was an insult to locals. You don't have to tell *cariocas* that water pollution is an issue in their city. To have Olympic luminaries take credit for consciousness-raising was galling. Eventually Rio Olympic honchos backpedaled and agreed to carry out viral testing of water at Olympic venues, but later they flip-flopped and refused to do the tests.[82]

The Associated Press's groundbreaking water investigation dramatically exposed Rio 2016's penchant for greenwashing. Guanabara Bay was supposed to be 80 percent clean by 2016, but Rio governor Luiz Fernando Pezão shoved back the timeline for cleanup to 2035.[83] For Jenny Barchfield, co-author of the AP investigation, the failure to properly clean up Guanabara Bay was "the most egregious" of all the broken environmental promises. As we sat in her apartment overlooking Guanabara Bay, the water's putrid stench wafted up through the windows. "This is a problem that has gone back for decades, everyone knows about it, it's widely acknowledged," she told me. "This was meant to be—after a whole series of failed attempts to clean up the Bay—*the* opportunity. If it couldn't be done for local people, at least you would think that the idea of receiving the world and being in the world's spotlight and having people compete here would be sufficient impetus to tackle this problem." For Barchfield, to have Rio 2016 honchos and Brazilian politicos squander "the perfect opportunity" was shocking. "The people of Rio have been cheated out of a chance to get their waterways back," she said. "It's inexcusable. It's a real tragedy for the city and especially for the people who live here."[84]

Smashed green dreams littered the city. Rio 2016 vowed to build eight "River Treatment Units" to clean up Guanabara Bay by filtering the main waterways that flowed into it. But a year before the Games, only one water treatment facility had been built, and even that one was not fully operational. Four more units were promised for the Barra da Tijuca lagoon system, but the projects became mired in red tape and were starved of the requisite funds.[85] Associated Press bureau chief Brad Brooks, Barchfield's co-author on the blockbuster investigative report, said to me, "They've done almost nothing to improve the water quality to the level that they promised in winning the Olympics in 2009." When I asked Brooks what grade he would give Rio officials on their efforts to clean up Rio's waterways in light of their original promises, he said without hesitation: "I would give them an F. They don't even talk about the subject in a serious manner. The notion that this is going to be a legacy for the people of Rio de Janeiro is a joke." He added: "What's happening here is an environmental crime. And they're holding the Olympics in it." [86]

Then there was Rio's Olympic golf course, built on an ecologically sensitive marshland. "I enjoy all sports but I'm really addicted to golf," Rudy Giuliani said when he parachuted into Rio in 2013 to collect a check for his firm's security consulting. "It's more than a hobby, more than a sport, more than fun, I'm really passionate about it."[87] Rio 2016 marked the return of golf to the Olympics after a 112-year hiatus. It also marked an audacious maneuver by Mayor Paes to trample public interest in the name of private gain. Class power trumped Olympic sustainability lingo.

Rio was already home to two golf courses and had staged numerous major tournaments, as advertised in the bid books. But Paes wanted to locate golf closer to the Olympic complex in the wealthy Barra da Tijuca suburb. In doing so, he teed up a staggering deal for the billionaire developer Pasquale Mauro. As long as Mauro's construction firm footed the bill for the golf course—between $20 million and $30 million—it would also win a contract to build 140 luxury apartments skirting the golf course, with units starting at $2 million. Penthouse condominiums cost upwards of $6 million. It was a multimillion-dollar giveaway, gift-wrapped by the mayor. In an emergency session just before Christmas in 2012, Paes slipped through a seemingly innocuous "Complementary Law 125." It allowed for the golf course to be built inside Marapendi Nature Reserve, home to a number of threatened species, including the Fluminense swallowtail butterfly, the barredtail pearlfish, and a rare tree iguana. Additional environmentally sensitive land was parceled into the development project, and the height limit of the luxury condos was allowed to increase from six stories to twenty-two. The golf-course project would not be slowed down by environmental impact reports or public hearings. It was full steam ahead for the mayor and his cronies. Alberto Murray Neto, an attorney who formerly served on the Brazilian Olympic Committee, stated, "The whole thing is just a pretext for land speculation."[88]

Local prosecutors tried to halt construction on environmental grounds and considered laying corruption charges for the concessions gifted to the developer. The deal also led to the formation of Golfe Para Quem? (Golf for Whom?), an intrepid group of protesters who rose up in challenge. With Ocupa Golfe (Occupy Golf) as their rallying cry, protesters argued that the golf course was an environmental catastrophe.

They seized space near the golf course, rotating activists into the camp and sparking a violent reaction from the Municipal Guard. Then, in late February 2015, activists from Occupy Golf and other environmental groups stormed the luxury hotel along Copacabana Beach where Olympic VIPs were huddling for pre-Rio 2016 meetings. Demonstrators wielded signs like "Thomas Bach is a nature killer" and "The city is not for sale." Another sign demanded that the IOC—COI in Portuguese, Comitê Olímpico Internacional—head back to Lausanne: "COI Go Home." One activist said: "We're not against the Olympic Games. This is about the golf course."[89]

The following month Paes unveiled the city's new golf mecca, busing the international press corps to the site. Barchfield of the AP explained to me how the mayor "worked himself into a lather with a more-than-two-hour presentation" where he distributed thick packets of documents that supposedly rebuffed the claims of critics. It was as if the idea was to "drown them in transparency," she said. Barchfield described how the mayor "spread his arms wide and said: 'You call this is an environmental crime? Look at the green grass'," as if a monocropped putting green held the same ecological value as a landscape humming with biodiversity.[90]

Fernando Meirelles, the Oscar-nominated director famous for works like *City of God*, is helping to orchestrate the Rio 2016 opening ceremony. "Since we joined the project the money has been cut, cut, cut," he said in September 2015. "It won't be an extravaganza like Beijing or London ... Our budget is twenty times less than Beijing! So we're really struggling to be consistent, with no money." Meirelles, one of three Brazilian film luminaries doubling as creative directors for the opening ceremony, added: "But it makes sense, not spending a fortune on this opening. We're in a crisis and there are better places to put money in Brazil than just the opening."[91]

Reforming the Games: Agenda 2020

In fall 2014, after the *New York Times* published an essay I wrote on the need to reform the Olympics, I was invited by Franz Beckenbauer's academic liaison to articulate my vision at a meeting of the soccer legend's think tank, Camp Beckenbauer. I was flown on a business-class ticket to Kitzbühel, Austria, where I got a firsthand taste of the extravagant opulence that is de rigueur in the rarefied echelons of the sports world. Dozens of beautiful people scampered around to attend to every whim. Premium chocolate was placed on my pillow each afternoon when the comforter got its daily fluffing. At a gala fundraiser event, a ten-day yacht trip to the coast of Spain was auctioned off at a jaw-dropping price. Not once did I take a single euro from my pocket; to do so would have been uncouth. The power brokers of sport were on hand, from President Thomas Bach and VP Nawal El-Moutawakel of the IOC, to President Sepp Blatter of FIFA and his high-profile ally Tokyo Sexwale, the former South African political prisoner turned 2010 World Cup organizer. Sports stars like Germany goalkeeper Jens Lehmann and the German gold-medal-winning downhill skier Maria Höfl-Riesch milled about, hobnobbing with the other VIPs.

I appeared on a panel with Michael Vesper, director-general of the German Olympic Sports Confederation; FIFA auditor Domenico Scala; and the urban geographer Chris Gaffney, who had flown in from Rio. While wending our way through the lavish labyrinth of saunas and steam rooms—replete with an enormous tropical fish tank—Gaffney and I decided to divide our attention. He'd zero in on FIFA and the just-completed Brazil World Cup, and I'd focus on the Olympics. We both punched hard and often, not holding back critiques that both organizations needed to hear. For the IOC and FIFA, the view from atop the mega-event world might appear rosy; we aimed to shift the point of view to help them see sports mega-events from the ground up, where real people suffered serious, negative impacts. Both Vesper and Scala were open to significant reforms of their respective organizations. But when I proposed that the IOC engage transparency and publicly state which members voted for which host-city candidates, Vesper acted as if my suggestion stepped beyond the pale. That brand of democracy simply went too far.

At the end of our session, those in attendance used techno-clickers to vote on whether the bidding process for mega-events like the Olympics and World Cup needs to be significantly reformed. An overwhelming majority—94 percent—agreed with Gaffney and me that they did. Both the IOC and FIFA are in crisis, in different ways and to varying degrees, but the sharpest of the lot know that change is required. They realize their brands are in danger and they need to take action to protect them. It's a matter of self-interest. To be sure, the IOC is light-years ahead of the festering quagmire known as FIFA, showing far more openness to reform. But the overall experience gave me a deeper understanding of the gobsmacking disconnect that exists between the taken-for-granted extravagance of sports-world power brokers and the significant challenges faced by workaday folks in the sports mega-event city. Too often the honchos don't comprehend how their glitzy spectacles affect everyday people, and if they do, they don't seem to care.

The question is what sorts of actions will the modern-day Olympic barons take? Power isn't simply a matter of getting people to do things in your interest; it's also about keeping certain items off the agenda entirely and reinforcing values that limit the scope of debate. One thing's for sure: sport honchos will do their utmost to narrow the range of reform possibilities, advancing the most cosmetic changes possible. The *appearance* of change may just do the trick, allowing the predatory, extractive business model to continue unabated under a shimmering veneer of reform. The IOC's much-vaunted "Olympic Agenda 2020" is one such mirage.[92]

In December 2014, the IOC huddled in Monaco to consider the Olympic Agenda 2020 reforms. Olympic officials luxuriated in palatial surroundings, courtesy of Prince Albert, an IOC member since 1985. Thomas Bach injected a sense of urgency among the delegates. The forty recommendations—freighted with jargon about "synergies" and "stakeholders"—passed in unanimous lockstep.

The news media was awash in platitudes about Agenda 2020 being a defining moment for the Olympic movement, even though the IOC had passed nothing more than a set of recommendations. The proposals themselves fell well short of substantive reform, but the press acted more like IOC stenographers than impartial recorders of events. Instead of critical journalism we got credulous churnalism repeating the IOC's own declaration that its Agenda 2020 was a game-changer.

To his credit, Bach acknowledged that the Olympic Games are mired in crisis. In the wake of the $51 billion Sochi 2014 Winter Games, interest in the 2022 Winter Olympics dried up. Voters in referendums in Stockholm, Munich, and Krakow, Poland, emphatically said no to the 2022 Winter Games, as did voters by a narrow margin in St. Moritz and Davos, Switzerland. Norwegian politicians, meanwhile, killed Oslo's bid, leaving only Beijing and Almaty, Kazakhstan, in the running. Both China and Kazakhstan are human-rights nightmares. No matter which city won, the Olympic movement would lose. The IOC ended up selecting Beijing, making it the first city chosen to host both the Summer and Winter Olympics. In crowning the Chinese city, the IOC gave the lie to the claim that holding the Games in authoritarian countries accelerates progress towards a more democratic future, as Beijing bidders claimed back in 2001 when applying for the 2008 Summer Games.

As we've seen, the Olympics have become a five-ring fiscal fiasco. Agenda 2020 addresses the need to corral spending. In the name of cost cutting, Olympic hosts will be allowed to stage events outside the host city and—in rare instances—even outside the host country. The bidding process has been streamlined in an attempt to reduce the forest of paperwork previously required. Candidate cities are encouraged to use existing athletic facilities and to construct temporary venues. All this is designed to placate a burgeoning chorus of fiscal critics. Unfortunately, much of it is merely optics.

The IOC also amended the Olympic Charter to bar discrimination based on sexual orientation. But such prejudice was already forbidden under the sixth fundamental principle of Olympism, which declares, "Any form of discrimination ... on grounds of race, religion, politics, gender or otherwise is incompatible with belonging to the Olympic Movement." This apparent reform is more an alibi for IOC inaction in Sochi than a meaningful change. The IOC already had the power to compel action in the face of Russian laws that discriminated against LGBTQ people, but it opted for shameful silence.

Similar pusillanimity occurred when the inaugural European Games were staged in the repressive state of Azerbaijan in June 2015. The IOC did not make a peep, despite Olympic Agenda 2020 tenets vowing to "strengthen ethics" and "ensure compliance." The IOC's reticence allowed the Azerbaijani dictator, Ilhem Aliyev, to conceal his crimes with Olympic luster. Though the European Games are not an official IOC event, the European Olympic Committees that run them abide by the Olympic Charter and claim to promote the ideals of Olympism. Numerous IOC members attended the Games in Baku, flouting the human rights principles enshrined in the group's own charter.[93]

Amid the slate of Agenda 2020 reforms, the IOC did not adopt a single measure that will immediately enforce accountability. Its Ethics Committee will now be elected by the IOC session, but it still lacks true independence, since it reports to the Executive Board. The IOC remains accountable only to itself. For everyday people in the Olympic city, it's a free-floating para-state—complete with tax-free status, special driving lanes, and mandatory five-star accommodations—that too frequently resembles a freeloading parasite.

In short, the IOC's self-proclaimed munificence demands our healthy skepticism. After all, one of the first recommendations the IOC has pursued with any urgency is the creation of an Olympic TV Channel to broadcast its brand. This is hardly something for which the movement's critics have clamored.[94] Until the IOC proves otherwise, Agenda 2020 should be seen as the polished patter of a well-heeled sports bureaucracy, lodged in what the *Guardian* sportswriter Owen Gibson calls "the shallow, platitudinous soup of what passes for international sporting diplomacy."[95] Unfortunately, Olympic Agenda 2020 is no watershed of momentous reform for the Olympic movement. Rather, it is a strategic rebranding, more aspirational than inspirational, baby steps where bold strides are required.

An Ambitious Plan

The Olympic movement has descended into a slow-motion crisis. Fewer and fewer cities are game for the Games. For too long host cities have worked in service of the Olympics. It's time for the Olympics to start working in service of host cities. A serious rethink is long overdue.

As we have seen, in their heyday, luminaries from the International Olympic Committee could trot out a cluster of cookie-cutter promises for surefire upticks in tourism, jobs, and economic growth. But in recent years these assurances have been debunked as a marketing scam, a formulaic charade. History and research have caught up with Olympic myth-making. Even Mitt Romney, the former Massachusetts governor who helped nudge the scandal-wracked 2002 Salt Lake City Olympics across the finish line, cautioned, "It's really not a money-making opportunity."[96] Romney's candor points to a seismic shift in the way we've come to understand sports mega-events like the Olympics over the past decade. Now is the time to think big, while the general public is more aware than ever of the Olympics' downside and while the IOC president is open to change.

If the Olympic Movement wants real reform, controlling the ever-vaulting cost of hosting the Games is the place to start.[97] As we have seen, IOC officials have long fretted about the threat of "gigantism": the transformation of the Olympics into an unwieldy spectacle with an exorbitant price tag. Today, "gigantism" is the new normal. Meanwhile, lowballing five-ring cost estimates to help rally the public support necessary to secure a bid has almost become an Olympic sport in itself. The Etch-A-Sketch economics must stop.

The Olympics cost too much, and host populations derive insufficient benefit in part because the Games are plagued by inept economic impact studies that enable fiscal fantasies of kick-started investment and growth that never materialize. These in turn allow ambitious politicians to push prestige projects that are ripe for corruption. But the price of hosting the Games is also sky-high because Olympic development is often disconnected from city and regional planning. The IOC should create an independent body comprising respected sports economists, urban planners, and political scholars who can objectively assess whether bids' construction plans fulfill long-view development strategies. The Olympic Charter already allows for outside experts to assist with evaluating bids. This panel—let's call it the Independent Bid Review Board—would meticulously analyze host cities' filings and make recommendations to the IOC's key decision-making body, the Evaluation Commission. The Board would make sure Olympic development went with the flow of a city's long-term plan. Meaningful public participation should be part of the process.

Ballooning Olympic costs can cripple host cities. In the wake of the Games, taxes that might have paid for infrastructure projects to benefit the whole community must go instead to service debt. Meanwhile, the IOC jets off to the next venue. An independent panel could reverse this trend by ensuring that spending goes to real needs like public transportation, and especially, sustainable systems like subways, light-rail, and bus networks. The Olympic Games should benefit the workaday people of a host city, not simply cater to the diktats of local elites and the whims of the peripatetic IOC. One concrete way to do this would be to make it standard practice to convert the Olympic Village into public housing that addresses the needs of low-income residents, perhaps as a first-time home-buyers program. The IOC should lend a bigger fiscal hand, paying for the independent panel and a whole lot more. After all, the IOC's Olympic Foundation reserve fund reached $980 million in 2014.[98] Furthermore, the IOC and its "Worldwide Partners" from the corporate world should not receive a single penny in tax breaks from the host city or country. This only diverts funds that should go to host communities back into the pockets of the corporate class.

Behind the smokescreen of reform, the IOC has made furtive power moves to fortify its own future while under-cutting the ability of local Olympic organizing committees to raise funds. In March 2015, the IOC colonized a new sponsor category—"mobility partner"—and named Toyota as the inaugural holder of the post. This was a subtle kick in the gut to local organizing committees. For instance, Tokyo 2020 Olympic organizers could no longer capture big-money sponsorship funds directly from car companies. Instead, that money would be funneled through the IOC. Then in August 2015 the IOC announced it was considering adding a new "professional services" category of top-tier sponsorship, with three firms in the running: Ernst & Young, Deloitte, and PricewaterhouseCoopers.[99] PricewaterhouseCoopers has been involved in auditing numerous aspects of previous Olympic Games. How could a firm be both an impartial auditor and corporate sponsor? The synchronized skimming has to cease.

In 2015 the IOC announced a set of cost-saving measures for aspiring host cities bidding on the Olympics. It lowered the Summer Games bidding fee from $650,000 to $250,000. Yet at the same time, the IOC ditched its shortlisting process, thereby setting up more cities to be strung along to the bitter end of the process. Commenting on changes to the bid process, the Olympic critic Janice Forsyth wrote: "The IOC needs to foster the illusion that the Games are worth the risk … It's like a twisted version of the Hunger Games."[100]

Every two years, Olympic boosters channel their inner Al Gore, claiming the mantle of "the greenest Games ever." But the reality has not lived up to the PR. When the likes of BP and Dow can be passed off as "sustainability partners," we know we're drowning in deceit. The term "sustainability" appears twenty-one times in Olympic Agenda 2020, and in the fuzziest of fashions. One recommendation aims to "include sustainability in all aspects of the Olympic Games" without offering any specifics. In IOC pronouncements, "sustainability" tends to appear alongside "legacy"—another conveniently mushy term—as a vague goal to strive for. But this brand of sustainability is nothing more than weak green tea.

Rather than a pay-to-play program with environmental rogues who double as IOC corporate sponsors, the Olympic movement needs independent monitors to keep local organizing committees in check. This watchdog must have the power to enforce sustainability promises and impose penalties if need be. It has become too easy to make big green promises only to ignore them at crunch time. Another innovation to reduce the Olympics' ecological footprint would be to encourage creative bids from multiple cities and even neighboring countries, sharing the burden and requiring less construction. As mentioned above, the IOC has cracked open this door by suggesting that it might be okay to organize "preliminary competitions outside the host city, or in exceptional cases, outside the host country." We should make multi-city and even multi-country Games standard practice.

The IOC also needs to address its severe democracy deficit. For too long it has proffered what the French philosopher Jacques Ranciere calls a "double discourse on democracy," singing its praises while ignoring its complicated practice.[101] The IOC should move aggressively to democratize its organizational structure. As we have seen, democracy has never been the IOC's strong suit. IOC power brokers like Avery Brundage were outspoken in their opposition to making the group more democratic. Women were not allowed to become IOC members until 1981. Fast-forward to September 2015: of the one hundred IOC members, only twenty-two were women. Meanwhile the group has managed to maintain its aristocratic flavor. In 2015, ten members were barons, princes, princesses, dukes, or sheikhs. The IOC needs to broaden its membership, especially with respect to class and gender. And unless the anachronistic royalty has a direct connection to sport, it's time for them to go back to their palaces and castles. Finally, when it comes to voting for which city will host the Games, IOC members are notoriously capricious, ignoring technical reports and voting for the bid with the shiniest promises. The IOC should publish the records of voting members, so that there's transparency about who is siding with the expert evidence and who is not.

There is precedence for greater transparency. In early 2015, the IOC's Ethics Committee made public the per diem and reimbursement costs for its members, offering some eye-popping numbers. Although President Bach does not draw a salary, he enjoys 225,000 Euros ($242,000) per year "to cover some of the President's personal costs related to the execution of his function" as well as complementary lodging in a suite at the Lausanne Palace luxury hotel and spa. When an IOC member is working on Olympic business, all travel, lodging, and accommodation expenses are fully covered by the IOC. On top of that, IOC members enjoy $450 per diem, while Executive Board members and commission chairs get $900 per day. Each IOC member can get an additional $7,000 a year for "annual administrative support." These numbers give us another glimpse at the affluence and privilege that the Olympic elite enjoy. Meanwhile, the average monthly income in Rocinha—Rio's largest favela—is $240, according to the BBC.[102]

The IOC should also move to democratize its sports program, and not simply by shifting from "a sport-based to an event-based" approach, as suggested in Agenda 2020. Competitions drenched in privilege, like the equestrian events, should be ditched (with apologies to Mitt and Ann Romney's horse Rafalca, a dressage competitor at London 2012). How many countries put forth teams in the anachronistic pentathlon? (In London, only around twenty-five.) How many people can even name the five sports that comprise the pentathlon? (It's fencing, swimming, horse show jumping, pistol shooting, and a cross-country run). Events with high start-up costs could be swapped for those requiring fewer resources. Why not bring back tug-of-war? It was a hotly contested event in the early twentieth century. The Official Report for the 1912 Olympics in Stockholm correctly called it "a form of sport which is found in nearly every country."[103] The IOC ought to consider adding more running events as well, like trail running and cross-country. These sports do not require expensive, sophisticated equipment.

The Olympics deserves credit for shining a spotlight on women's sport, providing female athletes a chance to gain wider acclaim. The 2012 London Games brought numerous landmarks vis-à-vis gender: women competed in every sport, no countries excluded female athletes, and they comprised 44 percent of all participants, a higher percentage than at any previous Summer Games.[104] One Agenda 2020 recommendation is to "foster gender equality" by lifting the participation of women to 50 percent, although the IOC does not specify the time frame for achieving that aspiration. It has also failed to abolish the horrific "sex-testing" of Olympic athletes.

A longtime baseline assumption of many sports administrators is that sex is a stable binary. The IOC has conceded that there is no biological binary. However, they argue that the categories for Olympic competition are binary and that they therefore need a policy for demarcating a border between men and women. Further, the IOC oscillates between conflating sex and gender and presuming that one's biological sex traits should always align with a particular gender. Intersexuality troubles their dogged boundary-making. It doesn't fit their rules for who can rightfully be considered a woman. Since the mid-twentieth century, female Olympians have been forced to endure an array of "gender verification tests." The International Association of Athletics Federations (IAAF) made female track athletes parade naked in front of ogling doctors. The IOC has carried out cheek-swabbing for chromosome analysis and tests for high natural levels of testosterone, or hyperandrogenism. The issue came to the fore in 2009 when the IAAF required the South African track star Caster Semenya to undergo so-called gender verification tests after she won gold in the women's 800-meter run at the World Athletics Championships. After orchestrating the humiliating and invasive process, the IAAF banned her from competition. This forced her to miss nearly a year of racing, though the IAAF eventually reinstated her. She competed in the London 2012 Games, where she won silver.[105]

The case of Indian sprinter Dutee Chand raised the issue again. In 2014, Chand was banned from competition when tests found she had hyperandrogenism. She refused to undergo the IAAF-recommended hormone or surgical "therapy" to reduce her testosterone levels, arguing she had done nothing wrong: the high levels of testosterone in her body were natural.

She appealed the regulation to the Court of Arbitration for Sport, and in summer 2015 the court overturned her suspension, asserting that the policy discriminates against women. The court gave athletics officials two years to come up with evidence for the policy they installed in 2011.[106] In late 2015 the IOC is supposed to decide whether intersex athletes and those with hyperandrogenism will be allowed to compete at Rio 2016.

The IOC needs to get out of the business of patrolling sex and gender. The IOC Medical Commission should not enable pseudo-science that serves as a pretext for challenging women's identity or sex. When I asked Katrina Karkazis, senior research scholar at the Center for Biomedical Ethics at Stanford University, how the IOC might adopt a forward-thinking policy that isn't rooted in oversimple binaries, she replied: "Policy for what? If women like men need to prove legal sex, what more do we need and why?" She added: "Sports governing bodies need to stop policing women athletes under the guise of fairness. Everyone agrees the women under investigation are women, and CAS has said there is no evidence women with naturally high testosterone have unfair advantage, so these policies are a solution in search of a problem."[107] Strong leadership from the IOC is long overdue.

Finally, the IOC needs to align its host city selections with the lofty principles of the Olympic Charter: human rights violators should not host the Olympics. There are some terrific ideas in the Olympic Charter. It's time the IOC honored them. All countries should be placed under the human-rights microscope—no exceptions.[108]

Every time the Olympics approach, some suggest permanently lodging the Summer Games in one city, typically Athens. But it's unclear whether the people of Athens actually want the sports festival. After all, many blame the debt incurred from the 2004 Olympics for stoking Greece's disastrous economic woes. Venues in Athens are modern-day ruins, decrepit monuments to catastrophic misspending. Refurbishing them would not be cheap. The idea of anchoring the Games in Athens has historical appeal, but it's hard to imagine the IOC agreeing to settle in one place, given its seemingly unquenchable penchant for bringing the Games to new terrain. Plus, mooring the Games in one metropolis would give that city tremendous leverage over the IOC. Finally, we'd need to see hard evidence that giving the Games permanently to Athens would actually benefit the everyday people of that city and not just a privileged sliver of Athenian elite.

A more tenable notion floated by reformers is to rotate the Games among a small stable of Olympic cities spanning the globe. This would cut down on fresh construction, although the local venues would still demand maintenance. Plus, sports facilities quickly become obsolete. Exhibit A: the onetime state-of-the-art Olympic stadium in Atlanta was deemed an architectural relic and set for demolition merely two decades after the 1996 Games. Moving the Olympics through a handful of cities—say, five each for the Winter and Summer Games— would likely be more attractive to IOC bigwigs accustomed to the cosmopolitan high life. But because of ever-changing geopolitics, an erstwhile global good guy could become a human rights bête noire; this could mean cementing a global villain into a permanent-host status.

A Moment of Movements

"Olympism is a great, quiet piece of machinery," Baron Pierre de Coubertin proclaimed, with his relentless blend of optimism and hyperbole. "Its gears do not screech and its movement never stops, despite the handfuls of sand that certain individuals throw on it in a persistent but unsuccessful attempt to impede its operation."[109] There have been a number of sharp curves in the road during the history of the Olympics, often due to the efforts of political activists. With forebears like the protesters during the Great Depression in California who held signs reading "Groceries Not Games! Olympics Are Outrageous!" a wave of dissident citizens across the globe are today just saying no to the Games. The momentum of anti-Olympics dissent is especially remarkable given that there is no established transnational anti-Olympic movement organized to challenge the Games and their adverse impacts. Rather than a "movement of movements" we have a "moment of movements." During a city's Olympic moment—whether it be the bidding process or the actual Games—activist groups come together using the Olympic Games as their fightback focal point. We don't yet have a transnational hub that has lasted through time, despite some valiant efforts.

In a sense, mobilizing to challenge the Games is an activist version of Whack-a-Mole. The Olympics pop up in one city, generating protest, and then promptly plunge underground, rearing their head in a different city two years later. Activists then return to their pre-Games protest patterns, refocusing on their central targets and objectives. The London-based activist and anthropologist Isaac Marrero-Guillamón was explicit about this. "I don't think you can say there's a movement against the Olympics in London—there are different groups doing projects and trying to link those projects together," he told me. "It's a very monadic structure—very loose, very networky."[110]

Nevertheless, even without a formal movement, activists have helped create a massive shift in the way the Olympics are talked about. Even *The Economist*, the standard-bearer for neoliberal capitalism, recently wrote, "Hosting the Olympics and the World Cup is bad for a city's health."[111] No longer can Olympic boosters yammer on about the alleged benefits of hosting the Games without challenge from activists, academics, community groups, and money-minded politicians. Left-right coalitions are plausible, with progressives uniting with fiscal conservatives to spurn the Olympics. The game has changed.

Nowhere was this clearer than in Boston, the city that in January 2015 was picked by the United States Olympic Committee as its candidate for the 2024 Summer Games. The move catalyzed an intensification of the resistance that had already coalesced during Boston's bid battle with Los Angeles, San Francisco, and Washington, DC. Activists took to Twitter, where they sprayed criticism of the Boston bid and the Games more generally and where they put pressure on city officials to embrace transparency and deepen public dialogue. Meanwhile, they ramped up public records requests to pry the truth from behind the paper wall and unveil the bidders' clandestine machinations. They made political hay of doozies like the $7,500-a-day fee for Olympics work paid to the former governor, Deval Patrick. The activists' strategy worked: Patrick announced that he would forgo the outrageous wage. Feeling the heat, Boston 2024 bid jockeys agreed to a series of public meetings, where they encountered stiff criticism, even though organizers controlled the agenda and the flow of information. Protesters successfully reshaped the media narrative and ultimately brought about the end of the bid. In July 2015, the USOC rescinded its offer after Mayor Marty Walsh balked at signing the host-city contract that would put Boston on the hook for cost overruns. As if to affirm the activists' prescience, the organizers of the failed bid were left with a multimillion-dollar debt.[112]

Jilted at the Olympic altar by Boston, the USOC repaired relations with Los Angeles, which eventually was named the USOC's candidate. Los Angeles joined Budapest, Hamburg, Paris, and Rome in a five-city race for the 2024 Summer Olympics. Hamburg voters made it a four-city race in November 2015 after torpedoing the bid in a referendum. The IOC will convene in Lima, Peru, in September 2017 to make its selection. Activists in Boston and Hamburg offered a vital takeaway to everyday people in the other four cities: to fend off the Olympics, protest early and often, *before your city is awarded the Games*. Fill the corridors of power, the public streets, and the quicksilver lanes of social media with your message that enough is enough.

Music aficionados have pointed out that Beethoven wrote his piano sonatas for a piano that wasn't invented until some fifty years later. Technology simply wasn't up to speed with the composer's quickfire mind. It's fun to fathom what the great minds of the Olympic Project for Human Rights could have accomplished with social media. Just think what John Carlos, Harry Edwards, and Tommie Smith could have done with Twitter at their fingertips. Kareem Abdul-Jabbar, who opted to boycott the 1968 Olympics, has said he would have relished a direct pipeline to the press and fans. Social media "would have been great," he remarked. "It would've been nice to really be able to explain myself in the way I wanted to explain myself."[113]

Today there is more space for athlete activism than ever. Even the power brokers are clearing the way for athletes to take public stands on politics. When Barack Obama was asked by *People* magazine what he thought of the basketball star LeBron James, a two-time Olympic gold-medal winner, taking the court wearing an "I Can't Breathe" T-shirt, he replied: "I think LeBron did the right thing. We forget the role that Muhammad Ali, Arthur Ashe, and Bill Russell played in raising consciousness. I'd like to see more athletes do that— not just around this issue, but around a range of issues."[114]

Despite the IOC's vise-like grip on power, despite the privilege threaded thick through the history of the Games, despite the multifarious ways everyday people in Olympic city after Olympic city have been marginalized and manipulated, the struggle continues. In some ways, activists and Games critics of today are empowered like never before. Momentum has shifted. "Hegemony," as the great Stuart Hall reminds us, "is never forever."[115] Three cheers for that.

Bibliography

Adams, C., "Fighting for Acceptance: Sigfrid Edstrom and Avery Brundage: Their Efforts to Shape and Control Women's Participation in the Olympic Games," *Sixth International Symposium for Olympic Research*, 2002, 143–8.

Adorno, T., "Commitment," in E. Bloch, G. Lukács, B. Brecht, W. Benjamin, and T. Adorno, *Aesthetics and Politics*, Trans. R. Taylor, London: Verso, 1980, 177–95.

"Africa and the XXIst Olympiad," *Olympic Review*, no. 109–110, November-December 1976, 584–5.

Agamben, G., *State of Exception*, Trans. K. Attell, Chicago and London: University of Chicago Press, 2005.

"Agenda 21 of the Olympic Movement," *Olympic Review*, vol. 26, no. 30, 1999, 42–3.

Alfred, T., "Deconstructing the British Columbia Treaty Process," *Balayi: Culture, Law and Colonialism*, vol. 3, 2001, 37–65.

Amnesty International, "China: The Olympics Countdown – Crackdown on Activists Threatens Olympic Legacy," April 2008.

Amnesty International, "You Killed My Son: Homicides by Military Police in the City of Rio de Janeiro," August 2015.

Andrejevic, M., *iSpy: Surveillance and Power in the Interactive Era*, Lawrence, Kansas: University Press of Kansas, 2007.

Associação de Moradores e Pescadores da Vila Autódromo, "Plano Popular da Vila Autódromo: Plano de Desenvolvimento Urbano, Econômico, Social e Cultural," 2012.

Athens 2004 Organising Committee for the Olympic Games, "Official Report of the XXVIII Olympiad," November 2005.

Baade, R. A., and V. Matheson, "Bidding for the Olympics: Fool's Gold?" in *Transatlantic Sport: The Comparative Economics of North American and European Sports*, C. P. Barros, M. Ibrahímo, and S. Szymanski (eds.), Cheltenham, UK, and Northampton, MA: Edward Elgar, 2002, 127–51.

Bibliography

Baade, R. A., and V. A. Matheson, "Home Run or Wild Pitch?: The Economic Impact of Major League Baseball's All-Star Game," *Journal of Sports Economics*, vol. 2, 2001, 307–26.

Bandy, S. J., "The Olympic Celebration of the Arts," in J. O. Segrave and D. Chu (eds.), *The Olympic Games in Transition*, Champaign, Illinois: Human Kinetics, 1988, 163–9.

Barbassa, J., *Dancing with the Devil in the City of God: Rio de Janeiro on the Brink*, New York: Touchstone, 2015.

Barcelona Holding Olímpic S. A. (HOLSA), "Los Juegos Olímpicos Como Generadores de Inversión (1986–1992)," Barcelona, June 1992.

Barcelona Olympic Organizing Committee, "Official Report of the XXV Olympiad, Barcelona 1992," 1993.

Barney, R. K., S. R. Wenn, and S. G. Martyn, *Selling the Five Rings: The International Olympic Committee and the Rise of Olympic Commercialism*, Salt Lake City: University of Utah Press, 2004.

Barney, R. K., "Resistance, Persistence, Providence: The 1932 Los Angeles Olympic Games in Perspective," *Research Quarterly for Exercise and Sport*, vol. 67, no. 2, 1996, 148–60.

Barney, R. K., "The Olympic Games in Modern Times," in G. P. Schaus and S. R. Wenn (eds.), *Onward to the Olympics: Historical Perspectives on the Olympic Games*, Waterloo, Ontario: Wilfrid Laurier University Press, 2007, 221–41.

Barney, R. K., and A. T. Bijkerk, "Carl Diem's Inspiration for the Torch Relay?: Jan Wils, Amsterdam 1928, and the Origin of the Olympics Flame," in G. P. Schaus and S. R. Wenn (eds.), *Onward to the Olympics: Historical Perspectives on the Olympic Games*, Waterloo, Ontario: Wilfrid Laurier University Press, 2007, 253–9.

Barral, W., and A. Haas, "Public-Private Partnership (PPP) in Brazil," *The International Lawyer*, vol. 41, no. 3, 2007, 957–73.

Barreiro, F., J. Costa, and J. M. Vilanova, "Impactos Urbanísticos, Económicos y Sociales de los Juegos Olímpicos de Barcelona '92," Barcelona: Centre D'Iniciatives, Recerques Europees a la Mediterrania (CIREM), June 1993.

Bergvall, E., and Swedish Olympic Committee, "The Official Report of the Olympic Games of Stockholm 1912," Stockholm: Wahlström and Widstrand, 1913.

Bolanki, A., "The Olympic Flag: Its History and Use," *Bulletin du Comité International Olympique*, no. 27, June 1951, 42–3.

Booth, D., *The Race Game: Sport and Politics in South Africa*, London and Portland, Oregon: Frank Cass Publishers, 1998.

Bibliography

Boulongne, Y., "Pierre de Coubertin and Women's Sport," *Olympic Review*, vol. 26, no. 31, March 2000, 23–26.

Boykoff, J., "Celebration Capitalism and the Sochi 2014 Winter Olympics," *Olympika: The International Journal of Olympic Studies*, vol. 22, 2013, 39–70.

Boykoff, J., *Celebration Capitalism and the Olympic Games*, London: Routledge, 2013.

Boykoff, J., *Activism and the Olympics: Dissent at the Games in Vancouver and London*, New Brunswick, NJ: Rutgers University Press, 2014.

Boyle, P., "Securing the Olympic Games: Exemplifications of Global Governance," in H. J. Lenskyj and S. Wagg (eds.), *The Palgrave Handbook of Olympic Studies*, New York: Palgrave Macmillan, 2012, 394–409.

Brady, A. M., "The Beijing Olympics as a Campaign of Mass Distraction, *China Quarterly*, vol. 197, March 2009, 1–24.

Braithwaite, J., *Regulatory Capitalism: How It Works, Ideas for Making It Work Better*, Cheltenham, UK: Edward Elgar, 2008.

Brenner, N., and N. Theodore, "Cities and the Geographies of 'Actually Existing Neoliberalism'," in N. Brenner and N. Theodore (eds.), *Spaces of Neoliberalism: Urban Restructuring in North America and Western Europe*, Oxford: Blackwell, 2002, 2–32.

Broudehoux, A., "Civilizing Beijing: Social Beautification, Civility and Citizenship at the 2008 Olympics," in G. Hayes and J. Karamichas (eds.), *Olympic Games, Mega-Events and Civil Societies: Globalization, Environment, Resistance*, New York: Palgrave Macmillan, 2012, 46–67.

Broudehoux, A., "The Social and Spatial Impacts of Olympic Image Construction: Beijing 2008," in H. J. Lenskyj and S. Wagg (eds.), *The Palgrave Handbook of Olympic Studies*, New York: Palgrave Macmillan, 2012, 195–209.

Bruce, T., and E. Wensing, "'She Is Not One of Us': Cathy Freeman and the Place of Aboriginal People in Australian National Culture," *Australian Aboriginal Studies*, no. 2, 2009, 90–100.

Brunet, F., "Analysis of the Economic Impact of the Olympics Games," in E. F. Peña, B. Cerezuela, M. G. Benosa, C. Kennett, and M. de Moragas Spà (eds.), *An Olympic Mosaic: Multidisciplinary Research and Dissemination of Olympic Studies*, Barcelona: Centre d'Estudis Olímpics, Universitat Autònoma de Barcelona, 2009, 211–31.

Brunet, F., "The Economic Impact of the Barcelona Olympic Games, 1986–2004," Barcelona: Centre d'Estudis Olímpics UAB, 2005.

Bibliography

Brunet, F., *Economy of the 1992 Barcelona Olympic Games*, Barcelona: Centre d'Estudis Olímpics, Universitat Autónoma de Barcelona, in cooperation with the IOC, 1993.

Carlos J., and D. Zirin, *The John Carlos Story: The Sports Moment that Changed the World*, Chicago: Haymarket Books, 2011.

Carrington, B., *Race, Sport, and Politics: The Sporting Black Diaspora*, London: Sage, 2010.

Castro, D. G., C. Gaffney, P. Ramos Novaes, J. Rodrigues, C. Pereira dos Santos, and O. A. Santos Junior, "O Projeto Olímpico da Cidade do Rio de Janeiro: Reflexões sobre os Impactos dos Megaeventos Esportivos na Perspectiva do Direito à Cidade," in O. A. Santos Junior, C. Gaffney, and L. C. Q. Ribeiro (eds.), *Brasil: Os Impactos Da Copa Do Mundo 2014 e Das Olimpíadas 2016*, Rio de Janeiro: Observatório Das Metrópoles, 2015, 409–35.

Carter, J., *Keeping the Faith: Memoirs of a President*, New York: Bantam Books, 1982.

Center on Housing Rights and Evictions (COHRE), "Barcelona 1992: International Events and Housing Rights: A Focus on the Olympic Games," Geneva: COHRE, 2007.

Center on Housing Rights and Evictions (COHRE), "Atlanta's Olympic Legacy," Geneva: COHRE, 2007.

Centre on Housing Rights and Evictions (COHRE), "One World, Whose Dream?: Housing Rights Violations and the Beijing Olympic Games," Geneva: COHRE, 2008.

Chappelet, J. L., and B. Kübler-Mabbott, *The International Olympic Committee and the Olympic System: The Governance of World Sport*, London and New York: Routledge, 2008.

Chorianopoulos, I., T. Pagonis, S. Koukoulas, and S. Drymoniti, "Planning, Competitiveness and Sprawl in the Mediterranean City: The Case of Athens," *Cities*, vol. 27, 2010, 249–259.

Clarke, J., "Living with/in and without Neo-liberalism," *Focaal*, vol. 51, 2008, 135–47.

Collins, T., *Sport in Capitalist Society: A Short History*, London and New York: Routledge, 2013.

Colomé G., and J. Sureda, "Sports and International Relations (1919–1939): The 1936 Popular Olympiad," Barcelona: Centre d'Estudis Olímpics UAB, 1994, 1–25.

Commission for a Sustainable London 2012, "Breaking the Tape: Commission for a Sustainable London 2012 Pre-Games Review (Annual Review 2011)," 2011.

Consejo Rector de la Candidatura de Barcelona a los Juegos Olímpicos de 1992, *Solicitud de Candidatura al Comité Olímpico Internacional para la Celebración en Barcelona de los Juegos de la XXV Olímpiada*. n.d.

Coubertin, P. D., "The Meeting of the Olympian Games," *North American Review*, vol. 170, no. 523, June 1900, 802–11.

Coubertin, P. D., "Through Coubertin's Writings: Coubertin on Amateurism," *Olympic Review*, no. 91–92, May–June 1975, 160–1, 178.

Coubertin, P. D., "Olympic Memoires XXI: The Eighth Olympiad (Paris 1924)," *Olympic Review*, no. 129, July 1978, 434–8.

Coubertin, P. D., "The Olympic Games of 1896," *Century Magazine*, vol. 53, November 1896, 39–55.

Coubertin, P. D., T. J. Philemon, N. G. Politis, and C. Anninos, *The Olympic Games, B.C. 776 – A.D. 1896*, London: H. Grevel and Co., 1897.

Coubertin, P. D., *The Olympic Idea: Discourses and Essays*, Schorndorf, Germany: Druckerei and Verlag Karl Hofmann, 1967.

Cremer, R., "Professionalism and Its Implications for the Olympic Movement," *Olympic Review*, vol. 26, no. 14, April 1997, 23–4.

Crompton, J. L., "Economic Impact Studies: Instruments for Political Shenanigans?" *Journal of Travel Research*, vol. 45, 2006, 67–82.

"Culture and Power: Interview Stuart Hall," *Radical Philosophy*, vol. 86, Nov–Dec 1997, 24–41.

Curi, M., J. Knijnik, and G. Mascarenhas, "The Pan American Games in Rio de Janeiro 2007: Consequences of a Sport Mega-Event in a BRIC Country," *International Review for the Sociology of Sport*, vol. 46, no. 2, 2011, 140–56.

Daniels, S., and A. Tedder, *"A Proper Spectacle": Women Olympians 1900–1936*, Petersham, Australia: Wall Wall Press, 2000.

De Moragas, M., "The Cultural Olympiad of Barcelona '92: Lights and Shadows, Lessons for the Future," in E. F. Peña, B. Cerezuela, M. G. Benosa, C. Kennett, and M. de Moragas Spà (eds.), *An Olympic Mosaic: Multidisciplinary Research and Dissemination of Olympic Studies*, Barcelona: Centre d'Estudis Olímpics, Universitat Autònoma de Barcelona, 2009, 103–14.

De Oliveira, F., "Lula in the Labyrinth," *New Left Review*, vol. 42, Nov–Dec 2006, 5–22.

Dean, J., *Democracy and Other Neoliberal Fantasies: Communicative Capitalism and Left Politics*, Durham and London: Duke University Press, 2009.

Debord, G., *The Society of the Spectacle*, Trans. D. Nicholson-Smith, New York: Zone Books, 1995.

Department of Culture, Media and Sport—Strategy Unit, "Game Plan: A Strategy for Delivering Government's Sport and Physical Activity Objectives," London, December 2002.

Dickinson, E., *The Complete Poems of Emily Dickinson*, New York: Little Brown, 1961.

Durry, J., "Art and Sport: 'Hohrod and Eschbach' a Mystery Finally Solved," *Olympic Review* vol. 26, no. 32, 2000, 26–8.

Dyreson, M., "The 'Physical Value' of Races and Nations: Anthropology and Athletics at the Louisiana Purchase Exhibition," in S. Brownell (ed.), *The 1904 Anthropology Days and Olympic Games: Sport, Race, and American Imperialism*, Lincoln and London: University of Nebraska Press, 2008, 127–55.

Edwards, H., "The Olympic Project for Human Rights: An Assessment Ten Years Later," *The Black Scholar*, March–April 1979, 2–8.

Edwards, H., *The Revolt of the Black Athlete*, New York: The Free Press, 1969.

Eichberg, H., "Olympic Anthropology Days and the Progress of Exclusion: Toward an Anthropology of Democracy," in S. Brownell (ed.), *The 1904 Anthropology Days and Olympic Games: Sport, Race, and American Imperialism*, Lincoln and London: University of Nebraska Press, 2008, 343–82.

Feddersen A., and W. Maennig, "Mega-Events and Sectoral Employment: The Case of the 1996 Olympic Games," *Contemporary Economic Policy*, vol. 31, no. 3, 2013, 580–613.

Ferguson, E., "South Africa and the Olympics: An Interview with Dennis Brutus," *Ufahamu: A Journal of African Studies*, vol. 13, no. 2–3, 1984, 40–59.

Floridis, G., "Security for the 2004 Athens Olympic Games," *Mediterranean Quarterly*, vol. 15, no. 2, 2004, 1–5.

Flyvbjerg, B., and A. Stewart, "Olympic Proportions: Cost and Cost Overruns at the Olympics 1960–2012," University of Oxford Said Business School Working Papers, June 2012, 1–23.

Forsyth, J., "Teepees and Tomahawks: Aboriginal Cultural Representation at the 1976 Olympic Games," in *The Global Nexus Engaged: Past, Present, Future Interdisciplinary Olympic Studies: Sixth International Symposium for Olympic Research*, K. Wamsley, R. K. Barney, and S. G. Martyn (eds.), London, Ontario: International Centre for Olympic Studies, 2002, 71–5.

Freeman, J., "Raising the Flag over Rio de Janeiro's Favelas: Citizenship and Social Control in the Olympic City," *Journal of Latin American Geography*, vol. 13, no. 1, 2014, 7–38.

Bibliography

Fussey, P., "Surveillance and the Olympic Spectacle," in A. Richards, P. Fussey, and A. Silke (eds.), *Terrorism and the Olympics: Major Event Security and Lessons for the Future*, London and New York: Routledge, 2011, 91–117.

Gaffney, C., "Between Discourse and Reality: The Un-Sustainability of Mega-Event Planning," *Sustainability*, vol. 5, 2013, 3926–3940.

Gaffney, C., "Securing the Olympic City," *Georgetown Journal of International Affairs*, vol. 13, no. 2, 2012, 75–82.

Gaffney, C., "Segurança Pública e os Megaeventos no Brasil," in O. A. Santos Junior, Christopher Gaffney, and L. C. Q. Ribeiro (eds.), *Brasil: Os Impactos Da Copa Do Mundo 2014 e Das Olimpíadas 2016*, Rio de Janeiro: Observatório Das Metrópoles, 2015, 165–84.

Garcia-Roza, L. A., *December Heat: An Inspector Espinosa Mystery*, New York: Henry Holt, 2003.

Gerlach, L., "An Uneasy Discourse: Salt Lake 2002 and Olympic Protest," *Pathways: Critiques and Discourse in Olympic Research*, 2008, 141–50.

Gessen, M., *Words Will Break Cement: The Passion of Pussy Riot*, New York: Riverhead Books, 2014.

Ginsberg, A., *Howl and Other Poems*, San Francisco: City Lights Books, 1993 [1956].

Gruneau, R., and H. Cantelon, "Capitalism, Commercialism, and the Olympics," in J. O. Segrave and D. Chu (eds.), *The Olympic Games in Transition*, Champaign, Illinois: Human Kinetics, 1988, 345–64.

Guiney, D., "The Olympic Council of Ireland," *Citius, Altius, Fortius*, vol. 4, no. 3, Autumn 1996, 31–3.

Guoqi, X., *Olympic Dreams: China and Sports, 1895–2008*, Cambridge, MA, and London: Harvard University Press, 2008.

Guttmann, A., *The Games Must Go On: Avery Brundage and the Olympic Movement*, New York: Columbia University Press, 1984.

Guttmann, A., *The Olympics: A History of the Modern Games*, 2nd ed., Urbana and Chicago: University of Illinois Press, 2002 [1992].

Hahn, G. M., "Russia in 2012: From 'Thaw' and 'Reset' to 'Freeze'," *Asian Survey*, vol. 53, no. 1, 2013, 214–23.

Hall, S., "Life and Times of the First New Left," *New Left Review*, vol. 61, Jan–Feb 2010, 177–96.

Hampton, J., *The Austerity Olympics: When the Games Came to London in 1948*, London: Aurum Press, 2008.

Harlan, H. V., *History of Olympic Games: Ancient and Modern*, London: Foster Press, 1931.

Bibliography

Hart-Davis, D., *Hitler's Games: The 1936 Olympics*, New York: Harper & Row, 1986.

Hartmann, D., *Race, Culture, and the Revolt of the Black Athlete: The 1968 Olympic Protests and Their Aftermath*, Chicago and London: University of Chicago Press, 2003.

Harvey, D., *A Brief History of Neoliberalism*, New York: Oxford University Press, 2005.

Hayes G., and J. Horne, "Sustainable Development, Shock and Awe?: London 2012 and Civil Society," *Sociology*, vol. 45, no. 5, 2011, 749–64.

Henry, B., "After the Games of the XIVth Olympiad, London 1948," *Olympic Review*, no. 13, January 1949, 21–3.

Hill, C. R., "The Cold War and the Olympic Movement," *History Today*, January 1999, 19–25.

Hill, C. R., *Olympic Politics*, 2nd ed., Manchester and New York: Manchester University Press, 1996.

Hitler, A., *Mein Kampf*, New York: Reynal & Hitchcock, 1941.

Hoberman, J., *The Olympic Crisis: Sport, Politics and the Moral Order*, New Rochelle, NY: Aristide D. Caratzas, 1986.

Hohrod, G., and M. Eschbach, "Ode to Sport," *Olympic Review*, vol. XXVI, no. 32, April–May 2000, 29.

Hom, S. K., "The Promise of a 'People's Olympics'," in M. Worden (ed.), *China's Great Leap: The Beijing Games and the Human Rights Challenges*, New York: Seven Stories Press, 2008, 59–71.

Horne, J., and G. Whannel, *Understanding the Olympics*, London and New York: Routledge, 2012.

Hotchkiss, J. L., R. E. Moore, and S. M. Zobay, "Impact of the 1996 Summer Olympic Games on Employment and Wages in Georgia," *Southern Economic Journal*, vol. 69, no. 3, 2003, 691–704.

Hughes-Hallett, L., *Gabriele D'Annunzio: Poet, Seducer, and Preacher of War*, New York: Alfred A. Knopf, 2013.

International Olympic Committee, "Brand Protection: Olympic Marketing Ambush Protection and Clean Venue Guidelines," Lausanne, Switzerland, 2005.

International Olympic Committee, "Factsheet: Women in the Olympic Movement," Lausanne, Switzerland, May 2014.

International Olympic Committee, "Final Report, 2005–2008," Lausanne, Switzerland, 2009.

International Olympic Committee, "IOC and NOCs of Israel and Palestine Hold Third Joint Meeting in Ramallah," Lausanne, Switzerland, October 27, 2011.

Bibliography

International Olympic Committee, "IOC Marketing Media Guide, Beijing 2008," Lausanne, Switzerland, 2008.

International Olympic Committee, "IOC Marketing Media Guide: Vancouver 2010," Lausanne, Switzerland, 2010.

International Olympic Committee, "Olympic Agenda 2020: 20+20 Recommendations," Lausanne, Switzerland, December 2014.

International Olympic Committee, "Olympic Marketing Fact File," Lausanne, Switzerland, 2014.

International Olympic Committee, "XII Olympic Congress," Paris, 1994.

International Olympic Committee, *Olympic Charter*, Lausanne, Switzerland, September 9, 2013.

International Olympic Committee, *Olympic Charter*, Lausanne, Switzerland, August 2, 2015.

International Olympic Committee, "The Olympic Flag," *Lettre d'informations / Newsletter (Olympic Review)*, no. 2, November 1967, 15–16.

"IOC Approves All Recommended Reforms," *Journal of Olympic History*, January 2000, 57–8.

James, C. L. R., *Beyond a Boundary*, Durham: Duke University Press, 1993.

Jenkins, R. *The First London Olympics 1908*, London: Piatkus Books, 2008.

Jennings, A., *The New Lord of the Rings: Olympic Corruption and How to Buy Gold Medals*, London: Pocket Books, 1996.

Karamichas, J., *The Olympic Games and the Environment*, New York: Palgrave Macmillan, 2013.

Karkazis, K., R. Jordan-Young, G. Davis, and S. Camporesi, "Out of Bounds? A Critique of the New Policies on Hyperandrogenism in Elite Female Athletes," *American Journal of Bioethics*, vol. 12, no. 7, 2012, 3–16.

Kasimati, E., and P. Dawson, "Assessing the Impact of the 2004 Olympic Games on the Greek Economy: A Small Macroeconometric Model," *Economic Modelling*, vol. 26, 2009, 139–46.

Keating, L., and C. A. Flores, "Sixty and Out: Techwood Homes Transformed by Enemies and Friends," *Journal of Urban History*, vol. 26, no. 3, 2000, 275–311.

Keech, M., "The Ties that Bind: South Africa and Sports Diplomacy 1958–1963," *The Sports Historian*, vol. 91, no. 1, 2001, 71–93.

Kennett, C., and M. de Moragas Spà, "Barcelona 1992: Evaluating the Olympic Legacy," in A. Tomlinson and C. Young (eds.), *National*

Bibliography

Identity and Global Sports Events: Culture, Politics, and Spectacle in the Olympics and Football World Cup, Albany, NY: State University of New York Press, 2006, 177–95.

Kidd, B., "The Aspirations of Olympism: A Framework for Considering the Athlete's Experience in the Olympic Movement at the Close of the Twentieth Century," Barcelona: Centre d'Estudis Olímpics UAB, 2000, 1–14.

Kidd, B., "The Culture Wars of the Montreal Olympics," *International Review for Sociology of Sport*, vol. 27, no. 2, 1992, 151–61.

Killanin, L., *My Olympic Years*, London: Secker & Warburg, 1983.

Kingfisher, C., and J. Maskovsky, "The Limits of Neoliberalism," *Critique of Anthropology*, vol. 28, no. 2, 2008, 115–26.

Klein, N., *The Shock Doctrine: The Rise of Disaster Capitalism*, New York: Metropolitan Books, 2007.

Kouvelakis, S., "The Greek Cauldron," *New Left Review*, vol. 72, Nov–Dec 2011, 17–32.

Kristof, N., "A Lever for Change in China," in M. Worden (ed.), *China's Great Leap: The Beijing Games and the Human Rights Challenges*, New York: Seven Stories Press, 2008, 17–21.

Krüger, A., "The German Way of Worker Sport," in A. Krüger and J. Riordan (eds.), *The Story of Worker Sport*, Champaign, Illinois: Human Kinetics, 1996, 1–25.

Krüger, A., "The Unfinished Symphony: A History of the Olympic Games from Coubertin to Samaranch," in J. Riordan and A. Krüger (eds.), *The International Politics of Sport in the Twentieth Century*, London and New York: E & FN Spon, 1999, 3–27.

Krüger, A., "The Origins of Pierre de Coubertin's *Religio Athletae*," *Olympika: The International Journal of Olympic Studies*, vol. 2, 1993, 91–102.

Large, D. C., "The Nazi Olympics: Berlin 1936," in H. J. Lenskyj and S. Wagg (eds.), *The Palgrave Handbook of Olympic Studies*, New York: Palgrave Macmillan, 2012, 60–71.

Lauermann, J., and M. Davidson, "Negotiating Particularity in Neoliberalism Studies: Tracing Development Strategies Across Neoliberal Urban Governance Projects," *Antipode*, vol. 45, no. 5, 2013, 1277–1297.

Leigh, M. H., and T. M. Bonin, "The Pioneering Role of Madame Alice Milliat and the FSFI in Establishing International Trade and Field Competition for Women," *Journal of Sport History*, vol. 4, no. 1, 1977, 72–83.

Bibliography

Lennartz, K., "The 2nd International Olympic Games in Athens 1906," *Journal of Olympic History*, 2002, 3–25.

Lenskyj, H. J., *Sexual Diversity and the Sochi 2014 Olympics: No More Rainbows*, New York: Palgrave Macmillan, 2014.

Lenskyj, H. J., *Olympic Industry Resistance: Challenging Olympic Power and Propaganda*, Albany: State University of New York Press, 2008.

Lenskyj, H. J., *The Best Olympics Ever?: Social Impacts of Sydney 2000*, Albany: State University of New York Press, 2002.

Light, M., "Migration, 'Globalised' Islam and the Russian State: A Case Study of Muslim Communities in Belgorod and Adygeya Regions," *Europe-Asia Studies*, vol. 64, no. 2, 2012, 195–226.

Loewenstein, A., *Disaster Capitalism: Making a Killing Out of Catastrophe*, London and New York: Verso, 2015.

Loland, S., "Coubertin's Ideology of Olympism from the Perspective of the History of Ideas," *Olympika: The International Journal of Olympic Studies*, vol. 4, 1995, 49–78.

London Organising Committee, "The Official Report of the Organising Committee for the XIV Olympiad," London, 1951.

Los Angeles Olympic Organizing Committee, *Official Report of the Games of the XXIIIrd Olympiad Los Angeles, 1984*, vol. 1, 1985.

Los Angeles Organizing Committee, "Xth Olympiad Los Angeles 1932: Official Report," Xth Olympiade Committee of the Games of Los Angeles, U. S. A. 1932, LTD., 1933.

Lucas, J., "1987: Admirers of Pierre de Coubertin and Avery Brundage Mark the Year," *Olympic Review*, no. 239, September 1987, 451–2.

Lucas, J., "American Involvement in the Athens Olympian Games of 1906: Bridge Between Failure and Success," *Stadion*, vol. 6, 1981, 217–28.

Ludwig, J., *Five Ring Circus: The Montreal Olympics*, New York and Toronto: Doubleday, 1976.

Lutan, R., and F. Hong, "The Politicization of Sport: GANEFO—A Case Study," *Sport in Society*, vol. 8, no. 3, 2005, 425–39.

MacAloon, J. J., *This Great Symbol: Pierre de Coubertin and the Origins of the Modern Olympics*, London and New York: Routledge, 2008.

Mackin, B., *Red Mittens & Red Ink: The Vancouver Olympics*, Vancouver: Smashwords, 2012.

Madden, J. R., "Economic and Fiscal Impacts of Mega Sporting Events: A General Equilibrium Assessment," *Public Finance and Management*, vol. 6, no. 3, 2006, 346–94.

Mallon, B., "The Olympic Bribery Scandal," *Journal of Olympic History*, vol. 8, no. 2, 2000, 11–27.

Mallon, B., *The 1906 Olympic Games: Results for All Competitors in All Events, with Commentary*, London: McFarland, 1999.

Mandell, R. D., *The First Modern Olympics*, Berkeley, CA: University of California Press, 1976.

Mandell, R. D., *The Nazi Olympics*, Urbana and Chicago: University of Illinois Press, 1987 [1971].

Maraniss, D., *Rome 1960: The Olympics that Changed the World*, New York: Simon and Schuster, 2008.

Marx, K., "Contribution to the Critique of Hegel's Philosophy of Law, Introduction," in *Karl Marx, Frederick Engels Collected Work, Volume 3*, London: Lawrence & Wishart, 1974 [1844].

Mascarenhas, G., *Entradas e Bandeiras: A Conquista do Brasil pelo Futebol*, Rio de Janeiro: Ed. UERJ, 2014.

Mascarenhas, G., "Desenvolvimento Urbano e Grandes Eventos Esportivos: O Legado Olímpico nas Cidades," in G. Mascarenhas, G. Bienenstein, and F. Sánchez (eds.), *O Jogo Continua: Mega-eventos Esportivos e Cidades*, Rio de Janeiro: Ed. UERJ, 2011, 27–39.

Matheson, V., "Economic Impact Analysis," in W. Andreff and S. Szymanski (eds.), *Handbook on the Economics of Sport*, Cheltenham, UK, and Northampton, MA: Edward Elgar, 2006, 137–42.

M'Bodj, S., "ISL Marketing AG," *Olympic Review*, vol. 25 no. 2, April–May 1995, 27–8.

McCann, B., *Hard Times in the Marvelous City: From Dictatorship to Democracy in the Favelas of Rio de Janeiro*, Durham and London: Duke University Press, 2014.

McFee, G., "The Promise of Olympism," in J. Sugden and A. Tomlinson (eds.), *Watching the Olympics: Politics, Power, and Representation*, London and New York: Routledge, 2012, 36–54.

McIntire, M., "National Status, the 1908 Olympic Games and the English Press," *Media History*, vol. 15, no. 3, 2009, 271–86.

McRoskey, S. R., "Security and the Olympic Games: Making Rio an Example," *Yale Journal of International Affairs*, Spring–Summer 2010, 91–105.

Merrifield, A., *Henri Lefebvre: A Critical Introduction*, New York: Routledge, 2006.

Miller, D., *The Official History of the Olympic Games and the IOC: Athens to London 1894 to 2012*, Edinburgh: Mainstream Publishing Company, 2012.

Miraftab, F., "Public-Private Partnerships: The Trojan Horse of Neoliberal Development?," *Journal of Planning Education and Research*, vol. 24, 2004, 89–101.

Mol, A. P. J., and L. Zhang, "Sustainability as Global Norm: The Greening of Mega-Events in China," in G. Hayes and J. Karamichas (eds.), *Olympic Games, Mega-Events and Civil Societies: Globalization, Environment, Resistance*, New York: Palgrave Macmillan, 2012, 126–50.

Montréal 1976, Games of the XXI Olympiad, "Official Report," Ottawa: COJO, 1978.

Müller, M., "(Im-)Mobile Policies: Why Sustainability Went Wrong in the 2014 Olympics in Sochi," *European Urban and Regional Studies*, vol. 22, no. 2, 2015, 191–209.

Müller, M., "State Dirigisme in Megaprojects: Governing the 2014 Winter Olympics in Sochi," *Environment and Planning A*, vol. 43, 2011, 2091–2108.

Müller, N., "Coubertin's Olympism," in Pierre de Coubertin, *Olympism: Selected Writings*, Lausanne, Switzerland: International Olympic Committee, 2000, 33–48.

Muñoz, F., "Olympic Urbanism and Olympic Villages: Planning Strategies in Olympic Host Cities, London 1908 to London 2012," *Sociological Review*, vol. 54, no. 2, 2006, 175–87.

Murray, W., "The Worker Sport Movement in France," in A. Krüger and J. Riordan (eds.), *The Story of Worker Sport*, Champaign, Illinois: Human Kinetics, 1996, 27–42.

Nixon, R., "Apartheid on the Run: The South African Sports Boycott," *Transitions*, vol. 58, 1992, 68–88.

O'Bonsawin, C. M., " 'No Olympics on Stolen Native Land': Contesting Olympic Narratives and Asserting Indigenous Rights within the Discourse of the 2010 Vancouver Games," *Sport in Society*, vol. 13, no. 1, 2000, 143–56.

Orttung, R. W., and S. Zhemukhov, "The Sochi Olympics Mega-Project and Political Economy," *East European Politics*, vol. 30, no. 2, 2014, 175–19.

Orwell, G., "The Sporting Spirit," in *Shooting an Elephant and Other Essays*, New York: Harcourt, Brace & World, 1950.

Owen, C. G., "Estimating the Cost and Benefit of Hosting Olympic Games: What Can Beijing Expect from Its 2008 Games?" *Industrial Geographer*, vol. 3, no. 1, 2005, 1–18.

Parezo, N. J., "A 'Special Olympics': Testing Racial Strength and Endurance at the 1904 Louisiana Purchase Exhibition," in S. Brownell (ed.), *The 1904 Anthropology Days and Olympic Games: Sport, Race, and American Imperialism*, Lincoln and London: University of Nebraska Press, 2008, 59–126.

Pauker, E., "Ganefo I: Sports and Politics in Djakarta," *Asian Survey*, vol. 5, no. 4, 1965, 171–85.

Paul, J., "The Great Progression: A Content Analysis of the *Lake Placid News* and the *Los Angeles Times*' Treatment of the 1932 Olympics," in G. P. Schaus and S. R. Wenn (eds.), *Onward to the Olympics: Historical Perspectives on the Olympic Games*, Waterloo, Ontario: Wilfrid Laurier University Press, 2007, 261–71.

Payne, M., *Olympic Turnaround: How the Games Stepped Back from the Brink of Extinction to Become the World's Best Known Brand – And a Multi-Billion Dollar Global Franchise*, London: London Business Press, 2005.

Peck, J., "Geography and Public Policy: Constructions of Neoliberalism," *Progress in Human Geography*, vol. 28, no. 3, 2004, 392–405.

Perelman, M., *Barbaric Sport: A Global Plague*, Trans. J. Howe, London and New York: Verso, 2012.

Perelman, R. B., *Olympic Retrospective: The Games of Los Angeles*, Los Angeles: Los Angeles Olympic Organizing Committee, 1985.

Perryman, M., *Why the Olympics Aren't Good for Us and How They Can Be*, London: OR Books, 2012.

Pound, R., "Olympian Changes: Seoul and Beijing," in M. Worden (ed.), *China's Great Leap: The Beijing Games and the Human Rights Challenges*, New York: Seven Stories Press, 2008, 85–97.

Pound, R. W., "The IOC and the Environment," *Olympic Message*, 35, 1993, 14–21.

Pound, R. W., *Inside the Olympics: A Behind-the-Scenes Look at the Politics, the Scandals, and the Glory of the Games*, Canada: Wiley, 2004.

Pouret, H., "Art and the Olympics," in L. Killanin and J. Rodda (eds.), *The Olympic Games: 80 Years of People, Events and Records*, New York: Macmillan, 1976, 160–64.

Preuss, H., *The Economics of Staging the Olympics: A Comparison of the Games, 1972–2008*, Cheltenham, UK, and Northampton, MA: Edward Elgar, 2004.

Pujadas, X., and C. Santacana, "The Popular Olympics Games, Barcelona 1936: Olympians and Anti-Fascists," *International Review for the Sociology of Sport*, vol. 27, no. 2, 1992, 139–48.

Quinn, M., *The King of Spring: The Life and Times of Peter O'Connor*, Dublin: The Liffey Press, 2004.

Bibliography

Raco, M., "Delivering Flagship Projects in an Era of Regulatory Capitalism: State-led Privatization and the London Olympics 2012," *International Journal of Urban and Regional Research*, vol. 38, no. 1, 2014, 176–97.

Ranciere, J., *Hatred of Democracy*, Trans. S. Corcoran, London and New York: Verso, 2006.

Redmond, G., "Prologue and Transition: The 'Pseudo-Olympics' of the Nineteenth Century," in J. Segrave and D. Chu (eds.), *Olympism*, Champaign, Illinois: Human Kinetics, 1981, 7–21.

Reich, K., *Making It Happen: Peter Ueberroth and the 1984 Olympics*, Santa Barbara, CA: Capra Press, 1986.

Reising, R., "Jim Thorpe: Multi-Cultural Hero," *The Indian Historian*, vol. 3, issue 4, 1974, 14–16.

Reuth, R. G., *Goebbels*, Trans. K. Winston, New York: Harcourt Brace & Company, 1993.

Rich, D. Q., K. Liu, J. Zhang, et al., "Differences in Birth Weight Associated with the 2008 Beijing Olympic Air Pollution Reduction: Results from a Natural Experiment," *Environmental Health Perspectives*, vol. 123, no. 9, 2015, 880–7.

Riefenstahl, L., *A Memoir*, New York: Picador, 1992.

Rinehart, R. E., "'Fists Flew and Blood Flowed': Symbolic Resistance and International Response in Hungarian Water Polo at the Melbourne Olympics, 1956," *Journal of Sport History*, vol. 23, no. 2, 1996, 120–39.

Rio 2016, "Candidature File for Rio de Janeiro to Host the 2016 Olympic and Paralympic Games, Volume 1–3," 2009.

Riordan, J., "The Worker Sport Movement," in J. Riordan and A. Krüger (eds.), *The International Politics of Sport in the Twentieth Century*, London and New York: E & FN SPON, 1999, 105–17.

Riordan, J. "Introduction," in A. Krüger and J. Riordan (eds.), *The Story of Worker Sport*, Champaign, Illinois: Human Kinetics, 1996, vii–x.

Romney, M., and T. Robinson, *Turnaround: Crisis, Leadership, and the Olympic Games*, Washington, DC: Regnery Publishing Inc., 2004.

Roosevelt, T., *The Letters of Theodore Roosevelt, Volume 4*, Elting E. Morrison (ed.), Cambridge, MA: Harvard University Press, 1951.

Rosefielde, S., *The Russian Economy: From Lenin to Putin*, Oxford: Blackwell, 2007.

Rutheiser, C., *Imagineering Atlanta: The Politics of Place in the City of Dreams*, London: Verso, 1996.

Bibliography

Samatas, M., "Security and Surveillance in the Athens 2004 Olympics: Some Lessons From a Troubled Story," *International Criminal Justice Review*, vol. 17, 2007, 220–38.

Samatas, M., "Surveillance in Athens 2004 and Beijing 2008: A Comparison of the Olympic Surveillance Modalities and Legacies in Two Different Olympic Host Regimes," *Urban Studies*, vol. 48, no. 15, 2011, 3347–3366.

Santos Junior, O. A., "Metropolização e Megaeventos: Proposições Gerais em Torno da Copa do Mundo 2014 e das Olimpíadas 2016 no Brasil," in O. A. Santos Junior, C. Gaffney, and L. C. Q. Ribeiro (eds.), *Brasil: Os Impactos Da Copa Do Mundo 2014 e Das Olimpíadas 2016*, Rio de Janeiro: Observatório Das Metrópoles, 2015, 21–40.

Santos Junior, O. A., and C. G. R. Lima, "Impactos Econômicos dos Megaeventos no Brasil: Investimento Público, Participação Privada e Difusão do Empreendedorismo Urbano Neoliberal," in O. A. Santos Junior, C. Gaffney, and L. C. Q. Ribeiro (eds.), *Brasil: Os Impactos Da Copa Do Mundo 2014 e Das Olimpíadas 2016*, Rio de Janeiro: Observatório Das Metrópoles, 2015, 57–77.

Sarantakes, N., *Dropping the Torch: Jimmy Carter, The Olympic Boycott, and the Cold War*, New York: Cambridge University Press, 2011.

Schaap, J. *Triumph: The Untold Story of Jesse Owens and Hitler's Olympics*, New York: Houghton Mifflin, 2007.

Schantz, O., "The Presidency of Avery Brundage," in *The International Olympic Committee—One Hundred Years: The Ideas – The Presidents – The Achievements, Volume 2*, Lausanne, Switzerland: International Olympic Committee, 1995.

Segrave, J. O., "Coubertin, Olympism, and Chivalry," *Olympika: The International Journal of Olympic Studies*, vol. 22, 2013, 1–38.

Segrave, J. O., and D. Foote, "'All Men Will Become Brothers': Beethoven's *Ninth Symphony* as Olympic Games Entertainment and Ideology," *Intersections and Intersectionalities in Olympic and Paralympic Studies*, London, Ontario: Western University, 2014: 24–9.

Senn, A. E., *Power, Politics, and the Olympic Games*, Champaign, Illinois: Human Kinetics, 1999.

Seoul Olympic Organizing Committee, "Official Report: Games of the XXIVth Olympiad Seoul 1988," September 1989.

Short, J. R., "Globalization, Cities, and the Summer Olympics," *City: Analysis of Urban Trends, Culture, Theory, Policy, Action*, vol. 12, no. 3, 2008, 321–40.

Bibliography

Short, J. R., *Global Metropolitan: Globalizing Cities in a Capitalist World*, London: Routledge, 2004.

Simri, U., *Women at the Olympic Games*, Netanya, Israel: Wingate Monograph Series, 1979.

Simonović, L., *Philosophy of Olympism*, Belgrade: Stručna Knjiga, 2004.

Singer, A., "Rebellion in Brazil: Social and Political Complexion of the June Events," *New Left Review*, vol. 85, Jan–Feb 2014, 19–37.

Simson, V., and A. Jennings, *Lord of the Rings: Power, Money and Drugs in the Modern Olympics*, London: Simon & Schuster, 1992.

Smith, T., and D. Steele, *Silent Gesture: The Autobiography of Tommie Smith*, Philadelphia: Temple University Press, 2007.

Stanton, R., "In Search Of the Artists of 1912," *Journal of Olympic History*, Spring 2001, 3–13.

Strenk, A., "Amateurism: The Myth and the Reality," in J. O. Segrave and D. Chu (eds.), *The Olympic Games in Transition*, Champaign, Illinois: Human Kinetics, 1988, 303–27.

Stump, A. J., "The Games That Almost Weren't," in J. O. Segrave and D. Chu (eds.), *The Olympic Games in Transition*, Champaign, Illinois: Human Kinetics, 1988, 191–9.

Sugden, J., "Watched by the Games: Surveillance and Security at the Olympics," in J. Sugden and A. Tomlinson (eds.), *Watching the Olympics: Politics, Power, and Representation*, London and New York: Routledge, 2012, 228–41.

Sullivan, J. E., "Anthropology Days at the Stadium," in J. E. Sullivan (ed.), *Spalding's Official Athletic Almanac for 1905*, New York: American Sports Publishing, 1905, 249–64.

Sullivan, J. E., *The Olympic Games at Athens, 1906*, New York: American Sports Publishing Company, 1906.

Sullivan, S. P., and R. A. Mechikoff, "A Man of His Time: Pierre de Coubertin's Olympic Ideology and the Via Media," *Olympika: The International Journal of Olympic Studies*, vol. 13, 2004, 27–52.

Sydney Organising Committee for the Olympic Games, "Official Report of the XXVII Olympiad," 2001.

Tang, W., "The 2008 Olympic Torch Relay in Hong Kong: A Clash of Governmentalities," *Human Geography*, vol. 1, no. 1, 2008, 106–10.

Tokyo Organizing Committee, "The Games of the XVIII Olympiad, Tokyo 1964: The Official Report of the Organizing Committee," 1964.

Tomlinson, A., "Olympic Survivals: The Olympic Games as a Global Phenomenon," in L. Allison (ed.), *The Global Politics of Sport: The Role of Global Institutions in Sport*, London and New York: Routledge, 2005, 46–62.

Tomlinson, A., "Olympic Values, Beijing's Olympic Games, and the Universal Market," in M. E. Price and D. Dayan (eds.), *Owning the Olympics: Narratives of the New China*, Ann Arbor: University of Michigan Press, 2008, 67–85.

Tomlinson, A., "The Disneyfication of the Olympics: Theme Parks and Freak-Shows of the Body," in J. Bale and M. K. Christensen (eds.), *Post-Olympism?: Questioning Sport in the Twenty-first Century*, Oxford: Berg Publishers, 2004, 147–63.

Toscano, R., *To Leveling Swerve*, San Francisco: Krupskaya, 2004.

Tsing, A. L., "Inside the Economy of Appearances," *Public Culture*, vol. 12, 2000, 115–44.

Ueberroth, P., R. Levin, and A. Quinn, *Made in America: His Own Story*, New York: William Morrow, 1985.

United States Government Accountability Office, "Olympic Security: US Support to Olympic Games Provides Lessons for Future Olympics," May 2005.

Vale, L. J., *Purging the Poorest: Public Housing and the Design Politics of Twice-Cleared Communities*, Chicago: University of Chicago Press, 2013.

Wamsley, K., and G. Schultz, "Rogues and Bedfellows: The IOC and the Incorporation of the FSFI," *Fifth International Symposium for Olympic Research*, 2000, 113–18.

Wang, T., et al., "Air Quality During the 2008 Beijing Olympics: Secondary Pollutants and Regional Impact," *Atmospheric Chemistry and Physics Discussions*, vol. 10, 2010, 12433–63.

Welky, D. B., "Viking Girls, Mermaids, and Little Brown Men: U.S. Journalism and the 1932 Olympics," *Journal of Sport History*, vol. 24, no. 1, 1997, 24–49.

Wenn, S., R. Barney, and S. Martyn, *Tarnished Rings: The International Olympic Committee and the Salt Lake City Bid Scandal*, New York: Syracuse University Press, 2011.

Wenn, S. R., "An Olympian Squabble: The Distribution of Olympic Television Revenue, 1960–1966," *Olympika: The International Journal of Olympic Studies*, vol. 3, 1994, 27–47.

Wheeler, R. F., "Organized Sport and Organized Labour: The Workers' Sport Movement," *Journal of Contemporary History*, vol. 13, no. 2, 1978, 191–210.

Bibliography

Whitelegg, D., "Going for Gold: Atlanta's Bid for Fame," *International Journal of Urban and Regional Research*, vol. 24, no. 4, 2000, 801–17.

Whitson, D., and D. Macintosh, "The Global Circus: International Sport, Tourism, and the Marketing of Cities," *Journal of Sport and Social Issues*, vol. 20, 1996, 278–95.

Wilcock, B., "The 1908 Olympic Marathon," *Journal of Olympic History*, vol. 16, no. 1, March 2008, 31–47.

Witte, J. C., et al., "Satellite Observations of Changes in Air Quality During the 2008 Beijing Olympics and Paralympics," *Geophysical Research Letters*, vol. 36, no. 17, 2009, 1–6.

Wright, G., "The Political Economy of the Montreal Olympic Games," *Journal of Sport and Social Issues,* vol. 2, 1978, 13–18.

Xiaobo, L., "Authoritarianism in the Light of the Olympic Flame," in M. Worden (ed.) *China's Great Leap: The Beijing Games and the Human Rights Challenges*, New York: Seven Stories Press, 2008, 263–72.

Young, A., *A Way Out of No Way: The Spiritual Memoirs of Andrew Young*, Nashville: Thomas Nelson, 1994.

Young, D. C., *The Modern Olympics: A Struggle for Revival*, Baltimore and London: Johns Hopkins University Press, 1996.

Yu, Y., F. Klauser, and G. Chan, "Governing Security at the Beijing Games," *The International Journal of the History of Sport*, vol. 26, no. 3, 2009, 390–405.

Yuankai, T., "Beijing Creates History," *Beijing Review*, issue 31, August 2001, 12–16.

Zimbalist, A., *Circus Maximus: The Economic Gamble Behind Hosting the Olympics and the World Cup*, Washington, DC: The Brookings Institution, 2015.

Zirin, D., *Brazil's Dance with the Devil: The World Cup, the Olympics, and the Fight for Democracy*, Chicago: Haymarket Books, 2014.

Zirin, D., *Welcome to the Terrordome: The Pain, Politics, and Promise of Sports*, Chicago: Haymarket Books, 2007.

Notes

Introduction

1. D. E. Sanger, "Obama Order Sped Up Wave of Cyberattacks Against Iran," *New York Times*, June 2, 2012, A1; P. Chatterjee, "The Urgency of a Computer Virus Nonproliferation Treaty," *Guardian*, June 27, 2012.
2. P. Hersh, "Rogge's Refusal to Comment on Bin Laden Death Sadly Speaks Volumes about IOC," *Chicago Tribune*, May 2, 2011.
3. T. Adorno, "Commitment," in E. Bloch, G. Lukács, B. Brecht, W. Benjamin, and T. Adorno, *Aesthetics and Politics*, Trans. R. Taylor, London: Verso, 1980, 177.
4. J. J. MacAloon, *This Great Symbol: Pierre de Coubertin and the Origins of the Modern Olympics*, London and New York: Routledge, 2008, 207.
5. A. Brundage, "Letter to Stanislaw Dabrowski," Avery Brundage Collection, 1908–1975 (hereafter cited as ABC), Box 179, Reel 103, February 7, 1969, International Centre for Olympic Studies, London, Ontario (hereafter cited as ICOS).
6. International Olympic Committee, "IOC and NOCs of Israel and Palestine Hold Third Joint Meeting in Ramallah," October 27, 2011.
7. J. Boykoff and D. Zirin, "The Sochi Paralympics, Ukraine, and the Olympic Truce," *The Nation*, March 16, 2014.
8. P. P. Pan, "China Using Rights Issue to Promote Olympic Bid; Potential Gains Cited as Inspectors Arrive," *Washington Post*, February 21, 2001, A18.
9. R. Pound, "Olympian Changes: Seoul and Beijing," in M. Worden (ed.), *China's Great Leap: The Beijing Games and the Human Rights Challenges*, New York: Seven Stories Press, 2008, 87.
10. For Reporters Without Borders rankings, see: rsf.org; Human Rights Watch, "China: Hosting Olympics a Catalyst for Human Rights Abuses," August 23, 2008, emphasis added.

11. M. Perelman, *Barbaric Sport: A Global Plague*, Trans. J. Howe, London and New York: Verso, 2012, 39–40.
12. K. Marx "Contribution to the Critique of Hegel's Philosophy of Law, Introduction," in *Karl Marx, Frederick Engels Collected Work, Volume 3*, London: Lawrence & Wishart, 1974 [1844], 174, emphasis in original.
13. J. Gilbert, "Pope Francis' Team Claims Argentine Title," *New York Times*, December 17, 2013, B14.
14. S. Kuper, "The World's Game Is Not Just a Game," *New York Times*, May 26, 2002, E36; S. Kuper, "Lost in Translation," *Financial Times Magazine*, February 1, 2008.
15. C. L. R. James, *Beyond a Boundary*, Durham: Duke University Press, 1993, 65.
16. R. Toscano, *To Leveling Swerve*, San Francisco: Krupskaya, 2004, 13.
17. E. Goddard, "In Sport All People Are Equal, Bach Tells United Nations," *Inside the Games*, April 15, 2015.
18. International Olympic Committee, "IOC Financial Summary," July 2014, 2.

1. Coubertin and the Revival of the Olympic Games

1. R. Stanton, "In Search of the Artists of 1912," *Journal of Olympic History*, 2001, 3–13; H. Pouret, "Art and the Olympics," in L. Killanin and J. Rodda (eds.), *The Olympic Games: 80 Years of People, Events and Records*, New York: Macmillan, 1976, 160–4.
2. J. Durry, "Art and Sport: 'Hohrod and Eschbach' a Mystery Finally Solved," *Olympic Review*, vol. 26, no. 32, April–May 2000, 26–8. In the Official Report for the Games, the gold-winning pseudo-duo was simply listed as participants from Germany, not France. See E. Bergvall and Swedish Olympic Committee, "The Official Report of the Olympic Games of Stockholm 1912," Stockholm: Wahlström and Widstrand, 1913, 808.
3. Stanton, "In Search of the Artists of 1912"; L. Hughes-Hallett, *Gabriele D'Annunzio: Poet, Seducer, and Preacher of War*, New York: Alfred A. Knopf, 2013. Hughes-Hallett notes that D'Annunzio also attracted the attention of the left, with Vladimir Lenin shipping him a jar of caviar and calling him the "only revolutionary in Europe," 5.
4. G. Hohrod and M. Eschbach, "Ode to Sport," *Olympic Review*, vol. 36, no. 32, April–May 2000, 29. For alternative translation,

see P. D. Coubertin, *The Olympic Idea: Discourses and Essays*, Schorndorf, Germany: Druckerei and Verlag Karl Hofmann, 1967, 39–40.

5. A. Guttmann, *The Olympics: A History of the Modern Games*, Urbana and Chicago: University of Illinois Press, 2002 [1992], 32. See also: Durry, "Art and Sport."

6. T. A. Cook and British Olympic Council, "The Fourth Olympiad, London 1908: Official Report," 1908, 383.

7. S. J. Bandy, "The Olympic Celebration of the Arts," in J. O. Segrave and D. Chu (eds.), *The Olympic Games in Transition*, Champaign, Illinois: Human Kinetics, 1988, 163–9.

8. Pouret, "Art and the Olympics," 162.

9. N. Müller, "Coubertin's Olympism," in P. D. Coubertin, *Olympism: Selected Writings*, N. Müller (ed.), Lausanne: International Olympic Committee, 2000, 43.

10. Coubertin, *The Olympic Idea*, 107; Müller, "Coubertin's Olympism," 37.

11. MacAloon, *This Great Symbol*, 197.

12. To be sure, there were international games that took place after the Olympics of Ancient Greece and before their modern-day incarnation. In the 1600s Robert Dover organized Olympic get-togethers in England. Versions of these events lasted through 1852, with less and less order and organization. A separate set of Olympics—sometimes replete with literature and art competitions—were organized in the mid-to-late 1800s astride the rise of organized sports like cricket and boxing. See: G. Redmond, "Prologue and Transition: The 'Pseudo-Olympics' of the Nineteenth Century," in J. O. Segrave and D. Chu (eds.), *Olympism*, Champaign, Illinois: Human Kinetics, 1981, 7–21.

13. "The Princeton French Debate," *New York Times*, December 23, 1895, 10.

14. R. D. Mandell, *The First Modern Olympics*, Berkeley: University of California Press, 1976, 52–3.

15. Baron P. D. Coubertin, "The Meeting of the Olympian Games," *The North American Review*, vol. 170, no. 523, June 1900, 803, 811.

16. Coubertin, *The Olympic Idea*, 51.

17. Cited in B. Kidd, "The Aspirations of Olympism: A Framework for Considering the Athlete's Experience in the Olympic Movement at the Close of the Twentieth Century," Barcelona: Centre d'Estudis Olímpics UAB, 2000, 13.

18. Coubertin, *The Olympic Idea*, 11.

19. Theodore Roosevelt, *The Letters of Theodore Roosevelt*, volume 4,

Elting E. Morrison (ed.), Cambridge, MA: Harvard University Press, 1951, 491.

20. Coubertin, *Olympism*, 405.
21. Ibid., *Olympism*, 174, 175.
22. Ibid., 114, 174–5.
23. Ibid., 580, emphasis in original.
24. Ibid., 548.
25. Ibid., 217.
26. Ibid., 202, 228, 567.
27. Roosevelt, *The Letters of Theodore Roosevelt*, 491.
28. Coubertin, *The Olympic Idea*, 107.
29. Coubertin, *Olympism*, 582–3, emphasis in original.
30. P. D. Coubertin, "Through Coubertin's Writings: Coubertin on Amateurism," Olympic Review, no. 91–2, May–June 1975, 160.
31. Coubertin, *Olympism*, 580, emphasis in original.
32. Coubertin, *The Olympic Idea*, 134.
33. Coubertin, *The Olympic Idea*, 11.
34. Coubertin, *Olympism*, 147.
35. J. O. Segrave, "Coubertin, Olympism, and Chivalry," *Olympika: The International Journal of Olympic Studies*, vol. 22, 2013, 14.
36. P. D. Coubertin, "The Olympic Games of 1896," *The Century Magazine*, vol. 53, November 1896, 53.
37. Coubertin, *Olympism*, 241.
38. Coubertin, *The Olympic Idea*, 134.
39. Coubertin, *Olympism*, 241.
40. Quoted in A. Krüger, "The Origins of Pierre de Coubertin's *Religio Athletae*," *Olympika: The International Journal of Olympic Studies*, vol. 2, 1993, 93.
41. Coubertin, *Olympism*, 595.
42. G. Orwell, *Shooting an Elephant and Other Essays*, New York: Harcourt, Brace & World, Inc., 1950, 152, 154.
43. Coubertin, *The Olympic Idea*, 132.
44. S. P. Sullivan and R. A. Mechikoff, "A Man of His Time: Pierre de Coubertin's Olympic Ideology and the Via Media," *Olympika: The International Journal of Olympic Studies*, vol. 13, 2004, 39.
45. Coubertin, *Olympism*, 711, 713.
46. Quoted in MacAloon, *This Great Symbol*, 103.
47. Quoted in K. B. Wamsley and G. Schultz, "Rogues and Bedfellows: The IOC and the Incorporation of the FSFI," Western Ontario University, Fifth International Symposium for Olympic Research, 2000, 113.
48. Coubertin, *Olympism*, 713.
49. Ibid., 583.

50. Coubertin, *Olympism*, 746.
51. Ibid., 582.
52. See, for example, G. McFee, "The Promise of Olympism," in J. Sugden and A. Tomlinson (eds.), *Watching the Olympics: Politics, Power, and Representation*, London and New York, Routledge, 2012, 44.
53. Coubertin, *Olympism*, 114.
54. Coubertin, "The Olympic Games of 1896," 50.
55. Quoted in L. Simonović, *Philosophy of Olympism*, Belgrade: Stručna Knjiga, 2004, 40.
56. Coubertin, *Olympism*, 498.
57. Ibid.
58. Coubertin, "The Meeting of the Olympian Games," 810.
59. J. Lucas, "1987: Admirers of Pierre de Coubertin and Avery Brundage Mark the Year," *Olympic Review*, no. 239, September 1987, 452.
60. Coubertin, "The Meeting of the Olympian Games," 808.
61. A. Guttmann, *The Olympics*, 4, 12–13.
62. Quoted in D. C. Young, *The Modern Olympics: A Struggle for Revival*, Baltimore and London: Johns Hopkins University Press, 1996, 40.
63. T. Collins, *Sport in Capitalist Society: A Short History*, London and New York: Routledge, 2013, 31.
64. Coubertin, "The Olympic Games of 1896," 53.
65. Coubertin, *Olympism*, 599.
66. A. Guttmann, *The Olympics*, 4; A. E. Senn, *Power, Politics, and the Olympic Games*, Champaign, Illinois: Human Kinetics, 1999, 9–10.
67. "Drastic Rules for American Oarsmen," *New York Times*, September 6, 1907, 7.
68. Coubertin, *The Olympic Idea*, 60.
69. Ibid.
70. Ibid., 51.
71. J. Hoberman, *The Olympic Crisis: Sport, Politics and the Moral Order*, New Rochelle, NY: Aristide D. Caratzas, 1986, 34.
72. Coubertin, *The Olympic Idea*, 97.
73. Coubertin, "Through Coubertin's Writings," 161.
74. "IOC Executive Committee Minutes," IOC Executive Committee Minutes, vol. 1 (1921–1948), Trans. W. Lyberg, Paris, July 12 and 23, 1922, 19.
75. A. Strenk, "Amateurism: The Myth and the Reality," in J. O. Segrave and D. Chu (eds.), *The Olympic Games in Transition*, Champaign, Illinois: Human Kinetics, 1988, 303–27.

76. Hoberman, *The Olympic Crisis*, 37, 43, 44.
77. A. Bolanki, "The Olympic Flag: Its History and Use," *Bulletin du Comité International Olympique*, no. 27, June 1951, 42–3; International Olympic Committee, "The Olympic Flag," *Lettre d'informations*, no. 2, November 1967, 15–16. International copyright laws dictated that copyright would expire fifty years after his death, on December 31, 1987.
78. Coubertin, *Olympism*, 594–5; R. K. Barney, S. R. Wenn, and S. G. Martyn, *Selling the Five Rings: The International Olympic Committee and the Rise of Olympic Commercialism*, Salt Lake City: The University of Utah Press, 2004, 160, 25.
79. Coubertin, *Olympism*, 298.
80. Ibid., 302.
81. Quoted in Young, *The Modern Olympics*, 90.
82. Coubertin, *Olympism*, 303.
83. Mandell, *The First Modern Olympics*, 86, 88.
84. MacAloon, *This Great Symbol*, 198–201.
85. J. L. Chappelet and B. Kübler-Mabbott, *The International Olympic Committee and the Olympic System: The Governance of World Sport*, New York: Routledge, 2008, 19; Young, *The Modern Olympics*, 108; quotation from MacAloon, *This Great Symbol*, 202.
86. Coubertin, *Olympism*, 587.
87. Mandell, *The First Modern Olympics*, 90–1.
88. Coubertin, "The Olympic Games of 1896," 39.
89. Mandell, *The First Modern Olympics*; Young, *The Modern Olympics*; a search of the New York Times historical database during the period of the 1896 Games turns up zero hits for "Coubertin."
90. Young, *The Modern Olympics*, 128; Mandell, *The First Modern Olympics*, 97, 100.
91. Young, *The Modern Olympics*, 116–26.
92. Ibid., 166–7.
93. C. R. Hill, *Olympic Politics*, 2nd ed., Manchester and New York: Manchester University Press, 1996, 29.
94. Mandell, *The First Modern Olympics*, 141.
95. Young, *The Modern Olympics*, 147.
96. R. K. Barney, "The Olympic Games in Modern Times," in G. P. Schaus and S. R. Wenn (eds.), *Onward to the Olympics: Historical Perspectives on the Olympic Games*, Waterloo, Ontario: Wilfrid Laurier University Press, 2007, 223.
97. A. Krüger, "The Unfinished Symphony: A History of the Olympic Games from Coubertin to Samaranch," in J. Riordan and A. Krüger (eds.), *The International Politics of Sport in the Twentieth Century*, London and New York: E & FN Spon, 1999, 6.

98. "The New Olympic Games," *New York Times*, April 26, 1896, 16.

99. "An Olympic Audience," *New York Times*, July 26, 1896, 22.

100. P. D. Coubertin, T. J. Philemon, N. G. Politis, and C. Anninos, *The Olympic Games, B.C. 776–A.D. 1896*, London: H. Grevel and Co., 1897, 107.

101. Letter reprinted in "Winners in the Stadium," *New York Times*, May 3, 1896, 3.

102. Coubertin, "The Olympic Games of 1896," 39.

103. Young, *The Modern Olympics*, 162–3.

104. Coubertin, *Olympism*, 388.

105. Ibid., 387–94; Guttmann, *The Olympics*, 21–2.

106. Coubertin, *Olympism*, 392.

107. Guttmann, *The Olympics*, 22–4; Senn, Power, Politics, and the Olympic Games, 25.

108. J. R. Short, *Global Metropolitan: Globalizing Cities in a Capitalist World*, London: Routledge, 2004, 88–9; Guttmann, *The Olympics*, 22; Senn, *Power, Politics, and the Olympic Games*, 19.

109. Coubertin, *Olympism*, 394.

110. "Millions of Americans Are Going in for Athletics," *New York Times*, July 23, 1905, SM4; Coubertin, *Olympism*, 401.

111. Coubertin, *Olympism*, 402, 408–9.

112. The number of reported participants varies, going as high as 687. See: A. Krüger, "The Unfinished Symphony," 7; Senn, *Power, Politics, and the Olympic Games*, 25–6; Guttmann, *The Olympics*, 24–7; N. J. Parezo, "A 'Special Olympics': Testing Racial Strength and Endurance at the 1904 Louisiana Purchase Exhibition," in S. Brownell (ed.), *The 1904 Anthropology Days and Olympic Games: Sport, Race, and American Imperialism*, Lincoln and London: University of Nebraska Press, 2008, 78.

113. Parezo, "A 'Special Olympics'," 78.

114. J. E. Sullivan, "Anthropology Days at the Stadium," in J. E. Sullivan (ed.), *Spalding's Official Athletic Almanac for 1905*, New York: American Sports Publishing, 1905, 249.

115. Parezo, "A 'Special Olympics'," 60.

116. Sullivan, "Anthropology Days at the Stadium," 257.

117. Parezo, "A 'Special Olympics'," 59.

118. H. Eichberg, "Olympic Anthropology Days and the Progress of Exclusion: Toward an Anthropology of Democracy," in S. Brownell, *The 1904 Anthropology Days and Olympic Games*, 344.

119. Parezo, "A 'Special Olympics'," 83.

120. Ibid.; M. Dyreson, "The 'Physical Value' of Races and Nations:

Anthropology and Athletics at the Louisiana Purchase Exhibition," in Brownell, *The 1904 Anthropology Days and Olympic Games*, 127–55.

121. Parezo, "A 'Special Olympics'."
122. Sullivan, "Anthropology Days at the Stadium," 251.
123. Parezo, "A 'Special Olympics'," 92.
124. Ibid., 89, 96.
125. Sullivan, "Anthropology Days at the Stadium," 257.
126. Ibid., 253.
127. Parezo, "A 'Special Olympics'," 97.
128. Quoted in Parezo, "A 'Special Olympics'," 112.
129. Sullivan, "Anthropology Days at the Stadium," 257.
130. Ibid., 249; Coubertin, *Olympism*, 695, 407, 409, 742.
131. Ibid., 695.
132. Ibid., 408–9.
133. H. V. Harlan, *History of Olympic Games: Ancient and Modern*, London: Foster Press, 1931, 89.
134. Dyreson, "The 'Physical Value' of Races and Nations," 149.
135. S. Loland, "Coubertin's Ideology of Olympism from the Perspective of the History of Ideas," *Olympika: The International Journal of Olympic Studies*, vol. 4, 1995, 66.
136. K. Lennartz, "The 2nd International Olympic Games in Athens 1906," *Journal of Olympic History*, March 2002, 8.
137. John Lucas, "American Involvement in the Athens Olympian Games of 1906: Bridge Between Failure and Success," *Stadion*, vol. 6, 1981, 218.
138. Bill Mallon prefers the term "intercalated" Olympics while Richard D. Mandell refers to them as the "'rump' Olympic Games." See B. Mallon, *The 1906 Olympic Games: Results for All Competitors in All Events, with Commentary*, London: McFarland & Company Inc., 1999 and Mandell, *The First Modern Olympics*, 167.
139. Mallon, *The 1906 Olympic Games*; Lennartz, "The 2nd International Olympic Games in Athens 1906."
140. Ibid., 8–9; Lennartz, "The 2nd International Olympic Games in Athens 1906," 12–13.
141. J. E. Sullivan, *The Olympic Games at Athens*, 1906, New York: American Sports Publishing Company, 1906, 7.
142. M. Quinn, *The King of Spring: The Life and Times of Peter O'Connor*, Dublin: The Liffey Press, 2004, 167–8.
143. Quinn, *The King of Spring*, 172. Ironically, O'Connor was born in England. Birth certificate on file, courtesy of Rosemarie O'Connor Quinn.

144. Lennartz, "The 2nd International Olympic Games in Athens 1906," 14; Mallon, *The 1906 Olympic Games*, 6.
145. Quinn, *The King of Spring*, 172.
146. Personal interview, June 23, 2014.
147. Mallon, *The 1906 Olympic Games*, 8.
148. Quinn, The King of Spring, 176; David Guiney, "The Olympic Council of Ireland," *Citius, Altius, Fortius*, vol. 4, no. 3, Autumn 1996, 33.
149. Quinn, *The King of Spring*, 179–84; Mallon, *The 1906 Olympic Games*, 51. Sullivan dismissed O'Connor's claims, asserting the judging was fair and Halpin was not the sole official on hand. See: Sullivan, *The Olympic Games at Athens, 1906*, 77.
150. *Limerick Leader*, August 25, 1956. Quoted in Quinn, *The King of Spring*, 183.
151. Mallon, *The 1906 Olympic Games*, 51.
152. Ibid.; David Guiney, "The Olympic Council of Ireland," 33; Quinn, *The King of Spring*, 184–5.
153. Peter O'Connor, letter to Seamus P. O'Ceallaigh, 27 August 1941, 1–2. On file, courtesy of Rosemarie O'Connor Quinn.
154. Quinn, *The King of Spring*, 184.
155. Personal interview, July 1, 2014.
156. Personal letter from Rosemarie O'Connor Quinn, May 1, 2015.
157. "The Olympic Games," *Daily Mail*, n.d., article found in Peter O'Connor, "Athletic Cuttings from Year 1904" (personal scrapbook), 45.
158. Quinn, *The King of Spring*, 191.
159. Ibid., 195.
160. Mallon, *The 1906 Olympic Games*, 5.
161. Lucas, "American Involvement in the Athens Olympian Games of 1906," 223.
162. "King Dines Athletes Who Won at Athens," *New York Times*, May 3, 1906, 4.
163. Lennartz, "The 2nd International Olympic Games in Athens 1906," 13–14; Lucas, "American Involvement in the Athens Olympian Games of 1906," 221.
164. Mallon, *The 1906 Olympic Games*, 15–17; Lennartz, "The 2nd International Olympic Games in Athens 1906," 20–1.
165. T. A. Cook and British Olympic Council, "The Fourth Olympiad, London 1908," 19, 20.
166. Matthew McIntire, "National Status, the 1908 Olympic Games and the English Press," *Media History*, vol. 15, no. 3, 2009, 271–86.
167. Coubertin, *Olympism*, 394.

168. Mandell, *The First Modern Olympics*, 172.

169. The distance of the marathon at the 1896 Athens Games was just under twenty-five miles. Historians differ on the amount of direct influence that the royal family had on the distance of the Olympic race in 1908. See: S. Halliday, "London's Olympics, 1908," *History Today*, vol. 58, issue 4, April 2008; Guttmann, *The Olympics*, 29; Mandell, *The First Modern Olympics*, 157; B. Wilcock, "The 1908 Olympic Marathon," *Journal of Olympic History*, vol. 16, no. 1, March 2008, 31–47.

170. R. Jenkins, *The First London Olympics 1908*, London, Piatkus Books, 2008, 109; Guttmann, *The Olympics*, 29.

171. Halliday, "London's Olympics, 1908"; Cook and British Olympic Council, "The Fourth Olympiad, London 1908."

172. Coubertin, *Olympism*, 425.

173. Cook and British Olympic Council, "The Fourth Olympiad, London 1908," 80–1; Jenkins, *The First London Olympics 1908*, 127–30.

174. "America's Triumph in Olympic Games," *New York Times*, July 26, 1908, S1.

175. S. Daniels and A. Tedder, *"A Proper Spectacle": Women Olympians 1900–1936*, Petersham, Australia: Wall Wall Press, 2000, 27.

176. Barney, "The Olympic Games in Modern Times," 221–41.

177. Coubertin, *Olympism*, 439.

178. "Sullivan Gets Home; Praises the Swedes," *New York Times*, August 11, 1912, S2.

179. Barney, "The Olympic Games in Modern Times," 224.

180. Guttmann, *The Olympics*, 32–3; Senn, *Power, Politics, and the Olympic Games*, 30.

181. R. Reising, "Jim Thorpe: Multi-Cultural Hero," *The Indian Historian*, vol. 3, issue 4, 1974, 14–16.

182. A. Brundage, "Olympic," in file "Notes on Art, Politics, Sports, 1968–1970, ABC, Box 246, Reel 143, ICOS.

183. A. Guttmann, *The Games Must Go On: Avery Brundage and the Olympic Movement*, New York: Columbia University Press, 1984, 30.

184. "Indian Thorpe in Olympiad," *New York Times*, April 28, 1912, C9; "America First as Olympics End," *New York Times*, July 16, 1912, 1; "Sullivan Gets Home; Praises the Swedes."

185. See, for example: "America First as Olympics End," *New York Times*.

186. For one version of the story, see E. Bergvall and Swedish Olympic Committee, "The Official Report of the Olympic Games of Stockholm 1912," 410–11.

187. R. Cremer, "Professionalism and its Implications for the Olympic Movement," *Olympic Review*, vol. 26, no. 14, April 1997, 23–4.

188. Coubertin, *Olympism*, 645, 457.

189. Young, *The Modern Olympics*, 41.

190. J. A. Haley, "Letter to Mr. Avery Brundage," June 18, 1969, ABC, Box 40, Reel 23, ICOS; H. Modell, Chairman for Fair Play to Jim Thorpe, "Letter to Avery Brundage," November 30, 1951, ABC, Box 40, Reel 23, ICOS; H. T. Cooke, "Letter to Mr. Avery Brundage," February 18, 1952, ABC, Box 40, Reel 23, ICOS.

191. A. S. Mike Monroney, "Letter to Mr. Avery Brundage," July 10, 1968, ABC, Box 40, Reel 23, ICOS.

192. A. Brundage, "Letter to Senator A.S. Mike Monroney," July 15, 1968, ABC, Box 40, Reel 23, ICOS.

193. A. Brundage, "Letter to Mr. Grantland Rice," June 25, 1949, ABC, Box 40, Reel 23, ICOS

194. A. Brundage, "Letter to Mr. H. T. Cooke," March 31, 1952, ABC, Box 40, Reel 23, ICOS. Brundage did have supporters. Hugh Harlan, who characterized Thorpe as "a personable but somewhat naïve American Indian," wrote that even if Thorpe broke the rule by "a paper-thin margin," the IOC's "only course of action" was to take away the medals. "Rules are rules," he wrote. "They must be enforced and no criticism should be directed at officials who are obligated to enforce them." H. V. Harlan, *History of Olympic Games*, 94.

195. G. Eskanazi, "Jim Thorpe's Olympic Medals Are Restored," *New York Times*, October 14, 1982, A1; R. Lindsey, "Thorpe's Medals Returned," *New York Times*, January 19, 1983, B13; J. McCallum, "The Regilding of a Legend," *Sports Illustrated*, October 25, 1982.

196. Brundage, "Letter to Mr. Grantland Rice." At least once Brundage referred to Thorpe as "a half-breed." See: A. Brundage, "Letter to Mr. Paul C. Sischo," June 6, 1968, ABC, Box 40, Reel 23, ICOS.

197. A. Brundage, "Letter to Mr. Henry Modell," December 5, 1951, ABC, Box 40, Reel 23, ICOS.

198. A. Brundage, "Stop, Look and Listen," 1948, ABC, Box 245, Reel 142, 2 ICOS.

199. Müller, "Coubertin's Olympism," 48; Young, The Modern Olympics, 115.

2. Alternatives to the Olympics

1. Coubertin, *Olympism*, 595.
2. Ibid., 469.
3. Ibid., 595.
4. Guttmann, *The Olympics*, 38; Coubertin, *Olympism*, 472.
5. Bolanki, "The Olympic Flag," 42–3; IOC, "The Olympic Flag," 15–16.
6. Coubertin, *Olympism*, 482.
7. Ibid., 465.
8. Ibid., 476.
9. "Crowd at Olympics Boos British Anthem," *New York Times*, August 28, 1920, 13.
10. See for example, "U.S. Athletes Win World Title at Games in Antwerp," *New York Times*, August 24, 1920, 1.
11. "Olympians Return, Condemn Officials," *New York Times*, September 12, 1920, S21; Senn, *Power, Politics, and the Olympic Games*, 38.
12. International Olympic Committee, "Factsheet: Women in the Olympic Movement," May 2014.
13. Quoted in Y. P. Boulongne, "Pierre de Coubertin and Women's Sport," *Olympic Review*, vol. 26, no. 31, February–March 2000, 23.
14. Coubertin, *Olympism*, 494.
15. Ibid., 488.
16. "Paris Council Accords Weak Support to Olympics, Which May Go Elsewhere," *New York Times*, March 12, 1922, 29; "Olympics May Yet Go to Los Angeles," *New York Times*, May 11, 1922, 24; "Olympics Money Voted by France," *New York Times*, June 16, 1922, 23.
17. "Value of Olympics Doubted by French," *New York Times*, July 23, 1924, 13; Senn, *Power, Politics, and the Olympic Games*, 40–1.
18. "Won't Ask Germans to 1924 Olympics," *New York Times*, April 13, 1923, 14.
19. 'British Want Empire System Used in Parade at Olympics," *New York Times*, April 13, 1924, S3.
20. "Value of Olympics Doubted by French."
21. "Italian Foilsmen Quit the Olympics," *New York Times*, July 1, 1924, 17; Guttmann, *The Olympics*, 43–4; "Go-As-You-Please Basis at Olympics," *New York Times*, February 24, 1922, 17.
22. "Value of Olympics Doubted by French."
23. P. D. Coubertin, "Olympic Memoires XXI: The Eighth Olympiad (Paris 1924)," *Olympic Review*, no. 129, July 1978, 435, 436.

24. Coubertin, *Olympism*, 486; Senn, *Power, Politics, and the Olympic Games*, 39–40.

25. For example, see A. Guttmann, *The Games Must Go On*, 55.

26. To be sure, Baillet-Latour's willingness should not be overstated. After all, in 1931 he voted to eliminate all women's athletics from the Olympics. Nevertheless, under his IOC presidency, women made great strides toward Olympic inclusion. Wamsley and Schultz, "Rogues and Bedfellows," 116.

27. Krüger, "The Unfinished Symphony," 12–13; R. K. Barney and A. T. Bijkerk, "Carl Diem's Inspiration for the Torch Relay?: Jan Wils, Amsterdam 1928, and the Origin of the Olympics Flame," in G. P. Schaus and S. R. Wenn (eds.), *Onward to the Olympics: Historical Perspectives on the Olympic Games*, Waterloo, Ontario: Wilfrid Laurier University Press, 2007, 253–9.

28. "Loan by Amsterdam Guarantees Olympics," *New York Times*, May 24, 1925, S5; "Dutch May Raise Fund for Olympics," *New York Times*, April 12, 1925, S7; "Dutch Olympic Appropriation Seems Doomed," *New York Times*, March 26, 1925, 26; "Dutch House Refuses Funds for Olympics," *New York Times*, May 7, 1925, 14.

29. D. Miller, *The Official History of the Olympic Games and the IOC: Athens to London 1894 to 2012*, Edinburgh: Mainstream Publishing Company, 2012, 100, 106–7; Guttmann, *The Olympics*, 51. In 2001 the IAAF changed its name to the International Association of Athletics Federations.

30. "IOC General Session Minutes," IOC *General Session Minutes*, vol. I (1894–1919) Trans. W. Lyberg, Paris, June 15–23, 1914, 84.

31. Wamsley and Schultz, "Rogues and Bedfellows," 113–18; C. Adams, "Fighting for Acceptance: Sifrid Edstrom and Avery Brundage: Their Efforts to Shape and Control Women's Participation in the Olympic Games," *Sixth International Symposium for Olympic Research*, 2002, 143–8; M.H. Leigh and T.M. Bonin, "The Pioneering Role of Madame Alice Milliat and the FSFI in Establishing International Trade and Field Competition for Women," *Journal of Sport History*, vol. 4, no. 1, 1977, 72–83.

32. "Year of 1922 Ranks High in Sports World," *New York Times*, December 31, 1922, 25, emphasis added.

33. "Girls Go to Prague," *New York Times*, August 24, 1920, E4.

34. U. Simri, *Women at the Olympic Games*, Netanya, Israel: Wingate Monograph Series, 1979, 28–9.

35. Leigh and Bonin, "The Pioneering Role of Madame Alice Milliat and the FSFI in Establishing International Trade and Field Competition for Women," 79. Others assert there were six countries at

the inception of the FSFI (Britain, France, Czechoslovakia, Italy, Switzerland, and the United States). See: Daniels and Tedder, "A Proper Spectacle," 52.

36. S. Edström, "Letter to Mr. Avery Brundage," March 7, 1935, 2, ABC, Box 42, Reel 24, ICOS.

37. S. Edström, "Letter to Mr. Avery Brundage," January 3, 1935, ABC, Box 42, Reel 24, ICOS.

38. "Allow Women in Olympics," *New York Times*, August 7, 1926, 8; Wamsley and Schultz, "Rogues and Bedfellows' 113–18.

39. "IOC Executive Committee Minutes," *IOC Executive Committee Minutes*, Vol. 1 (1921–1948), Trans. W. Lyberg, Paris, March 7–8, 1926, 31.

40. "Rogers Would Bar Women in Olympics," *New York Times*, January 5, 1929, 24.

41. "Greeks Were Right, Brundage Believes," *New York Times*, December 25, 1932, S1.

42. A. Brundage, "Letter to Mr. E. J. H. Holt," November 14, 1949, 2 ABC, Box 27, Reel 16, ICOS.

43. A. Brundage, "Circular Letter to Members of the IOC," August 31, 1957, 3 ABC, Box 70, Reel 39, ICOS.

44. "IOC General Session Minutes," *IOC General Session Minutes*, Vol. III (1948–1955), Trans. W. Lyberg, Mexico City, April 17–18 and 20, 1953, 300.

45. A. Daley, "More Deadly Than the Male," *New York Times*, February 8, 1953, S2.

46. Coubertin, *Olympism*, 604.

47. J. Riordan, "The Worker Sport Movement," in J. Riordan and A. Krüger (eds.), *The International Politics of Sport in the Twentieth Century*, London and New York: E & FN SPON, 1999, 105–17.

48. Olimpíada Popular de Barcelona, "Letter to the A.A.U.," ABC, Box 238, Reel 139, ICOS.

49. J. Riordan, "Introduction," in A. Krüger and J. Riordan (eds.), *The Story of Worker Sport*, Champaign, Illinois: Human Kinetics, 1996, vii–x.

50. Riordan, "The Worker Sport Movement."

51. Krüger and Riordan, *The Story of Worker Sport*, 167–70.

52. R. F. Wheeler, "Organized Sport and Organized Labour: The Workers' Sport Movement," *Journal of Contemporary History*, vol. 13, no. 2, April 1978, 200; A. Krüger, "The German Way of Worker Sport," in Krüger and Riordan, *The Story of Worker Sport*, 17; Riordan, "The Worker Sport Movement," 110–11.

53. W. Murray, "The Worker Sport Movement in France," in Krüger

and Riordan, *The Story of Worker Sport*, 31.

54. Wheeler, "Organized Sport and Organized Labour," 201; Riordan, "The Worker Sport Movement," 111–12.

55. "$1,000,000 Stadium Ready in Vienna," *New York Times*, July 19, 1931, E4.

56. Wheeler, "Organized Sport and Organized Labour," 201. The RSI was banned from participating. They staged their own sport extravaganzas in Moscow (1928) and Berlin (1931).

57. X. Pujadas and C. Santacana, "The Popular Olympics Games, Barcelona 1936: Olympians and Anti-Fascists," *International Review for the Sociology of Sport*, vol. 27, no. 2, 1992, 139–48; G. Colomé and J. Sureda, "Sports and International Relations (1919–1939): The 1936 Popular Olympiad," Barcelona: Centre d'Estudis Olímpics UAB, 1994, 1–25.

58. Wheeler, "Organized Sport and Organized Labour," 202; Riordan, "The Worker Sport Movement," 113.

59. Wheeler, "Organized Sport and Organized Labour," 204–7.

60. Riordan, "Introduction," ix.

61. See: ABC, Box 238, Reel 139, ICOS.

62. "IOC Executive Committee Minutes," *IOC Executive Committee Minutes, Vol. 1* (1921–1948), Trans. W. Lyberg, Paris, November 3–6, 1925, 29.

63. Coubertin, *Olympism*, 516, 517.

64. A. Brundage, "Letter to Honorable Herbert H. Hoover," September 14, 1931, ABC, Box 234, Reel 136, ICOS.

65. "3-Day Attendance Passes 1928 Total," *New York Times*, August 3, 1932, 19.

66. A. Tomlinson, "Olympic Survivals: The Olympic Games as a Global Phenomenon," in L. Allison (ed.), *The Global Politics of Sport: The Role of Global Institutions in Sport*, London and New York: Routledge, 2005, 60.

67. "Xth Olympiad Los Angeles 1932: Official Report," Xth Olympiade Committee of the Games of Los Angeles, U.S.A. 1932, LTD., 1933, 30; R.K. Barney, "Resistance, Persistence, Providence: The 1932 Los Angeles Olympic Games in Perspective," *Research Quarterly for Exercise and Sport*, vol. 67, no. 2, 1996, 148–60.

68. Barney, "Resistance, Persistence, Providence"; A. J. Stump, "The Games That Almost Weren't," in Segrave and Chu, *The Olympic Games in Transition*, 191–9.

69. "Los Angeles Water Hangs on Bond Sale," *New York Times*, May 15, 1932, E6.

70. "Xth Olympiad Los Angeles 1932: Official Report," 30.

71. Ibid., 235.
72. Coubertin, *Olympism*, 517.
73. D. B. Welky, "Viking Girls, Mermaids, and Little Brown Men: U.S. Journalism and the 1932 Olympics," *Journal of Sport History*, vol. 24, no. 1, Spring 1997, 24–49; J. Paul "The Great Progression: A Content Analysis of the *Lake Placid News* and the *Los Angeles Times*' Treatment of the 1932 Olympics," in G. P. Schaus and S. R. Wenn (eds.) *Onward to the Olympics: Historical Perspectives on the Olympic Games*, Waterloo, Ontario: Wilfrid Laurier University Press, 2007, 261–71.
74. Coubertin, *Olympism*, 518.
75. "Xth Olympiad," *Time*, vol. 20, issue 7, August 15, 1932.
76. Stump, "The Games That Almost Weren't," 199.
77. A. J. Daley, "Beccali of Italy Wins 1,500 Meters at Olympic Games," *New York Times*, August 5, 1932, 1; "Xth Olympiad."
78. D. C. Large, "The Nazi Olympics: Berlin 1936," in H. J. Lenskyj and S. Wagg (eds.), *The Palgrave Handbook of Olympic Studies*, New York: Palgrave Macmillan, 61.
79. A. Hitler, *Mein Kampf*, New York: Reynal & Hitchcock, 1941, 616. Hitler also suggested, "Not a day should pass during which the young man is not trained physically for at least an hour in the morning and again in the evening." The Nazis, he added, were not "breeding a colony of peaceful aesthetes and physical degenerates."
80. Guttmann, *The Games Must Go On*, 65; R. D. Mandell, *The Nazi Olympics*, Urbana and Chicago: University of Illinois Press, 1987 [1971], 235.
81. Mandell, *The Nazi Olympics*, 93–4.
82. A. Brundage, "Olympic," in file "Notes on Art, Politics, Sports, 1968–1970," ABC, Box 246, Reel 143, ICOS.
83. A. J. Daley, "A.A.U. Boycotts 1936 Olympics Because of the Nazi Ban on Jews," *New York Times*, November 21, 1933, 1; A. J. Daley, "Vote on Olympics Widely Approved," *New York Times*, November 24, 1933, 26.
84. A. J. Daley, "U.S. Will Compete in 1936 Olympics," *New York Times*, September 27, 1934, 28.
85. "Columbia Boycott on Olympics Urged," *New York Times*, October 3, 1935, 10; "Boycott of Olympics Favored by Battle," *New York Times*, October 28, 1935, 34; "Catholic Boycott on Olympics Urged," *New York Times*, July 31, 1935, 3; "Ask Olympics Boycott: Methodist Youth Spread Plea for Non-Participation," *New York Times*, September 10, 1935, 10.
86. Guttmann, *The Olympics*, 60.

87. "Brundage Favors Berlin Olympics," *New York Times*, July 27, 1935, 2. At the 1936 Winter Olympics in Garmisch-Partenkirchen, Rudi Ball, a top Germany hockey player, was Jewish. His inclusion stirred controversy.

88. J. S. Edström, "Letter to Avery Brundage," August 11, 1935, 1, ABC, Box 42, Reel 24, ICOS.

89. A. Brundage, "Letter to J. Sigfrid Edström," August 29, 1935, 1, ABC, Box 42, Reel 24, ICOS.

90. Guttmann, *The Games Must Go On*, 72.

91. J. S. Edström, "Letter to Avery Brundage," September 12, 1935, 1–2, ABC, Box 42, Reel 24, ICOS.

92. J. S. Edström, "Letter to Avery Brundage," August 11, 1935, 1, ABC, Box 42, Reel 24, ICOS.

93. "Honor U.S. Olympic Heads," *New York Times*, February 1, 1936, 10.

94. Large, "The Nazi Olympics," 64–5.

95. Coubertin, *Olympism*, 520.

96. Barney, Wenn, and Martyn, *Selling the Five Rings*, 54–5.

97. J. O. Segrave and D. Foote, "'All Men Will Become Brothers': Beethoven's Ninth Symphony as Olympic Games Entertainment and Ideology," *Intersections and Intersectionalities in Olympic and Paralympic Studies*, London, Ontario: Western University, 2014, 24–9.

98. R. G. Reuth, *Goebbels*, Trans. K. Winston, New York: Harcourt Brace, 1993, 213.

99. D. Hart-Davis, *Hitler's Games: The 1936 Olympics*, New York: Harper & Row, 1986, 139.

100. Mandell, *The Nazi Olympics*, 141–2.

101. "Olympic Games," *Time*, vol. 28, issue 8, August 24, 1936.

102. Quotes in J. Schaap, *Triumph: The Untold Story of Jesse Owens and Hitler's Olympics*, New York: Houghton Mifflin, 2007, 214, 215.

103. "Stoller Declares He Will Quit Track," *New York Times*, August 10, 1936, 13; Schaap, *Triumph*, 224.

104. L. Riefenstahl, *A Memoir*, New York: Picador, 1992, 229.

105. Ibid., 195.

106. Ibid., 179, 201–2, 187, 171, 580.

107. Guttmann, *The Games Must Go On*, 91.

108. Schaap, *Triumph*, 205.

109. Large, "The Nazi Olympics: Berlin 1936," 65.

110. Guttmann, *The Olympics*, 68; D. C. Large, "The Games the Nazis Played," *New York Times*, August 8, 2011; Schaap, *Triumph*, 211. Guttmann asserts Goebbels wished to edit out

some of the affirmative imagery involving Owens but was overruled by Hitler. The images remained in the film. But the story that Hitler refused to shake Owens's hand is a myth. In reality, Hitler stopped congratulating medal winners well before Owens won gold. IOC president Baillet-Latour insisted Hitler shake the hands of all victors, and so looking ahead to when black athletes would surely win, Hitler stopped the practice.

111. "A.A.U. Suspends Owens: He Refused to Go on Tour," *New York Times*, August 17, 1936, 1; Schaap, *Triumph*, 233; "Owens to Wait Until He Returns Home Before Making Decision on Pro Offers," *New York Times*, August 18, 1936, 23.

112. Schaap, *Triumph*, 234; Ryan Whirty, "The 1946 Portland Rose-buds," *Portland Monthly*, June 3, 2013; Steve Almasy, "Bidding for Jesse Owens' 1936 Gold Medal Tops $200,000," CNN, December 3, 2013; Darren Rovell, "Jesse Owens Gold Goes for $1.47M," ESPN, December 8, 2013.

113. Coubertin, *Olympism*, 519, 520.

114. F. T. Birchall, "Olympics Leave Glow of Pride in the Reich," *New York Times*, August 16, 1936, E5. In another article, the *New York Times* reported, "The strongest impression that visitors will carry away is the sense of having experienced exceeding courtesy, extreme consideration and hospitality organized to the last degree." See: F. T. Birchall, "Visitors to Olympics Carrying Away Highly Favorable Impression of Reich," *New York Times*, August 16, 1936, S2.

115. "Brundage Extols Hitler's Regime," *New York Times*, October 5, 1936, 9.

116. A. Brundage, "Memos, Notes, etc. by Avery Brundage on Sports, Art, Politics, 1952–1958," ABC, Box 245, Reel 142, ICOS.

117. A. Brundage, "Speech in Munich," n.d., 1–2, ABC, Box 249, Reel 144, ICOS.

118. A. Brundage, "The Wondrous Flame of the Olympics," 1938, 3, ABC, Box 248, Reel 143, ICOS.

119. "The Official Report of the Organising Committee for the XIV Olympiad," London, 1951, 17.

120. J. Hampton, *The Austerity Olympics: When the Games Came to London in 1948*, London: Aurum Press, 2008, 34.

121. D. Carew, "The Case Against the Olympics," *New York Times*, March 10, 1946, SM10.

122. B. Henry, "After the Games of the XIVth Olympiad, London 1948," *Olympic Review*, no. 13, January 1949, 22, 23.

123. A. Daley, "Not Quite Misogyny," *New York Times*, December 28, 1948, 27.

124. Barney, Wenn, and Martyn, *Selling the Five Rings*, 56.

3. Cold War Games

1. Orwell, *Shooting an Elephant and Other Essays*, 152.

2. J. Longman, "Pursuing Games, Boston Jumps in With One Foot," *New York Times*, January 10, 2015, D1.

3. A. Brundage, "Untitled," in folder "Avery Brundage Book—Politics U.S.A.," ABC, Box 243, Reel 141, ICOS.

4. A. Ginsberg, *Howl and Other Poems*, San Francisco: City Lights Books, 1993 [1956], 42–3.

5. Guttmann, *The Olympics*, 97.

6. H. E. Salisbury, "Russians Hail Olympic 'Victory' But Fail to Substantiate Claim," *New York Times*, August 5, 1952, 23.

7. Barney, Wenn, and Martyn, *Selling the Five Rings*, 57.

8. C. R. Hill, "The Cold War and the Olympic Movement," *History Today*, January 1999, 19.

9. A. Danzig, "Brundage Is Chosen Over Briton as Head of International Olympic Committee," *New York Times*, July 17, 1952, 28.

10. "Brundage Pledges to Bar Politics as He Takes Olympic Leadership," *New York Times*, August 15, 1952, 20.

11. A. Brundage, "Memorandum," March 18, 1950, emphasis added, ABC, Box 10, Reel 6, ICOS.

12. R. Butterfield, "Avery Brundage Close Up," *Life*, June 14, 1948, 118.

13. Miller, *The Official History of the Olympic Games and the IOC*, 144.

14. Butterfield, "Avery Brundage Close Up," 123.

15. A. Brundage, "Sport and Amateurism," in folder "Avery Brundage Book—Politics U.S.A.," ABC, Box 243, Reel 141, ICOS.

16. R. W. Pound, *Inside the Olympics: A Behind-the-Scenes Look at the Politics, the Scandals, and the Glory of the Games*, Canada: Wiley, 2004, 234–5.

17. Barney, "The Olympic Games in Modern Times," 230.

18. A. Brundage, "Remarks at the Foreign Correspondents Club Japan," June 29, 1968, Tokyo, Japan, ABC, Box 246, Reel 143, ICOS.

19. A. Brundage, "Remarks by Avery Brundage: 64th Session International Olympic Committee," Rome, Italy, April 24, 1966, ABC, Box 81, Reel 45, ICOS.

20. A. Brundage, "Address at the 67th Solemn Opening Session, Mexico City, Mexico," October 7, 1968, 6, ABC, Box 246, Reel 143, ICOS.

21. A. Brundage, "The Wondrous Flame of the Olympics," 1938, 15, ABC, Box 248, Reel 143, ICOS.

22. Brundage, "The Wondrous Flame of the Olympics," 3.

23. A. Brundage, "Letter to Hon. Franklin D. Roosevelt," September 25, 1933, ABC, Box 234, Reel 136, ICOS.

24. M. H. McIntyre, "Letter to Avery Brundage," October 9, 1933, ABC, Box 234, Reel 136, ICOS.

25. O. Schantz, "The Presidency of Avery Brundage," in *The International Olympic Committee—One Hundred Years: The Ideas – The Presidents – The Achievements, Volume 2,* Lausanne: International Olympic Committee, 1995, 189.

26. A. Brundage, "Memorandum," in folder "Memos, Notes, etc. by Avery Brundage on Sports, Art, Politics, 1952–1958," ABC, Box 245, Reel 142, ICOS.

27. A. Brundage, "Preliminary Report of Committee on Physical Fitness," 1944, ABC, Box 5, Reel 4, ICOS.

28. Guttmann, *The Games Must Go On*, 231, 110–131.

29. A. Brundage, "Circular Letter to Members of the I.O.C.," August 30, 1957, 5, ABC, Box 70, Reel 39, ICOS.

30. A. Brundage, "Speech in Munich," n.d., 4, ABC, Box 249, Reel 144, ICOS.

31. A. Brundage, "Football Memorandum," in folder "Avery Brundage: Notes and Memorandum, undated," n.d., ABC, Box 250, Reel 144, ICOS.

32. A. Brundage, "Circular Letter to Members of the I.O.C.," August 30, 1957, 2, ABC, Box 70, Reel 39, ICOS.

33. A. Brundage, "Address at the 67th Solemn Opening Session, Mexico City, Mexico," October 7, 1968, 9, ABC, Box 246, Reel 143, ICOS.

34. A. Brundage, "Remarks by Avery Brundage: 64th Session International Olympic Committee," Rome, Italy, April 24, 1966, ABC, Box 81, Reel 45, ICOS.

35. A. Brundage, "Circular Letter to I.O.C. Member," April 12, 1954, 8, ABC, Box 70, Reel 39, ICOS.

36. A. Brundage, "Remarks by Avery Brundage: 64th Session International Olympic Committee," Rome, Italy, April 24, 1966, 3, ABC, Box 81, Reel 45, ICOS.

37. A. Brundage, "Stop, Look and Listen," 1948, ABC, Box 245, Reel 142, 3, ICOS, emphasis added.
38. A. Brundage, "The Wondrous Flame of the Olympics," 1938, 15, ABC, Box 248, Reel 143, ICOS.
39. Brundage went on to argue, "These same qualities that led to the conquering of the wilderness, the founding of the Great Republic, and the development of science and invention, business and industry to the high levels of modern America, are responsible for the supremacy of American athletes [sic], who realize that their success depends on their own efforts." See: Brundage, "The Wondrous Flame of the Olympics," 16.
40. A. Brundage, "Address at the 67th Solemn Opening Session, Mexico City, Mexico," October 7, 1968, 7, ABC, Box 246, Reel 143, ICOS.
41. A. Brundage, "Circular Letter to Members of the I.O.C.," January 30, 1954, 3, ABC, Box 70, Reel 39, ICOS.
42. D. Maraniss, *Rome 1960: The Olympics that Changed the World*, New York: Simon and Schuster, 2008, 54.
43. A. Brundage, "Untitled," in folder "Avery Brundage Book— Politics U.S.A.," ABC, Box 243, Reel 141, ICOS, emphasis added.
44. A. Brundage, "Politics," in file "Notes on Art, Politics, Sports, 1968–1970," ABC, Box 246, Reel 143, ICOS, emphasis added.
45. Brundage, "Untitled."
46. A. Brundage, "Politics," in folder "Memos, Notes, etc. by Avery Brundage on Sports, Art, Politics, 1952–1958," ABC, Box 245, Reel 142, ICOS.
47. A. Brundage, "Politics," in file "Notes on Art, Politics, Sports, 1968–1970," ABC, Box 246, Reel 143, ICOS.
48. A. Brundage, "Politics," in folder "Memos, Notes, etc. by Avery Brundage on Sports, Art, Politics, 1952–1958," ABC, Box 245, Reel 142, ICOS.
49. A. Brundage, "The United States," in folder "Memos, Notes, etc. by Avery Brundage on Sports, Art, Politics, 1952–1958," February 11, 1955, ABC, Box 245, Reel 142, ICOS.
50. A. Brundage, "Politics," in folder "Memos, Notes, etc. by Avery Brundage on Sports, Art, Politics, 1952–1958," ABC, Box 245, Reel 142, ICOS.
51. Butterfield, "Avery Brundage Close Up," 118.
52. A. Brundage, "Memorandum," in folder "Avery Brundage Book— Politics U.S.A.," ABC, Box 243, Reel 141, ICOS.
53. A. Brundage, "Politics," in folder "Memos, Notes, etc. by Avery Brundage on Sports, Art, Politics, 1952–1958," ABC, Box 245, Reel 142, ICOS.

54. A. Brundage, "Politics," in file "Notes on Art, Politics, Sports, 1968–1970," ABC, Box 246, Reel 143, ICOS.
55. A. Brundage, "Memorandum," in folder "Memos, Notes, etc. by Avery Brundage on Sports, Art, Politics, 1952–1958," ABC, Box 245, Reel 142, ICOS.
56. A. Brundage, "Circular Letter to Members of the I.O.C.," August 30, 1957, 2, ABC, Box 70, Reel 39, ICOS.
57. A. Brundage, "Letter to Mr. Jim Sankovitz," May 23, 1955, ABC, Box 237, Reel 139, ICOS.
58. A. Brundage, "Letter to Mr. Harold Lord Varney," May 12, 1937, ABC, Box 41, Reel 24, ICOS; H. L. Varney, "Letter to Mr. Avery Brundage," May 21, 1937, ABC, Box 41, Reel 24, ICOS; A. Brundage, "Letter to Mr. Frederick Hanson," May 14, 1937, ABC, Box 41, Reel 24, ICOS; O. Meyer, "Letter to Avery Brundage," May 19, 1937, ABC, Box 41, Reel 24, ICOS.
59. S. Hall, "Life and Times of the First New Left," *New Left Review*, vol. 61, January–February 2010, 177.
60. "Lebanon Becomes Seventh Nation to Withdraw from Games at Melbourne," *New York Times*, November 11, 1956, 23.
61. "2 Nations Protest Actions of Russia," *New York Times*, November 7, 1956, 43.
62. "Nations that Withdrew Urged to Return to Olympic Games," *New York Times*, November 10, 1956, 22.
63. "A Sweet and Bloody Victory for Hungary," *Sports Illustrated*, December 17, 1956; R. E. Rinehart, "'Fists Flew and Blood Flowed': Symbolic Resistance and International Response in Hungarian Water Polo at the Melbourne Olympics, 1956," *Journal of Sports History*, vol. 23, no. 2, 1996, 120–39.
64. Senn, *Power, Politics, and the Olympic Games*, 108; Guttmann, *The Games Must Go On*, 163–4.
65. Xu Guoqi, *Olympic Dreams: China and Sports, 1895–2008*, Cambridge, MA, and London: Harvard University Press, 2008, 77–83.
66. A. Brundage, "Letter to Alfred R. Sanchez," October 1, 1952, ABC, Box 120, Reel 66, ICOS.
67. Guoqi, *Olympic Dreams*, 86.
68. Ibid., 89.
69. V. R. Edman, "Letter to Avery Brundage," June 9, 1959, ABC, Box 121, Reel 67, ICOS; W. Hartsfield, "Letter to Avery Brundage," June 8, 1959, ABC, Box 121, Reel 67, ICOS; E. S. Bibb, "Letter to Avery Brundage," June 8, 1959, ABC, Box 121, Reel 67, ICOS; J. Crane, "Letter to Avery Brundage," June 9, 1959, ABC, Box 121, Reel 67, ICOS.

70. "President Sees Politics in Olympics' China Step," *New York Times*, June 18, 1959, 14.

71. W. J. Jorden, "U.S. Scores Ban on Taiwan Team," *New York Times*, June 3, 1959, 9. Assistant Secretary of State J. Graham Parsons followed up with a private letter to Brundage: "I believe that an attempt to require athletes from the Republic of China to participate under a name which is unacceptable to them because it is incorrect cannot but be regarded as a political action." See: J. G. Parsons, "Letter to Avery Brundage," July 21, 1960, ABC, Box 121, Reel 67, ICOS.

72. "China and the Olympics," *New York Times*, May 30, 1959, 16. ABC, Box 121, Reel 67, ICOS.

73. O. Mayer, "Letter to John V. Grombach," June 17, 1959, ABC, Box 121, Reel 67, ICOS, underline and all-caps in original.

74. T. C. Hennings, "Letter to Avery Brundage," June 30, 1960, ABC, Box 120, Reel 66, ICOS.

75. R. Daley, "The Parade: History, Tragedy, and Politics," *New York Times*, August 26, 1960, 16; Guoqi, *Olympic Dreams*, 93–4.

76. Guoqi, *Olympic Dreams*, 164–96.

77. Quoted in E. Pauker, "Ganefo I: Sports and Politics in Djakarta," *Asian Survey*, vol. 5, no. 4, April 1965, 173. Also see "Jakarta Prepares for 'Emerging Nations' Games," *New York Times*, October 6, 1963, 16.

78. Quoted in Pauker, "Ganefo I," 174.

79. R. Lutan and F. Hong, "The Politicization of Sport: GANEFO—A Case Study," *Sport in Society: Cultures, Commerce, Media, Politics*, vol. 8, no. 3, 2005, 425–439; "Jakarta Prepares for 'Emerging Nations' Games," 16; Pauker, "Ganefo I."

80. "Jakarta Prepares for 'Emerging Nations' Games," 16.

81. T. P. Ross, "Sukarno's Lavish Ganefo Was Mostly Snafu," *Sports Illustrated*, December 2, 1963.

82. Pauker, "Ganefo I," 181.

83. Ibid., 179.

84. Ibid., 185.

85. However, an Asian GANEFO was staged in Cambodia in 1966, largely funded by China. Lutan and Hong, "The Politicization of Sport."

86. Guttmann, *The Olympics*, 103.

87. A. Brundage, "Letter to Mr. Hugh Weir," March 17, 1964, ABC, Box 64, Reel 38, ICOS.

88. "Olympics Rebuff South Africans," *New York Times*, January 28, 1964, 36.

89. "Boycotting South Africa," *Time*, vol. 91, March 8, 1968, 88.

90. "Newly Discovered 1964 MLK Speech on Civil Rights, Segregation and Apartheid South Africa," *Democracy Now!*, January 19, 2015.

91. M. Keech, "The Ties that Bind: South Africa and Sports Diplomacy 1958–1963," *The Sports Historian* vol. 91, no. 1, May 2001, 71–93; E. Ferguson, "South Africa and the Olympics: An Interview with Dennis Brutus," *Ufahamu: A Journal of African Studies* vol. 13, no. 2–3, 1984, 40–59.

92. Ferguson, "South Africa and the Olympics," 47.

93. G. Onesti, "Circular Letter to the IOC," March 29, 1968, 3, James Worrall Collection (hereafter JWC), Box 1, Folder 1b, ICOS.

94. D. Booth, *The Race Game: Sport and Politics in South Africa*, London and Portland, Oregon: Frank Cass Publishers, 1998, 61.

95. R. Nixon, "Apartheid on the Run: The South African Sports Boycott," *Transitions*, vol. 58, 1992, 77.

96. Booth, *The Race Game*, 78–9.

97. A. Brundage, "Letter to All IOC Members, All NOC Members, All International Federations," March 18, 1968, ABC, Box 70, Reel 40, 2, ICOS.

98. "Statement by Dennis Brutus," March 21, 1967, http://kora. matrix.msu.edu/files/50/304/32-130-FEE-84-GMH%20Brutus 67press.pdf

99. S. Ramsany, "Letter to the President of Organising Committee for the 21st Olympiad," May 31, 1976, JWC, Box 21, Folder 39, ICOS.

100. D. Brutus, "Letter to Mr. Duncan McSwain," January 10, 1970, JWC, Box D, Folder 87, ICOS.

101. L. Killanin, "Letter to Denis McIldowie," April 21, 1976, JWC, Box 21, Folder 39, ICOS.

102. B. Kidd, "Letter to Mr. Harry Kerrison," March 22, 1974, JWC, Box 17, Folder 5, ICOS.

103. Guttmann, *The Games Must Go On*, 239.

104. A. Brundage, "Cable to All Members of the IOC," n.d., ABC, Box 70, Reel 40, ICOS.

105. By the 1980s, inside the IOC, members including Richard Pound were pressing for the Committee to take a stronger stand against apartheid. As he wrote later in his autobiography, "I thought they were missing an opportunity to show that sport could find solutions to a difficult problem that had, to date, baffled the political leaders." Pound, *Inside the Olympics*, 123.

106. J. Carlos and D. Zirin, *The John Carlos Story: The Sports*

Moment that Changed the World, Chicago: Haymarket Books, 2011, 110.

107. H. Edwards, *The Revolt of the Black Athlete*, New York: The Free Press, 1969, 104.

108. J. Boykoff, "With Heads and Hands Held High: An Interview with John Carlos," *Street Roots*, November 23, 2012, 1.

109. A. Brundage, "Address at the 67th Solemn Opening Session, Mexico City, Mexico," October 7, 1968, 5–6, ABC, Box 246, Reel 143, ICOS.

110. Edwards, *The Revolt of the Black Athlete*, 58–9.

111. T. Smith with D. Steele, *Silent Gesture: The Autobiography of Tommie Smith*, Philadelphia: Temple University Press, 2007, 161.

112. H. Edwards, "The Olympic Project for Human Rights: An Assessment Ten Years Later," *The Black Scholar*, March–April 1979, 2.

113. "65 Athletes Support Boycott of Olympics on S. Africa Issue," *New York Times*, April 12, 1968, 28.

114. L. Koppett, "Robinson Urges So. Africa Ban," *New York Times*, February 9, 1968, 58.

115. V. X. Flaherty, "Letter to Avery Brundage," July 3, 1968, ABC, Box 179, Reel 103, ICOS.

116. A. Brundage, "Letter to Mr. Vincent X. Flaherty," July 14, 1968, ABC, Box 179, Reel 103, ICOS.

117. B. Carrington, *Race, Sport, and Politics: The Sporting Black Diaspora*, London: Sage, 2010, 4.

118. A. Daley, "The Incident," *New York Times*, October 20, 1968, S2.

119. B. Musburger, "Bizarre Protest by Smith, Carlos Tarnishes Medals," *Chicago American*, October 17, 1968, 43.

120. A. Daley, "The Incident."

121. "Statement of the US Olympic Committee," October 17, 1968, ABC, Box 179, Reel 103, ICOS.

122. A. Daley, "The Incident."

123. D. E. Jackson, "Letter to Avery Brundage," November 1968, ABC, Box 179, Reel 103, ICOS.

124. R. N. Kline, "Letter to Mr. Avery Brundage," October 19, 1968, ABC, Box 179, Reel 103, ICOS.

125. M. A. Rutter, "Letter to Olympic Committee," October 18, 1968, ABC, Box 179, Reel 103, ICOS.

126. D. A. Fox and E. M. Fox, "Letter to Mr. Avery Brundage," October 20, 1968, ABC, Box 179, Reel 103, ICOS.

127. Mrs. G. A. Johnson, "Letter to the International Olympic Committee," October 19, 1968, ABC, Box 179, Reel 103, ICOS.

128. R. Stevens, "Letter to the International Olympic Committee," October 18, 1968, ABC, Box 179, Reel 103, ICOS.

129. Athletex Welfare Association of Nigeria, "Telegram to the International Olympic Committee," October 20, 1968, ABC, Box 179, Reel 103, ICOS; Reverend J. L. Jackson, "Telegram to Tommy Smith, c/o the International Olympic Committee," October 23, 1968, ABC, Box 179, Reel 103, ICOS.

130. E. Howl, "Letter to Avery Brundage," October 21, 1968, ABC, Box 179, Reel 103, ICOS.

131. A. Brundage, "Letter to Mr. Farbes Norris," November 25, 1968, ABC, Box 179, Reel 103, ICOS.

132. A. Brundage, "Letter to Mrs. Wayne Fawks," November 15, 1968, ABC, Box 179, Reel 103, ICOS.

133. A. Brundage, "Letter to Joseph H. Pratt," November 13, 1968, ABC, Box 179, Reel 103, ICOS.

134. A. Brundage, "Letter to Mr. Thomas J. Dunne," November 13, 1968, ABC, Box 179, Reel 103, ICOS.

135. A. Brundage, "Letter to Arq. Pedro Ramirez Vasquez," August 20, 1969, ABC, Box 178, Reel 102, ICOS.

136. J. Clark, "Letter to Mr. Pedro Ramirez Vasquez," August 19, 1969, ABC, Box 178, Reel 102, ICOS.

137. P. R. Vasquez, "Letter to Mr. Avery Brundage," September 29, 1969, ABC, Box 178, Reel 102, ICOS.

138. Guttmann, *The Games Must Go On*, 245.

139. ESPN Films and Maggie Vision Productions, "Return to Mexico City," 2009.

140. D. Hartmann, *Race, Culture, and the Revolt of the Black Athlete: The 1968 Olympic Protests and Their Aftermath*, Chicago and London: University of Chicago Press, 2003, 166.

141. Thomas J. Hamilton, "Czechoslovak Team Going to Olympics as Difficulties of Occupation Ease," *New York Times*, September 15, 1968, S9.

142. Matt Rendell, "The Perfect Ten," *Observer*, July 4, 2014; Tim Weiner, "When the Games Became Political," *New York Times*, July 24, 2004, D1; Steve Cady, "A Citizen of Prague Speaks Her Mind," *New York Times*, February 1, 1969, 36.

143. A. Brundage, "Text of IOC President Brundage's Address of Memorial Services at Olympic Stadium on September 6, 1972," September 6, 1972, ABC, Box 249, Reel 144, ICOS.

144. "Munich, 1972 ..." *New York Times*, September 7, 1972, 42.

145. A. Brundage, "Press Statement," September 7, 1972, ABC, Box 249, Reel 144, ICOS.

146. K. Moore, "The Eye of the Storm," *Sports Illustrated*, August 12, 1991, emphasis in original.

147. N. Amdur, "Matthews Wins in 400," *New York Times*, September 8, 1972, 21.

148. "Matthews Takes a Stand and It Brings Him Trouble," *New York Times*, September 8, 1972, 21.

149. N. Amdur, "Matthews and Collett Banned from Olympics," *New York Times*, September 9, 1972, 17.

150. "IOC Executive Committee Minutes," *IOC Executive Committee Minutes, Vol. III* (1969–1981), Trans. W. Lyberg, Munich, August 18–22, September 1, 1972, 87.

151. Hartmann, *Race, Culture, and the Revolt of the Black Athlete*, 160–1, 241–2.

152. V. Matthews, "I'm an Athlete, Not a Politician," *New York Times*, September 9, 1972, 18.

153. Barney, Wenn, and Martyn, *Selling the Five Rings*, 106.

154. "IOC Executive Committee Minutes," *IOC Executive Committee Minutes, Vol. III* (1969–1981), Trans. W. Lyberg, Lausanne, May 27–30, 1972, 71.

155. R. Smith, "The Noblest Badger of Them All," *New York Times*, May 12, 1975, 48.

4. Commercialization of the Olympics

1. "Denver Triumph a 7-Year Effort," *New York Times*, May 13, 1970, 53.

2. "Colorado Drops Winter Games Bid," *New York Times*, November 9, 1972, 61.

3. "Montreal Olympics 1976: 'Self-financing?'" CBC, January 29, 1973.

4. R. Trumbull, "High Costs of Games Studied," *New York Times*, August 28, 1976, 35.

5. W. J. McNichols, Jr., "Letter to Avery Brundage," April 10, 1970, ABC, Box 191, Reel 110, ICOS.

6. Denver Committee of Candidature, n.d., ABC, Box 191, Reel 110, ICOS.

7. For letters of support, see ABC, Box 191, Reel 110, ICOS.

8. B. D. Ayres, Jr., "Invitation to Go Elsewhere," *New York Times*, November 12, 1972, E5.

9. J. Kirshenbaum, "Voting to Snuff the Torch," *Sports Illustrated*, November 20, 1972.

10. A. Nielson, "Letter to Mr. Avery Brundage," November 22, 1971, ABC, Box 192, Reel 110, ICOS; O. A. Payton, "Letter to Mr. Avery Brundage," December 10, 1971, ABC, Box 192, Reel 110, ICOS.

11. S. W. Brown, Jr., "Letter to Mr. Avery Brundage," January 18, 1972, ABC, Box 192, Reel 110, ICOS; R. D. Lewis, "Letter to Mr. Avery Brundage," December 9, 1971, ABC, Box 192, Reel 110, ICOS.

12. R. Worl, "Letter to Avery Brundage," May 5, 1972, ABC, Box 191, Reel 110, ICOS.

13. R. Griffin, "Letter to Comité International Olympique," January 28, 1972, ABC, Box 192, Reel 110, ICOS.

14. R. D. Lamm, "Letter to Avery Brundage," November 22, 1971, ABC, Box 192, Reel 110, ICOS.

15. R. D. Lamm, "Letter to James Worrall," April 4, 1972, JWC, Box 15, Folder 1, ICOS.

16. A. Brundage, "Untitled," May 8, 1972, ABC, Box 192, Reel 111, ICOS.

17. L. Killanin, "Letter to Clifford Buck," June 22, 1972, ABC, Box 191, Reel 110, ICOS.

18. "Minutes of the 71st Session of the International Olympic Committee," September 15–17, 1971, Luxemburg, 31–32, JWC, Box 2, ICOS.

19. R. J. Pringle, "Letter to Avery Brundage," January 4, 1972, ABC, Box 191, Reel 110, ICOS.

20. "Minutes of the 72nd Session of the International Olympic Committee," January 31–February 1, 1972, Sapporo, 23, JWC, Box 2, ICOS.

21. "IOC Executive Committee Minutes," *IOC Executive Committee Minutes, Vol. III* (1969–1981), Trans. W. Lyberg, May 27–30, 1972, Lausanne, 73.

22. "IOC Executive Committee Minutes," *IOC Executive Committee Minutes, Vol. III* (1969–1981), Trans. W. Lyberg, August 18–22, September 1, 5–8, 10–11, 1972, Munich, 85.

23. B. D. Ayres, Jr., " 'Ski-Town' Split on Winter Olympics," *New York Times*, November 6, 1972, 43.

24. Kirshenbaum, "Voting to Snuff the Torch."

25. Ibid.; "Colorado Drops Winter Games Bid," *New York Times*, November 9, 1972, 61.

26. C. M. Buck, "Cablegram Message to Lord Killanin," November 13, 1972, ABC, Box 191, Reel 110, ICOS.

27. Kirshenbaum, "Voting to Snuff the Torch."

28. J. Worrall, "Message of Munich," November 2, 1972, 10, JWC, Box 18, Folder 6, ICOS.

29. Quoted in Guttmann, *The Olympics*, 143.

30. R. Trumbull, "Olympic Advertising Is Planned," *New York Times*, October 15, 1974, 59.

31. J. Ludwig, *Five Ring Circus: The Montreal Olympics*, New York and Toronto: Doubleday, 1976, 35, emphasis added.

32. "Drapeau Offers Olympic Cost View," *New York Times*, January 23, 1975, 44; B. Kidd, "The Culture Wars of the Montreal Olympics," *International Review for Sociology of Sport*, vol. 27, no. 2, 1992, 151–61.

33. S. Cady, "High Cost of Staging Olympics Played Down Here by Drapeau," *New York Times*, September 27, 1975, 23.

34. Trumbull, "High Costs of Games Studied," 35; "Quebec's Big Owe Stadium Debt Is Over," CBC News, December 19, 2006.

35. E. Pilkington, "Childbirth: Transgender Man Has His Baby, Naturally," *Guardian*, July 5, 2008. According to Beatie's web site, he was "born female" and "transitioned to a male in his twenties" and kept his original reproductive organs.

36. J. Worrall, "Letter to Mr. Harold M. Wright," December 27, 1972, JWC, Box 18, Folder 7, ICOS.

37. J. Worrall, "Letter to His Excellency Roger Rousseau," December 25, 1972, JWC, Box 18, Folder 7, ICOS. In another missive, this one to Monique Berlioux of the IOC and dedicated entirely to the role of media, Worrall recommended she read the *Globe and Mail* and the *Star* but that "the Toronto SUN is a bit of a tabloid and it is quite anti-Olympics. You can subscribe to it if you wish, but I will send Lord Killanin any clippings which I think are of any significance." See: J. Worrall, "Letter to Mme Monique Berlioux," January 3, 1973, JWC, Box 18, Folder 7, ICOS.

38. J. Worrall, "Letter to John A. Fraser," December 28, 1972, JWC, Box 18, Folder 7, ICOS.

39. R. W. Pound, "Letter to Board of Directors, Comité Organizateur des Jeux Olympiques," January 15, 1975, JWC, Box 19, folder 12, ICOS.

40. G. Wright "The Political Economy of the Montreal Olympic Games," *Journal of Sport and Social Issues*, vol. 2, 1978, 17.

41. Trumbull, "Olympic Advertising Is Planned," 59; Senn, *Power, Politics, and the Olympic Games*, 164.

42. Kidd, "The Culture Wars of the Montreal Olympics," 158.

43. S. Burnton, "50 Stunning Olympic Moments," *Guardian*, December 14, 2011.

44. "IOC Head Bach Returns to Montreal, Site of 1976 Olympic Gold," Associated Press, July 9, 2015.

45. J. Nelson and B. Nelson, "The Jenners," *Track and Field News*, October 1975, 6–7.

46. F. Litsky, "Jenner Triumphs in Decathlon, Breaks World Mark," *New York Times*, July 31, 1976, L15.

47. B. Bissinger, "He Says Goodbye, She Says Hello," *Vanity Fair*, July 2015, 50–69, 105–6.

48. Guoqi, *Olympic Dreams*, 181.

49. S. Cady, "Egypt, Morocco Join Olympic Boycott," *New York Times*, July 21, 1976, 25.

50. "Africa and the XXIst Olympiad," *Olympic Review*, no. 109–10, November–December 1976, 584–5.

51. S. Cady, "Olympic Games Lose 17 Nations," *New York Times*, July 20, 1976, 1.

52. Guttmann, *The Olympics*, 150; N. Sarantakes, *Dropping the Torch: Jimmy Carter, The Olympic Boycott, and the Cold War*, New York: Cambridge University Press, 2011, 116–17.

53. J. Carter, *Keeping the Faith: Memoirs of a President*, New York: Bantam Books, 1982, 489.

54. Guttmann, *The Olympics*, 149–53; L. Killanin, *My Olympic Years*, London: Secker & Warburg, 1983, 192.

55. Personal interview via email, February 17, 2015.

56. W. O. Johnson, "A Contract with the Kremlin," *Sports Illustrated*, February 21, 1977, 14–19; Sarantakes, *Dropping the Torch*, 169.

57. "Video Rights Stir Olympic Dispute," *New York Times*, December 8, 1955, 53.

58. "Fascist Symbols Go for Rome Olympics," *New York Times*, August 9, 1960, 2.

59. S. R. Wenn, "An Olympian Squabble: The Distribution of Olympic Television Revenue, 1960–1966," *Olympika: The International Journal of Olympic Studies*, vol. 3, 1994, 47.

60. "The Games of the XVIII Olympiad, Tokyo 1964: The Official Report of the Organizing Committee," Tokyo, 1964, 66; Wenn, "An Olympian Squabble," 47.

61. Barney, Wenn, and Martyn, *Selling the Five Rings*, 101.

62. R. Reagan, "Letter to Mr. Avery Brundage," August 25, 1969, ABC, Box 194, Reel 112, ICOS.

63. E. G. Brown, "Letter to Mr. Avery Brundage," December 29, 1966, ABC, Box 194, Reel 112, ICOS.

64. R. Lindsey, "'84 Olympics Facing Financing Struggle," *New York Times*, August 19, 1979, 18; "1984 Olympics to Rely on Private Enterprise," *New York Times*, December 6, 1981, 31; "Los Angeles Appears Ready for Withdrawal of 1984 Olympics Bid," *New York Times*, July 19, 1978, 19.

65. N. Amdur, "Los Angeles Assured of Games," *New York Times*, February 11, 1979, S1.

66. P. Ueberroth, with R. Levin and A. Quinn, *Made in America: His Own Story*, New York: William Morrow, 1985, 9.

67. Ibid., 28, 60–1.

68. Ibid., 60. Barney, Wenn, and Martyn note the official price tag of $1.3 billion, as reported by Moscow officials as well as the $9 billion high-end estimate. See *Selling the Five Rings*, 148.

69. Senn, *Power, Politics, and the Olympics Games*, 191; R. Gruneau and H. Cantelon, "Capitalism, Commercialism, and the Olympics," in Segrave and Chu, *The Olympic Games in Transition*, 356; Ueberroth et al., *Made in America*, 121–2; R. Kennedy, "Miser with the Midas Touch," *Sports Illustrated*, November 22, 1982.

70. K. Reich, *Making It Happen: Peter Ueberroth and the 1984 Olympics*, Santa Barbara, CA: Capra Press, 1986, 12.

71. A. Zimbalist, *Circus Maximus: The Economic Gamble Behind Hosting the Olympics and the World Cup*, Washington, DC: The Brookings Institution, 2015, 18; Lindsey, "'84 Olympics Facing Financing Struggle," 18; J. Horne and G. Whannel, *Understanding the Olympics*, London and New York: Routledge, 2012, 7.

72. Los Angeles Olympic Organizing Committee, *Official Report of the Games of the XXIIIrd Olympiad Los Angeles, 1984*, Volume 1, 1985, 26.

73. R. B. Perelman, *Olympic Retrospective: The Games of Los Angeles*, Los Angeles: Los Angeles Olympic Organizing Committee, 1985, 119.

74. A. Brundage, "Stop, Look and Listen," 1948, ABC, Box 245, Reel 142, 1, 3, ICOS.

75. A. Tomlinson, "The Disneyfication of the Olympics: Theme Parks and Freak-Shows of the Body," in J. Bale and M. K. Christensen (eds.), *Post-Olympism?: Questioning Sport in the Twenty-first Century*, Oxford: Berg Publishers, 2004, 148.

76. Hill, *Olympic Politics*, 80.

77. Perelman, *Olympic Retrospective*, 94–107.

78. Ibid., 107.

79. Quoted in Barney, Wenn, and Martyn, *Selling the Five Rings*, 199.

80. Reich, *Making It Happen*, 246.

81. V. Simson and A. Jennings, *Lord of the Rings: Power, Money and Drugs in the Modern Olympics*, London: Simon & Schuster, 1992, 59.

82. Pound, *Inside the Olympics*, 140.

83. A. Jennings, *The New Lord of the Rings: Olympic Corruption and How to Buy Gold Medals*, London: Pocket Books, 1996, 12.

84. Seoul Olympic Organizing Committee, "Official Report: Games of the XXIVth Olympiad Seoul 1988," Volume 1, September 30, 1989, 222.

85. S. M'Bodj, "ISL Marketing AG," *Olympic Review*, vol. 25, no. 2, April–May 1995, 28.

86. Chappelet and Kübler-Mabbott, *The International Olympic Committee and the Olympic System*, 38.

87. V. Kortekaas, "Olympic Sponsors Seek Podium for Brands," *Financial Times*, September 3, 2011.

88. London 2012, "Partners," london2012.com.

89. International Olympic Committee, "Olympic Marketing Fact File," 2014 edition, 13.

90. K. Grohmann, "Olympics-IOC Extends Sponsor Deal with Atos to 2020," Reuters, February 8, 2014.

91. M. Bisson, "Toyota Olympic Sponsorship 'Game Changing'," *Around the Rings*, March 13, 2015.

92. Barney, Wenn, and Martyn, *Selling the Five Rings*, 302.

93. Ibid., 163. This put the IOC uncomfortably at the mercy and whim of the television companies. Acknowledging as well the LA organizing committee's power stemming from its position as the only city bidding to host the Games in 1984, IOC leaders knew they needed to seize back more control.

94. Horne and Whannel, *Understanding the Olympics*, 61.

95. Miller, *The Official History of the Olympic Games and the IOC*, 260.

96. H. Araton, "Barkley Putting Some Spin on the Ball Off the Court," *New York Times*, July 29, 1992, B14; D. DuPree, "Taking a Stand—In Reebok," *USA Today*, August 10, 1992, 6E.

97. F. Keating, "Barca the Best of the Global Fandangos," *Guardian*, August 10, 1992, 17.

98. G. Vecsey, "Heartfelt Adeu, Adeu: Barcelona Won Gold," *New York Times*, August 10, 1992, C4.

99. Zimbalist, *Circus Maximus*, 72–3.

100. F. Brunet, "Analysis of the Economic Impact of the Olympics Games," in E. F. Peña, B. Cerezuela, M. G. Benosa, C. Kennett, and M. de Moragas Spà (eds.), *An Olympic Mosaic: Multidisciplinary Research and Dissemination of Olympic Studies*, Barcelona: Centre d'Estudis Olímpics, Universitat Autònoma de Barcelona, 2009, 223; F. Brunet, *Economy of the 1992 Barcelona Olympic Games*, Centre d'Estudis Olímpics, Universitat Autónoma de Barcelona, in cooperation with the IOC, 1993, 51, 61. Comparatively, the Barcelona Holding Olímpic S.A. (HOLSA), made the following expenditure calculations: 33.8

percent of total Olympic activities were financed by private sector investment and 66.2 percent of total Olympic activities were financed by public sector investment. See: Barcelona Holding Olímpic S.A. (HOLSA), "Los Juegos Olímpicos Como Generadores de Inversión (1986–1992)," Barcelona, June 1992, 7; Andrew Zimbalist cites figures indicating that 60 percent ($6.9 billion) of funds came from private sources and 40 percent came from private sources. See *Circus Maximus*, 73.

101. Brunet, "Analysis of the Economic Impact of the Olympics Games," 220–3; F. Brunet, "The Economic Impact of the Barcelona Olympic Games, 1986–2004," Barcelona: Centre d'Estudis Olímpics UAB, 2005.

102. Coubertin, *Olympism*, 611.

103. M. de Moragas Spà, "The Cultural Olympiad of Barcelona '92: Lights and Shadows, Lessons for the Future," in E. F. Peña et al., *An Olympic Mosaic*, 103–14; "Official Report of the XXV Olympiad, Barcelona 1992," Vol. 2, 345–65.

104. Brunet, "Analysis of the Economic Impact of the Olympics Games," 222.

105. Zimbalist, *Circus Maximus*, 73.

106. Consejo Rector de la Candidatura de Barcelona a los Juegos Olímpicos de 1992, *Solicitud de Candidatura al Comité Olímpico Internacional para la Celebración en Barcelona de los Juegos de la XXV Olímpiada*, n.d., 93.

107. C. Kennett and M. de Moragas Spà, "Barcelona 1992: Evaluating the Olympic Legacy," in A. Tomlinson and C. Young (eds.), *National Identity and Global Sports Events: Culture, Politics, and Spectacle in the Olympics and Football World Cup*, Albany, NY: State University of New York Press, 2006, 180.

108. Centre on Housing Rights and Evictions (COHRE), "Barcelona 1992: International Events and Housing Rights: A Focus on the Olympic Games," Geneva: COHRE, 2007, 47. While COHRE found there were no forced evictions because of the Olympics, they did discover infringements on the right to adequate housing during the rehousing process. Transparency was lacking and people were resettled far from the Poblenou neighborhood where they had been living. This displacement largely impinged upon the poor; 624 families were affected. See: COHRE, "Barcelona 1992," 27, 56.

109. F. Barreiro, J. Costa, and J. M. Vilanova, "Impactos Urbanísticos, Económicos y Sociales de los Juegos Olímpicos de Barcelona '92," Barcelona: Centre D'Iniciatives, Recerques Europees a la Mediterrania (CIREM), June 1993.

110. F. Muñoz, "Olympic Urbanism and Olympic Villages: Planning Strategies in Olympic Host Cities, London 1908 to London 2012," *Sociological Review*, vol. 54, no. 2, 2006, 183.

111. Barreiro, Costa, and Vilanova, "Impactos Urbanísticos, Económicos y Sociales de los Juegos Olímpicos de Barcelona '92."

112. Kennett and Moragas, "Barcelona 1992: Evaluating the Olympic Legacy," 186.

113. COHRE, "Barcelona 1992," 55, italics in original.

114. B. Brown, "Critics of Mascot Ask Why Is It," *USA Today*, August 24, 1992, 1C; J. Longman, "One Year to Atlanta 1996," *New York Times*, July 19, 1995, B9; K. Sack, "No Medals for the Olympic Mascot," *New York Times*, June 30, 1996, Sec. 4, 5.

115. P. McKnight, "Mascot Bashing as an Olympic Sport," *Vancouver Sun*, August 14, 2004, C7.

116. H. Preuss, *The Economics of Staging the Olympics: A Comparison of the Games, 1972–2008*, Cheltenham, UK and Northampton, MA: Edward Elgar, 2004, 17; J. R. Short, "Globalization, Cities, and the Summer Olympics," *City: Analysis of Urban Trends, Culture, Theory, Policy, Action*, vol. 12, no. 3, 2008, 332. Writing before the Games, Rutheiser asserts that by 1995 more than $350 million in public funding had gone toward Atlanta 1996. See C. Rutheiser, *Imagineering Atlanta: The Politics of Place in the City of Dreams*, London: Verso, 1996, 231.

117. J. L. Hotchkiss, R. E. Moore, and S. M. Zobay, "Impact of the 1996 Summer Olympic Games on Employment and Wages in Georgia," *Southern Economic Journal*, vol. 69, no. 3, 2003, 691–704; A. Feddersen and W. Maennig, "Mega-Events and Sectoral Employment: The Case of the 1996 Olympic Games," *Contemporary Economic Policy*, vol. 31, no. 3, 2013, 580–613.

118. Feddersen and Maennig, "Mega-Events and Sectoral Employment," 598.

119. M. Turner, "Olympic Paychecks Increase," *Atlanta Journal and Constitution*, October 12, 1995, A1.

120. G. Collins, "Coke's Hometown Olympics," *New York Times*, March 28, 1996, D1.

121. Barney, Wenn, and Martyn, *Selling the Five Rings*, 251; Pound, *Inside the Olympics*, 190.

122. M. Turner, "Centennial Olympic Park: Patching Together the 'Landscape Quilt'," *Atlanta Journal and Constitution*, September 15, 1995, 6D.

123. B. Roughton, Jr., "Heavenly Purpose to Games?" *Atlanta Journal and Constitution*, May 14, 1994, B10; A. Young, *A Way Out of*

No Way: The Spiritual Memoirs of Andrew Young, Nashville: Thomas Nelson, 1994, 147.

124. "The Olympic Stadium Debate: The King Speech," *Atlanta Journal and Constitution*, March 4, 1993, C4.

125. M. Hiskey and M. Turner, "ACOG Wins with New Ordinance," *Atlanta Journal and Constitution*, September 1, 1994, F4.

126. Rutheiser, *Imagineering Atlanta*, 178; COHRE, "Atlanta's Olympic Legacy," Geneva, 2007; L. Keating and C. A. Flores, "Sixty and Out: Techwood Homes Transformed by Enemies and Friends," *Journal of Urban History*, vol. 26, no. 3, 2000, 275–311.

127. L. J. Vale, *Purging the Poorest: Public Housing and the Design Politics of Twice-Cleared Communities*, Chicago: University of Chicago Press, 2013, 150.

128. "Techwood and Olympics," *Atlanta Journal and Constitution*, May 28, 1992, A14.

129. Rutheiser, *Imagineering Atlanta*, 178; COHRE, "Atlanta's Olympic Legacy"; Keating and Flores, "Sixty and Out."

130. COHRE, "Atlanta's Olympic Legacy," 32.

131. Ibid., 7.

132. E. Harrison, "Mountain of Racist History Casts Shadow on Olympics," *Los Angeles Times*, July 19, 1995.

133. D. Whitelegg, "Going for Gold: Atlanta's Bid for Fame," *International Journal of Urban and Regional Research*, vol. 24, no. 4, 2000, 809.

134. M. Arsenault, "Atlanta Games' Venues Left Some Lessons for Boston," *Boston Globe*, August 3, 2014.

135. S. Dewan, "Bomber Offers Guilty Pleas, And Defiance," *New York Times*, April 14, 2005, A2.

136. H. Pousner, "The Closing Ceremony," *Atlanta Journal and Constitution*, August 5, 1996, 19S.

137. B. Mallon, "The Olympic Bribery Scandal," *Journal of Olympic History*, vol. 8, no. 2, 2000, 20–21.

138. W. Drozdiak, "Olympic-Size Debts Plague Hosts," *Washington Post*, January 27, 1992, A12; C. Dickey, "Ski Developments Blamed for Ecological Imbalance," *Vancouver Sun*, December 31, 1999, D9.

139. United Nations Environment Programme, "Rio Declaration on Environment and Development," in "Report of the United Nations Conference on the Human Environment," Stockholm, June 5–16, 1972.

140. R. W. Pound, "The IOC and the Environment," Olympic Message 35, 1993, 14, 18.

141. International Olympic Committee, "XII Olympic Congress, Paris," 1994.
142. International Olympic Committee, Olympic Charter, June 15, 1995, 13.
143. "Agenda 21 of the Olympic Movement," Olympic Review, vol. 26, no. 30, 1999, 42–3.
144. International Olympic Committee, "Final Report, 2005–2008," Lausanne, Switzerland, 2009, 28.
145. Personal interview, November 22, 2011.
146. C. Gaffney, "Between Discourse and Reality: The Un-Sustainability of Mega-Event Planning," Sustainability, Vol. 5, 2013, 3929.
147. G. Hayes and J. Horne, "Sustainable Development, Shock and Awe?: London 2012 and Civil Society," Sociology, vol. 45, no. 5, 2011, 761.
148. J. Karamichas, The Olympic Games and the Environment, New York: Palgrave Macmillan, 2013, 203.
149. International Olympic Committee, Sport and Environment Commission, "Olympic Movement's Agenda 21: Sport for Sustainable Development."
150. Sydney Organising Committee for the Olympic Games, "Official Report of the XXVII Olympiad, Vol. 1, Preparing for the Games," 2001, 353.
151. Ibid., 352–63.
152. Ibid., 362.
153. J. Shaw, "The Budget and the Public Nag," New York Times, May 10, 1999, D4.
154. J. Shaw, "Bondi Blues: Plan Elicits a Protest," New York Times, May 9, 2000, D8.
155. H. J. Lenskyj, The Best Olympics Ever?: Social Impacts of Sydney 2000, Albany: State University of New York Press, 2002, 197.
156. M. Devine, "Sun, Sand and Angry Hippies," Daily Telegraph (Sydney), May 10, 2000, 39.
157. V. Walker, "Outnumbered Protesters Dig in for Battle of Bondi," The Australian, May 9, 2000, 3.
158. M. Grattan, D. Jopson, and M. Metherell, "Freeman Reignites the Anger," Sydney Morning Herald, July 18, 2000, 1.
159. J. Huxley, "The Race of Our Lives," Sydney Morning Herald, September 25, 2000, 1.
160. E. Brady, "Freeman Lights Up Games: Aboriginal Star Runs to Glory for Her People, All Australians," USA Today, September 26, 2000, 1C.
161. Miller, The Official History of the Olympic Games and the IOC, 19, 338.

162. T. Bruce and E. Wensing, "'She Is Not One of Us': Cathy Freeman and the Place of Aboriginal People in Australian National Culture," *Australian Aboriginal Studies*, no. 2, 2009, 94–5.

163 Personal interview, April 5, 2015.

164. Barney, "The Olympic Games in Modern Times," 238.

165. "After Sydney Burned Bright, Athens Comes Under Fire," *Washington Post*, October 3, 2000, D2.

166. Mallon, "The Olympic Bribery Scandal," 17.

167. S. Wenn, R. Barney, and S. Martyn, *Tarnished Rings: The International Olympic Committee and the Salt Lake City Bid Scandal*, New York: Syracuse University Press, 2011, 27, 48.

168. Mallon, "The Olympic Bribery Scandal," 11–12.

169. G. J. Mitchell et al., "Report of the Special Bid Oversight Commission," US Senate, March 1, 1999, 9.

170. Mallon, "The Olympic Bribery Scandal," 14–15; Wenn, Barney, and Martyn, *Tarnished Rings*, 22–3, 47.

171. M. Payne, *Olympic Turnaround: How the Games Stepped Back from the Brink of Extinction to Become the World's Best Known Brand – And a Multi-Billion Dollar Global Franchise*, London: London Business Press, 2005, 233–4.

172. Wenn, Barney, and Martyn, *Tarnished Rings*.

173. Payne, *Olympic Turnaround*, 166–7.

174. S. Springer, "What the Olympics Did to My City," *Boston Globe*, April 7, 2015.

175. Payne, *Olympic Turnaround*, 186.

176. M. Romney with T. Robinson, *Turnaround: Crisis, Leadership, and the Olympic Games*, Washington, DC: Regnery Publishing, 2004, 226, 234; D. L. Bartlett and J. B. Steele, "Snow Job," *Sports Illustrated*, December 10, 2001; L. Gerlach, "An Uneasy Discourse: Salt Lake 2002 and Olympic Protest," *Pathways: Critiques and Discourse in Olympic Research*, 2008, 144.

177. Gerlach, "An Uneasy Discourse,"; "New Salt Lake Law Bans Masks During Olympics," *Deseret News*, January 23, 2002.

178. Romney with Robinson, *Turnaround*, 376.

179. Chappelet and Kübler-Mabbott, *The International Olympic Committee and the Olympic System*, 17–18.

180. "IOC Approves All Recommended Reforms," *Journal of Olympic History*, January 2000, 57–8.

181. Jennings, *The New Lord of the Rings*, 250–63.

5. The Celebration Capitalism Era

1. Collins, *Sport in Capitalist Society*, 13.
2. J. Boykoff, *Celebration Capitalism and the Olympic Games*, London: Routledge, 2013.
3. D. Harvey, *A Brief History of Neoliberalism*, New York: Oxford University Press, 2005, 3, 70.
4. N. Brenner and N. Theodore, "Cities and the Geographies of 'Actually Existing Neoliberalism',", in N. Brenner and N. Theodore (eds.), *Spaces of Neoliberalism: Urban Restructuring in North America and Western Europe*, Oxford: Blackwell, 2002, 2–32; Jamie Peck, "Geography and Public Policy: Constructions of Neoliberalism," *Progress in Human Geography*, vol. 28, no. 3, 2004, 394.
5. See, for example, Horne and Whannel, *Understanding the Olympics*, 135.
6. M. Raco, "Delivering Flagship Projects in an Era of Regulatory Capitalism: State-led Privatization and the London Olympics 2012," *International Journal of Urban and Regional Research*, vol. 38, no. 1, 2014, 177.
7. J. Braithwaite, *Regulatory Capitalism: How It Works, Ideas for Making It Work Better*, Cheltenham, UK: Edward Elgar, 2008.
8. Raco, "Delivering Flagship Projects in an Era of Regulatory Capitalism," 193, 179.
9. On this point, see J. Clarke, "Living with/in and without Neoliberalism," *Focaal*, vol. 51, 2008, 135–47.
10. N. Klein, *The Shock Doctrine: The Rise of Disaster Capitalism*, New York: Metropolitan Books, 2007, 181.
11. Klein, *The Shock Doctrine*, 14, 15, 466.
12. A. Loewenstein, *Disaster Capitalism: Making a Killing Out of Catastrophe*, London and New York: Verso, 2015, 307, 9.
13. J. Lauermann and M. Davidson, "Negotiating Particularity in Neoliberalism Studies: Tracing Development Strategies Across Neoliberal Urban Governance Projects," *Antipode*, vol. 45, no. 5, 2013, 1293.
14. A. L. Tsing, "Inside the Economy of Appearances," *Public Culture*, vol. 12, 2000, 143.
15. G. Agamben, *State of Exception*, Trans. K. Attell, Chicago and London: University of Chicago Press, 2005, 7.
16. Agamben, *State of Exception*, 50, emphasis added.
17. Hayes and Horne, "Sustainable Development, Shock and Awe?," 759.

18. See Harvey, *A Brief History of Neoliberalism*, 76–8.
19. To be sure, many have pointed out that deregulation is largely a myth. See, for instance, C. Kingfisher and J. Maskovsky, "The Limits of Neoliberalism," *Critique of Anthropology*, vol. 28, no. 2, 2008, 115–26. Yet scholars continue to slot highly regulated activities under the label of neoliberalism. This raises the question: what line would need to be crossed for neoliberalism to no longer be neoliberalism? For too many, this line is forever blurred and thus impossible to traverse.
20. Klein, *The Shock Doctrine*, 20.
21. Personal interview, February 5, 2010.
22. F. Miraftab, "Public-Private Partnerships: The Trojan Horse of Neoliberal Development?" *Journal of Planning Education and Research*, vol. 24, 2004, 91.
23. Ibid., 92.
24. Ibid., 98.
25. See Braithwaite, *Regulatory Capitalism*; Raco, "Delivering Flagship Projects in an Era of Regulatory Capitalism."
26. J. L. Crompton, "Economic Impact Studies: Instruments for Political Shenanigans?" *Journal of Travel Research*, vol. 45, 2006, 67, 73–5.
27. V. Matheson, "Economic Impact Analysis," in W. Andreff and S. Szymanski (eds.), *Handbook on the Economics of Sport*, Cheltenham, UK, and Northampton, MA: Edward Elgar, 2006, 140. See also R. A. Baade and V. Matheson, "Bidding for the Olympics: Fool's Gold?" in C. P. Barros, M. Ibrahímo, and S. Szymanski (eds.), *Transatlantic Sport: The Comparative Economics of North American and European Sports*, Cheltenham, UK, and Northampton, MA: Edward Elgar, 2002, 127–51.
28. Crompton, "Economic Impact Studies," 73–5; Zimbalist, *Circus Maximus*, 36.
29. J. R. Madden, "Economic and Fiscal Impacts of Mega Sporting Events: A General Equilibrium Assessment," *Public Finance and Management*, vol. 6, no. 3, 2006, 349; J. Barclay, "Predicting the Costs and Benefits of Mega-Sporting Events: Misjudgement of Olympic Proportions?" *Economic Affairs*, June 2009, 63.
30. R. A. Baade and V. A. Matheson, "Home Run or Wild Pitch?: The Economic Impact of Major League Baseball's All-Star Game," *Journal of Sports Economics*, vol. 2, 2001, 307–26.
31. Zimbalist, *Circus Maximus*, 38.
32. D. Whitson and D. Macintosh, "The Global Circus: International Sport, Tourism, and the Marketing of Cities," *Journal of Sport and Social Issues*, vol. 20, 1996, 283, emphasis in original.

33. London Assembly, Budget and Performance Committee, "Policing Costs for the London 2012 Olympic and Paralympic Games," November 1, 2011, 2–3.

34. R. Booth and N. Hopkins, "Olympic Security Chaos: Depth of G4S Security Crisis Revealed," *Guardian*, July 12, 2012.

35. D. Zirin, *Brazil's Dance with the Devil: The World Cup, the Olympics, and the Fight for Democracy*, Chicago: Haymarket Books, 2014, 170.

36. J. Longman, "Athens Wins a Vote for Tradition, and the 2004 Olympics," *New York Times*, September 6, 1997, 33.

37. Zimbalist, *Circus Maximus*, 41.

38. E. Kasimati and P. Dawson, "Assessing the Impact of the 2004 Olympic Games on the Greek Economy: A Small Macroeconometric Model," *Economic Modelling*, vol. 26, 2009, 140.

39. Athens 2004 Organising Committee for the Olympic Games, "Official Report of the XXVIII Olympiad, Vol. 2," November 2005, 518. The surplus was calculated at €7,021,116, to be precise.

40. R. Blitz, "2012 Olympics: The Gains from the Games," *Financial Times*, January 12, 2012.

41. Zimbalist, *Circus Maximus*, 50.

42. I. Chorianopoulos, T. Pagonis, S. Koukoulas, and S. Drymoniti, "Planning, Competitiveness and Sprawl in the Mediterranean City: The Case of Athens," *Cities*, vol. 27, 2010, 253.

43. S. Bloor, "Abandoned Athens Olympic 2004 Venues, 10 Years On—In Pictures," *Guardian*, August 13, 2014.

44. M. Perryman, *Why the Olympics Aren't Good for Us and How They Can Be*, London: OR Books, 2012, 46.

45. "Olympic Stadium Opens Doors to Athens Homeless," Ekathimerini.com, February 1, 2012; Adam Taylor, "Greece's Abandoned Olympic Stadiums Get a Second Life: Housing Refugees," *Washington Post*, October 1, 2015.

46. See S. Kouvelakis, "The Greek Cauldron," *New Left Review*, vol. 72, November–December 2011, 17–32; H. Smith, "Athens 2004 Olympics: What Happened after the Athletes Went Home?," *Guardian*, May 9, 2012. Hosting the Games may have slightly helped to curb unemployment in the lead-up to the Olympics. See Kasimati and Dawson, "Assessing the Impact of the 2004 Olympic Games on the Greek Economy."

47. Athens 2004 Organising Committee for the Olympic Games, "Official Report of the XXVIII Olympiad," 525.

48. M. Samatas, "Security and Surveillance in the Athens 2004 Olympics: Some Lessons From a Troubled Story," *International Criminal Justice Review*, vol. 17, 2007, 225; J. Sugden, "Watched

by the Games: Surveillance and Security at the Olympics," in J. Sugden and A. Tomlinson (eds.), *Watching the Olympics: Politics, Power and Representation*, London and New York: Routledge, 2012, 231–2; P. Boyle, "Securing the Olympic Games: Exemplifications of Global Governance," in Lenskyj and Wagg, *The Palgrave Handbook of Olympic Studies*, 394.

49. Chappelet and Kübler-Mabbott, *The International Olympic Committee and the Olympic System*, 46.
50. Samatas, "Security and Surveillance in the Athens 2004 Olympics," 224, 221. Also see: D. L. Bartlett and J. B. Steele, "Washington's $8 Billion Shadow," *Vanity Fair*, March 2007.
51. Samatas, "Security and Surveillance in the Athens 2004 Olympics," 224.
52. Athens 2004 Organising Committee for the Olympic Games, "Official Report of the XXVIII Olympiad," 190.
53. Samatas, "Security and Surveillance in the Athens 2004 Olympics," 224.
54. Horne and Whannel, *Understanding the Olympics*, 136.
55. C. Migdalovitz, Congressional Research Service Report RS21833, "Greece: Threat of Terrorism and Security at the Olympics," July 9, 2004. Released by WikiLeaks on February 2, 2009.
56. United States Government Accountability Office, "Olympic Security: US Support to Olympic Games Provides Lessons for Future Olympics," May 2005, 1–31.
57. G. Floridis, "Security for the 2004 Athens Olympic Games," *Mediterranean Quarterly*, vol. 15, no. 2, Spring 2004, 5. He also noted, "The same applies to the Firefighting Corps and to other forces that are being similarly equipped and modernized."
58. M. Samatas, "Surveillance in Athens 2004 and Beijing 2008: A Comparison of the Olympic Surveillance Modalities and Legacies in Two Different Olympic Host Regimes," *Urban Studies*, vol. 48, no. 15, 2011, 3351.
59. A. Shipley, "To Beijing or Not to Beijing?," *Washington Post*, July 13, 2001, D1.
60. Quoted in Amnesty International, "China: The Olympics Countdown—Crackdown on Activists Threatens Olympic Legacy," April 2008, 29.
61. N. Kristof, "A Lever for Change in China," in M. Worden (ed.)., *China's Great Leap: The Beijing Games and the Human Rights Challenges*, New York: Seven Stories Press, 2008, 21.
62. L. Xiaobo, "Authoritarianism in the Light of the Olympic Flame," in M. Worden, *China's Great Leap*, 265.
63. Amnesty International, "China: The Olympics Countdown—

Crackdown on Activists Threatens Olympic Legacy," 1, 2, 28.

64. Human Rights Watch, "China: Hosting Olympics a Catalyst for Human Rights Abuses," August 23, 2008.

65. Estimates range between $2 billion and $12 billion. See A. M. Broudehoux, "The Social and Spatial Impacts of Olympic Image Construction: Beijing 2008," in Lenskyj and Wagg, *The Palgrave Handbook of Olympic Studies*, 204; N. Klein, "The Olympics: Unveiling Police State 2.0," *Huffington Post*, August 7, 2008.

66. P. Fussey, "Surveillance and the Olympic Spectacle," in A. Richards, P. Fussey, and A. Silke (eds.), *Terrorism and the Olympics: Major Event Security and Lessons for the Future*, London and New York: Routledge, 2011, 103; Samatas, "Surveillance in Athens 2004 and Beijing 2008," 3356; Y. Yu, F. Klauser, and G. Chan, "Governing Security at the Beijing Games," *The International Journal of the History of Sport*, vol. 26, no. 3, 2009, 394.

67. Guoqui, *Olympic Dreams*, 252; Samatas, "Surveillance in Athens 2004 and Beijing 2008," 335.

68. K. Bradsher, "China Finds American Allies for Security," *New York Times*, December 28, 2007.

69. Yu, Klauser, and Chan, "Governing Security at the Beijing Games," 396–7.

70. Ibid., 397–8.

71. Bradsher, "China Finds American Allies for Security"; P. Fussey, "Surveillance and the Olympic Spectacle," in Richards, Fussey, and Silke, *Terrorism and the Olympics*, 104.

72. S. Wade, "Did Olympics Improve Human Rights in China?" Associated Press, March 13, 2009; Amnesty International, "China: The Olympics Countdown—Crackdown on Activists Threatens Olympic Legacy," April 2008, 18–21; A. M. Broudehoux, "Civilizing Beijing: Social Beautification, Civility and Citizenship at the 2008 Olympics," in G. Hayes and J. Karamichas (eds.), *Olympic Games, Mega-Events and Civil Societies: Globalization, Environment, Resistance*, New York: Palgrave Macmillan, 2012, 64.

73. Zimbalist, *Circus Maximus*, 120; COHRE, "One World, Whose Dream?: Housing Rights Violations and the Beijing Olympic Games," Geneva, July 2008, 8.

74. A. M. Brady, "The Beijing Olympics as a Campaign of Mass Distraction," *China Quarterly*, vol. 197, March 2009, 18–19.

75. COHRE, "One World, Whose Dream?," 6.

76. M. Fan, "China Defends Relocation Policy," *Washington Post*, February 20, 2008, A14.

77. Payne, *Olympic Turnaround*, 3.

78. A. Tomlinson, "Olympic Values, Beijing's Olympic Games, and the

Universal Market," in M. E. Price and D. Dayan (eds.), *Owning the Olympics: Narratives of the New China*, Ann Arbor: University of Michigan Press, 2008, 67–85; M. Godfrey, "Going for Gold," *Enterprise China*, June 2004.

79. International Olympic Committee, "IOC Marketing Media Guide, Beijing 2008," Lausanne, 2008, 8.

80. S. K. Hom, "The Promise of a 'People's Olympics'," in Worden, *China's Great Leap*, 64.

81. R. Blumenstein, "Venture to Focus on Managing Crises in China," *Wall Street Journal*, September 25, 2007.

82. J. G. Owen, "Estimating the Cost and Benefit of Hosting Olympic Games: What Can Beijing Expect from Its 2008 Games?," *Industrial Geographer*, vol. 3, no. 1, 2005, 12.

83. Zimbalist, *Circus Maximus*, 41

84. Broudehoux, "Spectacular Beijing," 386.

85. Zimbalist, *Circus Maximus*, 65–6; B. Demick, "Beijing's Olympic Building Boom Becomes a Bust," *Los Angeles Times*, February 22, 2009; D. Bond, "Did Beijing's Olympic Leave a Lasting Legacy?," BBC News, May 15, 2012.

86. "Ai Weiwei: China's Dissident Artist," BBC News, July 20, 2012.

87. Zimbalist, *Circus Maximus*, 50.

88. Reporters Without Borders, "Olympic Prisoners," July 31, 2009; J. Magnay, "Censors Make News," *Sydney Morning Herald*, August 14, 2008, 1; Reporters Without Borders, "Press Freedom Index 2008,"; Reporters Without Borders, "World Press Freedom Index 2014," rsf.org.

89. Committee to Protect Journalists, "Falling Short: Olympic Promises Go Unfulfilled as China Falters on Press Freedom," New York, June 2008, 10.

90. T. Boswell, "They Made the Buses Run on Time," *Washington Post*, August 25, 2008, E9.

91. T. Yuankai, "Beijing Creates History," *Beijing Review*, issue 31, August 2, 2001, 12–16.

92. A. P. J. Mol and L. Zhang, "Sustainability as Global Norm: The Greening of Mega-Events in China," in Hayes and Karamichas, *Olympic Games, Mega-Events and Civil Societies*, 134–6.

93. T. Wang et al., "Air Quality During the 2008 Beijing Olympics: Secondary Pollutants and Regional Impact," *Atmospheric Chemistry and Physics Discussions*, vol. 10, 2010, 12433–12463.

94. D. Q. Rich, K. Liu, J. Zhang et al., "Differences in Birth Weight Associated with the 2008 Beijing Olympic Air Pollution Reduction: Results from a Natural Experiment," *Environmental Health Perspectives*, vol. 123, no. 9, 2015, 880–7.

95. J. C. Witte et al., "Satellite Observations of Changes in Air Quality During the 2008 Beijing Olympics and Paralympics," *Geophysical Research Letters*, vol. 36, no. 17, 2009, 1–6.

96. M. Lederman, "Vancouver Orders Removal of Anti-Olympic Mural," *Globe and Mail*, December 11, 2009.

97. J. Boykoff, *Activism and the Olympics: Dissent at the Games in Vancouver and London*, New Brunswick, NJ: Rutgers University Press, 2014, 58.

98. International Olympic Committee, "Brand Protection: Olympic Marketing Ambush Protection and Clean Venue Guidelines," Lausanne, Switzerland, 2005.

99. B. Yaffe, "PM's Strategy of Controlling Message Fails to Silence Opponents," *Vancouver Sun*, February 12, 2010, B2.

100. H. J. Lenskyj, *Olympic Industry Resistance: Challenging Olympic Power and Propaganda*, Albany: State University of New York Press, 2008, 65.

101. Personal interview, February 5, 2010.

102. D. Bramham, "Olympics Bill Tops $6 Billion—So Far," *Vancouver Sun*, January 23, 2009; D. Inwood, "City Spent $550 Million on Olympics," *Vancouver Province*, April 16, 2010; B. Mackin, *Red Mittens & Red Ink: The Vancouver Olympics*, Vancouver: Smashwords, 2012, 204.

103. G. Mason, "Vancouver's Big Games Turning into a Big Owe," *Globe and Mail*, January 10, 2009, A7; G. Mason, "Athletes Village to Get $100-Million Loan," *Globe and Mail*, November 6, 2008, A15; Boykoff, *Celebration Capitalism and the Olympic Games*, 71–2.

104. Frontier Centre for Public Policy, "The 6th Annual Demographia International Housing Affordability Survey: 2010 Ratings for Metropolitan Markets," 39.

105. A. Merrifield, *Henri Lefebvre: A Critical Introduction*, New York: Routledge, 2006, 69–70, emphasis in original.

106. Personal interview, August 18, 2010.

107. "Vancouver Police Get Sonic Crowd Control Device," CBC News, November 10, 2009.

108. I. Austen, "Security at the Games and Its Cost Are Heavy," *New York Times*, February 18, 2010, B17; D. Lawson, "Project Management and the RCMP Security Mission for the Vancouver 2010 Olympic Games: Safe and Secure Games through Integrated Security Model," February 16, 2011.

109. D. Hansen, "Victoria Cop Infiltrated Anti-Games Group, Jamie Graham Says," *Vancouver Sun*, December 2, 2009; personal interview, August 17, 2010.

110. Montréal 1976, Games of the XXI Olympiad, "Official Report," Volume 1, Ottawa: COJO, 1978, 306; J. Forsyth, "Teepees and Tomahawks: Aboriginal Cultural Representation at the 1976 Olympic Games," in K. Wamsley, R. K. Barney, and S. G. Martyn (eds.), *The Global Nexus Engaged: Past, Present, Future Inter-disciplinary Olympic Studies: Sixth International Symposium for Olympic Research*, London, Ontario: International Centre for Olympic Studies, 2002, 72.

111. Mukmuk, a "sidekick" mascot, was also First Nations–inspired, but it only appeared online.

112. Vancouver Organizing Committee for the 2010 Olympic and Paralympic Winter Games (VANOC), "Vancouver 2010 Sustainability Report, 2009–2010," 18.

113. Personal interview via email, June 8, 2015.

114. T. Alfred, "Deconstructing the British Columbia Treaty Process," *Balayi: Culture, Law and Colonialism*, vol. 3, 2001, 42; K. Pemberton, "Aboriginal Groups Divided on Whether to Support Olympics," *Vancouver Sun*, February 6, 2010.

115. C. M. O'Bonsawin, "'No Olympics on Stolen Native Land': Contesting Olympic Narratives and Asserting Indigenous Rights within the Discourse of the 2010 Vancouver Games," *Sport in Society*, vol. 13, no. 1, 2000, 152.

116. Personal interview, August 18, 2010.

117. Personal interviews with Nathan Crompton, Dave Diewert, and Harsha Walia, August 17 and 18, 2010.

118. Personal interview with Dave Diewert, August 17, 2010; personal interview with Harsha Walia, August 18, 2010.

119. "Amy Goodman Detained at Canadian Border, Questioned about Speech ... and 2010 Olympics," Democracy Now!, November 30, 2009.

120. M. Andrejevic, *iSpy: Surveillance and Power in the Interactive Era*, Lawrence, Kansas: University Press of Kansas, 2007, 2.

121. J. Dean, *Democracy and Other Neoliberal Fantasies: Communicative Capitalism and Left Politics*, Durham and London: Duke University Press, 2009, 49, 24, emphasis in original.

122. International Olympic Committee, "IOC Marketing Media Guide: Vancouver 2010," Lausanne, 2010, 35.

123. Personal interview, August 17, 2010.

124. C. C. Bryant, "Canada Aims to 'Own the Podium' at Vancouver Olympics," *Christian Science Monitor*, February 10, 2010; personal interview with Harsha Walia, August 18, 2010; Personal interview with Gord Hill, August 18, 2010.

125. See wikileaks.org.

126. WikiLeaks, "Public Policy Question for Coca-Cola," June 2, 2009, EMAIL-ID 5413843.

127. WikiLeaks, "Bhopal update—03–07–11," March 7, 2011, EMAIL-ID 389943; WikiLeaks, "DOW CONFIDENTIAL: Bhopal Monitoring Report Friday, November 18, 2011," November 19, 2011, EMAIL-ID 407784.

128. Personal interview, May 10, 2012.

129. Personal interview, August 2, 2012.

130. B. Johnson, "Put a Sock in It, We're On To a Winner," *The Sun*, July 20, 2012.

131. Romney with Robinson, *Turnaround*, 222.

132. T. Gardner, "London 2012 Organisers Switched Traffic Lights Green to Ease Gridlock for Olympic VIPs During Bid to Host the Games," *Daily Mail*, May 13, 2012; M. J. Gross, "Jumping Through Hoops," *Vanity Fair*, June 2012.

133. J. Ball, "Torchbearers Picked by Sponsors Keep Flame of Commerce Alive," *Guardian*, June 6, 2012; M. Easton, "Empty Seats and the Privilege of the Games," BBC, August 3, 2012.

134. R. Syal, "Cherie Blair: London's Secret Lobbying Weapon," *Guardian*, July 22, 2012; Moody's Investors Service, "Olympics Will Give Only Short-Term Boost to Corporates," May 1, 2012. The firm also commented, "The benefits are likely to be largely short-lived, providing only a temporary fillip to corporate earnings."

135. IOC, Olympic Charter, 91; London Olympic Games and Paralympic Games Act 2006, 47–8.

136. T. Peck, "Father of Olympic Branding: My Rules Are Being Abused," *Independent*, July 21, 2012.

137. *The Andrew Marr Show*, BBC, May 13, 2012.

138. M. Hickman, "Britain Flooded with 'Brand Police' to Protect Sponsors," *Independent*, July 16, 2012; S. Goodley, J. Moulds, and S. Rogers, "London 2012: Olympic Sponsors Waive Tax Break," *Guardian*, July 18, 2012; S. Rogers, "London 2012 Olympic Sponsors List: Who Are They and What Have They Paid?" *Guardian*, July 19, 2012.

139. W. Dooling, "Corporate 'Sin Washing'—Embracing the Olympic Brand Pays Off for Sponsors," *Truthout*, August 11, 2012.

140. LOCOG, "London 2012 Sustainability Report," 87; Commission for a Sustainable London 2012, "Breaking the Tape: Commission for a Sustainable London 2012 Pre-Games Review," 3.

141. R. Neate, "Olympic Medal Pollution Protesters Disrupt Rio Tinto Meeting," *Guardian*, April 19, 2012.

142. The bail conditions for one activist were shared with me.

143. D. Chivers, "BP or Not BP, That Is the Question," *London Late*, August 7, 2012, 16.

144. E. Dickinson, *The Complete Poems of Emily Dickinson*, New York: Little Brown, 1961, 506; personal interview, August 9, 2012; personal interview, August 6, 2012.

145. Personal interview, July 20, 2012.

146. Personal interview, August 5, 2012.

147. I. Steadman, "Olympic Protesters Suspended from Twitter over Trademark Violation," *Wired*, May 23, 2012; S. Malik, "Twitter Suspends Account for Using London 2012 Olympics Logo," *Guardian*, May 23, 2012.

148. Documents available at spacehijackers.org.

149. Ibid.

150. HM Revenue & Customs, "Accredited Individuals and 2012 Partner Workers: Business Profits Exemption," n.d.; T. Hunt, "The Great Olympics Tax Swindle," *Ethical Consumer*, July 5, 2012.

151. Hunt, "The Great Olympic Tax Swindle"; Goodley, Moulds, and Rogers, "London 2012: Olympic Sponsors Waive Tax Break"; 38 Degrees, "Hurray! Now What Next?" July 26, 2012; A. Lezard, "Coca Cola Decides to Pay their Olympic Taxes," *New Statesman*, July 18, 2012.

152. IOC, Olympic Charter, 75.

153. A. Shergold, "Athletes Launch 'Gag' Protest Against the Olympic Rule that Bans them from Promoting Their Own Sponsors," *Daily Mail*, July 31, 2012.

154. K. Belson, "Olympians Take to Twitter to Protest Endorsement Rule," *New York Times*, July 31, 2012, B11.

155. IOC, Olympic Charter, 91.

156. M. Staniforth, "Australian Damien Hooper Escapes Punishment after Wearing Tee-shirt Displaying Aboriginal Flag," *Independent*, July 30, 2012.

157. P. Hennessy and B. Leapman, "Ministers Plan 'Big Brother' Police Powers," *Telegraph*, February 4, 2007.

158. N. Hopkins, R. Booth, and O. Gibson, "MoD to Set Up Temporary Base for Troops," *Guardian*, July 13, 2012.

159. M. Robinson, "Welcome to London! Royal Navy's Largest Warship Sails Down the Thames as Armed Forces Put on Show of Strength for Olympics," *Daily Mail*, July 13, 2012.

160. S. Laville, "Metropolitan Police Plastic Bullets Stockpile up to 10,000 after UK Riots," *Guardian*, May 3, 2012; B. Quinn, "Fast-track Court System Planned for London Olympics," *Guardian*, June 25, 2012.

161. G. Thomas, "Sonic Device Deployed in London During Olympics," BBC, May 12, 2012.

162. J. O'Mahony, "London 2012 Olympic Security Visualized," *Telegraph*, June 21, 2012; S. Laville, "Olympics Welcome Does Not Extend to All in London as Police Flex Muscles," *Guardian*, May 4, 2012.

163. Personal interview, August 3, 2012.

164. J. Cheyne, "The Aftermath 2012," Games Monitor, July 11, 2011; A. Oliver, "Cost of Olympics to spiral to £24bn," *Daily Mail*, January 27, 2012.

165. House of Commons, Culture, Media, and Sport Committee (CMSC), "London 2012 Olympic Games, Vol. 1," 3, emphasis added.

166. O. Gibson and D. Milmo, "Olympic Chief David Higgins Quits to Run Network Rail," *Guardian*, September 28, 2010; O. Gibson, "Olympic Village Complex Seeks Private Investors," *Guardian*, October 1, 2010; O. Gibson, "Olympic Village to Be Fully Funded by Taxpayers," *Guardian*, May 13, 2009.

167. J. Kollewe, "Olympic Village Snapped Up by Qatari Ruling Family for £557m," *Guardian*, August 12, 2011.

168. Department of Culture, Media and Sport—Strategy Unit, "Game Plan: A Strategy for Delivering Government's Sport and Physical Activity Objectives," London, December 2002, 66, emphasis added.

169. J. Wilson, "Russia Wins 2014 Cold War," *Herald Sun* (Melbourne), July 6, 2007, 105.

170. R.W. Orttung and S. Zhemukhov, "The 2014 Sochi Olympic Mega-Project and Russia's Political Economy," *East European Politics*, vol. 30, no. 2, 2014, 184.

171. B. Flyvbjerg and A. Stewart, "Olympic Proportions: Cost and Cost Overruns at the Olympics 1960–2012," University of Oxford Said Business School Working Papers, June 2012, 1–23.

172. Russian deputy prime minister and Olympic executive Dmitry Kozak quizzically asserted that "The real cost is about 3.5 billion dollars for Russian taxpayers." Previously, President Putin put the cost of the Games at $6.9 billion. See: E. Hula III, "Kozak Says Sochi Broke 'Ice of Skepticism,' Offers New Sochi Cost," *Around the Rings*, February 22, 2014.

173. M. Müller, "(Im-)Mobile policies: Why Sustainability Went Wrong in the 2014 Olympics in Sochi," *European Urban and Regional Studies*, vol. 22, no. 2, 2015, 191–209; Human Rights Watch, "Race to the Bottom: Exploitation of Migrant Workers

Ahead of Russia's 2014 Winter Olympic Games in Sochi," February 2013.

174. S. Rosefielde, *The Russian Economy: From Lenin to Putin*, Oxford: Blackwell, 2007, 166, 170.

175. J. Boykoff, "Celebration Capitalism and the Sochi 2014 Winter Olympics," *Olympika: The International Journal of Olympic Studies*, vol. 22, 2013, 39–70.

176. M. Müller, "State Dirigisme in Megaprojects: Governing the 2014 Winter Olympics in Sochi," *Environment and Planning A*, vol. 43, 2011, 2092.

177. Boykoff, "Celebration Capitalism and the Sochi 2014 Winter Olympics."

178. N. Butler, "Medals 'Secretly Awarded' by Putin to Major Sochi 2014 Investors," *Inside the Games*, June 3, 2014.

179. O. Gibson, "Sochi 2014: The Costliest Olympics Yet but Where Has All the Money Gone?," *Guardian*, October 9, 2013.

180. M. Weiss and O. Khvostunova, "Whose Idea Was It to Build a Winter Resort in the Warmest Part of Russia?," *The Atlantic*, June 17, 2013.

181. B. Quinn, "Boris Nemtsov Murder: Putin 'Politically Responsible'—Daughter," *Guardian*, March 12, 2015.

182. Orttung and Zhemukhov, "The 2014 Sochi Olympic Mega-Project and Russia's Political Economy," 183–6.

183. Sochi 2014 Candidature File, "Volume 1: Political and Economic Climate and Structure," 2007.

184. Human Rights Watch, "Laws of Attrition: Crackdown on Russia's Civil Society after Putin's Return to the Presidency," April 2013, 1.

185. Human Rights Watch, "Laws of Attrition," 14–17.

186. G. M. Hahn, "Russia in 2012: From 'Thaw' and 'Reset' to 'Freeze'," *Asian Survey*, vol. 53, no. 1, 2013, 221; F. Weir, "Russian NGOs in Panic Mode over Proposed 'High Treason' Law," *Christian Science Monitor*, September 26, 2012; Weir, F. "Many Russian NGOs Face 'Foreign Agent' Label," *Christian Science Monitor*, July 5, 2012.

187. Human Rights Watch, "Laws of Attrition," 25.

188. F. Weir, "Putin Warns of Growing Terror Risks as Kremlin Arrests Opposition Leader," *Christian Science Monitor*, October 17, 2012; M. Idov, "Putin Rival's Sentence Forces the Question: What Next for Opposition?" *Guardian*, July 18, 2013; "Alexei Navalny Freed by Russian Court but Conviction for Theft Is Upheld," Reuters, October 16, 2013.

189. "Sochi, Sport and Security: Russia Bans Protests During Winter

Olympics, Limits Access," *Russia Today*, August 24, 2013; D. M. Herszenhorn, "A Russian Protest Zone Where Almost No One Registers a Complaint," *New York Times*, February 14, 2014, A12.

190. A. E. Kramer, "Russia Passes Bill Targeting Some Discussions of Homosexuality," *New York Times*, June 12, 2013, A5.

191. H.J. Lenskyj, *Sexual Diversity and the Sochi 2014 Olympics: No More Rainbows*, New York: Palgrave Macmillan, 2014, 81; IOC, Olympic Charter, 12.

192. O. Gibson and A. Luhn, "Calls to Boycott Winter Olympics over Laws 'That Treat Gays as Hitler Did Jews'," *Guardian*, August 8, 2014, 9.

193. "Obama Names Billie Jean King as One of Two Gay Sochi Olympic Delegates," Associated Press, December 17, 2013.

194. C. Brennan, "U.S. Delegation Delivers Strong Message in Sochi," *USA Today*, February 7, 2014.

195. IOC, Olympic Charter, 93.

196. J. Boykoff and D. Zirin, "Sochi Games Are Apt Venue for Athlete Activism," *San Francisco Chronicle*, January 24, 2014, A20.

197. K. Whiteside, "Wagner, Miller Slam Russia's Anti-Gay Laws," *USA Today*, October 1, 2013, 3C.

198. M. Brigidi, "Sochi 2014: Brian Burke Calls Russia's Anti-Gay Law 'Repugnant'," SB Nation, August 27, 2013.

199. O. Gibson and S. Walker, "Olympians Urge Russia to Reconsider 'Gay Propaganda' Laws," *Guardian*, January 30, 2014.

200. A. Brundage, "Address: 67th Solemn Opening Session, Mexico City, Mexico."

201. L. Dillman, "A Pussy Riot Homage? Alexey Sobolev's Olympics Board Raises Questions," *Los Angeles Times*, February 6, 2014.

202. T. Ziller, "Out Snowboarder Cheryl Maas Displays Rainbow Glove in Sochi," SB Nation, February 7, 2014.

203. "US Ski Team Member Andrew Newell and 105 Winter Olympians Call for Climate Action," Protect Our Winters, February 10, 2014; "In the Olympic Spirit, Shut Up and Ski," *Investor's Business Daily*, February 14, 2014, A14.

204. International Olympic Committee, "Olympic Truce," olympic.org.

205. Boykoff and Zirin, "The Sochi Paralympics, Ukraine, and the Olympic Truce."

206. B. Pinelli and E. Hula III, "Sochi Scene," *Around the Rings*, February 20, 2014; E. Hula III, "Gold Medal Matchup Set; Moment of Silence for Ukraine," *Around the Rings*, February 21, 2014.

207. S. Walker, "Pussy Riot Members among Group of Activists Arrested in Sochi," *Guardian*, February 18, 2014; M. Gessen, *Words Will Break Cement: The Passion of Pussy Riot*, New York: Riverhead Books, 2014; A. Roth, "Members of Russian Protest Group Attacked by Cossacks in Sochi," *New York Times*, February 20, 2014, A4; "Deputy Prime Minister Dmitry Kozak Defends Pussy Riot Treatment in Sochi," *Independent*, February 18, 2014.

208. N. Vasilyeva "Rebel Leader Urges Fighters to Derail Sochi Olympics," Associated Press, July 4, 2013.

209. M. Light, "Migration, 'Globalised' Islam and the Russian State: A Case Study of Muslim Communities in Belgorod and Adygeya Regions," *Europe-Asia Studies*, vol. 64, no. 2, 2012, 211.

210. M. Light, "Sochi and the Northwest Caucasus—II," *Global Brief: World Affairs in the 21st Century*, April 12, 2010.

211. Personal interview, July 29, 2012.

212. Personal interview, October 21, 2014.

213. Ibid.; O. Bullough, "Sochi 2014 Winter Olympics: The Circassians Cry Genocide," *Newsweek*, May 21, 2012.

214. Boykoff, *Activism and the Olympics*, 171.

215. I. Watson, G. Somra, and D. Filippova, "Russia Arrests Leader of Circassian Ethnic Minority," CNN, February 17, 2014. Nalchik sits in the south of Russia, east of Sochi, while Maykop is to the north of the Olympic city.

216. Personal interviews with Dana Wojokh and Zack Barsik, October 21, 2014.

217. U. Bacchi, "Sochi Winter Olympics: Circassian Protest Website NoSochi2014 Hacked on Games' Eve," *International Business Times*, February 7, 2014; personal interview, October 21, 2014.

218. B. Pinelli, "Ski President Addresses IOC Concerns, Slams FIFA, Norway," *Around the Rings*, October 25, 2014.

6. The 2016 Rio Summer Olympics and the Path Ahead

1. J. Barbassa, *Dancing with the Devil in the City of God: Rio de Janeiro on the Brink*, New York: Touchstone, 2015, xviii–xix; J. Macur, "Rio Wins 2016 Olympics in a First for South America," *New York Times*, October 3, 2009, A1.

2. Macur, "Rio Wins 2016 Olympics in a First for South America."

3. "Brazil Takes Off," *The Economist*, November 12, 2009.

4. "Reagan 'Burned' During Toast," Associated Press, December 2, 1982.
5. Zirin, *Brazil's Dance with the Devil*, 63.
6. F. D. Oliveira, "Lula in the Labyrinth," *New Left Review*, vol. 42, Nov–Dec 2006, 10, 18.
7. Rio 2016 Candidate City Bid, Volume 1, 18, 27.
8. Rio 2016 Candidate City Bid, Volume 3, 175.
9. Rio 2016 Candidate City Bid, Volume 1, 23.
10. Barbassa, *Dancing with the Devil in the City of God*, 151; Rio 2016 Candidate City Bid, Volume 1, 21; P. Kuitenbrouwer, "Fears of a Pan Am Games Flop," *Financial Post*, July 3, 2015.
11. M. Curi, J. Knijnik, and G. Mascarenhas, "The Pan American Games in Rio de Janeiro 2007: Consequences of a Sport Mega-Event in a BRIC Country," *International Review for the Sociology of Sport*, vol. 46, no. 2, 2011, 147.
12. T. V. Barreto and J. Kfouri, "Interview," *Coletiva*, 2012.
13. Simon Jenkins, "The World Cup and Olympics Threaten to Overwhelm Rio," *Guardian*, April 23, 2014; Gaffney, "Between Discourse and Reality," 3931; Zimbalist, *Circus Maximus*, 23–4.
14. Barreto and Kfouri, "Interview."
15. G. Mascarenhas, *Entradas e Bandeiras: A Conquista do Brasil pelo Futebol*, Rio de Janeiro: Ed. UERJ, 2014, 233.
16. A. Singer, "Rebellion in Brazil: Social and Political Complexion of the June Events," *New Left Review*, vol. 85, Jan–Feb 2014, 19–37.
17. Barbassa, *Dancing with the Devil in the City of God*, 233.
18. Singer, "Rebellion in Brazil," 29.
19. J. Boykoff, "Why You Should Root for the World Cup Protesters," *Guardian*, June 10, 2014.
20. B. Homewood, "FIFA Is the Real President of Brazil, Says Romario," Reuters, June 22, 2013.
21. C. Gaffney, "Global Parties, Galactic Hangovers: Brazil's Mega Event Dystopia," *Los Angeles Review of Books*, October 1, 2014.
22. J. G. Castañeda, "What We Learned from the World Cup," *Fusion Soccer*, July 14, 2014.
23. O. A. Santos Junior, "Metropolização e Megaeventos: Proposições Gerais em Torno da Copa do Mundo 2014 e das Olimpíadas 2016 no Brasil," in O. A. Santos Junior, C. Gaffney, and L. C. Q. Ribeiro (eds.), *Brasil: Os Impactos Da Copa Do Mundo 2014 e Das Olimpíadas 2016*, Rio de Janeiro: Observatório Das Metrópoles, 2015, 31, 21–2.
24. W. Barral and A. Haas, "Public-Private Partnership (PPP) in Brazil," *The International Lawyer*, vol. 41, no. 3, Fall 2007, 957–73.

25. R. V. Gaier and S. Eisenhammer, "Brazil Labor Ministry Stops Construction at Two Rio 2016 Venues," Reuters, April 29, 2015.

26. "Rio 2016: IOC Vice-President Says Preparations Are 'Worst' Ever," BBC, April 29, 2014.

27. "Sobriety at the Carnival," *The Economist*, April 25, 2015.

28. Zimbalist, *Circus Maximus*, 102.

29. C. Radnedge, "Mayor: Rio Ready for World Cup Lessons," *Around the Rings*, July 14, 2014.

30. "Rio Mayor Admits He Is Worried One Year Before the 2016 Olympics," Reuters, August 5, 2015.

31. A. Bauer, "One Year Out, IOC President Reaffirms Support for Rio 2016," *Around the Rings*, August 5, 2015; T. Ribas, "Rio-2016 Terá Legado Melhor que o de Barcelona, Diz Eduardo Paes," *Folha de São Paulo*, March 16, 2015; A. Bauer, "Mayor: Rio Will Set Benchmark for Olympic Legacy," *Around the Rings*, August 12, 2015.

32. S. Wade, "A Year Away, Olympic Organizers Counting on Sun and Samba," Associated Press, July 28, 2015.

33. S. Wade, "IOC on Rio: 'Lot of Progress' But Schedule 'Tight'," Associated Press, October 1, 2014.

34. "Enquete: 68,8% Não Acreditam que Olimpíadas Deixarão Legado para o Rio," *O Dia*, August 11, 2015.

35. "Rio Mayor: Olympics 'Wasted' Chance for Water Cleanup," Associated Press, March 23, 2015.

36. "Sobriety at the Carnival," *The Economist*, April 25, 2015.

37. For example, see: A. Bauer, "One Year Out, IOC President Reaffirms Support for Rio 2016," *Around the Rings*, August 5, 2015.

38. O. A. Santos Junior and C. G. R. Lima, "Impactos Econômicos dos Megaeventos no Brasil: Investimento Público, Participação Privada e Difusão do Empreendedorismo Urbano Neoliberal," in Santos Junior, Gaffney, and Ribeiro, *Brasil*, 71; Kelly Phillips Erb, "World Cup Mania: Figuring Out FIFA, Soccer, and Tax," *Forbes*, June 16, 2014.

39. Personal interviews, September 4 and September 26, 2015.

40. S. Wade, "Unpaid Volunteers Worth Millions to Olympic Games," Associated Press, October 25, 2014.

41. Gaffney, "Global Parties, Galactic Hangovers."

42. Personal interview with Stephen Wade, September 7, 2015.

43. Rio 2016 Candidate City Bid, Volume 2, 203, 205.

44. J. Watts, "The Rio Property Developer Hoping for a $1bn Olympic Legacy of His Own," *Guardian*, August 4, 2015; Gaffney, "Global Parties, Galactic Hangovers"; "MP Resgata 11 Trabalhadores Escravos em Obras para as Olimpíadas," *O Dia*, August 14, 2015;

B. Schmidt, "Rio Olympics Developer Carvalho Becomes 13th-Richest in Brazil," *Bloomberg*, August 21, 2015.

45. L. A. Garcia-Roza, *December Heat: An Inspector Espinosa Mystery*, New York: Henry Holt, 2003, 30.

46. K. Rosen, "Rio Offers 'Embarrassment of Riches' for NBC TV Coverage," *Around the Rings*, August 6, 2015; K. Rosen, "NBC Sports Chairman: Network 'Aligned with IOC Year Round'," *Around the Rings*, July 17, 2015.

47. T. Mickle and J. Ourand, "NBC Deal Shows Focus by Bach, IOC on Loyal Partners," *Sports Business Journal*, May 12, 2014, 1.

48. A. Bauer, "Anti-Government Protests Consume Copacabana Beach," *Around the Rings*, August 16, 2015.

49. M. Ill-Raga, "Camelôs Protestam Contra Violência e Repressão Enquanto o Rio Caminha Para os Jogos Olímpicos," *Rio On Watch*, September 4, 2015.

50. Personal interview, September 18, 2015.

51. Personal interview, September 26, 2015.

52. J. Barbassa, *Dancing with the Devil in the City of God*, 40.

53. J. Freeman, "Raising the Flag over Rio de Janeiro's Favelas: Citizenship and Social Control in the Olympic City," *Journal of Latin American Geography*, vol. 13, no. 1, 2014, 7–38.

54. C. Gaffney, "Securing the Olympic City," *Georgetown Journal of International Affairs*, vol. 13, no. 2, 2012, 79, 81.

55. D. G. Castro, C. Gaffney, P. R. Novaes, J. Rodrigues, C. P. Santos, and O. A. Santos Junior, "O Projeto Olímpico da Cidade do Rio de Janeiro: Reflexões Sobre os Impactos dos Megaeventos Esportivos na Perspectiva do Direito à Cidade," in Santos Junior, Gaffney, and Ribeiro, *Brasil*, 429.

56. C. Gaffney, "Segurança Pública e os Megaeventos no Brasil," in Santos Junior, Gaffney, and Ribeiro, *Brasil*, 180.

57. Ministério da Defensa, Força Aérea Brasileira, "Aeronáutica Esclarece Medidas de Restrição de Voos Nas Cidades-sede," March 21, 2014, www.fab.mil.br/noticias/mostra/18005/.

58. S. R. McRoskey, "Security and the Olympic Games: Making Rio an Example," *Yale Journal of International Affairs*, Spring–Summer 2010, 102; Rio 2016 Organizing Committee, "Rudolph Giuliani Visits Rio 2016 Committee and Praises the Games Project," September 11, 2013.

59. G. Mascarenhas, "Desenvolvimento Urbano e Grandes Eventos Esportivos: O Legado Olímpico nas Cidades," in G. Mascarenhas, G. Bienenstein, and F. Sánchez (eds.), *O Jogo Continua: Megaeventos Esportivos e Cidades*, Rio de Janeiro: Ed. UERJ, 2011, 37.

60. Castro et al., "O Projeto Olímpico da Cidade do Rio de Janeiro,"

411, emphasis added. Gaffney, "Segurança Pública e os Meg-aeventos no Brasil," 411, emphasis added.

61. Rio 2016 Candidate City Bid, Volume 3, 43.

62. "Rio 2016 Olympics to Hire 85,000 Security Staff," BBC, July 31, 2015.

63. Rio 2016 Candidate City Bid, Volume 3, 27; "More than 1,500 Anti-terrorism Troops to Guard Rio Olympics," AFP, September 10, 2015.

64. B. McCann, *Hard Times in the Marvelous City: From Dictatorship to Democracy in the Favelas of Rio de Janeiro*, Durham and London: Duke University Press, 2014, 13.

65. Amnesty International, "You Killed My Son: Homicides by Military Police in the City of Rio de Janeiro," August 3, 2015, 33–5.

66. Rio 2016 Candidate City Bid, Volume 3, 33.

67. R. Martins, "Obras das Olimpíadas Podem Tirar Até 100 Mil de Suas Casas," *Exame*, August 30, 2015.

68. Personal interview, September 14, 2015.

69. Ibid.

70. Associação de Moradores e Pescadores da Vila Autódromo, "Plano Popular da Vila Autódromo: Plano de Desenvolvimento Urbano, Econômico, Social e Cultural," 2012; F. Clarke, "Vila Autódromo Creates Upgrading Plan in Fight Against Olympic Eviction," *Rio On Watch*, July 26, 2012; K. Steiker-Ginzberg, "Vila Autódromo People's Plan Wins Deutsche Bank Urban Age Award," *Rio On Watch*, December 20, 2013; J. Watts, "Favela Residents Protest Forced Olympic Relocation by Blocking Rio Roadway," *Guardian*, April 1, 2015.

71. Personal interview, September 12, 2015. Also see: "Candomblecista da Vila Autódromo Descreve o Terror do Processo de Remoção," *Rio On Watch*, September 17, 2015.

72. E. Paes, "The 4 Commandments of Cities," TED Talk, February 2012; Instituto de Arquitetos do Brasil, "Lançado no IAB-RJ o Concurso Nacional Morar Carioca," October 15, 2010.

73. F. Mena, "A Favela e a Olimpíada—Legado Para Quem?" *Folha de São Paulo*, August 21, 2015.

74. B. Parkin and K. Steiker-Ginzberg, "Mayor Eduardo Paes on the 2016 Olympic Games Legacy," *Rio On Watch*, May 3, 2014.

75. Rio 2016 Candidate City Bid, Volume 1, 33.

76. Gaffney, "Between Discourse and Reality," 3932.

77. Rio 2016 Candidate City Bid, Volume 1, 33; Rio 2016 Organizing Committee, "Rio 2016 and Dow to Implement Most Comprehensive Carbon Programme in Olympic Games History," September 23, 2014; V. Konchinski, "RJ Prometeu 34 Milhões de Árvores

para Rio-2016. Deve Plantar 8 Milhões," *UOL*, May 22, 2015.

78. Rio 2016 Candidate City Bid, Volume 1, 33.

79. S. Wade, "Rio Olympic Head Says Venue with Fish Die-Off Will Be Safe," Associated Press, April 17, 2015.

80. S. Romero and C. Clarey, "Note to Olympic Sailors: Don't Fall in Rio's Water," *New York Times*, May 19, 2014, A1.

81. B. Brooks and J. Barchfield, "Olympic Teams to Swim, Boat in Rio's Filth," Associated Press, July 30, 2015; J. Barchfield, "Away from Olympics, Sewage Blights Vast Swaths of Rio," Associated Press, September 10, 2015.

82. J. Barchfield, "IOC Rules Out Viral Testing of Rio's Olympic Waters," Associated Press, August 12, 2015; R. Harris, "Rio Head Vows to Introduce Viral Testing in Olympic Waters," Associated Press, September 1, 2015.

83. Barchfield, "Away from Olympics, Sewage Blights Vast Swaths of Rio."

84. Personal interview, September 18, 2015.

85. Rio 2016, "Sustainability Management Plan: Rio 2016 Olympic and Paralympic Games," March 2013, version 1, 43; Rio 2016 Candidate City Bid, Volume 1, 33; Brooks and Barchfield, "Olympic Teams to Swim, Boat in Rio's Filth."

86. Personal interview, September 21, 2015.

87. Rio 2016, "Rudolph Giuliani Visits Rio 2016 Committee and Praises the Games Project."

88. E. Hodges, "The Social and Environmental Costs of Rio's Olympic Golf Course," *Rio On Watch*, August 22, 2014; J. Barchfield, "Rio Mayor Unveils Controversial Olympic Golf Course," Associated Press, March 25, 2015; Barbassa, *Dancing with the Devil in the City of God*, 154–5; S. Wade, "2016 Athletes' Village Set to Become Luxury Housing," Associated Press, March 21, 2015.

89. L. Resende, "Ativistas Denunciam Agressão de Guardas Municipais," *O Dia*, January 11, 2015; S. Wilson and S. Wade, "Rio Ruckus: IOC, Olympics Targeted by Environmental Protest," Associated Press, February 28, 2015.

90. Personal interview, September 18, 2015.

91. J. Yamato, "Brazil's Olympics Maestro Talks Rio 2016: 'We're Really Struggling to Be Consistent with No Money'," *Daily Beast*, September 12, 2015.

92. International Olympic Committee, "Olympic Agenda 2020: 20+20 Recommendations," December 2014. Some of the following critiques of Agenda 2020 first appeared in J. Boykoff, "Boston Beware: The Olympics Are a Destroyer of Cities," Al Jazeera America, January 15, 2015.

93. J. Boykoff, "Europe's Leaders Should Boycott Autocratic Azerbaijan's Mini-Olympics," *Guardian*, June 3, 2015.

94. J. Boykoff, "Beijing and Almaty Contest Winter Olympics in Human Rights Nightmare," *Guardian*, July 30, 2015.

95. O. Gibson, "Sebastian Coe: Athletics Is About More than Drugs, Blood, and Urine," *Guardian*, September 3, 2015.

96. J. Clarke, "Mitt Romney Backs Boston Olympics But Warns It Won't Make Money," *Forbes*, November 1, 2013.

97. Some of the following ideas first appeared in J. Boykoff, "A Bid for a Better Olympics," *New York Times*, August 14, 2014, A23.

98. International Olympic Committee, "IOC Financial Summary," July 2014, 2. The IOC's "Revised Olympic Games Framework" released in September 2015 stated, "The IOC will bear costs linked to the visit of its Evaluation Commission." This is a step in the right direction, although it is remarkable that the IOC wasn't paying these costs before. See: International Olympic Committee, "Revised Olympic Games Framework," September 15, 2015, 18.

99. K. Nutley, "IOC Seeks 13th TOP Sponsor," *Around the Rings*, August 29, 2015.

100. R. Livingstone, "IOC Drops Applicant Phase and Short List From 2024 Olympic Bid as Part of Sweeping Changes to Process," GamesBids.com, August 2, 2015; J. Forsyth, "2024 Olympic Bid Process Suffers from a Lack of Transparency," *Huffington Post*, September 4, 2015.

101. J. Ranciere, *Hatred of Democracy*, Trans. S. Corcoran, London and New York: Verso, 2006, 4.

102. IOC Ethics Commission, "IOC Indemnity Policy," Rio de Janeiro, February 26–28, 2015; J. Carneiro, "Favela Life: Rio's City Within a City," BBC, June 9, 2014.

103. Bergvall and the Swedish Olympic Committee, "The Official Report of the Olympic Games of Stockholm 1912," 292.

104. P. Donnelly and M. K. Donnelly, "The London 2012 Olympics: A Gender Equality Audit," Centre for Sport Policy Studies Research Report, Toronto: Centre for Sport Policy Studies, Faculty of Kinesiology and Physical Education, University of Toronto, 2013, 12.

105. K. Karkazis, R. Jordan-Young, G. Davis, and S. Camporesi, "Out of Bounds? A Critique of the New Policies on Hyperandrogenism in Elite Female Athletes," *American Journal of Bioethics*, vol. 12, no. 7, 2012, 3–16.

106. M. Slater, "Sport and Gender: A History of Bad Science and 'Biological Racism'," BBC, July 28, 2015.

107. Personal interview via email, September 22–3, 2015.

108. D. Zirin and J. Boykoff, "The US Is Not Fit to Host the Olympics," *Al Jazeera America*, September 10, 2015.

109. Coubertin, *Olympism*, 484.

110. Personal interview, June 19, 2012.

111. "Sporting Mega-Events: Just Say No," *The Economist*, February 28, 2015, 74.

112. J. Cohn and R. Jacks, "Hey, LA: Here's How You Say 'No' to the Olympics," *The Nation*, August 27, 2015; M. Arsenault, "Patrick to Forgo $7,500 Daily Fee for Olympic Work," *Boston Globe*, March 20, 2015; M. Arsenault, "Olympic Bid Left Debt of Millions," *Boston Globe*, September 11, 2015.

113. J. C. Kang, "What the World Got Wrong about Kareem Abdul-Jabbar," *New York Times Magazine*, September 20, 2015, MM57.

114. "The Obamas Talk to *People*: We Can Still Make A Difference," *People*, December 29, 2014, 59.

115. "Culture and Power: Interview Stuart Hall," *Radical Philosophy*, 86, November/December 1997, 30.

Index

Index